Books by Mary Summer Rain

Spirit Song
Phoenix Rising
Dreamwalker
Phantoms Afoot
Earthway

EARTHWAY

MARY SUMMER RAIN

POCKET BOOKS

New York London Toronto Sydney Tokyo Singapore

POCKET BOOKS, a division of Simon & Schuster Inc.
1230 Avenue of the Americas, New York, NY 10020

Summer Rain, Mary, 1945–
    Earthway / by Mary Summer Rain.
        p.   cm.
    ISBN 0-671-70666-7 : $19.95
    1. Naturopathy.   2. Holistic medicine.   3. No-Eyes, 1892?–1984.
    I. Title.
    RZ440.S86   1990
    615.5′35—dc20   90-7593
                                                                    CIP

First Pocket Books hardcover printing September 1990

10 9 8 7 6 5 4 3 2 1

Design by Stanley S. Drate/Folio Graphics Co. Inc.

POCKET and colophon are registered trademarks of
Simon & Schuster Inc.

Printed in the U.S.A.

To my Earth Mother, who never stops caring and giving all she has to her many children.

My gratitude and love remain endless for all you've sacrificed and endured. Your constant blessings enkindle the flame of my heartlight; may you always perceive its radiating glow.

My Earth Mother, as it should be, I present you with the only Give-Away I have . . . *Earthway.*

TABLE OF CONTENTS

SECTION I
THE BODY
The Soil of Sacred Ground   *1*

vii

TABLE OF CHARTS AND LISTS

FOREWORD

In 1977, my husband and I, and our three daughters, were living in a suburb of Detroit when a voice whispered the words of a new destiny to us. These words resonated within our very souls; they struck a harmonious chord that rang of truth and gave our hearts a new reason for joy. We prepared to set out in a new direction that would ultimately be a journey of the spirit.

We sold our house and most of our meager possessions, leaving our old life behind for the high mountains of Colorado. From that point on, our lives would never be the same.

It took five years for that voice of destiny to speak to us again. But when it did, it came from the being of an aged Native American woman by the name of No-Eyes.

As the high-country seasons passed, I spent as much time as I could with the Old One, for she had much wisdom to impart and she called me her new messenger. The Visionary knew only two more wintercounts were left to her. And so she wanted to pass the wisdom and power of her years to another.

This book represents a portion of the Old One's vast knowledge of natural health, the knowledge she called Earthway.

The range of subject matters that comprises the Earthway knowledge No-Eyes shared with me is virtually encyclopedic, covering everything from minerals and geology to botanicals and other forms of living matter. I have brought all this information together for the first time in this volume. My hope is to provide an eye-opening look at how these widely various truths about the earth coalesce into a powerful Healing Way.

The Egyptians had some of this knowledge. So did the Aztecs and the Mayans. Some even believe the Atlanteans had similar knowledge. Native

Americans of today and the wise ones of antediluvian cultures all recognized the value of these earth treasures. How is it that such diverse cultures share this esoteric knowledge?

The question can best be answered by looking at the world of physics. Scientists of all countries work from a data base of established and accepted facts that serve as the foundation to their individual developmental theories. The basic knowledge—or set of truths that define the science of physics—is recognized by all who work within or are familiar with the field.

So, too, is there a "data base" of truths concerning the vibrationary fields of matter and nonmatter. Throughout the ages, certain sensitive individuals could intuitively draw from this foundation to formulate specific concepts that appeared to be immutable. It is this foundation of unalterable truths that the wise ones of various cultures drew from when they had moments of illumination, whether in the form of periods of altered states, visions, or sparks of enlightenment. Hence, a Native American wise one becomes cognizant of the vibratory rates of differing stones just as her ancient Mayan counterpart did thousands of years before her.

These truths are not selective. They do not choose who will discover them, for the wisdom is as a living current, available to all to perceive when their time is right. The wisdom is universal. It is collective and immutable. It has no name, no race or gender. It just *is*. It exists in a giving state, ready to impart itself to all those who would open themselves to it. . . . No-Eyes was such a one. She was an adept medicine woman who treated all those who came to her for medical help and advice.

Bearing this in mind, I have not presented personal cure-alls within the following pages of this book. What I have done is simply to record the knowledge that I have gained through my comprehensive lessons with the wise visionary. This book is therefore a product of the knowledge I gained from her—the knowledge of the invisible, yet strong and inherent, bond of genetic coding that man shares with all nature and the great cosmos.

No-Eyes was the practitioner. I am not. Therefore, I do not represent myself as one. I do not claim to be able to diagnose illness or cure the sick, but rather I am one who is still learning on the Earthway path.

In the case of all serious illnesses, I strongly advise the individual to seek professional help. This book shares with you the Indian way, the natural way, the Earth Mother's way, to health. Reap what you can from it; always remember, it is filled with valuable health concepts "new" to our modern society.

There's a lot of current interest in Native American traditions. Consequently, an increasing number of writers are producing books on the subject. Some of these works have gained acceptance by the Native People, while others have not. I'm fortunate to have had many, many Native correspondents who've written to encourage my continued writings and who have expressed a deep appreciation for my not having divulged the more sacred aspects of No-Eyes' teachings. Indeed, I would never do that, for those precious experiences are for my heart only.

Because my time with the Visionary, No-Eyes, was a very special part of my life, and because she wished me to share the knowledge she gave me with the public, I sat down to record the events. I had intended to fulfill my promise to the Old One by writing one book. That was *Spirit Song*. But as it turned out, that initial book was a mere outline that only touched upon the many subjects we discussed. After *Spirit Song* was published, I was concerned that such a simplistic sketch of my experiences left out too much valuable material. The second book, *Phoenix Rising,* was my attempt to give a more detailed account of No-Eyes' vision of the coming changes. *Phoenix Rising* was difficult to write, but I felt that people deserved to know what was about to become their reality. People needed to be aware so they could use their own free wills to choose a course of action and reevaluate their own individual paths.

After *Phoenix Rising* was published, I began getting letters asking about the Visionary's herbal remedies. This issue was very important to my teacher and we'd spent many, many weeks on it. But her botanical remedies were only a minuscule part of her healing techniques, and I needed to get that across to people. I knew I had to devote a book to the subject, but I also knew compiling the material would take time; in many ways it is the backbone of what No-Eyes shared with me. I began the work, but in the meantime also wrote *Dreamwalker,* a book about the many beautiful lessons I had learned from No-Eyes' former student, Brian Many Heart. I hoped to have the material on No-Eyes' Healing Way ready to do as my next book.

But things didn't work out that way, for my dear friend and teacher knew she had no more wintercounts left to her on this earth. She went home to die. Although she was gone from my physical realm of reality, she remained a living presence and continued to bring other learning experiences to me. It was immediately after her leaving that I realized the new direction I had to take. This was the time to concentrate my learning on working with wayward and lost spirits. And so I penned those experiences in *Phantoms Afoot.*

Afterward I was at last free to turn my full attention to the health notes I had amassed, and to work on pulling them together so that the Visionary's Healing Way could be presented in the enlightening manner in which it was given to me. Thus *Earthway* came into being. And looking back, I feel there must have been a force I knew nothing about deciding the course of my work, for indeed, now is the time for *Earthway.*

My hope is that the precious knowledge in this book will enlighten and help all who read it. But before you begin, I must forewarn you about some concerns that are crucial to me.

After the publication of *Spirit Song,* I began receiving letters from all over the world, a beautiful outpouring that increased with the publication of each subsequent work in the No-Eyes series. Although the readers who wrote to me always expressed a heartfelt fondness and love for No-Eyes, they also evidenced an undercurrent of admiration for me, Summer Rain. I feel I must address this sentiment by underscoring the fact that I am only the messenger of the teacher. I do not come as another teacher. I only share the message I received from the Visionary. Mine is simply the story of an ordinary woman who met a most extraordinary teacher; now it is my duty to share her knowledge with the world. And so a promise is kept.

I have also been concerned because many of my correspondents tend to zero in on the ethnic aspect of my teachings. This is a mistake. Although my teacher was Native American, the wisdom she gained over the many years of her life went far beyond Native American tradition. Accordingly, I do not mean to misrepresent the knowledge I share with you here as being solely based on Native American teachings. Much of No-Eyes' wisdom grew out of her childhood among the Chippewa in Minnesota, but she was also a unique individual and visionary, and the ultimate knowledge she shared with me came from many other sources. If you are in search of purely traditional Native American teachings, I suggest you turn to a Native teacher or the history books.

This is very important to me. All the phases of my life were only preparing me for my meeting with No-Eyes. She was my intended destiny. She was the reason my spirit led me to the Colorado mountains. The day my footfalls led me into the Visionary's forest, all the past sorrows of my life vanished like mist on mountains upon a shining daybreak. No-Eyes became the light of my life and the eternal beacon for my spirit. Our time together was the visible trailhead of my purpose.

The Indian People are a noble race, and within each specific tribe, certain wise ones are recognized for their great knowledge. These men and women demand and deserve high respect; they are deeply concerned about protecting and preserving their sacred traditions. I sympathize with and honor that concern. Hence, I do not come as a representative of any specific Native American People. I do not come to teach Native American traditions. I come merely as one who wants to share her experiences with one Native American teacher and visionary. I am simply one who hopes to bring to the public a message that exemplifies the importance and beauty of the Native People and the Native way, so that the consciousness of all will awaken to their vital presence and harken to the viability of their age-old wisdom.

As one who benefited so deeply from her education, I hope to awaken all to listen to the voices of the Native wise ones. Pay close attention to their words, for through their gentle ways the children of the earth can once again recognize their bond with all living things. Through them—not me. I am only the messenger.

And through the gift of No-Eyes, *Earthway* is the message.

INTRODUCTION

My old friend No-Eyes was a most extraordinary lady. Her bizarre teaching methods were both absolute and effective. Her mannerisms could be quite crude at times, and her appearance was usually eccentric. Occasionally she completely forgot to tie her hair back; some days she didn't wear her moccasins; other days she omitted her stockings. But never, never was she ever without her deerskin pouch—her treasured medicine bundle.

One crisp alpine morning, when we were sitting in front of her warming fire, I innocently asked her what was in it.

Her eyes remained closed as the corners of her mouth lifted ever so slightly. She slowly opened one dark eye and peered at me.

"That be secret," she whispered. "No-Eyes share all stuff with Summer but this one thing. Medicine bundles be sacred. Stuff inside be special power, they be good medicine for owner." She closed her eye and sighed as the fire crackled and snapped within her smoky fireplace.

Later that same day, the Old One sank into a heavy melancholy. She loved me as I also loved her, and she began gently removing each precious article from the worn skin bundle.

They were beautiful things, not in their outward appearance, but because of the personal sentiments that were attached to them. One by one, she laid them before me: a stone from her homeland, a shell from her mother's necklace, a string of beads her father had made her, a falcon feather, an eagle's claw, all kept close together with some homeland soil within the pouch. There were other things, too.

She laid them all out upon her lap as she lovingly detailed the fascinating stories behind each treasured object. Then she did a curious thing. She slowly pulled out her knife, reached over by my ear, and whisked off a piece of my hair.

"This gonna be last thing for my bundle," she said softly as the firelight reflected off her glistening eyes. "This gonna mark the completed circle of No-Eyes' medicine way. Now I gonna walk into woods a happy woman. I gonna be able to take last walk as a woman with big heart." She then carefully placed all her objects back into the soft sack, tightly drew up the drawstring, and attached it to the belt encircling her tiny waist.

"Summer," she continued in a whisper, "peoples need to change ways. They got bad medicine ways. They gonna need to live better. They need to see how they be always connected to Earth Mother's birth cord, to sky, to stars, an' to each other even. Peoples gonna need to live inside hoop with all spirits of life. They need to go back an' live the Earthway once again."

I looked up into the glistening dark pools of her eyes that had no sight. I saw within them a wisened being who was tired of humankind's erring and fumbling ways. I looked into her tender heart and found a great sadness dwelling there. I held her small hands.

"I'll tell people all the beautiful things you've taught me. I'll tell them how the Earth Mother cares for them. I'll tell them how to return to the earth, how to love one another, and how to become one with All That Is."

She patted my hand. "Promise?"

This book contains the healthful concepts that my wise friend taught me. Earthway reveals the way that man is intended to live with nature, in tune with the earth's vibrations, and among his fellow men. I do not claim to practice medicine, nor do I profess to be a learned doctor; I leave that to the qualified physicians. I have in *Earthway* merely set down the wise one's knowledge for all to benefit from.

This book represents a natural method of total healthful living—the Earthway.

SECTION

ONE

THE

B·O·D·Y

The Soil of
Sacred Ground

THE COSMIC UMBILICAL
Sharing the Celestial Genetic Coding of the Sky and Heavens

Mountain living, especially remote mountain living, can afford a person many opportunities for glances into life's esoteric facets. It bestows a peacefulness that envelops the core of one's being. This peacefulness mellows and smooths out man's rough edges, giving him an altered and expansive outlook on life—a view into infinity. It is because of this tranquil solitude that Bill and I treasure the stillness of our mountain nights.

The nights of a new moon can be quite comical to walk through. With no neighboring house lights, streetlamp beacons, or car beams to light our way, we can barely see our hands in front of our faces. But with the new moon we always make it a point to pick our way up and around the twisting ridge paths to one of our favorite clearings. There we sit in silence, his warm arm encircling me. It is on that high mountain ridge that we practice an inner joy—we softly step into the glittering cosmos of the endless universe.

The vibrant heavens on a moonless mountain night are one of our most valued treasures. They were created for man, and we delight in their undulating reality as we step into the beyond and become two of the minuscule specks floating on endless wavering oceans of brilliantly pulsating orbs. The deep blackness of night wraps its elongated arms around us in a friendly gesture of welcome, and we, in turn, are comforted.

3

These routine journeys into our dark highlands have bestowed upon us a clear sense of who we are and how we are part of the thriving pattern that comprises the grand scheme of all life. Together, we enjoy an epiphany of the mystical experience of man's bonded interrelationship with the Grand Cosmic Lifeforce. We know we are of the same genetic coding.

The first time we ventured out on a moonless night, we cowered beneath the massive sky. We were overwhelmed and felt a humbled insignificance by comparison. We were but two inconsequential people sitting in the inky-black solitude staring up into an infinity of twinkling stars and planets. We felt like nothing more significant than ants. Yet, as we stared deeper into the heavens' expansiveness, we perceived a magnetic sensation pulling at our consciousness. Silently we continued to observe our shimmering canopy, and soon we were drawn up into the Living Core of the slowly rotating universe.

This initial melding of our consciousness with that of the Cosmic Lifeforce instilled a new awareness within us, a warm and comforting knowledge that we are *not* viewed as mere ants, that we are loved and thought about all the time, that within us dwells a Presence brighter than the most brilliant pulsing star—within us lives the universe, the Grand Cosmic Lifeforce of the Source itself.

From this revealing experience came an enlightened perception: We understood each of our fellow men as a facet of that Living Cosmic Force, too. One's individual belief systems, social attitudes, ethnic background, mode of dress, or class are meaningless. There are no differences between us, for the blinding Presence is beautiful in all those we see. The experience bestowed upon us an acceptance of our life and our fellow men. The vast mountain night, with its multitude of stars, drew us into its swirling vortex, up through its nebulous portal and into its very beating heart, where we were touched with compassion, acceptance, and a deeper love for all mankind. The darkened mountain night had parted reality's gossamer veil, allowed us to enter, and revealed the sacred dwelling place where we humbly reached out our trembling hands and were permitted to touch the outstretched finger of God.

We ventured many times to that mountain ridge. While we did not always find the ultimate "touch," the Presence was always felt.

One day, while I was with the Old One, I brought up the experience. I recounted to her how we had initially felt so lowly beneath the grandeur of the night sky.

She cut me short before I could explain any further.

"Why Summer an' Bill feel so low?"

"Because the sky appeared so massive and overpowering. Everything was so beautiful and bright, and the largeness appeared to go on and on into forever."

The Old One leaned forward and shoved a bony finger against my chest. Her head swayed from side to side as she clicked her tongue.

"Tsk-tsk. What matter with Summer, huh? All that beautiful bright-sky stuff be right in there!"

I looked down at myself and turned her words over in my head. Then I stared up into her eyes, as dark as obsidian pools.

"I knew that," I replied softly. "I knew the Spirit was within me, just as It's within all people. What I was talking about was the *sky,* the *stars,* all the celestial objects together as a *whole.* "

No-Eyes sighed as she rested her sweet frailness back into her rocker.

"Summer must think No-Eyes be dumb," she whispered in exasperation as she began the slow creak-and-thud of her impaired rocker.

"What do you mean?" I asked respectfully.

The creaking rhythm paused while she threw her arms up.

"I no speak only 'bout Great Spirit here. No-Eyes be talkin' 'bout *sky* stuff, *star*stuff. Summer got *all* starstuff here!" she exclaimed, pounding her own thin chest.

"I'm sorry, I thought you meant—"

"Listen! Summer be assuming again." She appeared to relax after admonishing me. The rhythm of the chair resumed its slow-measured meter.

"Summer, peoples be so dumb. They not know what in own bodies even. They not know how sky stuff, that *star*stuff, influence bodies." She cryptically peered down at me. *"Summer* know 'bout that stuff?"

"I know that the moon phases affect the body. I know that certain planet alignments affect the sun, which, in turn, affects our physical systems." I hesitated. "And I guess that's about all I do know about it."

"Humph! That be more than most know. Summer, what 'bout planets? What 'bout them, huh?"

"You mean astrology?"

Her black eyes widened. "Summer got smart mouth again. What that word mean anyway?"

"I'm sorry," I said. "Astrology is the study of how different planets affect an individual's personality. It's based on calculating the precise positions of the planets in relation to the time and location of one's birth."

Silence. Thinking.

Waiting.

"Yup," she confirmed with a bright spark, "that be right. No-Eyes not think peoples be that smart." She grinned.

I didn't.

She frowned then, bringing her wispy brows together. "What's the matter?"

"No-Eyes, astrology is . . . well, most people don't take it seriously. They think it's just—a superstition." I was reluctant to call it that because I knew it would upset her. Mankind's ignorance of life's realities always did.

No-Eyes pursed her lips and slumped her shoulders.

"See?" she mumbled. "No-Eyes know all 'long how dumb peoples really be."

I let her silently ponder her disappointment while the rocking began anew. I was proud of her wisdom and I hated it when I had to inform her of another aspect of man's backwardness.

After a few minutes had passed, I broke the silence. "No-Eyes, maybe things will change," I said, trying to sound encouraging. "Maybe these things will be accepted as proven fact one day."

She was disheartened, but I knew she also foresaw the changes in man's view of reality that had to come.

"Yup, they gonna be all right. Too bad that that day not be here yet. It gonna be. It no can stay away." She sighed. "Summer, peoples need to see how all sky stuff, starstuff, an' earth stuff an' peoples be one big living thing. They be all in together living and breathing like one. See?"

"Yes. I do see." While she had been speaking, I had envisioned a great double helix out in space slowing rotating, its shimmering strands holding humankind, animals, plants, stars, and other intelligent beings. It was a beautiful image.

She spoke again, softly.

"All sky stuff affect all other living things. Sky actions give off different magnet energy strengths of power. This great energy, it push and pull on *all* living things. It have big effect on *every*thing. Even planets' little circles, planets' big circles, an' planets' slants have great bearing on movements an' actions of all others. See?"

"You're talking about planets' rotations, orbits, and the degrees of axis, right?"

"Yup, that's what No-Eyes just say all right."

I smiled, but then a question struck me. "No-Eyes, when the Phoenix is rising and the earth is altering, what will affect the earth's new axis-degree position?"

In answering me, she became animated, her arms flailing the air in emphasis. "Many, many big troubles out in sky gonna make earth's magnet field no good for minute, maybe more minutes. Earth gonna be in upset state from violent change in atmosphere. Earth gonna go like this"—she wobbled her head loosely—"then it gonna settle down into new slant position."

"What sort of new slant position? I mean, how much difference in degrees will there be from the present position?"

She raised her wrinkled hand. "No-Eyes see it gonna go from here"— she tilted her hand from one side to the other—"to here."

"That looks like it'll switch twenty-two degrees or so, only in the reverse direction." I showed her what I meant.

"That be 'bout right," she agreed. "That how it gonna settle." She paused momentarily before beginning again. "Peoples need to do much learning 'bout sky stuff, 'bout magnet planet fields, 'bout moon energies even, 'bout sun spears—what you call flares. Every sky thing leave big effects on peoples." She released a long and weary sigh. "Guess peoples not know they got sky stuff inside, guess they not know that they always been connected to stars like some big mother's cord, huh, Summer?"

I too sighed. "Guess not, No-Eyes. Guess they will someday though."

"Yup," she said confidently as the slow swaying of the creaky chair began. "They gonna wise up, they gonna find out. They not ready yet." Creak-thud. Creak-thud. "But they gonna be—someday."

After I had taken time to ponder all No-Eyes had later explained to me regarding the body's connection to the Cosmos, what struck me as being most unique was what she taught me about the weather's influence on our physiological systems. What impressed me most was not that the information was so new or foreign, but that it was all so logical, so totally right.

It's a common thing to hear someone predict a cold front or say that it will soon rain because their old joints are aching. It's also pretty well known that people's sinuses are aggravated when the humidity level goes up. But what impressed me about what No-Eyes taught me was not the *fact* of the subject, but rather the massive *extent* to which the weather affects our health.

Ages ago, when I was still unaware of so many enlightening facts of nature, I heard someone make an offhanded statement that, at the time, I had considered most ridiculous. The gentleman said, "Look at all those cows lying down. Must be a big storm on its way."

I gave the speaker a sidelong glance, as if to question his sanity. The sky was perfectly clear at the time. But within two hours, a thunderstorm engulfed the area.

So ignorance certainly doesn't do a thing to change the facts; the ways of nature are immutable.

I remember thinking at the time that those wide-eyed cows were smarter than I was. They were weather sensitive and had read the obvious signs that nature was sending. Their biological systems were responding to their own weather-wise perceptions.

The whole experience taught me a valuable lesson: Never disbelieve anything that sounds farfetched or unusual until you find out more about it; otherwise, you just might be exposing your ignorance for all the world to see!

In this first section of *Earthway*, I will share with you the knowledge No-Eyes gave me about how our whimsical weather actually plays an all-important role in determining how well or how unwell we feel physically and emotionally.

It's certainly no secret that the weather affects us emotionally. I'm sure you've noticed that on overcast days you feel gloomy, and when the sun breaks through and the clouds dissipate, you have a more happy disposition and enjoy a burst of energy. Since emotions are so closely tied to our physical state, weather-induced psychological changes give rise to corresponding physical conditions. However, these physical changes cannot be blamed solely upon the emotions, for as I will explain, many of our physical complaints are a direct result of the weather, not merely the *present* weather conditions but climatic conditions that existed as much as two to three days earlier.

No-Eyes said that our bodies are made of "earth stuff." We are children of the earth, and the weather is one tie that binds the human system to the cosmic life forces that surround and support it.

You don't need to be a meteorologist to realize that the weather affects us physically and emotionally. When you casually say that "you are under the weather," you are already acknowledging that your system is weather sensitive.

Our earthly atmospheric environment is inescapable. Our bodies have direct responses to the meteorological stimuli of such changing conditions as barometric pressure, air temperature, density of ionization, wind velocity and direction, light density, relative humidity, intensity of the magnetic field, and the unnatural pollutants that permeate the air we breathe.

The continually moving weather systems are in a constant state of metamorphosis. They flow over us, sometimes hovering for extended periods of time, but then they always move on, replaced by a different type of system. These weather cycles can be likened to the ever-changing tides of nature that influence the subtle inner tides of our own physiological systems.

Our own biological rhythms are in a closely corresponding state of fluctuation. Climatic conditions affect our respiration rate and capacity, thermoregulatory balance, blood pressure stability, acid/alkaline ratio, endocrine equilibrium, fluid circulation, metabolic rate, and our psychological state of mind.

It would greatly serve mankind's general health if we all made ourselves more aware of how our individual bodies respond to the meteorological changes . . . for we are also starstuff. We need to not only be aware of this connection, but we also need a more acute sense of ourselves. It's not that more research needs to be done on this unique aspect of human health; what we need are more cognizant physicians and patients. Modern health care needs to take into account the way weather systems affect us; it should become an automatic and permanent part of all professional diagnoses.

As the children of the earth, as beings melded of starstuff, we must begin to recognize the pulsing umbilical cord that connects us to the powerful meteorological forces of the womb that encloses us. Even though these omnipotent forces are inescapable, by recognizing them and understanding their effect upon us, we can discover the vibrational climate that is best for each of us, individually.

Just as we have internal time clocks that silently tick off the seconds and hours that correspond to our days and nights, we also have highly sensitive internal mechanisms that connect us to nature and the cosmos. Just as all living organisms respond to the external stimuli of such elements as light, pressure, and heat, so too we all react to the more subtle forces upon and above the earth such as magnetic fields, planetary configurations, and solar flares.

If we analyze the fundamental components of the human biological system, we find mostly water and a variety of minerals—in other words, *earth stuff.* As beings composed of this elemental earth stuff, we respond to the natural influences of the earth's own energies upon us.

All life-forms exist in a perpetual rhythm of cycles—these being the grand time clocks of nature. Planting, blooming, hibernation, the seasons, the tides, birthing times, gathering times, and the like are all directly affected by the specific cycles of nature and the universe. Many of us can accept that these smaller cycles are influenced by the larger ones. Why then is it so difficult for us to accept the ways in which the interrelationship of these cycles allows us to predict the future?

Most of us do not believe it is possible to predict the future. Yet we continue to strut about like a royal bantam that has no equal in the barnyard empire. We leer with self-importance as we primp into the mighty mirror of life; we perceive ourselves as the species perched on a gilded throne atop the pinnacle of the evolutionary pyramid.

But if we were to look a little more closely into that deceptive and warped mirror, if we were to scrutinize ourselves honestly, we would find a void in that reflection, for we have greatly hindered our evolutionary advancements by denying our inherent instincts. If you doubt that we are yet incomplete in awareness, remember that those cows know more about predicting the weather—*telling the future*—than you do.

Every autumn, a horse or dog will go through natural physiological changes. They insulate their bodies with a thicker layer of fat and a heavier outer coat in order to better withstand the coming winter. How do these animals know the coming season will be colder than normal? Why don't *we* know? The animal's instincts are just responding to nature's clear indicators. Their inner time clock reads the signs and automatically enacts the necessary physiological adjustments.

We, as human beings, are not without these inner sensing mechanisms, nor are we exempt from the biological effects of the cycles and forces of the cosmos. We are supposedly the highest form of life, the greatest achievement of the earth. We had better *act* as we *see* ourselves. We are made up of earth stuff and we possess the delicate sensors that allow us to attune our minds and our bodies to the fine undulating vibrations of the cosmos. Modern man has wasted too many valuable years in ignorance. The time has come for us to open our eyes and see the magnificent pulsing beauty of the cosmic umbilical cord.

1

STARSTUFF
Sharing the Celestial DNA
of the Sun and Planets

The Anasazi. A noble and peaceful People. A People of the stars. Starborn.

And so it came to be that a Native race in the American Southwest was established and settled for a specified span of time.

Knowledge was theirs, for their blood heritage coursed in metered time with the rhythmic movements of the far constellation from whence they came.

Wisdom was theirs. The heavenly aspects, naturally being a major concern in their lives, were fully integrated into their daily life and dominated the People's traditional ceremonies.

The Anasazi's knowledge of their World Above was complete in every aspect. They lived their truths and taught their young ones how closely they were bonded to the stars and the circling planets. From birth, the children were schooled in the sacred ways and influential effects each planet had on their physiological systems, their emotions, and the land they now populated. In this way, the Anasazi greatly differed from many other former Native tribes, for they lived by the stars rather than only by the earth. The earth, to them, was merely a temporary abode. Their star belief system was passed down to the surviving tribes and were incorporated into their cultural traditions, which some still practice to this day.

The Anasazi People adopted star legends. Each planet, along with the sun and moon, was accorded a ruling ancestor from the tribe's distant

11

beginnings. All the chosen notables were famous elders, for only the old ones were honored in such a sacred manner. The one exception was earth, and it was known as The Child, Maa-ru.

The Anasazi was a race that lived a simple material life, for they cared not for elaborate possessions. Their physical needs were few, for they were a highly spiritual race enlightened through years of ancestral wisdom. They knew of complex concepts that modern civilization has yet to envision. And when they gathered around the nightly communal fire, talk was frequently of their distant brothers. They revered the night, for it was then when they were free to dream of home . . . a home they knew they'd someday return to. This had been a traditional belief that lived within the hearts of the People. It would come to pass. This they knew, for their days on Maa-ru had been prophesied by their ancestors. One day, the Starborn Tribe would return home.

The following astronomy section represents how the Anasazi People perceive the heavenly bodies and their vibrational and gravitational effects on the fragile human systems, both biologically and psychologically. No-Eyes provided me with this information and in sharing it with you now, I am bringing it to the public for the first time. Since archaeologists have uncovered so little about this beautiful ancient race, this material represents a monumental breakthrough that provides a small opening we can peer through to perceive a small portion of the Anasazi's ancient wisdom.

The general theory of the Anasazi's planetary beliefs is roughly similar to present-day astrology, but only superficially. The Anasazi based their planetary concepts on knowledge received from their star ancestors; therefore, their knowledge is naturally far more accurate and advanced than ours today. For example, the Anasazi accord one heavenly body to a whole month and call these "seasons," instead of fragmenting the planet's influence between months or splitting months. Their healing techniques are correlated with the affecting planet's magnetic pull and vibrational frequency.

The following planetary section is presented in the pure Anasazi Native way. You will notice similarities to current concepts, but you will also notice the differences. Yet the fact of the matter remains—the biological and psychological vibrationary effects of the planets are real. These principles have stood the test of time. They still hold true today just as they did for the wise Anasazi of A.D. 650.

The above information along with the rest of this section represents a portion of No-Eyes' knowledge of the Anasazi's planetary concepts as they pertain to the effects on humankind.

PLANETARY CONCEPT OF THE ANASAZI

Planet	Symbol	Ruling Ancestor	Identity	Magnetic Season	Season Name	Month
Mercury		Waa-pu	The Spiritual Father	Moon of Little Changes	Aa-nu-qu-taa	May & Aug.
Venus		Mee-yaa-nu	The Dream Giver	Moon of Big Changes	Nu-raa-taa	April & Sept.
Mars		Qu-say-u	The Ancient Warrior	Talking Wind Moon	Yu-aa-nu-taa	March
Jupiter		Quaa-qu	The Provider	White Woman Moon	Maa-ee-tay-taa	Dec.
Saturn		Saa-qu-ya	The Wise One	Moon of Many Fires	Raa-qu-taa	Nov.
Uranus		Kaa-nu	The Philosopher	Wolf Moon	Tay-ee-taa	Jan.
Neptune		Aaqu-waa	The Magic Giver	Moon of Long Counts	Taa-yaa-nu	Feb.
Pluto		Yo-naa	The Healer	Cold Moon	Mee-ee-taa	Oct.
Sun		Qu-nu	Eternal Grandmother	Moon of Thirsty Ground	Taa-qu-aa-pu	July
Moon		Naa-yu	The Spiritual Mother	Moon of Many Gifts	Su-aa-ee-taa	June

WAA-PU
(Mercury)

Mercury's ruling ancestor of Anasazi legend was Waa-pu (*Wah*-poo). He was the highly respected aged elder who was the Spiritual Father of the People.

SPECIFICATIONS

Position from Sun: 1st
Distance from Sun: 47.2 million miles
Orbital revolution: 88 days
Orbital velocity: 29.75 miles per second
Rotation period: 58 days 21 hours 58 minutes
Equatorial diameter: 3,032 miles
Surface temperature: 620°F
Surface gravity* 0.38
Volume* 0.0559
Mass* 0.0553
Density* 0.99

INFLUENTIAL MAGNETIC SEASON

Aa-nu-qu-taa (*Ah* new *coo* tah), meaning Moon of Little Changes (May and August).

INFLUENCE ON HUMAN PERSONALITY

During the time of Waa-pu's strongest influence, the Anasazi wise woman, Saa-qu-ya, counseled people of her tribe who came to her with an inner restlessness. She advised them to calm their sudden onset of wanderlust by centering on the importance of family and home, and to participate more often in the many community activities available to them. In this manner their feelings of boredom would dissipate.

Saa-qu-ya knew that, during the season of Aa-nu-qu-taa, many were afflicted with a critical temperament, and she frequently had to be the impartial negotiator to settle family disagreements or be the wise sounding board for individuals with internal conflicts.

INFLUENCE ON HUMAN PHYSIOLOGY

The Anasazi healer, Yo-naa, treated a greater number of respiratory ailments during this season of Aa-nu-qu-taa. Also those clan members suffering from chronic arthritis came to see him for their aching finger joints, for Waa-pu (Mercury) affects the hands and arms.

Yo-naa gave special potions to tranquilize and ease tension and disorders of the central nervous system that had been aggravated by this planet's influence. For this ailment he prescribed increased rest and a well-balanced diet.

*Surface gravity, volume, mass, and density throughout this section are in relation to Earth's.

MEE-YAA-NU
(Venus)

Venus's ruling ancestor of Anasazi legend was Mee-yaa-nu (Me *yah* new). She was the beautiful ancient one who was the Dream Giver of the People.

SPECIFICATIONS

Position from Sun: 2nd
Distance from Sun: 67.2 million miles
Orbital revolution: 224.7 days
Orbital velocity: 21.76 miles per second
Rotation period: 243 days (retrograde)
Equatorial diameter: 7,520 miles
Surface temperature: 900°F
Surface gravity: 0.88
Volume: 0.8541
Mass: 0.8150
Density: 0.95

INFLUENTIAL MAGNETIC SEASON

Nu-raa-taa (New *rah* tah), meaning Moon of Big Changes (April and September).

INFLUENCE ON HUMAN PERSONALITY

The wise one, Saa-qu-ya, found few clients to counsel during the time of Mee-yaa-nu (Venus), for the planet tended to emit a calming influence that brought about a wonderful sense of belonging to the People. She saw how content most of them were. She loved the atmosphere of human love and generosity that flowed between the clan members.

Yet the season of Nu-raa-taa did not leave her idle. Clients still came to her because Mee-yaa-nu's calming effect frequently confused one's ability to remain strong in respect to chosen life goals. Tribe members were often overcome with a nonchalance they neither understood nor liked.

INFLUENCE ON HUMAN PHYSIOLOGY

Yo-naa, the healer, treated an increased number of throat and thyroid complaints during Mee-yaa-nu's influence. He saw patients suffering from tonsillitis, laryngitis, and earaches. He knew these conditions were aggravated by the changing weather patterns and the atmospheric alterations of the season of Nu-raa-taa (Moon of Big Changes); therefore he cautioned his patients to dress appropriately, eat well, and increase the frequency of their sweat baths.

QU-SAY-U
(Mars)

Mars's ruling ancestor of Anasazi legend was Qu-say-u (Coo *say* oo). He was an ancient elder who was the protecting Warrior of the People.

SPECIFICATIONS

Position from Sun: 4th
Distance from Sun: 141.6 million miles
Orbital revolution: 687 days
Orbital velocity: 14.9 miles per second
Rotation period: 24 hours 37 minutes 23 seconds
Equatorial diameter: 4,220 miles
Surface temperature: -10°F
Surface Gravity: 0.38
Volume: 0.15
Mass: 0.1074
Density: 0.71

INFLUENTIAL MAGNETIC SEASON

Yu-aa-nu-taa (*You* ah *new* tah), meaning Talking Wind Moon (March).

INFLUENCE ON HUMAN PERSONALITY

Saa-qu-ya was busy during Qu-say-u's Talking Wind Moon season. Her clients mainly consisted of those tribe members who were faced with obstacles found along their life paths. Those clients were of strong constitution and needed advice on how to overcome these frustrating difficulties that appeared to hamper their forward progress.

During this season of Yu-aa-nu-taa, the wise one was also visited by those who were themselves wise but thirsted for deeper understanding. Saa-qu-ya's upper-level room was frequently filled with a circle of young and bright minds eager to gain more of their teacher's wisdom.

INFLUENCE ON HUMAN PHYSIOLOGY

Yo-naa was frequented by the "marked" clients of the tribe during the season of Yu-aa-nu-taa. These ones had birthmarks or facial moles, yet also possessed more defined bone structure and had thicker hair. These experienced increased head ailments during this season, such as headaches, sinus complaints, or ear and eye conditions.

The healer knew how to treat these conditions borne of the great winds of Qu-say-u (March). He was knowledgeable of atmospheric pressure and treated his loyal patients accordingly.

**QUAA-QU
(Jupiter)**

Jupiter's ruling ancestor of Anasazi legend was Quaa-qu
(Coo *ah* coo). He was the ancient Provider of the People.

SPECIFICATIONS

Position from Sun: 5th
Distance from Sun: 483.7 million miles
Orbital revolution: 11.86 years
Orbital velocity: 8.12 miles per second
Rotation period: 9 hours 3 minutes 30 seconds
Equatorial diameter: 88,983 miles
Surface temperature: -240°F
Surface gravity: 2.64
Volume: 1,403
Mass: 317.83
Density: 0.23

INFLUENTIAL MAGNETIC SEASON

Maa-ee-tay-taa (*Mah* ee *tay* tah), meaning White Woman Moon (December).

INFLUENCE ON HUMAN PERSONALITY

The White Woman Moon of December was the season Saa-qu-ya loved
best. It was during this Maa-ee-tay-taa season when all the Anasazi elders
gathered in the wise one's warm quarters to discuss the deeper spiritual and
esoteric concepts of their star heritage. It was a wonderful time of sharing. It
was regarded as the time for recounting and preserving the sacred knowledge of their distant ancestors.

Quaa-qu (Jupiter) imparts an influence that intensifies the desire for
knowledge, and so it was that the wise ones naturally gathered to speak of
such things when the White Woman Moon shone down round and cold from
the December nights.

INFLUENCE ON HUMAN PHYSIOLOGY

Many came to rap on the door of the lower-level end room of the healer
during this season. They had complaints of hip-joint and liver ailments as
well as sciatica, for Quaa-qu affected these as well as the pituitary gland.

Yo-naa cheerfully treated all who came to his door. These patients, he
knew, would heal well and quickly recuperate because the White Woman
Moon of Maa-ee-tay-taa blessed the sick in this manner.

SAA-QU-YA
(Saturn)

Saturn's ruling ancestor of Anasazi legend was Saa-qu-ya (Sah *coo* yah). She was an old one who was the Wise One of the People. All the Anasazi wise ones were called Saa-qu-ya.

SPECIFICATIONS:

Position from Sun: 6th
Distance from Sun: 886.7 million miles
Orbital revolution: 29.5 years
Orbital velocity: 5.99 miles per second
Rotation period: 10 hours 29 minutes 20 seconds
Equatorial diameter: 74,560 miles
Surface temperature: -300°F
Surface gravity: 1.15
Volume: 832
Mass: 95.16
Density: 0.11

INFLUENTIAL MAGNETIC SEASON

Raa-qu-taa (Rah *coo* tah), meaning Moon of Many Fires (November).

INFLUENCE ON HUMAN PERSONALITY

Those who visited Saa-qu-ya during the time of Raa-qu-taa needed advice regarding their high level of ambition. These clients were driven by an inner drive to accomplish all tasks and goals to perfection. This resulted from their trait of strong responsibility, which frequently caused many inner conflicts.

The wise one had to counsel these ones by cautioning them to refrain from taking their responsibilities too far, for these clients most always got themselves into trouble by interfering in the personal lives of others.

INFLUENCE ON HUMAN PHYSIOLOGY

During the season of Raa-qu-taa, the healer could expect to see an increased number of patients suffering from a variety of orthopedic ailments. These included flare-ups of normally inactive conditions such as trick knees, rheumatism, and arthritis. Yo-naa attributed these complaints to the Moon of Many Fires, for November was well known for fooling people with its damp chill that crept into rooms where the fires were not attended well.

KAA-NU
(Uranus)

Uranus's ruling ancestor of Anasazi legend was Kaa-nu
(*Kah* new). He was an ancient one who was the
Philosopher of the People.

SPECIFICATIONS

Position from Sun: 7th
Distance from Sun: 1,783 million miles
Orbital revolution: 84.02 years
Orbital velocity: 4.23 miles per second
Rotation period: 15 hours 36 minutes (retrograde)
Equatorial diameter: 31,600 miles
Surface temperatures: -340°F
Surface gravity: 1.15
Volume: 63
Mass: 14.50
Density: 0.23

INFLUENTIAL MAGNETIC SEASON

Tay-ee-taa (Tay *ee* tah), meaning the Wolf Moon (January).

INFLUENCE ON HUMAN PERSONALITY

Tay-ee-taa, the Wolf Moon of January, would find Saa-qu-ya counseling
her tribe members who were viewed as the free thinkers. These represented
a broad scope of psychological aspects, for they extended to the far reaches
of the issue.

Some clients came to the wise one with innovative ideas and concepts.
They were eager to hear her opinion and sought her acceptance. Yet there
were also those who came full of burning concerns that revealed their inner
doubts of traditional beliefs. Some of these latter ones were pained to be
experiencing such open skepticism and it added to their confusion—but
only for a time, for such was the influence of the planet Kaa-nu.

INFLUENCE ON HUMAN PHYSIOLOGY

The circulatory system affected those calling on Yo-naa during the
January Wolf Moon. Patients complained of ailments in their extremities. Leg
cramps, varicose veins, cold and numb fingers. This planet's influence also
brought the healer those who had accidental mishaps with their arms or
legs.

The old healer expected an increase in this type of ailment, for the tribe
members were extremely active during this season. He cautioned them
against staying out in the cold for prolonged periods of time. He warned
them to shorten the length of time they spent outside in their Sky Watches.

AAQU-WAA
(Neptune)

Neptune's ruling ancestor of Anasazi legend was Aaqu-waa (Ah *coo* wah). She was an ancient one who was the Magic Giver of the People.

SPECIFICATIONS

Position from Sun: 8th
Distance from Sun: 2.8 billion miles
Orbital revolution: 164.8 years
Orbital velocity: 3.38 miles per second
Rotation period: 18 hours 26 minutes
Equatorial diameter: 30,200 miles
Surface temperature: -370°F
Surface gravity: 1.12
Volume: 55
Mass: 17.20
Density: 0.31

INFLUENTIAL MAGNETIC SEASON

Taa-yaa-nu (Tah *yah* new), meaning Moon of Long Counts (February).

INFLUENCE ON HUMAN PERSONALITY

This was the season Saa-qu-ya expected more visitations from the younger ones, especially the bright youth who were learning the tribe's esoteric knowledge. Because of their young age they had a highly sensitive emotional nature. Their egos were fragile aspects of their blossoming personalities.

Taa-yaa-nu, the Moon of Long Counts, imparted a heightened sensitivity to these young seekers of knowledge, and the wise one had her hands full as she counseled them. Guiding their frequently overfilled minds was a difficult task that she managed with much love and patience.

INFLUENCE ON HUMAN PHYSIOLOGY

When the February season of Taa-yaa-nu was upon the clan, the healer treated the lower extremities of his many patients. Foot problems were affected by this Long Count Moon because of the cold and bitter temperatures. Frostbite was most common, but other foot ailments increased during this time such as athlete's foot, bunions, and foot accidents.

Yo-naa cautioned his patients to change their footwear frequently and, when indoors, walk barefoot, take footbaths, and keep the feet warm.

YO-NAA
(Pluto)

Pluto's ruling ancestor of Anasazi legend was Yo-naa (*Yo nah*). He was the old wise man who was the Healer of the People. All the Anasazi healers were called by the name of Yo-naa.

SPECIFICATIONS

Position from Sun: 9th
Distance from Sun: 2.8 million miles at perihelion
                       4.6 million miles at aphelion
Orbital revolution: 247.7 years
Orbital velocity: 2.9 miles per second
Rotation period: 6 days 9 hours 18 minutes (retrograde)
Equatorial diameter: 1,980 miles
Surface Temperature: -446°F
Surface Gravity: 0.04
Volume: 0.01
Mass: 0.0025
Density: 0.25

INFLUENTIAL MAGNETIC SEASON

Mee-ee-taa (Me *ee* tah), meaning Cold Moon (October).

INFLUENCE ON HUMAN PERSONALITY

Saa-qu-ya counseled an increased number of budding intellectuals during the season of Mee-ee-taa. The October Cold Moon enhanced the inquisitiveness of many minds. This influence brought about a deeper comprehension of concepts for many of the tribe's members. These would be the future teachers. They would become the wise one's students, for their keen perception and analytical abilities were evidenced early on in their lives. The influence of Yo-naa enhanced these intellectual traits to the point of making these students stand out and claim their life direction.

INFLUENCE ON HUMAN PHYSIOLOGY

The healer treated genital ailments that were affected by the season of Mee-ee-taa. These included urinary and reproductive complaints. Infections were on the rise during this time, as well as the number of consultations given regarding sexual matters and conception.

For the Cold Moon time, Yo-naa prescribed all manner of potions. He was not only the tribe's healer during this season, he was also the matchmaker.

QU-NU
(Sun)

The Sun's ruling ancestor of Anasazi legend was Qu-nu (*Coo* new). She was the ancient one who was the Eternal Grandmother of the People.

SPECIFICATIONS

Distance from Earth: 93 million miles
Equatorial diameter: 865,120 miles
Rotation period: 24 days 16 hours 48 minutes
Core temperature: 23,000,000°F
Core pressure: 1 million million pounds per square inch
Photosphere temperature: 11,000°F
Surface gravity: 27.9
Volume: 1,303,730
Mass: 332,830
Density: 0.26

INFLUENTIAL MAGNETIC SEASON

Taa-qu-aa-pu (*Tah* coo *ah* poo), meaning Moon of Thirsty Ground (July).

INFLUENCE ON HUMAN PERSONALITY

Taa-qu-aa-pu was the season when the Sun imparted its greatest force. In Qu-nu (July) the wise one advised her clients against being overly optimistic, for logic and wisdom needed to be used also in their bright perceptions.

Saa-qu-ya also counseled those of the clan who were the extroverts. These required words of admonishment to temper their excessive energies and exuberance, for frequently these were sources of irritation to the other members.

INFLUENCE ON HUMAN PHYSIOLOGY

Moon of Thirsty Ground in July affected the digestive system. The healer treated patients afflicted with conditions that evidenced a disruption of the body's normal assimilation functions. This was not unusual for the Taa-qu-aa-pu season as the clan was extremely active and many didn't take the time to eat properly.

NAA-YU
(Moon)

The Moon's ruling ancestor of Anasazi legend was Naa-yu (*Nah* you). She was an ancient elder who was the Spiritual Mother of the People.

SPECIFICATIONS

Distance from Earth: 221,463 miles at perigee
 252,710 miles at apogee
Orbital revolution: 27 days 7 hours 43.2 minutes
Orbital velocity: 2,300 miles per hour
Equatorial diameter: 2,160 miles
Rotation period: same as orbital revolution
Surface temperature: Bright side: 260°F
 Dark side: -280°F
Surface gravity: 0.17
Volume: 0.020
Mass: 0.0123
Density: 0.62

INFLUENTIAL MAGNETIC SEASON

Su-aa-ee-taa (*Soo* ah *ee* tah), meaning Moon of Many Gifts (June).

INFLUENCE ON HUMAN PERSONALITY

The Bright Side: Saa-qu-ya saw clients whose empathetic nature had been emphasized during the time when the Moon of Many Gifts showed its bright side. To these, friendships and family were extremely important aspects of their lives; therefore the concern for some was a high priority. The empaths were also blessed by the Su-aa-ee-taa season by being gifted with a higher degree of determination that served to grant these clients a greater measure of perseverance.

The Dark Side: During the faceless Naa-yu phase, the wise one counseled those people troubled with a combination of nonchalance and a restlessness to begin new projects or proceed with goals. These clients frequently had the additional tendency to overwork themselves and a leaning toward intolerance. The wise one cautioned these people to remember the importance of others and to refrain from centering solely on their own path in deference to others along the way.

INFLUENCE ON HUMAN PHYSIOLOGY

The Bright Side: "Energetic" is the word for patients Yo-naa saw during this moon phase of the Su-aa-ee-taa season. These were the people of the tribe who, although they came to the healer with a variety of physical complaints, had an uncommon reservoir of inner strength and will to fight off physical ills. It was well known that Naa-yu's bright side gifted humans with this increased healing power.

The Dark Side: The faceless side of Naa-yu brought the healer patients whose emotional states were highly volatile. This volatility leaves the body's immune system vulnerable. Yo-naa addressed the root cause of these various emotional states first, for he was well schooled in the damaging effects of stress and emotional negativity when internalized. These, he knew, were the ones who self-generated their bodily ills—these were frequently the psychosomatic patients who couldn't deal with life.

2

SKY STUFF

Sharing Earth's Amniotic Atmosphere

HOW TEMPERATURE AND HUMIDITY AFFECT DRUGS

Our physiological systems are affected by variations in climatic conditions, which in turn means that these same varying conditions also have a direct effect upon our systems' absorption of ingested chemicals.

Many of our common kitchen cleansers come with specific instructions about proper storage; they usually specify that you keep them in a cool, dry place. This is because warm temperatures and high humidity can cause a chemical breakdown of a substance's active components. It can either lose its original composition, thereby becoming virtually inactive, or it can undergo a chemical reaction and become dangerously potent—all depending on the temperature and degree of dampness.

Drugs are no different from your kitchen collection of solvents, cleansers, powders, and antiseptic disinfectants. Drugs have a specifically balanced chemical composition and are subject to temperature and moisture in the same way cleansers are. Substances such as alcohol, caffeine, and nicotine have a more intense reaction upon the physical system when ingested in warm weather, during sudden heat waves or extended hot spells. If you live in geographically warm and humid areas such as Florida and South Carolina, you need to take your climate into account by having your physician adjust prescription dosages accordingly.

In *hot* weather or climates, *decrease* the intake or recommended dosage of the following:

alcohol
anticoagulants
antispasmodics
atropine (and all derivatives)
cortisone (and all derivatives)
diuretics
sedatives

In *cold* weather or climates, *decrease* the intake or recommended dosage of the following:

analgesics
barbiturates
hallucinogens
narcotics
sulfa
tranquilizers

No-Eyes recommends the above adjustments because the external temperature will *increase* the effectiveness of the drugs; therefore you should *decrease* the dosage.

HOW HUMIDITY AFFECTS OUR HEALTH

All manner of confusion can arise when one attempts to define adequately what humidity is. But for our purpose here, all we need understand is that humidity is the amount of moisture in the air at any given time.

Just as humidity affects the chemical content of the kitchen cleansers and prescription drugs, it also affects the chemical balance within our own biological systems.

Geographical areas where *high* humidity is the norm will see evidence of all types of illnesses with its people. This is intensified if the location has the high humidity in conjunction with warm or hot air temperatures, and it is even further intensified if all of the above are found in a *low*-altitude area. This dangerous climatic combination slows or restricts blood flow, which in turn raises the incidence of circulatory problems, places an additional strain on the cardiovascular system, increases respiratory congestion, and submits the entire physiological system to an increased amount of atmospheric pressure. High humidity, when accompanied by *warm* or *hot* air temperatures, will *increase* the body's thermoregulatory system into a cycle of rapid heat transference (increased perspiration). This adds surface moisture and creates a more uncomfortable situation, increasing the probability of heat prostration.

High humidity, when accompanied by *cool* or *cold* air temperatures, will *decrease* the body's natural thermoregulatory system in an attempt to retain its inner heat adequately. Remember that high humidity conducts and intensifies air temperatures, making the summer heat appear stifling and the winter cold appear bitter.

People who make their permanent residence in a humid clime are generally less healthy, more often lethargic with accompanying spells of extreme tiredness or exhaustion, are more timid, and experience a higher ratio of heart and circulatory problems, diabetes, and respiratory ailments.

A hot and humid climate is the last place an elderly person should live. Rather, they should move to a warm and dry region.

HOW BAROMETRIC PRESSURE AFFECTS OUR HEALTH

Barometric pressure is simply the amount of air pressure that is bearing down on a specific geographical location as calculated by a measuring instrument called a barometer.

The amount of this pressure is affected by the air temperature of surrounding areas, humidity, and wind current, direction, and velocity.

When the barometric pressure falls, the fluids in the body thicken, blood flow is slowed, circulation is restricted, pregnant women near to term begin the first stage of labor, more suicides are contemplated and carried out, and blood-sugar levels fall.

The following are physiological and psychological ailments that are directly aggravated by *falling* and *low* barometric pressure readings:

Abdominal cramps	Epilepsy
Accidents	Headaches/Migraines
Allergies	Heart ailments
Appendicitis	Menstrual pain and flow
Arthritis	Phlebitis
Asthma	Rheumatism
Blood circulation	Sinus Problems
Bronchitis	Tiredness/Exhaustion
Cancer	Tonsillitis
Depression	Tumors
Diabetes	Ulcers

HOW WIND TEMPERATURE AND DIRECTION AFFECT OUR HEALTH

Wind variations are caused by fluctuating solar radiation, land and water placement, and the earth's own rotation. Water masses heat more slowly than land masses, which creates a great differential in temperature. This difference in temperature creates our winds.

Not only does the wind's temperature and velocity affect our physiological systems, it also influences our psychological functioning. For example, the chinook and the Santa Ana winds bring an overabundance of positively charged ions with them. These excessive ions create a marked decrease in our mental well-being, causing us to be irritable and restless.

While No-Eyes and I never had time to review this information fully, the following is a partial list of ailments that are aggravated by the different types of wind:

Cold Northerly: aging, diabetes, gall bladder dysfunctions, and kidney ailments.

Cold Westerly: arthritis, bursitis/bone stiffness, muscle aches/cramps, and rheumatism.

Warm Southerly: allergies, appendicitis, asthma/bronchitis, depression, emphysema, excitability, heart/circulatory ailments, infections, insomnia, pleurisy, respiratory ailments, and tonsillitis.

Warm Westerly: anemia/blood pressure, cancer, circulation, colitis, convulsions, depression, epilepsy, fevers/exhaustion, glands, headaches/migraines, hemorrhaging, irritability/suicide, liver ailments, phlebitis, and tumors.

HOW ALTITUDE (GEOGRAPHIC ELEVATION) AFFECTS OUR HEALTH

Geographical locations high in altitude (6,500 feet and above) bestow many beneficial effects upon the human biological system. However, dangerous reactions are in store for those unfamiliar and unadjusted to the ways of "mountain sickness."

Mountain sickness is generally characterized by headaches (often severe), increased weakness, nausea, and vomiting. It is important for low-altitude dwellers to be mindful that the higher-altitude regions will have a markedly lower content of oxygen and carbon dioxide in the atmosphere. This "thinner air" places an increased demand on the respiratory system; breathing becomes more labored.

The human physiological system is not constant. It automatically makes internal adjustments to external atmospheric changes. Thus, a low-altitude dweller who travels to altitudes above 6,000 feet will perhaps be temporarily affected by the thinner atmosphere, but after several days of moderate rest, the biological systems begin to make their instinctive adjustments. The rate of respiration switches from shallow to deep. The blood chemical composition turns from acid to alkaline, which increases the concentration of erythrocytes (oxygen-carrying hemoglobins). Both of these changes contribute to a better overall and lasting health.

High altitudes are beneficial for several other reasons: less physical energy is required for normal exercise; the air contains fewer chemical pollutants (above 8,000 feet); and the body's metabolic rate is more efficient. Those individuals who are fortunate enough to dwell year-round at an altitude of 7,000 feet or higher are blessed with a continued increase of energy and have more stamina, and they are generally healthier and tend to be slimmer.

This last benefit is especially healthful to the human system. Over-weight low-altitude dwellers who move their permanent residence to an altitude above 7,000 feet will soon begin to lose their excess weight and feel generally healthier through the addition of increased energy.

HOW THUNDERSTORMS AFFECT OUR HEALTH AND EMOTIONS

Thunderclouds create an intensely powerful electricity within them. This power is generated through the explosive reaction between the highly charged negative and positive ions. Each ion becomes so charged that there soon becomes an overload, which discharges in a bursting release of electrons. This sudden release creates a channel through the air in which the individual charges unite in a great force of light and sound. This is lightning.

Thunderstorms produce a massive amount of *positively* charged ions in our atmosphere. Whenever the atmosphere is overbalanced with *positive* ions, our mental awareness dulls, our moods depress, and we begin to feel physically under the weather. After a thunderstorm has passed, the atmosphere is left with an abnormally high level of *negatively* charged ions, thereby giving us a renewed psychological uplift.

HOW THE EARTH'S MAGNETIC FIELD AFFECTS OUR HEALTH

The earth's magnetic field is in a state of perpetual movement. It is not constant nor is its intensity stable. In general, wherever the field is strongest, a cooler climate results. A weaker section of the field produces a warmer climate.

Historical records show that the earth's magnetic poles have made complete reversals many times in the past. This has been verified by the analysis of layers of sedimentary rock, which contained particles with differing magnetic polarities. During the pausing moments between these pole reversals, the earth was temporarily subjected to the highly destructive radioactive cosmic rays that penetrated the exposed atmosphere.

The earth's magnetic field is markedly disturbed whenever major sunspots and solar flares are in evidence. And whenever the earth's magnetic field is disturbed, there results a correspondingly radical increase in human psychological aberrations. Psychiatric hospital admissions increase, human behavior becomes erratic and irrational, mental awareness decreases, and reflexes are dulled.

Evidence of the human physiological reaction to the earth's magnetic field can be seen in the measured heartrate fluctuations of a person walking over ground with a magnetic field of varying intensity.

Since the earth's magnetic field is affected by planet positions and solar flares and sunspots, it is clearly evidenced that our physiological and psychological systems are deeply connected, intertwined, with the powerfully intense forces of nature and the cosmos.

THE EARTH MOTHER'S UMBILICAL
The Womb's Life Force of Earthway Living

While driving out to No-Eyes' place one clear mountain morning, I found myself in a contemplative mood. The warmth of the high-country air brought a feeling of contentedness, and as I glanced around at the tall jack pines along the road, my heart was near to bursting with happiness.

My thoughts meandered back to the time ten years ago when we were still living in Westland, a suburb of Detroit. I recalled the day Bill and I had realized that our life was incomplete, that there was an emptiness that kept us constantly in a state of restlessness and discontent. That void forced us to recognize that we were not living in the geographic location that was best for our bodies and spirits. We decided to move away, to go wherever we belonged, to seek out that right location—regardless of the objections of our friends and relations. When I think back to all the problems our decision caused, I am soothed by the comforting fact that it eventually turned out so well—it had been so right.

Thinking about those times as I drove along also reminded me of a conversation I had overheard recently while sitting in a restaurant one morning in my current home, Woodland Park, Colorado. Some tourists were discussing the possibility of moving to the Pikes Peak region from their home state. The gentleman wanted very much to rush right back home and sell their house and belongings so they could settle up in the mountains as soon as possible. His wife, on the other hand, seemed to be adamantly opposed to the idea. She, too, loved our little wooded town on the high mountain pass, but she kept saying that her husband just *couldn't* leave his "good job," and they couldn't desert their friends, relatives, and all their years of "built-up security." When the couple left the café, he was still excitedly talking about his plans while she continued shaking her head and saying, "No, it just can't be done!"

This wasn't the first time I had overheard that kind of discussion from the summer tourists about moving here. One partner would be full of excited plans while the other would be just as stern and dour in their opposition. Then there were those people we knew who lived here for a long, long time and decided to move elsewhere in the nation . . . only to return six months later.

It has been said that the mountains get in one's blood. It certainly appears to be that way with many folks: I know it's that way with Bill and me. This line of thought weaved in and out of my mind as I made my way to the remote cabin of my dear, old teacher.

When I reached my destination, No-Eyes was sitting on one of the frail pine-branch chairs that had been pulled out in the sun of her yard. As I parked the car and approached her, I greeted her excitedly. She remained still, but raised one hand in recognition.

I pulled up one of the chairs to face her.

"Sit there," she commanded gently. "Summer no put back to sun this day."

I repositioned my chair next to hers and leaned my head back to face the warming rays. We were silent for several minutes while we listened to the raucous chirping and chatterings of the surrounding forest people. The stream below gushed forth its never-ending song, harmonizing with the hushed whisperings of the tall ponderosa pines as they bent their heads together and swayed in the morning breeze. It was so peaceful. And the peace filled my heart.

When No-Eyes spoke, her soft voice blended with nature's music, creating a gentle harmony.

"Summer be full of happy today," the wise one whispered.

I smiled. "Yes, it's very beautiful."

"Then what the matter?"

I remained in my position of rest, soaking up the warm sun and the tender woodland sounds.

"What makes you think there's anything the matter?"

She straightened up and faced me. "No-Eyes know. No-Eyes *feel* that there be some special thought in Summer's head this fine morning."

I hadn't particularly wished to shatter the gentleness of nature's music with our coarse spoken voices. I didn't move. I didn't answer. Silence prevailed.

Listening.

Remaining silent.

Suddenly the Visionary slapped my knee. "Get up! We gonna go for walk. We gonna talk."

I knew that, as usual, it would've been futile for me to object. I slowly got out of the chair and stretched.

"Where are we off to?"

"No-Eyes think we go down by stream. That gonna be right place for lesson today."

I held her arm as we strolled down toward the western slope of her hillside.

"What're we going to talk about?"

"We gonna speak 'bout stuff that circle round up in Summer's head. We gonna get that stuff straight today."

I tugged at her thin arm as I pulled up short.

"You've been nosing around in my head again," I teased.

Her narrow shoulders shrugged. "No-Eyes not be good teacher if she not know what stuff bother student. Anyway, this gonna be good lesson. This be stuff *all* peoples should know 'bout."

I placed a whisper-soft kiss on her wrinkled cheek and we descended the hill toward the sparkling stream.

We walked beside the rushing waters until we came to a clearing of soft wildgrass and sat down. After taking several moments to listen to the tranquillity of the cascading sounds, No-Eyes spoke.

"We gonna talk 'bout what be inside peoples. Then Summer gonna understand what make some peoples want to move and some others want to stay. Then we gonna talk 'bout colors and health. Last we gonna speak 'bout right way to eat. All this stuff be connected, one stuff lead to others, it be natural. It be *Earthway.*"

I didn't see how one's residential preference had anything to do with one's diet, but if she said it did, then it must be so. I reclined on my side in the cool grasses and rested my head in my hand.

She squinted down at me. "Summer not gonna get too comfortable here. Summer gonna listen good."

I assured her that I would.

"First we gonna settle why some peoples not be happy where they live. Maybe they got good job, some big moneys, many friends, long time secure, but they be much unhappy in here," she said, gently placing her hand over her heart, "they no be content, they no be at peace *here* either." She pointed to her head. "Now, why Summer think reason be for this big unrest in peoples?"

I grinned at her. "I thought *you* were going to tell *me* that."

Eyes twinkling, she poked my side and giggled. "I not gonna do *all* thinking here. Summer gonna do some, too!"

"Well," I tried, "it's obvious that these people have got some sort of an inner conflict raging within themselves. And I'd have to say its source probably isn't consciously recognized." I smoothed a blade of grass between my fingers. "Personally, I think this conflict has to do with an individual's basic purpose."

"Purpose?"

"Yeah, why they're *here*, what they need to *accomplish*. It's like they're physically not where they should be and their subconscious knows that. The subconscious nags and tugs at the consciousness creating a constant vague feeling of discontent."

She thought my theory over. "That be pretty good idea, that be pretty right. But Summer, what *make* that discontent? What single concept make that?"

It was now my turn to do some deeper thinking. She had said "concept," and I knew that to No-Eyes that word meant a rule of life, a rule that was a little-known fact that involved the realities of man.

I looked her straight in the eyes. "I don't know about this concept," I said. "I don't think we've ever talked about this one."

The old one raised her small chiseled profile to the clear turquoise sky. Her eyes were closed in deep contemplation.

I waited.

Slowly, thoughtfully, she returned and gazed at me.

"Summer, all things—living and not-living things—got movement. This inner movement be a fine vibration special to itself. See?"

"Like an individualized vibratory rate?"

"That right. Now, this vibratory rate be very different in each living and not-living thing. This be important stuff here, now listen." She cautioned me with a warning finger. "Each thing has got matching, near-matching, or different rates. When a living thing be located near matching rates of vibration, they be happiest. See?"

"Yes. You're saying that matching vibratory rates create harmony. And that unlike rates bring about a discontentment within the mind and spirit. Unlike rates would create a general restlessness."

She nodded. "All peoples got a Power Point up here," she said, pointing up to her forehead. "It be there where this vibration shimmers and waves in movement like oceans. It always be in motion, always. If people's surroundings not be in same rate of motion, they feel unhappy."

It was very clear to me. "So all people possess an individual rate of vibration that must be matched up with the rate of vibration of a specified geographical area in order for them to feel content. It's the matching vibratory rate that makes them feel they're where they should be and need to be for their life's purpose."

"Yup, that what No-Eyes just say all right."

I turned onto my back and placed my hands behind my head. A few wispy tufts of white had begun to drift over our deep sea-blue sky.

"You said that color enters in with this concept of vibrations. How's that?"

Her mercurial eyes bore deep into mine. "Summer tell No-Eyes that."

I returned my gaze to the floating clouds. "All right, I'll try." I considered the matter before continuing. "I know that everyone has a specific major aura color, and that colors themselves have individual vibratory rates. So, the aura color's rate of vibration and the individual's own vibratory rate must match if their systems are to be in healthful harmony." I waited for a confirmation.

Silence.

Waiting.

Finally the Visionary spoke. "So?"

I frowned. "So what? What else is there?" I questioned.

"Summer, that be right, but that be only top of stuff. Go deeper."

I thought for a minute or two. "People and colors have vibratory rates." I then stopped dead in my tracks because I wasn't quite sure where we were going with all of this.

No-Eyes nodded. "Go on."

I watched a raven perch atop the pinnacle of a wavering fir. Then, as my gaze traveled down the stately evergreen, the next connecting thought came to me.

"And all living and nonliving things have vibratory rates. That's it, isn't it, No-Eyes? *All* things have these rates. So, trees, mountains, bodies of water, deserts, rocks, *everything* can be properly matched to anyone's specific rate!" I sat up with the exuberance of my newfound knowledge.

No-Eyes grinned as she tossed me a small rock.

"Hold that," she said. "Place it in hand, close fingers gently but firmly round it. Tell No-Eyes what Summer feel."

I curiously looked down at the large stone and was beginning to inspect it.

"*Close* eyes! I not say to *study* rock. I say to *hold* it!"

I quickly shut my eyes. I allowed the world to drift away from me. There was nothing but myself and the entity of that rock. I waited within awareness. Soon I perceived an irritating sense of strangeness. My hand felt disconnected from the rest of my being. The rock and I didn't belong together.

"I feel separated," I said softly. "I'm not at peace with this. I don't like the feeling."

"Now Summer can look at rock—study it."

I opened my hand and found an unusual stone. "This isn't from around here," I said, turning it over and over. "Where'd you get this?"

The Visionary closed her eyes and smiled. She stretched out her hand to me.

"No-Eyes take back now." As she placed the stone back into her deerskin pouch, she added, "That come from long, long ways. That come from No-Eyes' homeland."

I grinned with new understanding. "Well, that certainly explains why I didn't feel comfortable with it. I've never liked Minnesota. I must not vibrate harmoniously with that area."

No-Eyes smiled. "That be right. Now Summer see how people's vibrations need to match right land vibrations. But," she said, cautioning with a thin finger, "if Summer be sick with too much body water inside, that stone gonna help to heal, see?"

I did . . . sort of.

"Listen," she expanded, "all stuff have these rates. Stones, minerals, flowers, trees, colors, planets, sounds, smells, *everything*. So, too, do different diseases of bodies. A flu have different rate than broken-bone rate. A measles have different rate than bad tonsils. And when peoples get sick, they need to match up right rates of all different surrounding stuff to get better fast. See, Summer?"

"This is fascinating! It's like everything has got to be in absolute alignment, all vibrations have to match correspondingly. And you're saying that when people are ill, they get better quicker if they use the right vibrations of color, sound, and other things to help cure themselves. This entire concept is new to me and we'll have to go into it very carefully. This is so incredibly fascinating!"

"Nope. It just be fact."

"But it *is* fascinating, No-Eyes. Why, if everyone knew the proper harmonizing vibratory alignments, they'd get well a heck of a lot faster and if—"

"Tsk-tsk," she clucked, "Summer forget most important health stuff here. All right matches do no good if *food* be all wrong. Food got rates too."

She was right. I'd forgotten how important our eating habits are as a foundation to good health. I sighed. "Guess I got carried away, huh?"

"Huh."

The sound of the watercourse carried my exuberance downstream as the gentle breeze brought a refreshed clarity to my thinking.

"People don't eat right, No-Eyes."

"Humph! Summer not give old No-Eyes news flash here. No-Eyes not be dumb. *Peoples* be dumb. Peoples eat all wrong stuff."

"I think they're coming around though," I said, hoping to soothe her sudden agitation. "Lots of folks are beginning to change their ways, they're—"

"Blah! Peoples cook in grease. Peoples eat too much sugar an' meats!" She bent to peer over at me. "They still killin' cattle?"

"Well, yes, but—"

"See! Peoples never gonna learn." Then she allowed a slow grin to curl up her face. "Well . . . they gonna learn *someday*, huh, Summer?"

I dropped my voice. "Yeah, someday."

She shook her head. "But now they be dumb. They ruin bodies, they be all acid. Nobody gonna be healthy when it be so bad in acid."

"No-Eyes, the body does require a certain percentage of acid for proper absorption and balance of various chemicals, vitamins, and minerals."

She nodded in agreement. "That be right, but bodies no can take more than this much acid," she said as she held her fingers up to demonstrate a minute measurement.

"Looks to me like about ten percent worth," I guessed.

She slightly enlarged the space between her fingers. "Maybe fifteen," she corrected.

"Fifteen percent acid and eighty-five alkaline is probably about right." Then I frowned. "That's difficult for the average person to maintain, No-Eyes."

"Blah! Summer do that. Bill and family do that. *All* peoples can do that, too."

She was beginning to lose control again.

"But it's hard for people when they don't realize this balance factor. They're too conditioned to eat french fries, fried hamburgers, red meat and sweet rolls and chocolate and—"

"Summer!"

Silence.

She calmed and spoke softly. "No-Eyes be sorry. No-Eyes not mean to shout." She paused before continuing. "Summer, peoples need to set better importance on stuff here. We not only speakin' 'bout health of bodies here, we speakin' 'bout greater stuff even. Would peoples put filth on altars in their churches?"

Her meaning was only too clear. "Of course not," I answered with a sigh.

"Then why they fillin' spirit's Sacred Ground with filth food stuff? People's bodies be house, be Sacred Ground of Great Spirit, and they fillin' it with bad vibrations from killed animals." She was becoming saddened. "Peoples need to see how close they be connected with Earth Mother, they need to see *good* foods that come to them through her great nourishing mother's cord."

"I know. Remember I told you about the high amount of antibiotics and growth hormones that are being injected into the cattle and the chemical additives in their feed?"

"Yup. Summer say peoples gettin' all that bad stuff in own systems, too, when they eat that bad meat."

"That's right. And now I just read where researchers are saying that because of that, our young people are physically maturing too soon, and they have also developed a greater resistance to antibiotics because of this high ingestion of those red meats."

"Summer, that only be new part. Peoples not meant to eat that meat stuff anyway. It be too heavy in people's system. It give bodies stuff like tumors, stuff like—"

"Yeah, I know, No-Eyes."

The old woman raised her tired head to the sun and received its warming Give-Away upon her face. She was silent for a long while. The stream splashed and rippled as it surged by us. The pines and firs wavered in the gentle breeze. And I remained quiet as my sweet friend thought thoughts of mankind and silently offered up her prayers to the Great Spirit on their behalf.

After No-Eyes finished with her prayers, we discussed the finer details of her concept of our interlocking vibratory rates of alignment. She talked about the correct diet for mankind and how well the Earth Mother provided for all our dietary needs. And this brought us to the subject of the natural, wild botanicals that nature has been providing for man's health from the beginning of time.

The old one listed specific diseases, their natural botanical curatives, and also their various vibratory rates, including those natural elements that best harmonized with them, such as color, sound, wind direction, moon phases, scents, light densities, and more. This lesson lasted long into the early evening hours.

The following material within this section on the body and its total physical health reflects her deep wisdom on the subject . . . wisdom passed on to her by the wind's breath, the mountain's whispers, the earth's own knowledge, and of course, her special cosmic friends.

HEARTSOUNDS
Our Homing Instincts
for Lifestyle Choices

Everything living and nonliving possesses molecules that move about within it. Some of these molecules move at an extremely slow rate, while others are accelerated to an incredibly rapid pace. However, within each and every individual exists a sensitive scanner that perceives the entire scale of vibratory rates. This finely tuned ability originates within the pineal gland located at the base of the brain's third ventricle.

Everyone possesses a "Mean Vibratory Rate," that is, a specific vibratory rate that is unique unto the individual. If an individual is not sensitive enough to attune his mental energies to his personal vibratory rate, there are certain indicators that supply the clues needed to discern one's own Mean Vibratory Rate. To assist you, I will put forth several searching questions you can use to zero in on your own specific rate of vibration. This will not reveal a vibrational number, but more important, it will clarify specific aspects in your life that are aligned—or not aligned—with your own rate.

What is your favorite geographical region?

Do you prefer a seasonal climate over a year-round one?

How would you describe your ideal living environment? Do you prefer the city or the country?

What period of furniture do you favor?

What exterior material would you like your home constructed of?

What style of architecture most pleases you?

What is your favorite type of wood?

What is your favorite color?

What clothing fabric do you prefer?

If you have answered the above questions honestly, perhaps you have found that you're not presently living as you would like. That's a sign that your lifestyle is not in tune with your individual Mean Vibratory Rate. Compare your true answers with those of your present living conditions. If they differ, then you have found the source of your uneasiness, your discontent—you are *not* living with compatible vibratory surroundings.

Let's first look at the question of geographical location. If you find you are not in harmony with your current location, you are facing a major life crossroads. Now you must decide whether or not you wish to correct your situation. If you do, then you must do everything within your power to make it a reality, to make your decision come into fruition, thereby giving yourself a pleasing and contented living condition whereby your spirit will be better attuned to its purpose.

Perhaps you wish to make this change but are held back by psychological rationalizations such as, "I can't move because I have good job security. My neighbors will think I'm crazy. My relatives will be upset." These are merely worn-out excuses you're using to hide your fear of the unknown and your personal insecurities. What possible benefits do you reap from job security if you are living a life of inner unhappiness? Such excuses are really just albatrosses in disguise. They are great heavy chains wrapped around your life to prevent you from being the person you were meant to be.

This concept is extremely important to understand. You, and you alone, are responsible for your life. You, and you alone, have to answer for the decisions you make in life. Your friends, your relatives, or your neighbors are *not* held accountable for *your* life. You are accountable. Don't let the attitudes or comments of others dictate your final decision. Are you going to take hold of your own future? Are you going to take control of your own life?

If you are unhappy, search out the true reason and be determined to correct it. You will be relieved that you did, no matter what temporary commotion may arise from your decision. Stand up for your life! Seek your *own* future! Search out your happiness in where you feel you belong and you will never regret it. Change your life if you need to. Change your surroundings to coincide with your own Mean Vibratory Rate so that you will become more in tune with the world, and most important, with your *self.*

The human need to belong is intense. Whether you feel the need to belong in the center of a bustling city, in a desert adobe, or in the middle of a pine forest atop a mountain, *get* there. Search out your true inner promptings and follow them.

Just as an individual's Mean Vibratory Rate should be in harmony with his geographical surroundings, so, too, should you align yourself with the vibratory rates of color.

As previously mentioned, all living and nonliving matter vibrates. Hence, all living and nonliving matter has a certain amount of energy it emits from its moving complexity of molecules. This energy emanates out and away from its primary source in a molecular force called the aura.

Everything has an aura of energy. Living organisms possess a greater and more colorful aura than inanimate objects. It is the activity of different organisms that contributes to the variations of color and movement in the aura itself.

Certain innovative scientists have developed a rather crude but serviceable mechanism that illustrates the activity of an aura. Kirlian photography has shown us what auras look like, and researchers have now begun to interpret the precise meanings of the various aura patterns emanating from different subjects.

Many of you who developed your spiritual awareness may have seen for yourselves the beauty of a shimmering aura surrounding the human form.

All individuals possess an aura of living energy that surrounds their physical forms. Its visual condition directly corresponds to the psychological mood and physical health of the individual. In depicting the current health of a subject, the aura can reveal specific areas of imbalance or disease.

One day, routine health care will include diagnostic technicians operating simple machines that will clearly illuminate the patient's aura. These technicians will be able to analyze the physical dysfunction by pinpointing the irregularities that will clearly be evident within the individual's aura emanations. However, we still have much to learn before this kind of medical technology becomes a time- and life-saving reality.

Just as you have a Mean Vibratory Rate, so, too, you possess a main aura color that is unique to you. Have you ever worn clothing of a color that just did not agree with you? Do you enjoy wearing one color more than others? Do you frequently feel *uncomfortable* wearing a certain color? Or do you simply *refuse* to wear a specific color altogether? Your answers to these questions relate directly to your unconscious awareness of your own main aura color.

For example, if the Mean Aura Color is predominately blue, you will naturally feel uncomfortable wearing red or any shade of red, such as pink, rose, and possibly orange. You will be most comfortable wearing the clothing colors that correspond or complement your Mean Aura Color. The recent faddish concept of having someone "match" your clothing colors to coordinate with your complexion and hair coloring is not helpful to one's total ease, for often your facial complexion has nothing whatsoever to do with your Mean Aura Color. In general, you will find you're productive and confident if your clothing complements your personal aura color.

So far we've seen that all individuals possess a Mean Vibratory Rate and a Mean Aura Color. We've dealt primarily with the inner functions of vibrations; now we'll direct our attention to the "outer" you.

The human body requires daily bathing. Actually, showers are preferred for total cleanliness. The hair also requires daily cleansing—and no, it *won't* dry up and fall out. You would be repulsed if you could see the multitude of infinitesimal germs that set up breeding grounds on your scalp, eyelids, and skin. These microorganisms, if left even for a few days, will continue to breed and multiply at an incredibly rapid rate, producing festering pustules that appear as acne, boils, rashes, sties, and the like. Some of these germs are friendly, yet there are those that need to be cleansed routinely. Take the same care of your personal hygiene as you would of a new and prized automobile.

Exercise is another way to treat your body with respect. Do not allow your beautiful physical form to become lax and waste away. There are many methods of exercise, and there's one for *you*. No-Eyes did not recommend running because it eventually does more damage than good to your body. Aerobics are excellent as long as you monitor your own specific pace *and* you're working under the direction of a well-qualified instructor. Even so, not all of the exercises done in an aerobics class are meant for *your* body, especially if you have knee, ankle, or hip problems.

Walking is highly recommended. Most people can do it safely. It's not strenuous, but it effectively increases respiration, expands lung capacity, stimulates circulation, increases the body's thermoregulatory exchange, maintains good muscle tone, and uplifts the spirit all at the same time. You should take a moderately paced walk daily.

Adequate rest is another important aspect of good health. Your body requires at least eight hours of sound sleep per night. I said "night" because the physical system is meant to be active during the daylight hours and restful during the night. We are not nocturnal creatures. Nighttime sleep is essential to you both physically *and* psychologically. Methods devised to alter the body's internal time clock will eventually prove to be highly detrimental.

A waterbed merely fools the human mind into believing that the physical body only needs five or six hours of rest per night. It lulls your body with a motion similar to that experienced by a fetus floating within the warm waters of the womb. This is, of course, excellent for a developing infant. But it is not meant for the adult form, as it will rob the body of the recommended hours of rest.

The placement of your bed is also important. No-Eyes explained that the human system performs at a peak of efficiency if during sleep the human form is in direct alignment to the direction of magnetic north. In other words, your *head* should be facing this important position. Through the ages, alignments have shown they have a powerful pull on the human body and mind. We have already seen some of this in the section dealing with the effects of weather and celestial objects on human health and temperament. This all-important concept remains true in regard to how the magnetic field interacts with our bodies.

By placing the head of the bed in direct alignment with the direction of magnetic north, you will experience a deeper sleep, awake more refreshed, and feel physically enhanced. All these benefits are a result of the natural "pull" of the earth in a straight line through your positioned body, which draws your energies up through the head instead of out from the feet or the side.

Just as your bed should be positioned properly, so also is the design of your house an important aspect of your overall health. I cringe when I see a decorating trend toward the ultramodern. This style most often uses various metals such as chrome, aluminum, steel, bronze, iron, and the like. These materials are most harmful to the sensitive human system, as they "draw" upon the human energies and cause highly erratic energies to be released in a haphazard manner. Such metals interact with the earth's natural magnetic field causing a wild disbursement of energy to be spewed back and forth throughout the rooms they occupy like a bombardment of damaging atoms or X rays.

Please understand that we, as the appointed children of the earth, were meant to live in harmony and unity with our Earth Mother. The *hardness* of metals prevents our gentle and soft union with the living entity of earth. Please replace your damaging metals with soft, warm woods. It is bad enough that most of mankind has opted for harsh, cold homes made up of straight lines and corners and boxes instead of the unifying form of circles. Don't compound the matter with detrimental metals.

For those who are contemplating building a new house, consider circular configurations in the planning. Circular houses and rooms hold one's valuable energies and can be highly beneficial to man's total health. Building materials should be as natural as possible; adobe interiors and exteriors, wood beams, logs over eight inches in diameter, natural paneling, wood-frame windows, stone or brick—anything other than the metals. Anything natural is best.

None of these concepts is complex or difficult to implement within your daily living. They are simple concepts for maintaining a healthful physical condition, simple concepts to provide us, the children of the earth, with a harmonious lifestyle—the Earthway style.

Choosing a lifestyle in harmony with the earth can facilitate a harmonious existence. But no adjustments you make in your lifestyle will be effective unless you first attend to your diet, the very foundation upon which all harmonious alignments are based. By "diet" I don't mean losing weight according to some faddish eating program. Rather, I am referring to the general dietary law prescribed for all mankind.

No-Eyes described earth's human inhabitants as being a collection of foolish beings who continually defile their spirit's encasement with filth in the form of damaging foods. She compared man's manner of food consumption to spitting on a sacred object such as the Bible or the Torah. She said man's physical body contained the brilliant essence of the living God, the Spirit. Consequently, man's poor eating habits were a direct desecration of that God Spirit within the self.

At this point, whether or not you believe your body contains a spirit is absolutely irrelevant. Whether or not you even believe in God is not the crucial point. The only thing that matters is that you realize the food you eat can be damaging your body. Perhaps the old saying "You are what you eat" has become a cliché, but it's still true.

Residual elements of everything you eat remain within your sensitive system. Some elements remain longer than others, some *never* leave. This is a particularly significant fact to keep in mind when you consider the various adverse chemicals that are added to most foods in the guise of chemical enhancers, preservatives, colorings, and flavorings. "But I feel great!" you claim. "I eat all the right foods," you continue to insist. But do you? Do you *really?*

The delicate and intricate systems of man are no different from other life-forms on our planet. Man was intended to ingest certain forms of food to maintain a peak state of health. You would not feed beef to your prized tropical fish. You would not continually give chocolates to your dog. Why then would you similarly misfeed yourself?

Think of the various diets that are prescribed for patients suffering from different physiological dysfunctions. Heart patients must follow one specific diet, those with diabetes must adhere to another. Overweight patients are placed on one strict diet regime, and those suffering from circulatory disorders are advised to follow another. Why? Because certain foods are *not* healthful for the human system.

The human body needs *care* to maintain good health. And just as psychological depression can lead to poor physical health, so, too, can poor health lead to depression. It is most important for our total being that we eat properly.

Negative emotions are often instigated by the chemicals added to foodstuffs. Researchers have found that hyperactive children become stabilized once they stop eating sugars, artificial colorings and flavorings, and artificial sweeteners. A spiraling chain of physical illness is frequently instigated by depressed emotions or hyperactivity, which, in turn, is caused by chemical and artificial additives in the food ingested.

You will also find in this section on man's diet some general information regarding vitamins and minerals. Vitamins and minerals naturally provide the building blocks that use the body's own energies to rejuvenate and rebuild the various organs. The gross absence of vital vitamins and minerals within the system will significantly reduce the body's effective functioning and result in atrophied or stiffened joints, delayed or poor involuntary muscle responses, weakened bone formation, impaired sensual perception, poor circulation and respiration, and mental confusion. If you are ingesting the proper foods in the correct balanced combinations, you should *never* need to take megavitamins. Remember, especially when it comes to vitamin and mineral supplements, more is not better. Only if you're suffering from an illness or have special dietary needs because you're pregnant should you take broad-spectrum multivitamin and mineral supplements. In order to facilitate complete absorption of such supplements, No-Eyes recommended the additional intake of gelatin. Gelatin tends to retain the vitamins and minerals within the system for an extended period of time because of its binding effect. Gelatin in itself contains nine of the amino acids that aid the system in the production of hemoglobin. In the technical material of this section you will find a listing of the essential vitamins and minerals and their specific benefits.

EARTHWAY GENETICS
Our Dietary Heritage

NATURE IN THE BALANCE

The "chemical balance factor" is vitally important to man's attainment and maintenance of good health. This balance comes naturally from consuming the right foods in the proper combinations. However, the concept itself requires an explanation for those who are not familiar with it.

All foods have a polarity. All foods, when ingested, either are acid producers or alkaline producers. An individual with too much acid in his system will experience all manner of adverse physical dysfunctions and a frequent susceptibility to colds and flu. Conversely, an individual whose system is mostly alkaline will experience good general health and well-being. This concept of the acid/alkaline ratio will be familiar to tropical fish breeders. The delicate balance between acidity and alkalinity in the water is a precarious thing in the maintenance of tropical fish, for an imbalance either way will result in fatalities. The delicate balance between acidity and alkalinity is just as important to the human physiological systems.

But how do you determine what the acid/alkaline ratio in your system is? It's very simple. You must learn which foods produce acid and which produce alkaline, and evaluate your diet accordingly.

The ideal balance for the human system is fifteen percent acid and eighty-five percent alkaline. Some of you might be thinking that a totally alkaline system would be best, since acid is harmful. Not so! Remember that more of a good thing does *not* constitute "best." Tropical fish would die in a

46

totally alkaline tank of water. Man's system, too, requires a delicate *balance* of the two conditions. We need a certain level of acidity in order to facilitate the proper absorption of various vitamins and minerals. Therefore, that certain level of allowable acid is fifteen percent—but *no more.*

Although No-Eyes was never able to give me a full listing, the following is a partial listing of acid- and alkaline-producing foods that you should find useful in your daily life:

Acid-Producing Foods	*Alkaline-Producing Foods*
Animal fats	Dairy products (yogurt, cheese, etc.)
Vegetable oils	
Egg whites	Fruits (except plums)
Legumes	Vegetables (except legumes)
Nuts (except almonds)	Seafood/shellfish
White flour/pasta	Poultry
Starches	Sunflower seeds
Chocolate	Almonds
Cane sugars	Hard grains/wheat
Alcohol	Honey
Artificial additives	Maple syrup
Plums	Egg yolk
Beef (steaks, burgers, liver, heart, etc.)	Raisins
	Granola
Pork (ham, ribs, bacon, hocks, etc.)	Herbal teas
Cranberries	
Animal organs	

Be sure to adjust your ratio of consumption accordingly. If you are frequently susceptible to colds and other minor illnesses, your system may be too acid. Mullein tea and/or fresh alfalfa sprouts help equalize the chemical balance factor and aid the system in returning to a healthful alkaline condition.

Please note that all forms of beef and pork are acid producers. Not only do they produce harmful acid within your system, they also invade it with a myriad of dangerous chemicals.

The ranchers enhance the cattle and swine feedlots with such fat-producing agents as powdered chemical additives, newspapers, and garbage fillers. They then give routinely scheduled injections of antibiotics to protect against diseases and inject hormones to facilitate rapid growth. Now these animals are plump and ready for the slaughterhouse. In the surrounding stockyard, a multitude of animals frequently die in the lots. These dead animals are not always culled, but are dragged into the processing plant regardless of their condition. Then all the meat is processed and sent to market where color enhancers are often added to the specific cuts of meat to make them look so much more appealing to the hungry shopper.

Now you go shopping. You see rich, red meat that is moist and tender looking. You purchase it, cook it, and eat it with mouth-watering relish. "Mmmm, great tasting steak!" you exclaim as you smack your lips. Better think again! You've just eaten newspaper, antibiotics, hormones, chemicals, and perhaps germs from a disease-ridden animal that was not separated at the slaughterhouse.

Is it any wonder that European countries are now refusing the beef we're trying to export to them? At least they are concerned enough for the health of their countrymen. Why aren't we?

If liver is your choice of meat, you've chosen the organ that filters chemicals and impurities consumed or injected into the animal it came from. They all concentrate in the liver. You might think it's good for you because it's high in iron, but it's even higher in pollutants.

Although the poultry industry is little better than the beef or pork, the contaminating agents in poultry can be killed by thorough cooking and proper culinary hygiene. Turkey is a good beef substitute. Why? Because turkey is an alkaline producer. Ground turkey can be a healthful beef substitute in lasagna, spaghetti, hamburgers, meat loaf, or just about anything ground beef can be used for. Also, you might keep in mind that turkey can lay claim to possessing one of the highest protein contents of *any* of the meats, even more than beef. And if you're concerned about not receiving enough protein by cutting out the beef, you might be interested to learn that a mere handful of sunflower seeds provides the protein equivalent of a medium-sized broiled steak.

Some foods are particularly beneficial to the human system. Potatoes are excellent. But please, stop *peeling* them. Would you cut the fat off a chicken and discard the meat? In essence, you are doing just that when you peel the potato and eat only the inside. Virtually all of the potato's best nutrients are within the skin.

The general dietary philosophy that No-Eyes taught was for the most part developed through her own leanings and instruction from her cosmic friendships. There is, of course, a great wealth of background material that served as a spiritual foundation for the advice she received. This material dealt in high philosophies and revelations of yet unenvisioned spiritual concerns. And since my time with her was cut short before I could gain the full facets of the material that she had begun sharing with me, it wouldn't be prudent of me to try explaining the many fragments that I did gain. However, suffice it to say, her dietary information disavowed the practice of absolute vegetarianism. Rather, she recommended fish and fowl be included in the diet. She excluded the four-legged, or hooved, animals as a food source because of their more developed spirit force.

My own experience has confirmed what No-Eyes taught me. The four-leggeds do indeed have higher spirits than the lesser beings of fin and feather; on many occasions I've felt a communication with a four-legged animal, as I'm sure many of you have. There is no way I could now eat a hooved being as I once did in the more ignorant days of my youth.

The wisdom of what No-Eyes taught me has also been confirmed by many of the letters I've received from readers since the publication of my first book, *Spirit Song*. One letter in particular stands out in my mind. It came from a woman who, thinking she had to be a complete vegetarian in order to walk the spiritual path, wrote with a heavy concern in her heart. She explained to me how deeply committed she was to her "spiritual" diet, and that she held to it so devotedly that she even excluded milk, eggs, and all dairy products. However, it appeared that her family physician diagnosed her infant as being malnourished to a degree of considerable concern. But she wrote to me not out of concern for the babe, but because she was worried about how to stay true to her spiritual convictions.

If any of you who have read of my not infrequent outbursts with No-Eyes, you would have no trouble envisioning my immediate outrage with this misguided mother. How could a mother hold her dietary philosophies more dear to her heart than the life-and-death condition of her own baby? What could she possibly be thinking? Needless to say, I told her as much, and I told her to get milk into that child before she took another breath! And eggs! And lots and lots of high-protein baby food!

The issue of vegetarianism is *not* a spiritual one. It has been taught by our cosmic brothers that the human systems are not made more spiritual by such a diet, but that fish and fowl are wonderful sources of protein and nutrients for our particular biological composition.

Our concern should not be with whether or not vegetarianism is spiritual, but rather with maintaining the rights of personal *preference* and *choice*. One who eats only vegetables is no more spiritual than one who eats fish and fowl. This was emphasized by No-Eyes more than once. You should eat only vegetables if you like, but don't claim to be enlightened because of it.

EARTHWAY DIETARY GUIDELINES

The following guidelines are recommended if you wish to live a healthful and contented life. The rules are not complex. They are simple and direct. They are the Earthway of eating.

1. *Eat only fruits and vegetables that have been grown in your local region.* Locally grown foods help the body build up a natural immunity to regional contaminants and impurities. This translates into a natural resistance to local allergenic agents. (Honey processed locally is especially helpful for the purpose of alleviating symptoms or building up immunization against seasonal botanical allergies.)

2. *Eat only vine-ripened products.* Fruits and vegetables that have been picked and shipped while green have not had adequate time to absorb sufficient nutrients from their living source.

3. *Never combine sugars with starches.* This combination causes adverse chemical reactions within the digestive tract, resulting in constipation, flatulence, and an irritated colon. It is like allowing a fermenting reaction to take place within the digestive tract—something akin to the process of homemade bread dough rising.

4. *Never consume starches with meats.* This harmful combination will produce an excessively long absorption time within the digestive tract, thereby causing an invasion of the bloodstream and organs by fermenting elements.

5. *Never mix citrus fruits or juices with milk.* This detrimental combination sours the ingested milk with the strong citric acid of the fruit, resulting in poor nutrient assimilation and aggravated digestive functioning.

6. *Never eat fried foods.* Broil, braise, bake, boil, stew, or steam, but never, ever fry.

7. *Never cook in copper or aluminum cookware.* Metal elements of these utensils enter all foods prepared in them. Cast-iron cookware is recommended because the iron mineral enters the food and benefits the system. This also applies to mixing bowls and the like. Throw out all uncoated aluminum and copper kitchen utensils. They may look pretty, but they're deadly.

And if you're using aluminum foil to wrap or cook food in—stop it! The same concept applies.

8. *Never consume preservatives or artificial additives.* These will prove to be the real tumor-inducing agents, especially nitrates and certain colorings.

9. *Never eat chocolate.* "Oh, no!" you cry. "Not my chocolate!" Yes, *chocolate.* Acid, acid, *acid!* What a pity the food producers have spoiled the wonderful nutritional value of granola bars by adding marshmallows and chocolate to them. They have literally transformed a healthful food snack into a harmful candy bar.

10. *Steam all fresh vegetables.* This is the only cooking method that retains the total nutrient value.

11. *Limit all sugar substitutes and chemically decaffeinated drinks.* Virtually all sugar substitutes are detrimental in some form or another. And unnatural methods use additional chemicals for the process of decaffeinating drinks. It would be more healthful to the physical system to ingest moderate amounts of regular coffee and drinks than larger amounts of the decaffeinated type, since No-Eyes taught that decaffeinated coffee would raise levels of serum cholesterol in the bloodstream. Of course, some illnesses prohibit the ingestion of caffeine; in this instance, you should always follow the advice of your physician.

12. *Avoid egg whites.* The yolk is the most nutritious part of an egg; it is alkaline. Eat the yolk and leave the acid white alone.

13. *Never eat pork, beef, or animal organs.* This has been thoroughly explained.

14. *Inspect eating utensils.* Never use a questionable glass or utensil. You may experience some embarrassment by asking for spotless replacements, but being embarrassed is better than spending six to eight weeks in bed because you've contracted a severe case of hepatitis or some other disease. Besides, a proprietor who provides setups that are anything other than spotless deserves to be reprimanded.

15. *Never eat when you're upset, nervous, or angry.* These negative emotions have a direct effect on your digestion. Negative mental attitudes can constrict the digestive tract and cause rhythmic contractions of the intestines and colon, resulting in cramps, diarrhea, and/or severe indigestion. Rather, you should wait to eat until your emotions have calmed.

16. *Limit sweets.* If you must have frequent goodies, munch on sunflower seeds, yogurt, granola bars, raisins, almonds, and the like. If you insist on topping off a meal with dessert, make it fresh fruit compotes or pies instead of cakes with rich frostings or gooey sweets.

17. *Limit alcoholic beverages.* This is self-explanatory.

18. *Be aware of your body's acid/alkaline balance.*

19. *Drink eight glasses of water per day.*

20. *Get at least eight hours of sleep a night and analyze your dreams.*

21. *Accept others as they are. Accept life.*

22. *Love yourself.* This last rule may sound a bit pretentious, but you cannot maintain physical health while harboring feelings of inferiority, inadequacy, ugliness, and the like. Good health is the direct result of good *thoughts.* Love must first fill the vessel within the self before it can overflow and encompass that which is without (your physical body).

THE EARTHWAY KITCHEN

The Earthway kitchen can be found in everyone's home, whether you live in an apartment or mobile home, condominium or houseboat. An Earthway kitchen is not solely the room in which you cook; it is a healthful way of cooking.

Food preparation can become so routine one begins to feel like an automaton going through the steps. This can make us thoughtless and lead to haphazard shortcuts. Many of these can be dangerous.

There are basic procedures you can follow to ensure a healthy kitchen. Some of these kitchen hints are quite common, but some will be new to you. All combine to make good healthy kitchen sense.

It's important to perceive your kitchen as a very special room of the home. As such, it demands a certain measure of attention to insure against health risks created by falling into habit, nonchalance, or shortcuts. Food preparation and the state of the entire preparation area need to be as healthful as possible. This is a minimum standard we all expect in the restaurants we frequent. We should expect no less in our own home.

Here are some Earthway kitchen hints:

1. Wash hands thoroughly before any food preparation.
2. When drawing tap water, allow it to run for a minute before filling a glass. This removes water with lead buildup accumulated in plumbing pipes.
3. Always thoroughly wash poultry before preparing it. Wash all counter surfaces with which the meat has come in contact. Likewise, wash anything you've touched with your meat-contaminated hands. Thoroughly wash hands with soap and water when done.
4. Never use a wooden butcher block or cutting surface. Food particles remain in the cut surfaces and breed germs.
5. Wooden kitchen utensils retain food particles that can also breed germs. Use Teflon or stainless steel, never aluminum or wood.
6. Store chopped onions and garlic in *glass* containers or jars. Plastic containers will retain odors.
7. An open box of baking soda placed in the refrigerator will help to absorb food odors.
8. Wash all fruit and vegetables before eating.
9. Wash can lids before opening. Otherwise, dirt particles will contaminate the contents during opening. Also, rodents and insects have been known to skitter across stocked foods either in the manufacturing plant or in private cupboards. These critters may have left more than dirt particles behind in the wake of their passing.
10. Before eating, mentally thank your food for the Give-Away of its life force.
11. Allow enough time for meals. Never eat when rushed or upset. Mealtimes should take place in a relaxing and pleasant atmosphere.
12. If you use Teflon cooking/baking utensils, replace them whenever the coating is broken through or worn off.
13. Clean tops of salt and pepper shakers daily.

14. When washing forks, clean well down *between* the tines.

15. Keep pets off kitchen surfaces. This may sound ridiculous, but there's many a bird cage cleaned in the kitchen, and more than one cat considers it his right to meander on kitchen counters. Folks love their animals, but they don't think about where those cute little paws have been.

16. Never leave leftover food out after the meal has been concluded. Take the time to properly store it away (especially meat).

17. Keep all foods covered. If you leave out your stick of butter, be sure the dish has a cover. Flies lay their eggs in food. Such exposed foodstuffs can be contaminated by various sources, including airborne particles.

18. Always use a *clean* spoon each time you taste-test while cooking. I've even seen TV cooks take a taste from a spoon and then return it to the pot! This is definitely *not* good kitchen hygiene.

19. Frequently examine all household plants placed in the kitchen area. They can become bug infested without your noticing.

20. If you wash and dry dishes by hand, be sure there is a *separate* dish towel and hand towel. A towel people wipe their hands on should *not* be the same one used to dry the clean dishes. Take out clean towels daily.

21. Remove all cellophane-wrapped grocery edibles from their original store packaging right after bringing them home. Fresh fruits and vegetables will go rotten faster if left wrapped.

22. Never refreeze any edibles.

23. Don't purchase or eat green-skinned potatoes.

24. Don't store medicines in cupboards near or above the stove.

25. Keep a fresh raw potato handy for accidental kitchen burns. By immediately placing a slice of potato on a burn, the burning sensation will be alleviated. Taping the potato over the injury will help to heal the wound.

26. Keep a fire extinguisher in the kitchen. Make sure it's rated for kitchen-type fires. Make sure everyone knows how to use it. Do routine refresher sessions with the family members.

27. Never serve pink poultry. If it's not an opaque white after cooking, then it's underdone. *All* meats need to be thoroughly cooked.

28. Give ice trays a routine washing with soap and hot water.

29. When the freshness of an edible is in doubt (as in meal leftovers or seldom-used refrigerator items), throw it out.

30. Never use strong cleansing solvents in the kitchen. Harmful vapors can be absorbed by foodstuffs. Simple baking soda is a wonderful cleansing agent for most kitchen chores.

31. Keep a bar of antibacterial hand soap in a soap dish on the kitchen sink. Rinse soap bar after each use. Bars of soap should never look dirty, nor should their dishes.

32. Never cook when you're upset. You're an accident waiting to happen.

VITAL SIGNS—THE EARTH'S VITAMINS AND MINERALS

Medically speaking, vital signs are physiological functions that are vital to one's life. These include heart rate and rhythm, blood pressure, respiratory rate, and the like. The word "vital" means any elements essential to the continued functioning of a system. I have thus called this section on vitamins and minerals "Vital Signs" because these substances are vital to our overall health and continued well-being.

Although a book on health wouldn't be complete without some portion devoted to vitamins and minerals, it would almost seem redundant to include it here (in view of the volumes written about it) if it weren't for the additional information No-Eyes shared with me about natural and wild foods.

The question of healthful vitamin and mineral intake has been an issue of many conflicting beliefs over the years. Some recommend the daily ingestion of megavitamins and minerals. Some adhere to the ingestion of only those found in foods eaten.

When I asked No-Eyes if she thought people should regularly take vitamin and mineral supplements, she responded that it depended on the individual. She said that although these nutrients were provided by the Earth Mother in food, some people didn't eat enough of the right varieties to benefit from them, and in this case supplements would appear to be indicated; but that ultimately people needed a physician to evaluate the situation and make qualified recommendations.

With the current tendency toward fad diets and hurried lifestyles, vitamins and minerals have become an issue relegated to the bottom of the priority list after fats, carbohydrates, and cholesterol. Although these three are indeed equally important, it's the vitamins and minerals that can most severely affect your vital signs.

<u>VITAMIN A</u>

What It Does: Vitamin A is essential for the healthy formation of bones, teeth, hair, and skin. It aids in the repair of bodily tissues and organs; maintains normal night vision; regulates the amount of moisture in the mucous linings of the throat, nose, lungs, and mouth; aids in the formation of rich blood; helps the digestive system to assimilate proteins properly; and acts as an antioxidant.

Deficiency Symptoms: loose teeth, gum disease, frequent infections, night blindness, brittle hair and nails, dry skin, sinus problems, allergies, loss of sense of smell, diarrhea, exhaustion, and loss of appetite.

Best When Taken With: zinc, calcium, and vitamins B-complex, C, D, and E.

Canceling Substances: alcohol, coffee, mineral oil, and excessive iron.

Food Sources for Vitamin A:

CEREAL, FLOUR, & BREADS

Banana bread	Raisin bran cereal
Bran flake cereal	Raisin bread
Buckwheat flour	Soy flour
Corn flake cereal	Wheat bran cereal
Cornmeal	Wheat flake cereal
Oat flake cereal	Wheat flour
Oatmeal	Whole wheat bread

DAIRY PRODUCTS

American cheese	Custard
Blue cheese	Eggnog
Butter	Egg yolk
Cheddar cheese	Goat's milk
Cheese sauces	Ice cream
Cottage cheese	Skim milk
Cow's milk	Sour cream
Cream	Swiss cheese
Cream cheese	Yogurt

FRUITS

Agave	Juniper
Apples	Kinnikinnick
Apricots	Lemons
Bananas	Nectarines
Blackberries	Oranges
Blueberries	Papaya
Boysenberries	Peaches
Cantaloupe	Persimmons
Cherries	Pineapple
Dates	Prunes
Elderberries	Raisins
Figs	Raspberries
Gooseberries	Strawberries
Grapefruit	Tangerines
Grapes	Watermelon
Jams/jellies	Yucca

MEATS

Chicken	Goose
Duck	Turkey

NUTS & SEEDS

Cashews	Pumpkin seeds
Hyssop	Saltbush
Mesquite	Sunflower
Pistachios	Walnuts
Pecans	Water lily

SEAFOOD

Clams	Mackerel
Cod	Oysters
Crabmeat	Salmon
Haddock	Sardines
Halibut	Shrimp
Herring	Swordfish
Lobster	Tuna

VEGETABLES

Asparagus	Milkweed
Beets	Mushrooms
Broccoli	Mustard greens
Brussels sprouts	Okra
Cabbage	Olives
Carrots	Onions
Cauliflower	Parsley
Celery	Peas
Collard greens	Peppers
Coltsfoot	Pumpkin
Corn	Radishes
Cucumber	Reindeer moss
Dandelion	Rhubarb
Eggplant	Sauerkraut
Fireweed	Sorrel
Green beans	Spinach
Lamb's-quarter	Squash
Leeks	Sweet potatoes
Lentils	Tomatoes
Lettuce	Turnip greens
Lima beans	Watercress

VITAMIN B COMPLEX

What It Does: The group of vitamins known as B complex includes B_1 (thiamine), B_2 (riboflavin), B_3 (niacin), B_6 (pyridoxine), B_{12} (cyanocobalamin), B_{13} (orotic acid), B_{15} (pangamic acid), B_{17} (laetrile), biotin, choline, folic acid, inositol, PABA (para-aminobenzoic acid), and pantothenic acid.

The B-complex group of vitamins is important for converting carbohydrates into glucose, which, in turn, the body burns in order to produce energy. The B complex serves as the body's regulator for proper metabolism and nervous system functioning, healthy skin, hair, eyes, and liver. It maintains normal functioning of the gastrointestinal tract.

Deficiency Symptoms: irritability, depression, hair loss, acne, poor appetite, exhaustion, insomnia, dry skin, constipation, and anemia.

Best When Taken With: not applicable.

Canceling Substances: alcohol, coffee, contraceptive pills, stress, excessive sugar, sleeping medication, and prescriptions containing sulfa.

Food Sources for the B Complex: All the above elements of B complex except B_{17} (laetrile) can be found in brewer's yeast and whole-grain cereals.

VITAMIN B_1 (THIAMINE)

What It Does: Vitamin B_1 is necessary for regulating the appetite and the body's assimilation of food. It converts carbohydrates into glucose and insulates the nerves. B_1 improves the brain's functioning by increasing the learning capacity. It is the vitamin responsible for maintaining good pulmonary and gastrointestinal muscle tone. It maintains healthful eyes, hair, liver, and mouth conditions. It relieves dental pain and quickens the healing process.

Deficiency Symptoms: impaired growth of children, weakness, exhaustion, loss of appetite, numbness in hands and/or feet, nervousness, shortness of breath, constipation, cardiac dysfunctions, depression, and forgetfulness.

Best When Taken With: manganese and vitamins B complex, C, and E.

Canceling Substances: alcohol, coffee, fever, tobacco, stress, and surgery.

Vitamin B_1 Food Sources:

CEREAL, FLOUR & BREADS

Banana bread	Cornmeal
Barley	Farina
Bran flake cereal	Oat flake cereal
Brewer's yeast	Oatmeal
Brown rice	Pumpernickel bread
Buckwheat flour	Raisin bran cereal
Corn flake cereal	Raisin bread

Rye bread
Soy flour
Wheat bran cereal

Wheat flake cereal
Wheat germ
Whole wheat bread

DAIRY PRODUCTS

Blue cheese
Buttermilk
Cheddar cheese
Cheese sauces
Cottage cheese
Cow's milk
Cream
Custard

Eggnog
Egg yolk
Goat's milk
Ice cream
Parmesan cheese
Skim milk
Sour cream
Yogurt

FRUITS

Apples
Apricots
Bananas
Blackberries
Blueberries
Boysenberries
Cantaloupe
Cherries
Dates
Elderberries
Figs
Grapefruit

Grapes
Oranges
Papaya
Pears
Persimmons
Pineapples
Prunes
Raisins
Raspberries
Saguaro cactus
Strawberries
Watermelon

MEATS

Chicken

Turkey

NUTS & SEEDS

Almonds
Amaranth
Blue cohosh
Brazil nuts
Bulrush
Cashews
Chestnuts
Hazelnuts
Hickory

Peanuts
Pecans
Pistachios
Pumpkin
Purslane
Sesame
Sunflower
Walnuts
White oak

SEAFOOD

Clams
Crabmeat
Flounder

Haddock
Halibut
Lobster

Mackerel	Sardines
Oysters	Shrimp
Perch	Swordfish
Red snapper	Trout
Salmon	Tuna

VEGETABLES

Adder's-tongue	Lettuce
Arrowhead	Mushrooms
Asparagus	Mustard greens
Beets	Onions
Broccoli	Potatoes
Brussels sprouts	Parsley
Burdock root	Parsnips
Cabbage	Peas
Carrot	Peppers
Cattail	Plantain
Cauliflower	Purslane
Celery	Reindeer moss
Coltsfoot	Sassafras
Corn	Soybean
Dandelion	Spinach
Eggplant	Squash
Feverbush	Squawberry vine
Fireweed	Tomatoes
Green beans	Tumbleweed
Horsetail	Turnip greens
Kidney beans	Watercress
Lamb's-quarter	Wild garlic
Leeks	Yerba santa
Lentils	Yucca

VITAMIN B$_2$ (RIBOFLAVIN)

What It Does: Vitamin B$_2$ is essential for the proper metabolism of fats, carbohydrates, and proteins. It must be present for enzymes to function properly to provide adequate oxygen to all the cells. B$_2$ is necessary for antibody and red-blood-cell formation, and it maintains healthy skin, hair, eyes, nails, and liver.

Deficiency Symptoms: dizziness, dermatitis, mouth cankers, inflammation of the tongue, flakes of skin around nose and forehead, excessive loss of hair, poor digestion, and eye problems.

Best When Taken With: phosphorus, vitamin B complex, and C.

Canceling Substances: alcohol, coffee, sugars, and tobacco.

Vitamin B₂ Food Sources:

CEREAL, FLOUR & BREADS

Barley   Rye bread
Brewer's yeast   Soy flour
Corn flake cereal   Wheat flake cereal
Oat flake cereal   Wheat germ
Oatmeal   Whole wheat bread

DAIRY PRODUCTS

American cheese   Custard
Blue cheese   Eggnog
Buttermilk   Egg yolk
Cheddar cheese   Goat's milk
Cheese sauces   Ice cream
Cottage cheese   Parmesan cheese
Cow's milk   Skim milk
Cream   Sour cream
Cream cheese   Yogurt

FRUITS

Apricots   Prunes
Avocados   Raisins
Bananas   Raspberries
Blueberries   Serviceberries
Boysenberries   Solomon's seal
Cherries   Strawberries
Chokecherries   Tangerines
Elderberries   Watermelon
Figs

MEATS

Chicken   Goose
Duck   Turkey

NUTS & SEEDS

Almonds   Pumpkin
Butternuts   Sesame
Cashews   Shepherd's purse
Chestnuts   Sunflower
Peanuts   Walnuts

SEAFOOD

Clams	Mackerel
Cod	Oysters
Crabmeat	Perch
Flounder	Salmon
Haddock	Sardines
Halibut	Shrimp
Herring	Swordfish
Kelp	Trout
Lobster	Tuna

VEGETABLES

Broccoli	Okra
Brussels sprouts	Parsnips
Cauliflower	Peas
Chickweed	Potatoes
Collard greens	Pumpkin
Corn	Purslane
Dandelion greens	Sorrel
Fireweed	Soybeans
Green peppers	Spinach
Lamb's-quarter	Squash
Leeks	Turnip greens
Lentils	White cedar
Lima beans	Yampa
Mushrooms	Yellow beans
Mustard greens	

VITAMIN B₃ (NIACIN)

What It Does: Niacin is important for reducing blood cholesterol, regulating the proper metabolism of the fat-carbohydrate-protein cycle, insulating the nerves, and the maintenance of healthy skin and digestive system functioning.

Deficiency Symptoms: dermatitis, muscle soreness or cramping, exhaustion, insomnia, indigestion, mental disturbances, mouth sores, loss of appetite, and skin dryness.

Best When Taken With: phosphorus and vitamins B_1 and C.

Canceling Substances: alcohol, coffee, excessive sugars and starches, and antibiotics.

Niacin Food Sources:

CEREAL, FLOUR & BREADS

Amaranth flour	Farina
Barley	Oat flake cereal
Bran flake cereal	Oatmeal
Bromegrass meal	Rice flake cereal
Brown rice	Rye bread
Buckwheat	Soy flour
Burdock flour	Wheat flake cereal
Corn flake cereal	Wheat germ
Cornmeal	Whole wheat bread

DAIRY PRODUCTS

American cheese	Egg yolk
Cheddar cheese	Goat's milk
Cottage cheese	Ice cream
Cow's milk	Swiss cheese
Custard	Yogurt
Eggnog	

FRUITS

Apricots	Juniper
Bananas	Oranges
Barberry	Peaches
Blackberries	Pineapples
Blueberries	Prunes
Boysenberries	Raisins
Cherries	Raspberries
Dates	Saguaro cactus
Grapefruit	Strawberries
Grapes	

MEATS

Chicken	Goose
Duck	Turkey

NUTS & SEEDS

Agave	Piñon
Almonds	Pistachios
Amaranth	Pumpkin
Cashews	Sesame
Hyssop	Sunflower
Peanuts	Walnuts

SEAFOOD

Cod	Haddock
Crabmeat	Kelp
Flounder	Lobster

Mackerel	Shrimp
Oysters	Swordfish
Perch	Trout
Salmon	Tuna

VEGETABLES

Adder's-tongue	Mustard greens
Amaranth	Navy beans
Asparagus	Nettle
Breadroot	Okra
Broccoli	Onions
Brussels sprouts	Parsley
Bulrush	Plantain
Burdock	Potatoes
Carrots	Sorrel
Cattail	Soybeans
Cauliflower	Spring beauty
Coltsfoot	Squash
Corn	Tumbleweed
Green peppers	Watercress
Lamb's-quarter	Wild leek
Mushrooms	Yampa

VITAMIN B_6 (PYRIDOXINE)

What It Does: Vitamin B_6 is essential for the regulation of fat, carbohydrate, and protein metabolism; it is necessary for the production of antibodies and red blood cells; it helps digestion; and it is necessary for proper assimilation of vitamin B_{12}. B_6 also aids in the body's regulation of potassium and sodium.

Deficiency Symptoms: dermatitis, nervousness, hair loss, acne, dry lips, arthritis, and learning disabilities.

Best When Taken With: B complex, magnesium, potassium, and pantothenic acid.

Canceling Substances: alcohol, coffee, contraceptive pills, and radiation.

Vitamin B_6 Food Sources:

CEREAL, FLOUR & BREADS

Barley	Farina
Bran flake cereal	Oat flake cereal
Corn flake cereal	Oatmeal

Pumpernickel bread	Wheat bran
Raisin bran cereal	Wheat flake cereal
Raisin bread	Wheat germ
Rice cereal	Whole wheat bread

DAIRY

American cheese	Eggnog
Buttermilk	Egg yolk
Cheddar cheese	Goat's milk
Cottage cheese	Skim milk
Cow's milk	Sour cream
Cream	Swiss cheese
Cream cheese	Yogurt

FRUITS

Agave	Grapes
Apples	Jams/jellies
Apricots	Nectarines
Bananas	Oranges
Blackberries	Peaches
Blueberries	Pears
Cantaloupe	Pineapples
Cherries	Raisins
Dates	Raspberries
Figs	Strawberries
Grapefruit	Watermelons

MEATS

Fowl

NUTS & SEEDS

Almonds	Peanuts
Brazil nuts	Walnuts

SEAFOOD

Clams	Perch
Crabmeat	Salmon
Halibut	Sardines
Mackerel	Smelt

VEGETABLES

Angelica	Brussels sprouts
Asparagus	Cabbage
Bergamot	Carrots
Blue cohosh	Cattail

Cauliflower	Onions
Celery	Parsley
Corn	Potatoes
Cucumber	Pumpkin
Dewberry	Rhubarb
Eggplant	Saguaro cactus
Green peppers	Sauerkraut
Hemlock	Soybeans
Hyssop	Spinach
Meadow fern	Squash
Mushrooms	Turnip greens
Mustard greens	Yampa
Okra	Yucca

VITAMIN B$_{12}$ (CYANOCOBALAMIN)

What It Does: Vitamin B$_{12}$ is essential in regulating fat, carbohydrate, and protein metabolism, important for the maintenance of healthy cells and nervous systems, is necessary for the formation of red blood cells, and aids in the body's assimilation of iron.

Deficiency Symptoms: poor appetite, nervousness, anemia, general tiredness, leg weakness, speaking difficulties, and brain damage.

Best When Taken With: potassium and vitamins B$_6$ and C.

Canceling Substances: alcohol, coffee, laxatives, tobacco, and contraceptive pills.

Vitamin B$_{12}$ Food Sources:

CEREAL, FLOUR & BREADS

Corn flake cereal	Cornmeal

DAIRY PRODUCTS

American cheese	Eggnog
Buttermilk	Egg yolk
Cheddar cheese	Goat's milk
Cottage cheese	Skim milk
Cow's milk	Swiss cheese
Cream	Yogurt
Cream cheese	

FRUITS

Feverbush	Serviceberry

MEATS
Chicken

NUTS & SEEDS
Amaranth   Piñon

SEAFOOD
Crabmeat   Lobster

VEGETABLES
Adder's-tongue   Peas
Corn   Spring beauty

VITAMIN C (ASCORBIC ACID)

What It Does: Vitamin C strengthens blood vessels; aids in the formation and maintenance of healthy gums, teeth, and bones; aids in the assimilation of iron; and helps the body's overall resistance to infections. It aids in protecting vitamins within the body so they can properly be assimilated. Vitamin C is instrumental in the healing of skin wounds and burns. It has an anticancer effect, assists in removing toxic heavy metals from the body, reduces oxidized cholesterol, and acts as an antioxidant.

Deficiency Symptoms: muscular weakness, bleeding gums, low infection resistance, slow fracture and wound healing, tendencies toward bruising easily, anemia, loss of appetite, swollen joints, and nosebleeds.

Best When Taken With: calcium and magnesium.

Canceling Substances: aspirin, antibiotics, cortisone, stress, tobacco, sulfa drugs, baking soda, and copper cooking utensils.

Vitamin C Food Sources:

CEREAL, FLOUR & BREADS
Amaranth flour   Raisin bran cereal
Bran flake cereal   Saltbush flour
Corn flake cereal   Yampa flour
Oat flake cereal

DAIRY PRODUCTS
Cow's milk   Ice Cream
Cream   Skim milk
Goat's milk   Yogurt

FRUITS

Apples	Lemons
Apricots	Muskmelon
Bananas	Oranges
Blackberries	Papaya
Blueberries	Peaches
Boysenberries	Pears
Cantaloupe	Pineapples
Cherries	Prickly pear
Feverbush	Prunes
Figs	Pumpkins
Gooseberries	Raspberries
Grapefruit	Strawberries
Grapes	Watermelon

MEATS

Chicken	Turkey

NUTS & SEEDS

Amaranth	Peanuts
Brazil nuts	Piñon
Hazelnuts	Saltbush

SEAFOOD

Clams	Herring
Crabmeat	Kelp
Flounder	Lobster
Haddock	Oysters
Halibut	Tuna

VEGETABLES

Arrowhead	Mustard greens
Asparagus	Peas
Broccoli	Pine needles
Brussels sprouts	Potatoes
Cabbage	Pumpkin
Carrots	Sorrel
Cauliflower	Soybeans
Collard greens	Spinach
Coltsfoot	Squash
Corn	Tomatoes
Dandelion greens	Turnip greens
	Watercress

VITAMIN D (CHOLECALCIFEROL)

What It Does: Vitamin D is essential for bone and teeth formation in children. It maintains a healthy nervous system and facilitates normal blood clotting. It is necessary for the body's assimilation of phosphorus and calcium, and it aids in the functioning of the thyroid gland.

Deficiency Symptoms: rickets in children, loss of energy, phosphorus retention within the kidneys, myopia, diarrhea, nervousness, poor metabolism, diabetes, and poor tooth formation.

Best When Taken With: calcium, phosphorus, and vitamins A and C.

Canceling Substances: mineral oil

Special Note: When some vitamins are taken in doses that are in great excess of our bodies' needs, they accumulate within the system. This buildup results in an actual poisoning and creates a highly toxic condition that evidences itself in a variety of harmful symptoms.

The symptoms of toxic overdose of Vitamin D are nausea, vomiting, dizziness, loss of appetite, frequent urination, calcification of the blood vessels and heart tissue, and anorexia.

Vitamin D Food Sources:

CEREAL, FLOUR & BREADS

Amaranth bread	Corn flake cereal
Banana bread	Fireweed flour
Bran flake cereal	Horsetail flour
Bromegrass meal	Raisin bran cereal

DAIRY PRODUCTS

Butter	Egg yolk
Cow's milk	Skim milk
Eggnog	

FRUITS

Bananas	Saguaro cactus

MEATS
Chicken

NUTS & SEEDS

Amaranth	Horsetail
Bromegrass	

SEAFOOD

Fish liver oils	Sardines
Salmon	Tuna

VEGETABLES

Amaranth	Fireweed
Breadroot	Milkweed

VITAMIN E (TOCOPHEROL)

What It Does: Vitamin E is instrumental in slowing down the aging process, increasing male potency, protecting the body's retention of fat-soluble vitamins, and maintaining healthy muscles and nerves. It dilates the blood vessels, protects the adrenal and pituitary hormones, and prevents edema. Vitamin E is important for the body's defense against the poisoning pollutants in foodstuffs and from the elements. It aids in the prevention of miscarriages.

Deficiency Symptoms: dull hair, impotency, miscarriages, heart disease, enlarged prostate, kidney and liver damage, gastrointestinal dysfunctions, infant anemia, male sterility, and cancer.

Best When Taken With: manganese, phosphorus, selenium, and vitamins A, B, and C.

Canceling Substances: contraceptive pills, chlorine, and mineral oils.

Special Note: For those with heart disease and high blood pressure, excessive Vitamin E will increase the blood pressure and complicate heart problems.

Vitamin E Food Sources:

CEREAL, FLOUR & BREADS

Arrowhead porridge	Mesquite meal
Banana bread	Reindeer moss flour
Brown rice	Rice flake cereal
Cornmeal	Wheat germ
Horsetail flour	

DAIRY PRODUCTS

Cream	Egg yolk
Eggnog	Ice cream

FRUITS
Apples   Oranges
Bananas   Serviceberries
Cantaloupe   Solomon's seal
Grapefruit   Strawberries

MEATS
Fowl

NUTS & SEEDS
Agave   Peanuts
Hyssop   Prickly pear
Mesquite

SEAFOOD
Shrimp

VEGETABLES
Arrowhead   Mustard greens
Cabbage   Parsley
Carrots   Reindeer moss
Corn   Spinach
Mesquite

VITAMIN K (PHYLLOQUINONE)

What It Does: Vitamin K is essential for normal liver functioning. It is an important factor in the body's production of prothrombin, which, in turn, is necessary for the regulation of blood clotting. Vitamin K is also helpful for extending the body's longevity.

Deficiency Symptoms: hemorrhaging, diarrhea, frequent nosebleeds, colitis, prolonged blood-clotting time, and miscarriages.

Best When Taken With: gelatin

Canceling Substances: aspirin, rancid fats, radiation, mineral oils, antibiotics, and air pollution.

Special Note: The symptoms of a toxic overdose of vitamin K are anemia, chest pain, sweating, and hot flashes.

Vitamin K Food Sources:

CEREAL, FLOUR & BREADS
Banana bread   Oatmeal
Cornmeal   Piñon meal

Raisin bran cereal	Wheat germ
Raisin bread	Whole wheat bread

DAIRY PRODUCTS

Cow's milk	Eggnog
Cream	Egg yolk

FRUITS

Bananas	Peaches
Barberry	Raisins
Feverbush	Saguaro cactus
Kinnikinnick	Strawberries
Oranges	Wintergreen

MEATS
Chicken

NUTS & SEEDS

Asparagus	Oak
Coffee bean	Piñon

SEAFOOD
Not applicable

VEGETABLES

Adder's-tongue	Mushrooms
Asparagus	Potatoes
Broccoli	Purslane
Cabbage	Soybeans
Carrots	Spring beauty
Cauliflower	Tomatoes
Corn	Tumbleweed
Green beans	Watercress
Miner's lettuce	Water lily

FOLIC ACID

What It Does: Folic acid is necessary for the healthy formation of red blood cells. It is important for the formation of nucleic acid, which promotes normal cell growth and reproduction. It helps the liver function properly and aids in the prevention of intestinal parasites.

Deficiency Symptoms: gastrointestinal disorders, poor assimilation, anemia, learning disabilities, retarded growth, and graying hair.

Best When Taken With: biotin, pantothenic acid, and vitamins B_{12} and C.

Canceling Substances: alcohol, coffee, stress, tobacco, sulfa drugs, and streptomycin.

Folic Acid Food Sources:

CEREAL, FLOUR & BREADS

Arrowhead flour
Barley
Bran cereal
Brewer's yeast
Brown rice
Corn flake cereal
Cornmeal
Horsetail flour
Oat flake cereal
Oatmeal
Piñon flour
Rye flour/bread
Soy flour
Wheat flake cereal
Wheat germ
Wild rice
Whole wheat bread

DAIRY PRODUCTS

American cheese
Cheddar cheese
Cottage cheese
Cow's milk
Eggnog
Egg yolk
Goat's milk
Honey

FRUITS

Apples
Apricots
Bananas
Blackberries
Blueberries
Cantaloupe
Cherries
Feverbush
Figs
Grapes
Grapefruit
Juniper
Oranges
Peaches
Pineapples
Raisins
Serviceberries
Strawberries
Watermelon
Wintergreen

MEATS

Chicken
Turkey

NUTS & SEEDS

Agave
Almonds
Barley
Hazelnuts
Peanuts
Pecans
Shepherd's purse
Walnuts
Water lily

SEAFOOD

Clams
Crabmeat
Mackerel
Salmon
Shrimp
Tuna

VEGETABLES

Angelica
Asparagus
Breadroot
Broccoli
Brussels sprouts
Burdock
Cabbage
Calamus
Cauliflower
Coltsfoot
Corn
Eggplant

Endive
Lettuce
Milkweed
Miner's lettuce
Onions
Parsley
Purslane
Sorrel
Spinach
Spring beauty
Wild lettuce

PANTOTHENIC ACID

What It Does: Pantothenic acid is a coenzyme that aids in the assimilation of riboflavin. It stimulates growth, helps in the formation of antibodies, stimulates the adrenal gland's hormone production for healthy skin and nerves, prevents premature aging and cell damage from radiation, and aids arthritis.

Deficiency Symptoms: hair loss, dry, itching skin, kidney problems, vomiting, low blood sugar, respiratory infections, depression, ulcers, constipation, and fatigue.

Best When Taken With: folic acid and vitamins B_6, B_{12}, and C.

Canceling Substances: alcohol, baking soda, coffee, and vinegar.

Pantothenic Acid Food Sources:

CEREAL, FLOUR & BREADS

Arrowhead flour
Barley
Bran flake cereal
Breadroot flour
Brewer's yeast
Brown rice
Buckwheat flour

Cornmeal
Rye bread
Soy flour
Wheat flake cereal
Wheat flour
Wheat germ
Whole wheat bread

DAIRY PRODUCTS

American cheese
Cheddar cheese
Cottage cheese

Cow's milk
Cream
Eggnog

Egg yolk	Ice cream
Goat's milk	Yogurt

FRUITS

Apples	Kinnikinnick
Bananas	Oranges
Cherries	Pineapple
Dates	Raspberries
Elderberries	Serviceberries
Grapefruit	Strawberries
Juniper	Watermelon

MEATS

Chicken	Turkey

NUTS & SEEDS

Agave	Peanuts
Almonds	Piñon
Cashews	Sunflower

SEAFOOD

Clams	Perch
Crabmeat	Salmon
Halibut	Sardines
Lobster	Shrimp
Oysters	

VEGETABLES

Arrowhead	Lentils
Breadroot	Milkweed
Broccoli	Mushrooms
Brussels sprouts	Peas
Cabbage	Potatoes
Calamus	Pumpkin
Cauliflower	Sorrel
Corn	Soybeans
Eggplant	Yampa

BIOTIN

What It Does: Biotin is essential in producing the body's fat, which is required for energy. Biotin aids in the body's assimilation of protein, vitamin B_{12}, folic acid, and pantothenic acid. It is a strong factor in promoting the body's overall growth and is required for healthy muscles, hair, and skin.

Deficiency Symptoms: loss of appetite, exhaustion, muscle aches, dermatitis, insomnia, depression, and poor skin color.

Best When Taken With: folic acid, pantothenic acid, and vitamins B_{12} and C.

Canceling Substances: not applicable.

Biotin Food Sources:

CEREALS, FLOUR & BREADS
Amaranth	Fireweed
Brewer's yeast	Piñon
Corn flake cereal	Shepherd's purse
Cornmeal	Soy flour

DAIRY PRODUCTS
American cheese	Cow's milk
Cheddar cheese	Egg yolk

FRUITS
Apples	Peaches
Bananas	Raisins
Cantaloupe	Serviceberries
Grapefruit	Strawberries
Oranges	Watermelon

MEATS
Poultry

NUTS & SEEDS
Agave	Pecan
Almond	Piñon
Hazelnuts	Walnuts
Peanuts	

SEAFOOD
Herring	Salmon
Mackerel	Sardines
Oysters	Tuna

VEGETABLES
Agave	Carrots
Arrowhead	Cauliflower
Asparagus	Corn
Bean sprouts	Feverbush
Beets	Green beans
Blue cohosh	Kinnikinnick
Borage	Lentils
Bromegrass	Mushrooms
Bulrush	Onions
Cabbage	Peas

Reindeer moss	Spring beauty
Shepherd's purse	Sweet potatoes
Soybeans	Turnip greens

PARA-AMINOBENZOIC ACID (PABA)

What It Does: Para-aminobenzoic acid acts as a coenzyme in the breakdown and utilization of proteins. It helps produce folic acid, aids in the body's formation of healthy red blood cells, helps maintain healthy hair and skin pigmentation. It also is a natural sunscreen.

Deficiency Symptoms: digestive disorders, chronic headaches, depression, exhaustion, anemia, and nervousness.

Best When Taken With: folic acid and vitamin C.

Canceling Substances: alcohol, coffee, and sulfa drugs.

Special Note: The toxic overdose symptoms of para-aminobenzoic acid are kidney disorders, heart and liver failure, nausea, and vomiting.
   The sources of food with the highest amount of PABA are brewer's yeast, molasses, and wheat germ.

INOSITOL

What It Does: Inositol is essential in helping the body reduce its cholesterol content in the blood. It aids in the formation of lecithin and is necessary for healthy hair growth. It is vital for the formation of healthy cells in the intestines, eyes, and bones.

Deficiency Symptoms: high cholesterol levels, constipation, eye disorders, and skin problems.

Best When Taken With: choline, phosphorus, and vitamins B_{12} and C.

Canceling Substances: alcohol, antibiotics, coffee, and sugars.

Inositol Food Sources:

CEREAL, FLOUR & BREADS

Amaranth flour	Corn grits
Bromegrass meal	Horsetail flour
Brown rice	Soy flour
Cattail flour	Wheat flake cereal

Wheat flour	Whole wheat bread
Wheat germ	

DAIRY PRODUCTS
Cow's milk

FRUITS

Apples	Oranges
Cherries	Raisins
Feverbush	Strawberries
Grapefruit	Watermelons
Kinnikinnick	

MEATS
Chicken

NUTS & SEEDS

Amaranth	Prickly pear
Bromegrass	Water lily
Peanuts	

SEAFOOD
Salmon

VEGETABLES

Arrowhead	Nettle
Beets	Peas
Cabbage	Potatoes
Carrots	Soybeans
Cattail	Turnip greens
Cauliflower	Wild rice
Lima beans	Yampa

<u>CHOLINE</u>

What It Does: Choline is important for the proper metabolism of the body's fat and cholesterol. It is vital in keeping the liver and kidney free from fat, and it insulates the nerves and aids in the transmission of nerve impulses. Choline helps in the regulation of the gall bladder, the formation of lecithin, and maintenance of a normally functioning thymus gland.

Deficiency Symptoms: cirrhosis of the liver, fatty liver deposits, bleeding stomach ulcers, hemorrhaging of the kidneys, high blood pressure, and hardening of the arteries.

Best When Taken With: inositol and vitamins A and B_{12}.

Canceling Substances: alcohol, coffee, and sugars.

Choline Food Sources:

CEREAL, FLOUR & BREADS
Brewer's yeast	Soy flour
Brown rice	Wheat flour
Cornmeal	Wheat germ
Fireweed flour	Whole wheat bread

DAIRY PRODUCTS
Cheddar cheese	Egg yolk
Cow's milk	Goat's milk
Eggnog	

FRUITS
Apples	Molasses
Feverbush	Saguaro cactus
Grapefruit	

MEATS
Chicken

NUTS & SEEDS
Peanuts	Pecans

SEAFOOD
Not applicable

VEGETABLES
Adder's-tongue	Green beans
Amaranth	Hyssop
Asparagus	Lentils
Bean sprouts	Mesquite
Bulrush	Mustard greens
Cabbage	Peas
Cattail	Potatoes
Chickpeas	Salsify

IRON

What It Does: Iron is an essential mineral for the regulation of the body's protein metabolism and the formation of hemoglobin in the blood and myoglobin in the muscle tissues. It aids in the body's ability to resist infections and flu viruses.

Deficiency Symptoms: respiratory difficulties, brittle and weak nails, anemia, fatigue, constipation, and frequent colds.

Best When Taken With: copper, folic acid, phosphorus, and vitamin C.

Canceling Substances: coffee, tea, lack of hydrochloric acid, and the excessive intake of phosphorus and zinc.

Special Note: The symptoms of toxic overdose of iron are diabetes, pancreas dysfunction, and cirrhosis of the liver.

Iron Food Sources:

CEREAL, FLOUR & BREADS
Amaranth bread	Mesquite flour
Arrowhead bread	Oat flake cereal
Barley	Oatmeal
Bran flake cereal	Piñon flour
Breadroot flour	Raisin bran cereal
Bulrush flour	Raisin bread
Burdock flour	Rye bread
Cattail flour	Soy flour
Corn flake cereal	Wheat flake cereal
Cornmeal	Wheat germ
Farina	Whole wheat bread

DAIRY PRODUCTS
All cheeses	Egg yolk
Cow's milk	Ice cream
Custard	Skim milk
Eggnog	

FRUITS
Apples	Oranges
Apricots	Papaya
Bananas	Peaches
Blackberries	Pears
Blueberries	Pineapple
Boysenberries	Prunes
Chokecherries	Pumpkin
Dates	Raisins
Elderberries	Raspberries
Grapefruit	Saguaro cactus
Grapes	Serviceberries
Juniper	Strawberries
Kinnikinnick	Watermelon
Nectarines	

MEATS
Chicken   Goose
Duck   Turkey

NUTS & SEEDS
Almonds   Pecans
Amaranth   Piñon
Brazil nuts   Pistachios
Cashews   Pumpkin
Chestnuts   Sesame
Coffee beans   Sunflower
Mesquite   Walnuts
Peanuts

SEAFOOD
Clams   Mackerel
Cod   Oysters
Crabmeat   Perch
Flounder   Salmon
Haddock   Sardines
Halibut   Shrimp
Kelp   Swordfish
Lobster   Tuna

VEGETABLES
Amaranth   Lettuce
Asparagus   Mesquite
Bean sprouts   Miner's lettuce
Broccoli   Mushrooms
Brussels sprouts   Parsley
Cauliflower   Peas
Chickweed   Potatoes
Collard greens   Sorrel
Corn   Soybeans
Dandelion greens   Spinach
Eggplant   Sweet potatoes
Endive   Tomatoes
Lentils   Turnip greens

CALCIUM

What It Does: Calcium effectively interacts with phosphorus to form and
maintain healthy bones and teeth. It aids in the body's normal blood-clotting
ability, regulates the muscle responses and heart rhythms, regulates the
blood's acid/alkaline balance, and maintains normal assimilation of iron

and other vital nutrients within the body's cells. It aids in the prevention of arthritis and rheumatism.

Deficiency Symptoms: teeth and bone malformation, weak bones, muscle cramps, joint pain, insomnia, slow blood clotting, heart palpitations, and excessive tooth decay.

Best When Taken With: iron, manganese, phosphorus, magnesium, and vitamins C, D, and F.

Canceling Substances: excessively alkaline system, lack of vitamins C and D, stress, lack of magnesium, chocolate, and the lack of exercise.

Special Note: The symptom of a toxic overdose of calcium is a condition called hypercalcemia, which is excessive calcium deposits within the body's soft tissues, bones, and organs. Another toxic symptom related to excessive calcium is renal failure.

The food sources for calcium are too numerous to list. However, especially high quantities are found in all grains, dairy products, meats, and seafoods.

MAGNESIUM

What It Does: Magnesium is an essential mineral for the healthful regulation of the body's acid/alkaline balance. It aids the body in assimilating the B complex and C and E vitamins, helps strengthen muscle functioning including the heart, aids in strong bone formation, and is an effective nerve insulator.

Deficiency Symptoms: heart disease, calcification of the blood vessels, kidney stones, nervousness, loss of muscular control, and vascular blood clots.

Best When Taken With: proteins, calcium, phosphorus, and vitamins C and D.

Canceling Substances: alcohol

Special Note: The symptoms of toxic overdose associated with magnesium are stroke, brittle bones, epileptic seizure, cardiac disturbances, and respiratory failure.

Magnesium Food Sources:

CEREAL, FLOUR & BREADS

Amaranth flour	Pumpernickel bread
Barley	Raisin bran cereal
Bran flake cereal	Raisin bread
Breadroot flour	Rye bread
Brown rice	Soy flour
Buckwheat flour	Wheat bran cereal
Corn flake cereal	Wheat flake cereal
Cornmeal	Wheat germ
Farina	Whole wheat bread
Mesquite meal	

DAIRY PRODUCTS

American cheese	Goat's milk
Cheddar cheese	Ice cream
Cow's milk	Parmesan cheese
Cream	Skim milk
Eggnog	Swiss cheese
Egg yolk	

FRUITS

Apples	Grapes
Bananas	Nectarines
Blackberries	Oranges
Blueberries	Peaches
Boysenberries	Pineapples
Cherries	Prickly pear
Chokecherries	Prunes
Dates	Raisins
Feverbush	Raspberries
Figs	Serviceberries
Gooseberries	Strawberries
Grapefruit	Watermelon

MEATS

Chicken	Turkey

NUTS & SEEDS

Agave	Hyssop
Almonds	Peanuts
Amaranth	Pecans
Brazil nuts	Piñon
Cashews	Pistachios
Hickory	Sesame

| Shepherd's purse | Walnut |
| Sunflower | |

SEAFOOD

Crabmeat	Oyster
Flounder	Salmon
Kelp	Shrimp
Lobster	Tuna

VEGETABLES

Adder's-tongue	Fireweed
Amaranth	Mesquite
Arrowhead	Mustard greens
Beets	Nettle
Breadroot	Onion
Broccoli	Parsnips
Brussels sprouts	Peas
Bulrush	Plantain
Carrots	Potatoes
Cattail	Salsify
Cauliflower	Sorrel
Collard greens	Squash
Coltsfoot	Tomatoes
Corn	Turnip greens
Eggplant	

PHOSPHORUS

What It Does: Phosphorus is an important mineral that aids in the effective utilization of the body's carbohydrate-fat-protein cycle. It maintains normal nerve responses, facilitates healthy cell growth and regeneration, and combines with calcium in the formation of strong teeth and bones. Phosphorus regulates the acid/alkaline balance within the blood, and it aids in the glandular regulation of hormones.

Deficiency Symptoms: arthritis, bone and teeth malformation, gum disease, exhaustion, obesity, loss of appetite, nervousness/excitability, and breathing difficulties.

Best When Taken With: calcium, iron, manganese, and the vitamins A and D.

Canceling Substances: excessive sugar intake, aluminum cookware, and the excessive ingestion of iron and magnesium.

Special Note: The symptom of a toxic overdose of phosphorus is renal failure.

Phosphorus can be found in all dairy products, most grains, meats, seafood, nuts, fruits, and vegetables.

POTASSIUM

What It Does: Potassium is an essential mineral that helps regulate the body's proper acid/alkaline ratio. It is important for normal kidney regulation, muscle contractions (including the heart), nerve insulation, and growth regulation.

Deficiency Symptoms: constipation, cardiac arrest, nervousness/excitability, insomnia, slowed heartrate, digestive dysfunctions, general weakness, and dry skin.

Best When Taken With: sodium.

Canceling Substances: alcohol, coffee, diuretics, excessive sugars, prolonged diarrhea, or excessive sweating.

Special Note: The symptoms of a toxic overdose of potassium are muscle paralysis and cardiac disturbances.

Potassium Food Sources:

CEREAL, FLOUR & BREADS
All domestic and wild grains

DAIRY PRODUCTS

Cheddar cheese	Eggnog
Cottage cheese	Egg yolk
Cow's milk	Goat's milk
Cream	Ice cream
Cream cheese	Skim milk
Custard	

FRUITS

Apples	Chokecherries
Apricots	Dates
Bananas	Elderberries
Blackberries	Gooseberries
Blueberries	Grapefruit
Boysenberries	Grapes
Cantaloupe	Juniper
Cherries	Lemons

Nectarines
Oranges
Papaya
Peaches
Pears
Pineapple
Prickly pear

Prunes
Raisins
Raspberries
Serviceberries
Strawberries
Watermelon

MEATS

Chicken
Duck

Goose
Turkey

NUTS & SEEDS

Almonds
Amaranth
Cashews
Peanuts

Pecans
Pistachios
Sunflower
Walnuts

SEAFOOD

Clams
Cod
Crabmeat
Flounder
Haddock
Halibut
Kelp
Lobster

Oysters
Perch
Red snapper
Salmon
Sardines
Shrimp
Tuna

VEGETABLES

Agave
Amaranth
Bean sprouts
Beets
Broccoli
Brussels sprouts
Bulrush
Cabbage
Carrots
Cattail
Cauliflower
Collard greens
Coltsfoot
Cucumber
Dandelion greens
Eggplant
Fireweed
Green beans
Green peppers

Lima beans
Miner's lettuce
Mushrooms
Mustard greens
Onions
Parsley
Parsnips
Peas
Potatoes
Pumpkin
Purslane
Spinach
Spring beauty
Squash
Tomatoes
Turnip greens
Wild leeks
Wild lettuce
Wild onions

COPPER

What It Does: Copper is an important mineral that aids in the body's healthy formation of red blood cells. It helps amino acid function, aids in the body's assimilation of vitamin C, and helps in the formation of elastin, which maintains healthy muscle tone and responses.

Deficiency Symptoms: respiration difficulties, weakness, dermatitis, anemia, and edema.

Best When Taken With: iron and zinc.

Canceling Substances: excessive zinc intake and chronic diarrhea.

Special Note: The symptoms of a toxic overdose of copper are abdominal pain, nausea, vomiting, and diarrhea.

Copper Food Sources:

CEREAL, FLOUR & BREADS

Banana bread	Rye bread
Bran flake cereal	Soy flour
Breadroot flour	Wheat flake cereal
Cornmeal	Wheat germ
Oatmeal	Whole wheat bread

DAIRY PRODUCTS

Cheddar cheese	Egg yolk
Cottage cheese	Goat's milk
Cow's milk	Ice cream
Cream	Skim milk
Eggnog	Swiss cheese

FRUITS

Apples	Feverbush
Apricots	Grapefruit
Bananas	Grapes
Blackberries	Oranges
Blueberries	Pears
Cantaloupe	Prunes
Cherries	Raisins
Dates	Strawberries

MEATS

Chicken	Turkey

NUTS & SEEDS

Almonds	Pistachios
Hyssop	Prickly pear
Peanuts	Sesame
Pecans	Sunflower
Piñon	Walnuts

SEAFOOD

Cod	Mackerel
Crabmeat	Oyster
Flounder	Perch
Haddock	Pike
Halibut	Red snapper
Kelp	Salmon
Lobster	Trout

VEGETABLES

Agave	Mushrooms
Breadroot	Parsley
Broccoli	Potatoes
Bulrush	Soybeans
Chickweed	Squash
Eggplant	Sunflower
Hyssop	Tomatoes
Lentils	

IODINE

What It Does: Iodine is an important mineral for the regulation of hormones from the thyroid gland. It is responsible for maintaining healthy skin tone, strong teeth, nails, and hair.

Deficiency Symptoms: dry and dull hair, cold hands and feet, nervousness and excitability, obesity, mental retardation, brittle nails, and heart palpitations.

Best When Taken With: not applicable.

Canceling Substances: excessive ingestion of nuts.

Iodine Food Sources: Trace amounts of iodine can be found in many foods. However, the greatest concentration can be found in fish oil, kelp, salmon, iodized salt, and turkey.

FLUORINE

What It Does: Fluorine is a mineral that aids in the body's proper assimilation of calcium, and it prevents the formation of acid in the mouth. However, excessive fluorine in drinking water may cause adverse physiological effects. Fluorine *is* beneficial, yet it is not the panacea that the dental profession makes it out to be. Please avoid excessive intake of this mineral. It is being added to drinking water, and treatments are given by dental hygienists as a routine part of a six-month checkup. No-Eyes recommends omitting the fluoride treatments and not using toothpastes with it as a component. Again, more is not always better.

Deficiency Symptoms: poor tooth formation and excessive decay.

Best When Taken With: not applicable.

Canceling Substances: insoluble calcium.

Special Note: The symptoms of a toxic overdose of fluorine are discoloration of tooth enamel, mongolism, stunted growth, hardening of ligaments, and functional losses of the heart, liver, and adrenal glands.

THE EARTH MOTHER'S FOOD PANTRY

Whenever I'm in a conversation where the subject of wild foods comes up, I'm amazed to hear how limited people's understanding tends to be. It seems that most people are not aware of the wide variety of edibles our Earth Mother provides us with.

From the bountiful earth soil come seventeen kinds of nuts and seeds, many used to make delicious bread and muffin flour. Coffee substitutes can be brewed from nine different sources. Eleven botanicals make excellent soup, and did you know that there are over thirty-eight sources that can be used for flour? Flavorful teas can be brewed from thirty-six botanicals. The earth supplies over fifty-one varieties of vegetables and seventeen more common fruits. Even butter and chewing gum are reaped from our giving earth. And for those who like to alternate with different flavors in their ceremonial pipes, the Earth Mother provides over seventeen botanicals that can be used in place of tobacco.

I feel wild foods need to be addressed in *Earthway* because so many people are not aware of the bounty that nature so generously provides. And that is as it should be, for the earth is indeed our mother. She provides well. How well? Turn the page and take a peek into the cupboards of *her* pantry.

(These foods can be obtained through your local health food store or through those listed in the Appendix.)

NUTS AND SEEDS

(roasted nuts are, of course, *un*salted)

Agave (bud) roasted
Almond (nut) raw or roasted
Amaranth (seed) roasted
Asparagus (seed) roasted
Barley (seed) roasted
Beech (nut) raw or roasted
Black Walnut (nut) roasted
Chestnut (nut) roasted
Hazelnut (nut) raw or roasted
Hyssop (seed) raw or roasted
Lamb's-quarter (seed) roasted
Piñon (nut) roasted
Prickly pear (seed) roasted
Pumpkin (seed) roasted
Shepherd's purse (seed) roasted
Sunflower (seed) raw or roasted
Water lily (seed) roasted

COFFEE SUBSTITUTES

(all of the following coffee substitutes are prepared by being first roasted, then ground)

Asparagus (seed)
Barley (seed)
Beech (nut)
Blue cohosh (seed)
Chicory (root)
Dandelion (root)
Douglas fir (needle)
Juniper (berry)
Sunflower (seed)

SOUPS

Angelica (leaf) boiled
Breadroot (tuber) boiled
Fireweed (stalk) boiled
Nettle (root) boiled
Pumpkin (pulp) simmered
Reindeer moss (moss) boiled
Sorrel (leaf) boiled
Sunflower (blossom head & seed) boiled
Watercress (leaf) boiled
Wild onion (bulb) simmered
Wild rice (grain) roasted and boiled

STEW FLAVORINGS AND NATURAL ADDITIVES

Angelica (leaf) simmered
Barberry (berry) dried & simmered
Bayberry (leaf) dried & simmered
Bergamot (leaf) dried & boiled
Birch (sap) boiled
Burdock (root) dried & simmered
Cherry (berry) raw & boiled
Cherry birch (inner bark) simmered
Coltsfoot (leaf) dried & burned for salt
Crab apple (fruit) raw & boiled
Feverbush (berry) dried & ground
Hickory (sap) boiled
Kinnikinnick (berry) dried & simmered
Maple (sap) boiled
Milkweed (buds) dried & steeped
Sarsaparilla (root) dried & simmered
Sassafras (leaf) dried & steeped
Shepherd's purse (seed) raw & boiled
Sorrel (leaf) raw & boiled
White oak (acorn) roasted & ground
Wild garlic (bulb) raw or roasted
Wild ginger (blossom) boiled
            (root) dried & ground
Wild mint (leaf) raw & steeped
Wild mustard (leaf) dried & ground
Wild onion (bulb) raw or simmered
Wintergreen (berry) raw & boiled

BREAD FLOUR

Alfalfa (stem) dried & ground
Amaranth (seed) roasted & ground
Arrowhead (tuber) roasted & ground or dried & ground for porridge
Beech (nut & inner bark) roasted & ground
Black walnut (nut) roasted & ground
Breadroot (tuber) roasted & ground
Bromegrass (seed) dried & ground for meal
Bulrush (blossom pollen) dried
            (seed) dried & ground
Burdock (root) roasted & ground
Butternut (nut) roasted & ground
Cattail (blossom) dried & ground
            (root) roasted & ground
Chestnut (nut) dried & ground
Fireweed (stalk) roasted & ground
Hemlock (inner bark) roasted & ground
Hickory (nut) roasted & ground
Horsetail (stem) roasted & ground

Jerusalem artichoke (tuber) roasted & ground
Juniper (berry) dried & ground
Lamb's-quarter (seed) roasted & ground
Leek (bulb) roasted & ground
Maize (kernel) roasted & ground
Mesquite (pod) dried & ground
        (seed) roasted & ground for meal
Piñon (nut) roasted & ground for meal
Prickly pear (seed) roasted & ground for porridge
Pumpkin (seed) roasted & ground
Purslane (seed) roasted & ground or dried & ground
Red clover (blossom) dried & ground
Reindeer moss (moss) dried & ground
Saguaro cactus (rind) dried & ground as porridge
Saltbush (seed) roasted & ground
Shepherd's purse (seed) dried & ground
Solomon's seal (root) roasted & ground
Sunflower (seed) roasted & ground
Water lily (root) roasted & ground
        (seed) dried & ground
White oak (acorn) roasted & ground
Wild rose (hip) roasted & ground
Yucca (fruit) roasted & ground

TEAS

Alfalfa (leaf) steeped
Barberry (leaf) steeped
Bergamot (leaf) steeped
Blackberry (leaf) boiled
Blue cohosh (root) boiled
Borage (leaf) steeped
Chamomile (blossom) steeped
Chicory (leaf) steeped
Clover (leaf & blossom) steeped
Coltsfoot (leaf & blossom) steeped
Comfrey (leaf & root) boiled
Dandelion (blossom) boiled
Dewberry (leaf) boiled
Douglas fir (twig) boiled
Elderberry (berry) boiled
Feverbush (leaf & bark) boiled
Goldenrod (leaf & blossom) boiled
Grape (berry) boiled
Ivy (leaf) steeped
Juniper (berry) boiled
Kinnikinnick (leaf) steeped
Meadow fern (leaf) boiled
Mint (leaf) boiled
Nettle (root) boiled

Pennyroyal (leaf) steeped
Pine (needle) crushed & boiled
Piñon (needle) crushed & boiled
Raspberry (berry) boiled
Sarsaparilla (root) boiled
Sassafras (leaf & root) boiled
Squawberry vine (leaf) steeped
Strawberry (berry) boiled
Violet (leaf) steeped
White cedar (twig) boiled
Wild rose (hip) boiled
Witch hazel (leaf) steeped

VEGETABLES

Adder's-tongue (leaf) steamed
                (corm) roasted
Agave (bud) roasted
Alfalfa (sprout) raw
       (twig) boiled
       (leaf) raw or steamed
Amaranth (stem) boiled
         (leaf) steamed
Angelica (stem) boiled
Arrowhead (tuber) raw or roasted
Asparagus (stalk) boiled
Black mustard (whole) boiled
Breadroot (tuber) baked or steamed
Bulrush (shoot) raw or boiled
Burdock (leaf) steamed
        (root) baked
        (shoot) boiled
Cabbage (leaf) raw or steamed
Calamus (shoot) raw or steamed
Chickweed (leaf) steamed
Chicory (leaf) raw or steamed
Coltsfoot (leaf) steamed
Dandelion (leaf) raw
Fireweed (shoot) boiled
         (leaf) raw or steamed
Hyssop (rootstalk) boiled
Jerusalem artichoke (tuber) roasted, baked, or boiled
Kelp (leaf) raw or steamed
Lamb's-quarter (leaf) raw or simmered
Lily (stem) raw
     (leaf) steamed
Maize (kernel) steamed
Mesquite (pod) raw or roasted

Milkweed (shoot) steamed
          (pod) boiled
Miner's lettuce (leaf) raw or steamed
Nettle (leaf) boiled
Parsnip (leaf) raw or steamed
          (root) boiled
          (stem) boiled
Pine (inner bark) raw
Plantain (leaf) raw or steamed
Purslane (leaf) steamed
            (stem) boiled
Raspberry (leaf) steamed
Red clover (blossom) raw or steamed
Salsify (root) roasted
          (leaf) boiled
Shepherd's purse (whole) boiled
Solomon's seal (root) raw
Sorrel (leaf) raw or steamed
Spring beauty (corm) raw or boiled
                (leaf) steamed
Sunflower (blossom head) boiled
Tumbleweed (root) boiled
Violet (leaf) raw or steamed
Watercress (leaf) raw or steamed
Wild garlic (bulb) raw or boiled
Wild leek (bulb) steamed
Wild lettuce (leaf) raw or steamed
Wild onion (bulb) raw or boiled
Wild rice (grain) steamed with fruit
Wintergreen (leaf) raw
Yampa (root) raw or roasted
Yucca (blossom) raw or boiled

FRUITS

Barberry (berry) raw or boiled for jam
          (root) raw
Blueberry (berry) raw or dried for pemmican additive
Cherry (berry) raw or dried for pemmican additive
Chokecherry (berry) raw
Crab apple (fruit) boiled for jelly & sauce
Cranberry (berry) raw or dried for pemmican additive
Feverbush (berry) dried, ground, & used for pepper
Gooseberry (berry) raw or boiled for sauce
Juniper (berry) dried for pemmican additive
Kinnikinnick (berry) raw
Prickly pear (ripe fruit) dried for pemmican additive
                (unripe fruit) boiled for sauce
Saguaro cactus (fruit) raw

Serviceberry (berry) raw or dried for pemmican additive
Solomon's seal (berry) raw or dried for pemmican additive
Wild plum (fruit) raw, boiled for jam, or dried for pemmican additive
Wild rose (hip) raw or boiled for jam
Wintergreen (berry) raw

CHEWING GUM

Chicory (root)
Dandelion (root)
Dogwood (twig)
Indian hemp (stem)
Licorice (root)
Marshmallow (root)
Milkweed (stem)
Plantain (root)
Salsify (stem & root)
White pine (sap)

BUTTER AND OILS

Beech (nut) ground & boiled
Black walnut (nut) ground & boiled
Sunflower (seed) mashed & boiled
White oak (acorn) crushed & boiled
Wintergreen (leaf) crushed & boiled

SMOKING TOBACCO

Angelica (leaf) dried
Clover (blossom) dried for tobacco flavoring
Coltsfoot (leaf) dried
Dogwood (inner bark) dried & ground
Everlasting (leaf) dried & smoked or raw & chewed
Goldenrod (leaf) dried
Henbane (leaf) dried
Jimsonweed (leaf) dried & crushed
Kinnikinnick (leaf) dried & smoked or raw & chewed
Lobelia (leaf) dried
Mullein (leaf) dried
Sassafras (root bark) dried & ground
Sumac (berry) dried & ground
        (leaf & root) dried
Sunflower (leaf) dried
Wild lettuce (leaf) dried
Yarrow (leaf) dried
Yerba santa (leaf) dried & ground

A MEDICINE WOMAN CALLED
EARTH MOTHER
A Guide to Botanical Healing

During the time No-Eyes was teaching me botanical healing, I was frequently confused and frustrated because I was unfamiliar with the terminology she used and I had little field experience. The latter would have been especially useful to me, but No-Eyes had so much she wished to share with me on so many subjects that we rarely had the golden time to go out into the mountains and valleys in search of the plants and herbs we were discussing. This made it more difficult for me in the long run.

This handicap was made more troublesome by the "language of No-Eyes." Her unique terminology and idiosyncratic style of speaking made it all the more difficult for me to follow my lessons. It was a long and arduous labor of love to identify properly the plants she spoke about. Since she neither knew nor cared about the "proper" names of these plants, she would call them by her own names.

There was a sense of logic to her terminology, though. Some plants were classed by fragrance, others by their habitat, shape, blossom time, or season of harvest. I quickly learned that in No-Eyes' lexicon all poisonous plants began with "bad."

And so it was that I had to learn her way of classification first and then work down through the subclasses and place the right names to everything. It would've been so easy to have simply used her unique names, but then *everyone* I tried to share this knowledge with would've been as confused as I was. I could never have completed the task of translating No-Eyes' knowl-

edge had it not been for the generous and wise Native American friends who
have assisted me in the process of straightening out the botanical terms. I
can never thank them enough for their help. They were not nearly as
confused by No-Eyes' terminology as I was; her plant "names" were not
unique unto herself and were indeed quite logical to those who were used to
living close to the earth, for they naturally spoke the Earthway language
themselves.

The following section is a collection of No-Eyes' knowledge concerning
"plant stuff." It does indeed serve as verification of the Earth Mother's
expertise as a wise and well-experienced physician.

AILMENTS AND THEIR BOTANICAL TREATMENTS

Since the beginning of time, people have recognized the healing value
of the various plants, trees, and flowers that grow in profusion around them.
From the flower blossoms of the tropical paradise islands to the mosses and
lichens of the frozen tundra, botanicals have played a major role in healing
arts of both primitive and technically advanced cultures. This is not voodoo
medicine. This is not folktale nonsense. This is real.

Many different plants can have curative effects on the same disease.
However, there are usually a specific few that have a greater effect because of
their chemical makeup. These are the ones that ultimately become the most
well-known treatment or remedy.

In this section, I will share these botanical remedies with you, just as
No-Eyes shared them with me. Please remember, however, that although the
botanicals are a very effective aspect in healing, they are only that—*one*
aspect. As you will see in a later chapter, *total* healing must encompass
many aspects of the Earth Mother's complete bounty. The botanical facet
must be viewed as only one part of the healing whole. To learn herbal
healing is to take but one small step on the road to becoming a full-fledged
Earthway physician. Just as an intern doctor rotates rounds in order to learn
about different fields of medicine, so, too, must the Earthway healer learn
one subject at a time to understand and assimilate properly *all* the facets
Earth Mother has to offer us in the form of Earthway healing.

The lists I've provided you with are easy to use.

1. First, you can look up the disease or discomfort you're concerned
about in this section entitled "Ailments and Their Botanical Treatments."

2. Next, you can look up information about how to apply the botanical
treatment you're interested in pursuing in the chart entitled "Wild Plants
Used by Native Americans," which is organized by plant name (page 116).

3. I recommend that you next check the list entitled "The Dark Side of
Nature" to inform yourself about any potential risks that might be involved
with the botanical treatment you've selected (page 158).

4. Finally, you can check "The Earth Mother's Pharmacy" to see the many ways modern medicine uses natural botanicals as the basis of their own pharmaceutical treatments (page 183).

To help introduce you to botanical healing, in "Ailments and Their Botanical Treatments" I have listed the full range of possible botanical remedies for various illnesses and conditions. However, some of these remedies are more effective than others. Thus, in the "Wild Plants Used by Native Americans" section, I have not repeated all the information in the "Ailments and Their Botanical Treatments" section; rather, in the "Wild Plants" section I have only listed the most effective botanical treatments. (You will also find later in the book, in the "Ailments and Their Gateway Treatments" section—which is the master healing section in the book—that I have refined the list of botanicals even further, listing only the most preferred treatments rather than all those that appear in "Ailments and Their Botanical Treatments" and "Wild Plants Used by Native Americans.")

ABRASIONS

barberry, bayberry, capsicum, comfrey, juniper, olive oil, plantain, sassafras, shepherd's purse.

ABSCESSES

adder's-tongue, alumroot, barberry, bitter root, cabbage, cattail, chicory, chokecherry, frostwort, garlic, goldenseal, Indian hemp, papaya, pine, plantain, prickly pear, puffball, red clover, shepherd's purse, slippery elm, starwort, stonecrop, walnut, wild onion, yucca.

ACIDITY BALANCER

alfalfa, blessed thistle, buckthorn, dandelion, motherwort, mullein, red clover, watercress, yarrow.

ACNE

chaparral, dandelion, elder, garlic, goldenrod, horseradish, juniper, mullein, palma christi, pine, pokeroot, red clover, saffron, sassafras, uva-ursi, walnut.

AFTERBIRTH

capsicum, cotton root, flatspine ragweed, golden ragwort, tansy, valerian, wild lettuce, yarrow.

AGING

alfalfa, black mustard, celery, echinacea, horehound, Indian hemp, mandrake, nettle, red clover, sage, watercress, wintergreen.

AGING SPOTS

black mustard, chaparral, gotu kola, palma christi, red clover, Siberian ginseng, Solomon's seal, white cabbage, white pond lily.

ALCOHOLISM

angelica, elecampane, goldenseal, hops, maize, mullein, parsley, plantain, red clover, Rocky Mountain maple, sage, wormwood, yellow dock.

ALLERGIES

aspen, black mustard, blessed thistle, cinquefoil, fireweed, goldenseal, hops, horehound, lichen, lobelia, mandrake, mountain ash, pleurisy root, pokeroot, skullcap, valerian root, wild lettuce, wild licorice, wild onion.

ANEMIA

alfalfa, aspen, bayberry, black mustard, chamomile, chicory, dandelion, fireweed, Indian lettuce, lobelia, mullein, pine, pokeroot, purslane, red clover, saxifrage, scurvy grass, serviceberry, shepherd's purse, sorrel, starwort, valerian, walnut, watercress, yellow dock.

ANTIBIOTIC

aspen, burdock, cabbage, capsicum, cattail, chokecherry, echinacea root, garlic, goldenseal, honey, horseradish root, oak, onion, papaya, pine, plantain, pokeroot, puffball, red clover, starwort, sumac, willow.

ANTIDEPRESSANT

capsicum, gotu kola, ginseng, Indian hemp, rosemary, sage, skullcap, valerian, watercress.

ANTISEPTIC

aloe, aspen, barberry, bayberry, birch, bitterroot, carrot, chokecherry, cinquefoil, clove, dandelion, echinacea root, elderberry, elecampane, frostwort, horsetail, juniper, mountain ash, pine, plantain, prickly pear, red clover, sage, sarsaparilla, sassafras, slippery elm, starwort, stonecrop, sumac, thyme, walnut, wild indigo, yucca.

ANTITOXIN

buckthorn, burdock, cascara-sagrada bark, chaparral, comfrey, echinacea, graperoot, mountain ash, mullein, parsley, peach bark, pokeroot, prickly ash, red clover, sarsaparilla, slippery-elm bark, starwort, wild licorice root, wormwood.

APPENDICITIS

angelica, birch, blue vervain, chamomile, chicory, cinquefoil, dandelion, goldenseal, horsetail, mullein, oak, parsley, pokeroot, prickly pear, red clover, sage, sarsaparilla, starwort, stonecrop, wild lettuce, wild onion, wormwood, yucca.

APPETITE

blessed thistle, buckthorn, dandelion, liverwort, lungwort, red clover, rhubarb, yarrow.

ARTHRITIS

alfalfa, bittersweet, black cohosh, burdock, celery, chaparral, comfrey, hawthorn, lobelia, nettle, parsley, peppermint, prickly ash, sunflower, thyme, walnut, wild licorice, wintergreen, wormwood, yucca.

ASTHMA

angelica, birch, boneset, buckthorn, chokecherry, coltsfoot, comfrey, eucalyptus, garlic, goldenseal, horehound, hyssop, jimsonweed, lungwort, mandrake, mullein, pleurisy root, pokeroot, purslane, rosemary, stillingia, walnut, yerba santa.

ASTRINGENT

aloe, alumroot, barberry, bitterroot, chokecherry, Indian hemp, juniper, parsley, shepherd's purse, squawberry, sumac, uva-ursi, walnut, willow, witch hazel, yarrow.

ATHLETE'S FOOT

black walnut, cascara-sagrada bark, castor bean, celery, chamomile, elder, gentian violet, goldenrod, juniper, uva-ursi.

BALDNESS

comfrey, horsetail, lobelia, sage.

BITES

Ant
garlic, onion, saltbush, snakeweed, spleenwort fern.
Bee
coneflower, goldenrod, honeysuckle, marigold, onion, plantain, purslane, snakeweed.
Insect
bayberry, elderberry, elecampane, garlic, hops, palma christi, plantain, wild onion.
Rattlesnake
jimsonweed, mandrake, plantain, white ash.
Snake
mandrake root, snakeroot, sunflower.
Spider
bladderpod, jimsonweed, prickly pear, sage, sunflower, wood lily.

Tick
amaranth, chestnut, oak.

BLADDER AILMENTS

birch, black cohosh, celery, gingerroot, goldenseal, horsetail, hyssop, juniper, lobelia, maize, mandrake, marshmallow, parsley, pipsissewa, saxifrage, uva-ursi, white pond lily, wormwood.

BLISTERS

peach-pit wash, pipsissewa, plantain, spleenwort fern, sumac, sunflower.

BLOOD BUILDER

alfalfa, barberry bark, bayberry bark, capsicum, dandelion root, garlic, gingerroot, ginseng, goldenseal, graperoot, parsley, yellow dock root.

BLOOD COAGULANT

alumroot, capsicum, cattail, juniper, shepherd's purse, sorrel, sumac, uva-ursi, wintergreen, yarrow.

BLOOD PRESSURE (high)

black cohosh, blue vervain, buckthorn, garlic, hyssop, maize, parsley, pokeroot, sassafras, skullcap, wild onion, wild rice.

BLOOD PRESSURE (low)

clove, gentian, strawberry leaves, watercress.

BLOOD PURIFIER

alfalfa, blue vervain, buckthorn, burdock, celery, chaparral, dandelion, echinacea, elder, gentian root, goldenseal, hyssop, mandrake root, mountain ash, mullein, myrrh, pokeroot, prickly ash, red clover, sarsaparilla, starwort, stillingia, uva-ursi, wild licorice, wormwood, yarrow, yellow dock.

BOILS

black walnut, chaparral, comfrey, echinacea, garlic, goldenseal, lobelia, myrrh, palma christi, pine, plantain, pokeroot, red clover, slippery-elm bark, sorrel, starwort, stonecrop, walnut, yellow dock.

BONES

aspen, boneset, comfrey, horsetail, lobelia, Solomon's seal, stillingia.

BOWEL CLEANSER

birch, bitterroot, boneset, buckthorn, butternut, cascara sagrada, chamomile, cotton root, elder, fennel, horehound, hyssop, peppermint, plantain, red clover, rhubarb, sassafras, slippery elm, starwort, tansy, thyme, uva-ursi, walnut, wild licorice, yucca.

BREASTS

Cracked/Sore
balsam fir, cinquefoil, comfrey, echinacea root, elderberry, goldenseal, lobelia, myrrh, palma christi, pasture brake, pokeroot, purslane, trillium, yarrow.
Promote Milk Flow
baneberry, blue lettuce, borage, caraway, fennel, prickly pear, skeleton weed, wintergreen.
Staunch Milk Flow
parsley, sage.
Tumors
adder's-tongue, chaparral, cramp bark, eucalyptus, frostwort, peach bark, pipsissewa, red clover.
Weaning
aloe massaged on nipples.

BRONCHITIS

angelica, buckthorn, burdock, chamomile, coltsfoot, comfrey, elecampane, eucalyptus, fennel, garlic, goldenseal, honey, hyssop, lichen, lobelia, lungwort, mullein, myrrh, nettle, pleurisy root, pokeroot, purslane, sarsaparilla, sassafras, skullcap, stillingia, sunflower, thyme, walnut, wild lettuce, wild licorice, witch hazel, wormwood, yerba santa.

BRUISES

aspen, barberry, cabbage, chaparral, cinquefoil, comfrey, jimsonweed, sassafras, shepherd's purse, Solomon's seal, sunflower, tansy, witch hazel, wormwood.

BURNS

aloe, beech, birch, blueberry, burdock, cattail, comfrey, echinacea, elderberry, horsetail, juniper, pine, potato, puffball, red clover, slippery elm, sumac, yarrow.

BURSITIS

black cohosh, black mustard, celery, chaparral, clove, gentian, magnolia, nettle, peppermint, pokeroot, slippery elm, stillingia, sunflower, wild licorice, wintergreen, yarrow, yellow dock, yerba santa, yucca.

CANCER

bayberry bark, blue vervain, buckthorn, burdock, chaparral, comfrey, cramp bark, dandelion, echinacea, frostwort, garlic, ginseng, goldenseal, graperoot, Indian hemp, mandrake root, Norwegian kelp, peach bark, pokeroot, prickly ash, red clover, starwort, stillingia, tansy.

CANKERS

camphor, comfrey, eucalyptus, goldenseal root, horsetail, myrrh, palma christi, plantain, slippery elm, sumac, thyme, white pond lily, yarrow, yellow dock.

CATARACTS

bayberry, borage, chamomile, eyebright, goldenseal, Rocky Mountain maple, sumac, tansy, witch hazel, yarrow.

CHAPPED SKIN

beech, black mustard, comfrey, hops, olive oil, palma christi, peanut oil, peppermint, plantain, slippery-elm bark.

CHEST PAIN

boneset, burdock, chamomile, dogbane, elecampane, hellebore, lobelia, mullein, pleurisy root, wahoo, wild licorice.

CHICKEN POX

adder's-tongue, aloe, aspen, beech, chamomile, cinquefoil, comfrey, dandelion, elecampane, goldenseal, hops, Indian hemp, oak, pine, purslane, slippery elm, spleenwort fern, starwort, walnut, wild lettuce, yarrow, yerba santa, yucca.

CHILDBIRTH

Induce
blue cohosh, mistletoe, squaw vine, tansy.
Ease
cotton root, golden ragwort, pipsissewa, Rocky Mountain raspberry, slippery elm, spleenwort fern.
Pain
black cherry, black cohosh, cinquefoil, cotton root, cramp bark, ginseng, jimsonweed, lady's-slipper root, pasture brake, skullcap, squawberry, sweet-rush root, valerian root.
Staunch Hemorrhaging
buckwheat, chokecherry, juniper, shepherd's purse, squawberry, sumac, uva-ursi, wintergreen, yarrow.
Post-partum
snakeweed, wild licorice.
To Heal Womb
goose grass, white pond lily.

CHILLS

black haw, capsicum, gooseberry, horehound, magnolia, pennyroyal, pleurisy root, sassafras, sunflower.

CHOLESTEROL (to remove from system)

capsicum, garlic, gingerroot, ginseng, goldenseal, mullein, parsley, yucca.

CIRCULATION

bayberry bark, black haw, blue vervain, capsicum, cinnamon, cloves, coriander, dandelion, garlic, gentian, gingerroot, ginseng, hawthorn, mandrake, mullein, parsley, peppermint, white pine.

COLDS

aspen, bayberry bark, boneset, capsicum, clove, elecampane, fennel, garlic, gingerroot, honey, horehound, lobelia, mullein, skullcap, thyme, white pine, wild cherry bark, wild onion, yarrow.

COLIC

angelica, bayberry, catnip, chamomile, clove, fennel, garlic, lobelia, pennyroyal, sweet-rush root, thyme, wintergreen.

COLITIS

barberry, birch, capsicum, cascara-sagrada bark, fennel, garlic, gentian, ginger, goldenseal root, lobelia, rhubarb, Rocky Mountain raspberry, wormwood.

COLON AILMENTS

barberry, capsicum, cascara-sagrada, fennel, Rocky Mountain raspberry.

CONGESTION

angelica, aspen, black mustard, camphor, chokecherry, coltsfoot, eucalyptus, fennel, garlic, honey, horehound, lobelia, mullein, pleurisy root, pokeroot, sassafras, stillingia, sunflower, wild onion, wintergreen.

CONJUNCTIVITIS

aspen, bayberry bark, borage, chokecherry, eyebright, goldenseal, oak, Rocky Mountain maple, Rocky Mountain raspberry, rosemary, sassafras, serviceberry, sumac, yarrow.

CONSTIPATION

barberry bark, birch, bitterroot, buckthorn, cascara sagrada, cotton root, elderberry, fennel, goldenseal, lobelia, plantain, red clover, rhubarb, Rocky Mountain raspberry, sassafras, slippery elm, starwort, wild licorice root, yucca.

CONTRACEPTION

amaranth, blue cohosh, cotton root, dogbane, flatspine ragweed, gingerroot, golden ragwort, hemlock, Indian paintbrush, milkweed, mistletoe, pennyroyal, sage, Solomon's seal, tansy, thistle, yarrow.

CONVULSIONS

black cohosh, blue vervain, cotton root, cramp bark, henbane, hops, jimsonweed, lady's slipper, lobelia, redroot, skullcap, valerian root.

COUGHS

angelica, birch, buckthorn, burdock, camphor, chokecherry, cinquefoil, comfrey, elecampane, eucalyptus, fennel, garlic, ginseng, honey, hops, horehound, lobelia, lungwort, purslane, sarsaparilla, skullcap, wild cherry, wild lettuce, wild licorice, witch hazel, yellow dock, yerba santa.

CRACKED LIPS

beech, comfrey, myrrh, olive oil, palma christi, plantain, slippery-elm bark.

CRAMPS

Abdominal
amaranth, bayberry, birch, capsicum, cinquefoil, clove, fennel, gingerroot, pennyroyal, skullcap, spleenwort fern, valerian root, white pine bark, wild lettuce.
Menstrual
blessed thistle, blue cohosh, capsicum, chamomile, cramp bark, false unicorn root, lady's-slipper root, marshmallow root, Rocky Mountain raspberry, skullcap, squaw vine, uva-ursi.

CROUP

angelica, aspen, barberry bark, capsicum, cascara-sagrada bark, chokecherry, eucalyptus, fennel, garlic, gingerroot, goldenseal, honey, lobelia, rhubarb, Rocky Mountain raspberry, wild onion.

CUTS

barberry bark, bayberry, capsicum, comfrey, juniper, olive oil, plantain, sassafras, shepherd's purse.

CYSTS

chaparral, comfrey, goldenseal, mandrake root, marshmallow root, mullein, pokeroot, red clover, slippery-elm bark, squaw vine, starwort, yellow dock.

DANDRUFF

birch, black mustard, burdock, chicory, cucumber root, dandelion, elderberry, fireweed, goldenseal, hops, Indian hemp, juniper, magnolia, nettle, peanut oil, pine, pokeroot, shepherd's purse, slippery elm, starwort, walnut hulls, willow.

DEODORANT

chamomile, coriander, elderberry, juniper, parsley, pennyroyal, pine, sage, thyme, willow.

DIABETES

bitterroot, dandelion, fennel, garlic, goldenseal, horehound, horsetail, pipsissewa, red clover, uva-ursi, yarrow.

DIARRHEA

bayberry, black haw, blueberry, cotton root, fireweed, garlic, goose grass, myrrh, nettle, oak, pasture brake, peppermint, serviceberry, slippery-elm bark, spleenwort fern, squawberry, white pond lily, yerba santa.

DIURETIC

alumroot, angelica, arrowhead, birch, black cohosh, buckthorn, cascara sagrada, chamomile, chaparral, dog grass, elderberry, goldenrod, horsetail, juniper, marshmallow root, nettle, parsley, rose hips, sunflower, uva-ursi.

DIVERTICULITIS

barberry, black haw, black walnut, cascara sagrada, fennel, garlic, gingerroot, goldenseal, lobelia, Rocky Mountain raspberry, wormwood.

EAR INFECTION

black cohosh, capsicum, echinacea, garlic, gingerroot, ginseng, goldenseal, lobelia, pokeroot, sassafras, wild licorice, wild onion.

ECZEMA

black walnut, dandelion, garlic, goldenseal, plantain, puffball, sassafras, serviceberry, shepherd's purse, slippery elm, spleenwort fern, sumac, yarrow.

EMOTIONAL STRESS

blue vervain, cotton root, cramp bark, ginseng, henbane, hops, Indian hemp, jimsonweed, lady's slipper, lobelia, redroot, skullcap, valerian root.

EMPHYSEMA

angelica, bergamot, coltsfoot, comfrey, fennel, garlic, honey, lichen, lobelia, lungwort, mullein, nettle, pleurisy root, pokeroot, poplar, wild lettuce, wormwood.

ENDURANCE

alfalfa, bitterroot, capsicum, ginseng, gotu kola, Indian hemp, watercress.

EPILEPSY

black cohosh, blue vervain, henbane, hops, jimsonweed, lady's-slipper root, lobelia, parsnip, skullcap, redroot, valerian.

EXHAUSTION

bitterroot, ginseng, gotu kola, Indian hemp, valerian, watercress.

EXPECTORANT

chokecherry, cinquefoil, coltsfoot, nettle, pleurisy root, purslane, yerba santa.

EYE AILMENTS

bayberry bark, borage, eyebright, Indian hemp, mesquite, Rocky Mountain maple, sassafras, serviceberry, sumac, yarrow.

FEVER

barberry, bayberry, birch, boneset, capsicum, clove, dogwood, echinacea, fennel, feverbush, garlic, gooseberry, lobelia, magnolia, nettle, pleurisy root, pokeroot, poplar, purslane, Rocky Mountain raspberry, sassafras, skullcap, stonecrop, tansy, white pine bark, wild licorice, willow, yucca.

FLATULENCE

bayberry, birch, dandelion, fennel, gingerroot, liverwort, pasture brake, pennyroyal, peppermint, pleurisy root, red clover, rhubarb, sage, sweet-rush root, thyme, wintergreen.

FLU

aspen, bayberry, black haw, capsicum, chokecherry, clove, eucalyptus, fennel, garlic, gooseberry, hemlock, honey, horehound, mullein, onion, pennyroyal, pine, pokeroot, sassafras, stillingia, sunflower, thyme, walnut, wild lettuce, wild licorice, wild onion.

FLY REPELLENT

bloodroot, elderberry, palma christi, rosemary, sage, wormwood.

FRACTURES (see Bones)

FRECKLES

black mustard, chaparral, palma christi, pokeroot, red clover, Solomon's seal, white cabbage, white pond lily.

FRIGIDITY (see Sexual Stimulant)

FROSTBITE

beech, capsicum, gingerroot, wild onion.

GALL BLADDER AILMENTS

blue vervain, buckthorn, chamomile, dandelion, goldenseal, graperoot, hops, lobelia, lungwort, papaya, red clover, rhubarb, tansy, wintergreen, yarrow.

GALLSTONES

bitterroot, blue vervain, buckthorn, dandelion, papaya, parsley, red clover, rhubarb, sage, salsify, yarrow.

GANGRENE

barberry, bitterroot, chokecherry, feverbush, horsetail, Indian hemp, pine, pokeroot, prickly pear, puffball, sarsaparilla, slippery elm, stonecrop, sumac, willow, yucca.

GUMS

cinquefoil, comfrey, frostwort, goldenseal, horsetail, myrrh, thyme, white pond lily, yerba santa.

HAIR

birch, chamomile, Indian hemp, jojoba, nettle, peppermint, pine, yucca.

HALITOSIS

barberry, buckthorn, cascara sagrada, fennel, geranium, gingerroot, lobelia, myrrh, parsley, pennyroyal, peppermint, Rocky Mountain raspberry, rhubarb, yerba santa.

HALLUCINOGENS

henbane, horse chestnut (opiate), Indian hemp (opiate), jimsonweed, mescal bean, morning glory, peyote (mescaline), red larkspur.

HAY FEVER (see Allergies)

HEADACHE

blue vervain, chokecherry, cotton root, dandelion, elderberry, lady's slipper, lobelia, mullein, peppermint, red clover, redroot, skullcap, tansy, valerian, wild lettuce, yucca.

HEART PALPITATIONS

black haw, blue vervain, horehound, parsley, pokeroot, skullcap, tansy, valerian, wild rice.

HEMORRHAGING

External
aloe, alumroot, barberry, bitterroot, chokecherry, horsetail, Indian hemp, juniper, parsley, puffball, shepherd's purse, squawberry, sumac, uva-ursi, walnut, witch hazel, willow, yarrow.
Internal
black haw, capsicum, comfrey, cotton root, cramp bark, parsley, plantain, Rocky Mountain raspberry, shepherd's purse, sorrel, squawberry, sumac, uva-ursi, wintergreen.

HEMORRHOIDS

alder bark, almond oil, alumroot, goldenseal, Indian hemp, lobelia, oak, palma christi, starwort, willow, yerba santa.

HEPATITIS

alfalfa, angelica, blue vervain, boneset, burdock, celery, chaparral, chicory, dandelion, elder, feverbush, hyssop, lobelia, mandrake, mountain ash, mullein, myrrh, nettle, palma christi, parsley, plantain, pokeroot, red clover, Rocky Mountain maple, sage, starwort, stillingia, uva-ursi, watercress, wormwood, yarrow, yellow dock root.

HIVES

adder's-tongue, aloe, aspen, beech, bitterroot, cattail, chamomile, chicory, cinquefoil, comfrey, dandelion, elecampane, goldenseal, hops, Indian hemp, oak, pine, purslane, sassafras, slippery elm, spleenwort fern, star-wort, sumac, walnut, wild lettuce, wild onion, yarrow, yerba santa, yucca.

HOARSENESS

bayberry bark, cloves, eucalyptus, ginger, myrrh, white pine.

HORMONE IMBALANCE

alfalfa, black cohosh, black mustard, celery, echinacea, fennel, ginseng, goldenseal, horehound, Norwegian kelp, papaya, red clover, sarsaparilla, watercress, wild licorice.

HYPERACTIVITY

bitterroot, black cohosh, blue vervain, hops, lady's slipper, lobelia, mistletoe, skullcap, valerian, wood betony.

HYPNOTIC

henbane, jimsonweed, lady's-slipper root, lobelia, redroot, wild lettuce.

HYPOGLYCEMIA

black cohosh, celery, dandelion, horseradish, juniper, wild licorice.

IMPETIGO

black mustard, chicory, dandelion, elderberry, fireweed, goldenseal, Indian hemp, juniper, nettle, palma christi, peanut oil, pine, slippery elm, starwort, walnut, willow.

IMPOTENCE(see Sexual Stimulant)

INDIGESTION

bayberry, birch, cramp bark, dandelion, fennel, gingerroot, liverwort, pasture brake, peppermint, pleurisy root, red clover, rhubarb, sweet-rush root.

INFECTION

adder's-tongue, aspen, burdock, cabbage, capsicum, cattail, chokecherry, echinacea root, garlic, honey, horseradish root, oak, papaya, plantain, pokeroot, puffball, starwort, sumac, willow.

INSECT BITES (see Bites)

INSOMNIA

black cohosh, blue vervain, celery, henbane, hops, jimsonweed, lady's-slipper root, mandrake, purslane, skullcap, valerian root.

ITCHING (see Hives)

JAUNDICE (see Hepatitis)

KIDNEY AILMENTS

alderbark, almonds, alumroot, angelica, arrowhead, birch, black cohosh, buckthorn, cascara sagrada, chaparral, dog grass, elderberry, goldenrod, horsetail, Indian hemp, juniper, marshmallow root, mullein, nettle, parsley, pipsissewa, red clover, rose hips, sassafras, saxifrage, slippery elm, snakeroot, sunflower, uva-ursi, white pond lily.

KIDNEY STONES

bitterroot, blue vervain, buckthorn, chaparral, cotton root, gooseberry, horsetail, parsley, sage, stonecrop, uva-ursi, watercress.

LARYNGITIS (see Hoarseness)

LAXATIVE

birch, bitterroot, boneset, buckthorn, butternut, cascara sagrada, chamomile, cotton root, elder, fennel, horehound, hyssop, peppermint, plantain, red clover, rhubarb, sassafras, slippery elm, starwort, tansy, thyme, uva-ursi, walnut, wild licorice, yucca.

LICE

Indian hemp, larkspur, walnut.

LIVER AILMENTS (see Hepatitis)

LONGEVITY (see Endurance)

LOWER-BACK PAIN

alder, arnica, black cohosh, black mustard, boneset, clove, elecampane, gentian, horsemint, mullein, pokeroot, sweet-rush root, tansy, thyme, wild licorice, wormwood, yellow dock.

LOWER-LEG PAIN

amaranth, aspen, beech, black haw, blue vervain, capsicum, chicory, comfrey, cramp bark, dandelion, fireweed, horsetail, lady's slipper, lobelia, purslane, sassafras, shepherd's purse, tansy, wintergreen, wormwood, yellow dock.

MEMORY

blessed thistle, blue vervain, capsicum, comfrey, gingerroot, ginseng, gotu kola, lobelia, rosemary.

MENSTRUATION

Cramps
blessed thistle, blue cohosh, capsicum, chamomile, cramp bark, false unicorn root, lady's slipper, marshmallow root, pasture brake, Rocky Mountain raspberry, skullcap, squaw vine, uva-ursi.
Promote Flow
angelica, black cohosh, black mustard, cedar, chamomile, fennel, flatspine ragweed, horsetail, pennyroyal, skullcap, tansy.
Reduce Flow
bayberry, black haw, capsicum, cotton root, cramp bark, juniper, plantain, Rocky Mountain raspberry, sage, shepherd's purse, sorrel, squawberry, sumac, thyme, uva-ursi, wintergreen.
Inhibit
amaranth.

MISCARRIAGE (preventive)

black haw, cotton root, cramp bark, plantain, Rocky Mountain raspberry, squawberry, uva-ursi.

MOSQUITO/MOTH REPELLENT

bloodroot, elderberry, palma christi, spleenwort fern (moth), tansy.

MUMPS (see Swelling)

NAILS (ingrown)

alumroot.

NAUSEA

adder's-tongue, basil, ginger, goldenseal, honey, peppermint, sage, wintergreen.

NERVOUS TENSION

bitterroot, black cohosh, blue vervain, cabbage, capsicum, chamomile, clove, comfrey, cotton root, cramp bark, hops, lady's slipper, lobelia, myrrh, redroot, rosemary, sage, valerian.

NEURALGIA

alder, alfalfa, black cohosh, celery, chamomile, clove, nettle, peppermint, thyme, wild licorice, wintergreen, yellow dock.

NOSEBLEEDS

cotton root, shepherd's purse, snakeroot, Solomon's seal, sorrel, sumac, willow.

OBESITY

alfalfa, black walnut, capsicum, echinacea, fennel, ginseng, gotu kola, mandrake root, Norwegian kelp, papaya, rhubarb, saffron, wild licorice root.

OPIATE

horse chestnut, Indian hemp.

PAIN RELIEVER

black cherry, black cohosh, capsicum, chamomile, cinquefoil, cramp bark, elderberry, hops, lady's slipper, lobelia, mullein, nettle, pasture brake, red clover, redroot, skullcap, sweet-rush root, thyme, valerian, wild lettuce, willow, yarrow, yucca.

PERSPIRATION (promote)

boneset, burdock, feverbush, horehound, pennyroyal, pleurisy root, sassafras, sunflower, thyme.

PLEURISY

angelica, aspen, birch, black cohosh, burdock, chokecherry, eucalyptus, horehound, lichen, lobelia, mullein, pine, pleurisy root, wintergreen.

PNEUMONIA

bayberry, black mustard, capsicum, clove, comfrey, echinacea, fennel, fenugreek, garlic, honey, lobelia, marshmallow root, mullein, onion, pine, pokeroot, wild onion.

POISON ANTIDOTE

Poisonous snakes/insects
mandrake root, plantain, sarsaparilla.
Pokeweed
blue vervain.

POISON IVY/OAK

blue vervain, mandrake root, plantain, sarsaparilla, soaproot, spleenwort fern, wild lettuce, wild onion, wormwood, yarrow, yellow dock.

PROSTATE AILMENTS

blackberry, capsicum, elder, ginger, goldenseal, juniper, marshmallow root, nettle, parsley, peach, sunflower, uva-ursi, white pond lily.

PYORRHEA

barberry, capsicum, cinquefoil, frostwort, goldenseal, horsetail, myrrh, sage, sumac, white pond lily, yerba santa.

RASHES (see Hives)

RELAXANT

black cohosh, blue vervain, cotton root, cramp bark, hops, jimsonweed, lady's-slipper root, lobelia, redroot, skullcap, valerian, wild lettuce.

RESPIRATORY AILMENTS

angelica, black mustard, burdock, chokecherry, coltsfoot, comfrey, elecampane, eucalyptus, fenugreek, feverbush, garlic, horehound, hyssop, lichen, lobelia, mandrake root, marshmallow root, mullein, pine, pleurisy root, pokeroot, starwort, stillingia, sunflower, thyme, walnut, wild lettuce, wild licorice, witch hazel, yerba santa.

RESTLESSNESS

fennel, hops, lady's-slipper root, lobelia, peppermint, redroot, skullcap, valerian.

RHEUMATISM

birch, black cohosh, black mustard, bloodroot, dandelion, eucalyptus, magnolia, nettle, peppermint, stillingia, sunflower, thyme, wintergreen, wormwood, yerba santa, yucca.

RINGWORM

birch, bitterroot, bloodroot, goldenseal, mandrake root, milkweed, nettle, plantain, pokeroot, purslane, Rocky Mountain maple, walnut, wild onion.

RODENT REPELLENT

peppermint.

ROUNDWORM

bitterroot, blackberry, mandrake root, nettle, pinkroot, plantain, pumpkin seed, purslane, wild onion, wormwood.

SCARS

olive oil, palma christi, peanut oil.

SCURVY

alfalfa, aspen, bayberry, chicory, cramp bark, cucumber root, dandelion, fireweed, Indian lettuce, lobelia, mountain ash, nettle, pennyroyal, pine, red clover, saxifrage, scurvy grass, serviceberry, shepherd's purse, sorrel, sunflower, uva-ursi, wild onion, yellow dock.

SEDATIVE

black cohosh, blue vervain, chamomile, cotton root, cramp bark, henbane, hops, jimsonweed, lady's slipper, lobelia, red clover, redroot, skullcap, valerian root, wild lettuce.

SEXUAL DEPRESSANT

hops, sage, skullcap, valerian root, willow bark.

SEXUAL STIMULANT

alfalfa, bitterroot, columbine, ginseng, gotu kola, lobelia, lupine, purslane.

SINUS

aspen, barberry, capsicum, cascara-sagrada bark, cherry bark, chicory, coltsfoot, echinacea, elderberry, eucalyptus, fennel, ginger, goldenseal, hyssop, lobelia, marshmallow root, mullein, nettle, pokeroot, rhubarb, Rocky Mountain raspberry, sage, wintergreen, yerba santa.

SKIN CANCER

adder's-tongue, bitterroot, cabbage, chaparral, dandelion, echinacea, frost-wort, garlic, goldenseal, lobelia, mandrake resin, mullein, palma christi, papaya, pokeroot, red clover, sage, slippery-elm bark, sorrel, stonecrop, tansy, walnut.

SORE THROAT

alumroot, aspen, bayberry, bitterroot, comfrey, eucalyptus, palma christi, redroot, red clover, stillingia, sumac, wintergreen, yerba santa.

SPLEEN AILMENTS

angelica, blue vervain, celery, chamomile, chicory, dandelion, elecampane, eucalyptus, mullein, parsley, pokeroot, Rocky Mountain maple, spleenwort fern, watercress, wintergreen, wormwood, yellow dock.

SPRAINS

amaranth, aspen, barberry, black mustard, burdock, chaparral, chicory, cinquefoil, jimsonweed, myrrh, onion, palma christi, plantain, sassafras, stillingia, tansy, wild onion, wintergreen, witch hazel, wormwood.

SUNBURN

aloe, aspen, beech, birch, cattail, comfrey, echinacea, elderberry, horsetail, juniper, red clover, slippery elm, sumac, tansy, yarrow.

SWELLING

alfalfa, amaranth, angelica, beech, blue vervain, boneset, burdock, celery, chaparral, chicory, coltsfoot, comfrey, dandelion, elder, feverbush, fireweed, henbane, hyssop, jimsonweed, lobelia, mandrake root, mountain ash, mullein, myrrh, nettle, palma christi, parsley, pipsissewa, plantain, pokeroot, red clover, Rocky Mountain maple, sassafras, starwort, stillingia, uva-ursi, watercress, wintergreen, witch hazel, wormwood, yarrow, yellow dock root.

TESTICLE SWELLING

black mustard, starwort.

TONSILLITIS

alfalfa, boneset, celery, chicory, feverbush, fireweed, horehound, mullein, nettle, oak, plantain, pipsissewa, red clover, Rocky Mountain maple, sage, starwort, stillingia, watercress, wormwood, yellow dock.

TOOTHACHE

black mustard, clove, elecampane, goldenseal, myrrh, plantain, sumac, thyme, white pond lily, wild lettuce, willow, yarrow.

ULCERATED WOUNDS

alumroot, anemone, aspen, barberry, birch, bitterroot, cabbage, cattail, chokecherry, comfrey, death camas, echinacea, elecampane, frostwort, garlic, goldenseal, horsetail, Indian hemp, oak, papaya, plantain, pokeroot, prickly pear, puffball, red clover, sarsaparilla, slippery elm, starwort, stone-crop, sumac, walnut, wild onion, willow, yellow dock, yucca.

ULCERS

adder's-tongue, birch, black walnut, bloodroot, cramp bark, echinacea, elderberry, elm bark, eucalyptus, frostwort, goldenseal, mullein, myrrh, palma christi, pine, pipsissewa, plantain, pokeroot, red clover, shepherd's purse, slippery elm, stonecrop, sumac, wintergreen, witch hazel, yellow dock, yerba santa, yucca.

UTERINE ULCERATION

white pond lily.

VAGINAL INFECTIONS

cramp bark, cranberry, garlic, goldenseal, myrrh, oak, plantain, Rocky Mountain maple, Rocky Mountain raspberry, white pond lily, willow.

VENEREAL DISEASE

bitterroot, lobelia, pine, prickly ash, sarsaparilla, sumac, willow.

VITAMIN DEFICIENCY

alfalfa, aspen, bayberry, black mustard, chicory, cramp bark, cucumber root, elderberry, fireweed, Indian lettuce, mountain ash, parsley, pine, pokeroot, purslane, red clover, saxifrage, scurvy grass, serviceberry, shepherd's purse, sorrel, starwort, walnut, watercress, wild onion, yellow dock.

WARTS

buckthorn, cabbage, chaparral, cowslip, dandelion, garlic, lobelia, man-drake, milkweed, mullein, pleurisy root, pokeroot, prickly pear, sage, sorrel, stonecrop, tansy.

WATER RETENTION

angelica, arrowhead, black cohosh, cascara sagrada, chaparral, dog grass, elderberry, gingerroot, goldenrod, horsetail, juniper, marshmallow root, net-tle, parsley, rose hips, sunflower, uva-ursi.

WHOOPING COUGH

black walnut, chestnut, coltsfoot, lichen, purslane, thyme, wild lettuce, wild onion, yerba santa.

WRINKLES

myrrh, olive oil, palma christi, peanut oil, sumac.

WILD PLANTS USED BY NATIVE AMERICAN HEALERS

The natural botanicals were recognized by Native Americans as medicine—pure and simple medicine. There were no synthetic, man-made substitutes that were deemed better. The Native people merely used whatever their Mother the Earth provided as medicine for Her People. And they did heal one another. How simple it was—so beautifully simple.

With no medical textbooks, with no pharmaceutical training, these people of mountains, plains, and prairies discovered for themselves their unique bond with the all-providing earth. And they experimented and learned all they needed to know of the wonderful healing ways that were so natural to them.

But that's only the beginning. A root dug up and ingested in one season will be a miraculous remedy, but if it's dug up and ingested in another season, it may be fatal. There were harvesting times to learn. And does one use the root, the stalk, the leaf, or the blossom? Will it become a poison if it's boiled?

The full extent of Native American remedy knowledge would fill a volume much larger than this offering. However, I offer the following section as a simple sampling of the wide range of botanicals and their various preparations and uses.

WILD PLANTS USED BY NATIVE AMERICANS

*denotes poison, narcotic, or abortifacient

Botanical	Part	How Prepared	Medicine Form	Remedy For	Foodstuff
ADDER'S-TONGUE	leaf	raw/mashed	paste	ulcers, tumors, abscesses	vegetable
	whole	boiled	wash	inflammations, hives	
	root	dried/steeped	tea	vomiting, hiccoughs	tea
ALFALFA	leaf	dried/steeped	tea	swollen glands, tonsillitis, spring tonic, blood purifier, hepatitis, aging, arthritis, sexual stimulant	tea
	leaf	raw	wild green	scurvy, acid balancer	salad
	seed	dried/ground			bread flour
ALOE	leaf juice	raw	salve	burns, sunburn, insect bite, on nipples for weaning	
ALUMROOT	root	dried/powdered	compress	external hemorrhaging	
	root	raw/mashed	compress	joints, hemorrhoids, sore feet	
	root	dried/steeped	tea	diuretic	tea
	root	raw/mashed	paste	thrush, ingrown nails	
	leaf	boiled	compress	sore throat	

117

WILD PLANTS USED BY NATIVE AMERICANS

*denotes poison, narcotic, or abortifacient

Botanical	Part	How Prepared	Medicine Form	Remedy For	Foodstuff
AMARANTH	flower	dried/steeped	tea	contraception, stops menstruation	tea
	leaf	boiled	compress	swellings, sprains, ticks	
	leaf	raw/steeped	tea	stomachache	tea
	leaf	boiled		high calcium & iron content	spinach
	seed	dried/ground		high in the amino acid lysine (almost a complete protein)	bread flour & seeds
ANGELICA	root	dried/steeped	tea	appendicitis, liver, spleen, colic, kidney, diuretic, hepatitis	bread flour & tea
	root	raw/mashed	compress	bronchitis, asthma	(leaf) smoke
ARROWHEAD	corm	roasted	chew & ingest	diuretic	bread flour, potato
ASPEN	leaf bud	raw/mashed	compress	wounds, sunburn, antibiotic, chicken pox	
	bud resin	steeped	tea	scurvy	tea
	root bark	raw	chewed	sore throat	
	root	raw/mashed	compress	bruises, sprains	

WILD PLANTS USED BY NATIVE AMERICANS

*denotes poison, narcotic, or abortifacient

Botanical	Part	How Prepared	Medicine Form	Remedy For	Foodstuff
ASPEN	bark	steeped	tea	colds, flu, allergies, anemia, antibiotic	tea
BARBERRY	berry	raw	chew & ingest	fever, colitis, diarrhea, blood builder	jam & fruit
	root	raw/boiled	wash	cuts, bruises, external hemorrhaging, sprains	stew flavoring
	root	raw/mashed	paste	ulcerated wounds	
BAYBERRY	bark	dried/powdered	tea	diarrhea, sore throat, fever, blood circulation, pneumonia, flu	tea
	bark	boiled/mashed	paste	cuts, insect bites	
	root	boiled	tea	blood builder, slows menstrual flow, cancer	tea
	leaf	dried/steeped	tea	scurvy	stew flavoring
	berry	raw	chew & ingest	flatulence, colic, stomach cramps	

119

WILD PLANTS USED BY NATIVE AMERICANS

*denotes poison, narcotic, or abortifacient

Botanical	Part	How Prepared	Medicine Form	Remedy For	Foodstuff
BEECH	leaf	raw/steeped	wash	frostbite, burns	
	leaf	raw/mashed	compress	swelling, leg pain	
	bark	raw/boiled	wash	skin inflammation, hives, chicken pox	
	bark	dried/ground			bread flour
	nut	dried/ground			coffee & oil
BIRCH	bark	raw/steeped	tea	ulcers, fever, colitis, flatulence, diuretic, ringworm	tea
	leaf	raw/steeped	wash	wounds, burns, shampoo	
	sap	boiled	syrup	cough, laxative, abdominal cramps, appendicitis, asthma, pleurisy	syrup & stew flavoring
BITTERROOT	root	raw	chew & ingest	sore throat	
	root	dried/steeped	tea	laxative, venereal disease, diabetes, worms, kidney stones, gallstones	tea

120

*denotes poison, narcotic, or abortifacient

Botanical	Part	How Prepared	Medicine Form	Remedy For	Foodstuff
BITTERROOT	root	raw/mashed	compress	ulcerated wounds, sores, hives, external hemorrhaging, skin cancer	
	seed	roasted		nervousness, exhaustion	coffee
BLACK COHOSH	root	dried/steeped	tea	sedative, rheumatism, diuretic, high blood pressure, convulsions, pleurisy, promotes menstruation	tea
BLACK HAW	root bark	raw/boiled	tea	chills, fever, dysentery, diarrhea, blood circulation, heart palpitation, miscarriage prevention	tea
BLACK MUSTARD	leaf	raw/mashed	poultice	toothaches	
	leaf	raw		vitamin deficiency, dandruff	wild green
	seed	dried/steeped	tea	aging, anemia, promotes menstruation, reduces testicle swelling	tea
	seed	raw/ground	paste	rheumatism, sprains, lower-back pain, impetigo	
	seed	raw/crushed	bath additive	draws out congestion, pneumonia	
	seed	raw/boiled with honey	salve	relieves dryness, reduces skin discoloration	

WILD PLANTS USED BY NATIVE AMERICANS

*denotes poison, narcotic, or abortifacient

Botanical	Part	How Prepared	Medicine Form	Remedy For	Foodstuff
BLESSED THISTLE	whole	raw/steeped	tea	balances acid in system, allergies, increases appetite, menstrual cramps, memory enhancer	tea
*BLOODROOT	root	raw/steeped	weak tea	rheumatism, ringworm, ulcers	tea
	root	raw/boiled	wash	insect repellent	
BLUE VERVAIN	root	raw/boiled	tea	nervousness, worms, spleen, liver, blood circulation, headache, epilepsy, insomnia, gall stones, kidney stones, high blood pressure, heart palpitations, hepatitis, appendicitis, cancer, memory enhancer	tea
	leaf	dried/steeped	tea	pokeweed antidote, convulsions	tea

WILD PLANTS USED BY NATIVE AMERICANS

*denotes poison, narcotic, or abortifacient

Botanical	Part	How Prepared	Medicine Form	Remedy For	Foodstuff
BONESET	leaf	raw/steeped	hot tea	bowel cleanser, increases perspiration, induces vomiting, colds	tea
	leaf	raw/steeped	cold tea	fever, jaundice, bone aches, hepatitis, swollen glands, tonsillitis, back pain	
BURDOCK	root	dried/steeped	tea	blood purifier, pleurisy, hepatitis, increases perspiration, swollen glands, cough, antibiotic, cancer	vegetable, tea
	root	raw/mashed	salve	burns, antitoxin, sprains	stew flavoring
	root	roasted			coffee & bread flour
CAPSICUM	fruit	dried/ground	tea	ear infection, fevers, blood circulation, slows menstrual flow, menstrual cramps, blood builder, colds, pneumonia, internal hemorrhaging, antibiotic, antidepressant, chills, sinus	tea
CATTAIL	cob down	raw	matting	absorbent material	
	root	raw/ground	salve	ulcerated wounds, sores, hives, blood coagulant	bread flour
	root	roasted			potato
	stem	raw/mashed	salve	burns	vegetable

123

WILD PLANTS USED BY NATIVE AMERICANS

*denotes poison, narcotic, or abortifacient

Botanical	Part	How Prepared	Medicine Form	Remedy For	Foodstuff
CELERY	seed	dried/ground	tea	bladder incontinence, blood cleanser, liver, hepatitis, tonsillitis, neuralgia, insomnia, spleen, swollen glands, aging, arthritis	tea
CHAMOMILE	flower	raw/mashed	juice tea	jaundice, dropsy, promotes menstrual flow	tea
	flower	dried/steeped	wash	liver & spleen pain, deodorant, athlete's foot, shampoo	
	leaf	dried/boiled	tea	colic, infant convulsions, measles, diuretic, gall bladder afflictions, anemia, appendicitis	tea
CHAPARRAL	leaf	raw/steeped	tea	diuretic, hepatitis, dissolves cancer tumors, blood purifier, arthritis	tea
	leaf	dried/boiled	wash	bruises, skin blemishes, boils, warts, sprains	

WILD PLANTS USED BY NATIVE AMERICANS

*denotes poison, narcotic, or abortifacient

Botanical	Part	How Prepared	Medicine Form	Remedy For	Foodstuff
CHESTNUT	nut	raw/boiled	paste	tick bites	syrup
	nut	dried/ground			bread flour
CHICORY	leaf	dried/steeped	tea	hepatitis, liver ailments, spleen ailments, tonsillitis, vitamin & mineral deficiency, anemia, appendicitis	tea
	leaf	raw	fresh greens	scurvy, dandruff	salad
	leaf	raw/mashed	compress	swelling, inflammations, hives, sprains	
	root	roasted			coffee & chewing gum
CHOKECHERRY	bark	raw/steeped	tea	lung congestion, colds, cough, jaundice, antibiotic	fruit (berry)
	bark	dried	smoked	headache	
	inner bark	dried/ground	compress	ulcerated wounds, external hemorrhaging, antibiotic, conjunctivitis	

WILD PLANTS USED BY NATIVE AMERICANS

*denotes poison, narcotic, or abortifacient

Botanical	Part	How Prepared	Medicine Form	Remedy For	Foodstuff
CINQUEFOIL	leaf	dried/steeped	tea	abdominal cramps, allergies, appendicitis, pain reliever	tea
	root	raw/mashed	paste	itching rashes, sores, bruises, sprains	
	root	juice	gargle	cough, bleeding gums	
	root	roasted			potato
COLTSFOOT	leaf	dried/steeped	tea	bronchitis, cough, asthma, whooping cough, sinus	tea & salad
	leaf	raw/mashed	compress	swellings	stew flavoring & smoke
	stem	roasted			salt
COMFREY	leaf	raw/mashed	compress	burns, ulcerated wounds, gum lesions, bruises, sore throats, boils, cough, arthritis	
	root	dried/boiled	tea	broken bones, nervousness, internal hemorrhaging, antitoxin	tea

WILD PLANTS USED BY NATIVE AMERICANS

*denotes poison, narcotic, or abortifacient

Botanical	Part	How Prepared	Medicine Form	Remedy For	Foodstuff
*COTTON ROOT	inner root	dried/boiled	weak tea	eases labor, internal hemorrhaging	tea
	root	dried/boiled	strong tea	contraception	
	leaf	raw/steeped	tea	diarrhea, kidney stones	tea
	seed	raw/boiled	tea	laxative, sedative, headache, convulsions	tea
*COWSLIP	sap	raw	drops	warts, tumors, skin growths	
CRAMP BARK	stem	raw/boiled	tea	internal hemorrhaging, miscarriage prevention, menstrual cramps, slows menstrual flow, indigestion	tea
	bark	raw/boiled	tea	sedative, convulsions	tea
	berry	raw	chew & ingest	scurvy	fruit
	berry	raw/mashed	compress	malignant ulcers & tumors	
CUCUMBER ROOT	leaf & shoot	raw	wild greens	scurvy, dandruff	salad

127

WILD PLANTS USED BY NATIVE AMERICANS

*denotes poison, narcotic, or abortifacient

Botanical	Part	How Prepared	Medicine Form	Remedy For	Foodstuff
DANDELION	leaf	raw	wild greens	eczema, hives, scurvy, blood cleanser, cancer, malignant skin tumors, blood circulation, acne, antiseptic, dandruff, warts	salad
	sap	dried		appetite stimulator	chewing gum
	root	raw/boiled	tea	rheumatism, liver & spleen ailments, gall bladder, blood builder, hepatitis, headache, appendicitis	tea
	root	roasted			coffee
ECHINACEA	root	raw/boiled	wash	burns, wounds, boils, skin cancer, ear infection	
	root	dried/steeped	tea	strong blood cleanser, antitoxin, pneumonia, sinus, ulcers, cancer, aging	tea
*ELDERBERRY	leaf	raw/mashed	salve	mosquito/fly repellent, deodorant	
	bark	raw/mashed	compress	ulcers, blisters, burns, athlete's foot	
	berry	raw		vitamin & mineral deficiency; diuretic, bowel cleanser	fruit & tea
	berry	raw/mashed	compress	headache	syrup
	root	raw/mashed	compress	sore breasts	

128

WILL PLANTS USED BY NATIVE AMERICANS

*denotes poison, narcotic, or abortifacient

Botanical	Part	How Prepared	Medicine Form	Remedy For	Foodstuff
ELECAMPANE	root	raw/boiled	wash	wounds, itching rashes	
	root	raw/steeped	tea	lower-back pain, toothache, worms, pancreas, spleen, pulmonary ailments, cough, alcoholism	tea
EUCALYPTUS	leaf	dried/steeped	tea	asthma, bronchitis, spleen, rheumatism, tumors, ulcers, worms, pleurisy, sore throats, sinus	tea
	leaf	raw/mashed	compress	chest colds, sore throat	
FEVERBUSH	bark	raw/boiled	tea	coughs, worms, fever, dysentery, jaundice, gangrene, tonsillitis, hepatitis, promotes perspiration	tea, fruit, stew flavoring
FIREWEED	sprout	boiled	wild greens	scurvy, anemia, dandruff	cooked greens
	stalk	boiled	wild greens	scurvy, anemia	soup
	stalk	dried/ground			bread flour
	root	raw/mashed	compress	swellings, leg pain	
	root & leaf	dried/steeped	tea	hay fever, diarrhea, tonsillitis	tea

WILD PLANTS USED BY NATIVE AMERICANS

*denotes poison, narcotic, or abortifacient

Botanical	Part	How Prepared	Medicine Form	Remedy For	Foodstuff
*FLATSPINE RAGWEED	leaf	dried/steeped	weak tea	promotes menstruation	tea
	leaf	dried/boiled	strong tea	contraception	
FROSTWORT	leaf	raw/mashed	compress	ulcerated wounds, skin cancer, tumors	tea
	leaf	dried/steeped	gargle	mouth & gum lesions	
	leaf	raw/steeped	tea	internal cancer tumors, ulcers	tea
GINSENG	leaf	dried/steeped	tea	cough, blood builder, sexual stimulant, exhaustion, memory	tea
	root	raw	chew & ingest	digestive aid, prostate aid, retards cancer growth	
	root	raw/boiled	tea	menstrual cramps, combats radiation effects in system	tea

130

WILD PLANTS USED BY NATIVE AMERICANS

*denotes poison, narcotic, or abortifacient

Botanical	Part	How Prepared	Medicine Form	Remedy For	Foodstuff
*GOLDEN RAGWORT	leaf	raw/mashed	compress	antidote for poison under skin	
	leaf	dried/steeped	weak tea	eases childbirth	tea
	leaf	dried/steeped	strong tea	contraception	
GOLDENSEAL	root	raw/mashed	paste	wounds, eczema, boils, sore breasts, gum lesions, skin cancer, toothache, gum disease, hemorrhoids	
	root	dried/steeped	tea	prostate ailments, asthma, cancer, jaundice, colitis, diabetes, ulcers, blood builder & purifier, bladder, abdominal complaints, alcoholism	tea
GOOSEBERRY	leaf	dried/steeped	tea	kidney stones	tea
	berry	cooked	porridge	fever, chills	fruit
GOOSE GRASS	stem & leaf	raw/steeped	tea	diarrhea	tea
	root	dried/boiled	tea	postpartum drink to heal womb	tea

WILD PLANTS USED BY NATIVE AMERICANS

*denotes poison, narcotic, or abortifacient

Botanical	Part	How Prepared	Medicine Form	Remedy For	Foodstuff
*HENBANE	leaf	raw	bath additive	swellings	
	leaf	dried	smoked	hypnotic, hallucinogen	smoke
	leaf	raw/steeped	weak tea	insomnia, sedative, convulsions	tea
HOPS	cone	dried/ground	tea	sedative, coughs, insomnia, gall bladder ailments, allergies	tea
	cone	raw/mashed	salve	itching skin, rashes, hives	
	root	dried/steeped	tea	jaundice, liver ailments	tea
HOREHOUND	leaf	dried/steeped	tea	coughs, pulmonary ailments, jaundice, asthma, worms, hoarseness, laxative, chills, tonsillitis, diabetes, promotes perspiration, aging	tea
HORSETAIL	leaf	raw/steeped	tea	diabetes, diuretic, kidney ailments, appendicitis	tea
	leaf	raw/mashed	compress	gangrene, ulcerated wounds, bones, burns	
	leaf	scorched in grease	salve	cankers, gum lesions	
	stem	raw/mashed	compress	external hemorrhaging	bread flour
	stem	dried/steeped	tea	promotes menstruation, dropsy	tea

132

WILD PLANTS USED BY NATIVE AMERICANS

*denotes poison, narcotic, or abortifacient

Botanical	Part	How Prepared	Medicine Form	Remedy For	Foodstuff
*INDIAN HEMP	leaf	raw/mashed	poultice	hemorrhoids, sties	
	leaf	dried/ground	paste	ulcerated sores, dissolves skin tumors	
	leaf	raw/steeped	wash	dandruff, lice, shampoo	
	root	raw/steeped	weak tea	kidney ailments, heart stimulant, antidepressant, blood circulation, aging, asthma, exhaustion	chewing gum & tea
INDIAN LETTUCE	leaf	raw	wild greens	scurvy, anemia	salad
*JIMSONWEED	leaf	dried	smoked	hypnotic, sedative, asthma, insomnia, hallucinogen, convulsions	smoke
	leaf	raw/mashed	compress	bruises, swellings, sprains, spider & rattlesnake bites	
JOJOBA	nut	roasted			coffee
	root	boiled	paste	hair shampoo	

133

WILD PLANTS USED BY NATIVE AMERICANS

*denotes poison, narcotic, or abortifacient

Botanical	Part	How Prepared	Medicine Form	Remedy For	Foodstuff
JUNIPER	leaf	raw/mashed	compress	burns	smoke
	twig	raw/mashed	compress	antiseptic, acne, athlete's foot, dandruff	
	berry	raw/steeped	paste	external hemorrhaging	coffee, tea, bread flour
LADY'S SLIPPER	root	dried/steeped	tea	sedative, pain reliever, insomnia, tranquilizer, headache, internal calmative, menstruation	tea
*LARKSPUR	root	raw/boiled	wash	head & body lice	
LICHEN	moss	raw/steeped	tea	cough, pleurisy, bronchitis	tea
*LOBELIA	leaf	dried/steeped	weak tea	hepatitis, spasms, colic, venereal disease, colitis, coughs, pleurisy, bronchitis, convulsions, arthritis, bladder	smoke
	shoot	raw	wild greens	scurvy, anemia, bones	salad
	root	dried/steeped	weak tea	hypnotic, insomnia, headache	tea
	root	raw/mashed	compress	hemorrhoids, skin cancer, draws out boils	

134

WILD PLANTS USED BY NATIVE AMERICANS

*denotes poison, narcotic, or abortifacient

Botanical	Part	How Prepared	Medicine Form	Remedy For	Foodstuff
MAGNOLIA	flower	boiled	oil wash	dandruff	
	root	dried/steeped	tea	rheumatism, fever, chills, bursitis	tea
MAIZE	kernel	cooked			vegetable, bread flour
	silk	raw/boiled	tea	bedwetting, high blood pressure	tea
	oil	boiled	tea	liver stimulant	oil
*MANDRAKE	root	dried/steeped	weak tea	bladder incontinence, liver ailments, asthma, blood circulation, insomnia, worms, poison antidote, aging	tea
	resin	raw/boiled	paste	warts, tumors, skin cancer	
*MESCAL BEAN	bean	raw	chewed	hallucinogen	
*MISTLETOE	leaf	dried/steeped	weak tea	induces labor	tea

135

WILD PLANTS USED BY NATIVE AMERICANS

*denotes poison, narcotic, or abortifacient

Botanical	Part	How Prepared	Medicine Form	Remedy For	Foodstuff
MOUNTAIN ASH	bark	raw/steeped	tea	blood purifier, hepatitis, allergies, antiseptic	tea
	berry	raw	chew & ingest	scurvy	fruit
MULLEIN	flower	raw/steeped	tea	pain reliever, headache	tea
	leaf	dried	smoked	asthma, lung congestion, pleurisy	smoke
	leaf	raw/mashed	compress	tonsillitis, ulcers, skin cancer, lower-back pain, acne, warts	
	leaf	dried/steeped	tea	blood purifier, balances acid in system, antitoxin for cancer, acne	tea
	root	raw/steeped	tea	liver & spleen ailments, hepatitis, swollen glands, appendicitis	tea
NETTLE	leaf	dried/steeped	tea	fever, bronchitis, scurvy, tonsillitis, aging	salad & tea
	leaf	raw/mashed	compress	rheumatism, neuralgia, arthritis	
	leaf	raw/crushed	juice	diarrhea, worms	
	root	raw/boiled	tea	jaundice, liver ailments, prostate ailments, hepatitis, diuretic, aging	soup & tea
	root	raw/mashed	compress	painful joints, bursitis	

136

WILD PLANTS USED BY NATIVE AMERICANS

*denotes poison, narcotic, or abortifacient

Botanical	Part	How Prepared	Medicine Form	Remedy For	Foodstuff
OAK	acorn mold	raw	compress	wound antibiotic, ticks, conjunctivitis	
	bark	raw/mashed	compress	hemorrhoids	
	bark	raw/boiled	tea	diarrhea, appendicitis	tea
	inner bark	raw/boiled	gargle/douche	tonsillitis, vaginal infection	
	acorn	roasted/ground			stew flavor, bread flour, oil
PALMA CHRISTI	whole	raw/boiled	wash	insect repellent	
	seed	raw/crushed	liniment	skin blemishes, skin growths, tumors, chapped skin, wrinkles	
	leaf	raw/mashed	compress	internal ailments, tumors, hepatitis	
	leaf	raw/boiled	compress	boils, swellings, sprains, inflamed breasts, sore throats, ulcers	

WILD PLANTS USED BY NATIVE AMERICANS

*denotes poison, narcotic, or abortifacient

Botanical	Part	How Prepared	Medicine Form	Remedy For	Foodstuff
PARSLEY	leaf	raw	chew & ingest	breath freshener	
	leaf	dried/steeped	tea	kidney stones, gallstones, heart palpitations, high in vitamin B & potassium, blood builder, blood circulation	tea
	leaf	raw/mashed	compress	swollen glands, insect bites & stings, dries breast milk	
	root	raw/boiled	tea	jaundice, diuretic, liver & spleen ailments, hepatitis, high blood pressure, arthritis	tea
PASTURE BRAKE	root	raw/boiled	tea	flatulence, diarrhea, menstrual cramps, nipple softener, indigestion	tea
PENNYROYAL	leaf	dried/steeped	tea	scurvy, flatulence	tea
	leaf	raw	chew & ingest	breath freshener	salad
	leaf	raw/boiled	strong tea	promotes perspiration, chills, relieves abdominal cramps, colic, promotes menstruation, contraception	

138

WILD PLANTS USED BY NATIVE AMERICANS

*denotes poison, narcotic, or abortifacient

Botanical	Part	How Prepared	Medicine Form	Remedy For	Foodstuff
*PEYOTE	heads	dried	chewed	hallucinogen (mescaline)	
PINE	bark	raw/mashed	compress	burn antibiotic	
	inner bark	boiled/mashed	compress	pleurisy	vegetable
	inner bark	boiled/mashed	paste	ulcerated wounds, boils, acne	
	sap	boiled	wash	antiseptic, deodorant, acne, dandruff	chewing gum
	nuts	roasted/ground		vitamin deficiency	bread flour
	needles	boiled	tea	scurvy, ulcers, venereal disease, anemia	tea
PIPSISSEWA	leaf	dried/steeped	tea	eases childbirth, diabetes, bladder	tea
	root	raw/mashed	compress	swollen glands, ulcers, tonsillitis, blisters, breast tumors	

WILD PLANTS USED BY NATIVE AMERICANS

*denotes poison, narcotic, or abortifacient

Botanical	Part	How Prepared	Medicine Form	Remedy For	Foodstuff
PLANTAIN	leaf	raw/mashed	compress	cuts, abrasions	
	leaf	boiled/crushed	paste	blisters, infection, boils, cracked lips	
	leaf	dried/steeped	tea	worms, slows menstrual flow	tea, vegetable
	leaf	raw/crushed	juice wash	rattlesnake bite, poisonous insect antidote, eczema, burns, ulcerated wounds, cracked lips	
	whole	crushed/boiled	compress	sprains	
	seed	raw/steeped	tea	laxative, ulcers, hepatitis, liver ailments, tonsillitis, swollen glands	tea
	root	raw/mashed	poultice	toothaches	
	sap	dried	chewed		chewing gum
PLEURISY ROOT	leaf	raw/boiled	tea	expectorant, fever, increases perspiration, induces vomiting, chest pain, chills	tea
	root	dried/boiled	tea	flatulence	tea
	root	roasted	chew & ingest	bronchitis, pleurisy, asthma	potato
	root	raw/mashed	paste	wounds	
	sap	raw	paste	warts	
	sap	dried	chewed		chewing gum

WILD PLANTS USED BY NATIVE AMERICANS

*denotes poison, narcotic, or abortifacient

Botanical	Part	How Prepared	Medicine Form	Remedy For	Foodstuff
*POKEROOT	shoot	boiled	wild greens	vitamin deficiency, anemia	asparagus
	seedling	boiled	wild greens	vitamin deficiency, anemia	spinach
	root	dried/steeped	tea	asthma, bronchitis, ulcers, swollen glands, ringworm, tumors, warts, spleen pain, heart palpitations, high blood pressure, hepatitis, appendicitis	tea
	berry	raw/mashed	paste	skin cancer, boils, ear infection, swollen breasts, ulcerated wounds, warts, acne, antitoxin	
PRICKLY PEAR	shoot	raw/mashed	compress	increases breast milk flow	seeds
	pulp	mashed/boiled	compress	infected sores, appendicitis, spider bites	dried fruit
	stems	peeled/mashed	compress	ulcerated wounds, warts	bread flour (seeds)

WILD PLANTS USED BY NATIVE AMERICANS

*denotes poison, narcotic, or abortifacient

Botanical	Part	How Prepared	Medicine Form	Remedy For	Foodstuff
PUFFBALL	whole	dried	powder	antibiotic, wounds, burns, external infections, bleeding	
PURSLANE	whole	raw	chew & ingest	vitamin deficiency, anemia	salad
	whole	boiled	wash	fever, skin inflammations, hives, itching rashes	
	stem	juice	gargle	cough, bronchitis, lung congestion	vegetable
	seed	raw/boiled	tea	insomnia, worms, sexual stimulant	tea, bread flour
RED CLOVER	flower	raw/boiled	tea	sedative, liver ailments, gall bladder ailments, ulcers, blood purifier, antitoxin, hepatitis, diabetes, tonsillitis, throat gargle, internal cancer, aging, appendicitis, bowel cleanser, headache	tea
	flower	raw/crushed	salve	ulcerated wounds, tumors, boils, skin cancer, aging spots	bread flour
	leaf	raw	chew & ingest	scurvy, appetite	salad
	leaf	raw/boiled	compress	abscesses, burns, boils, skin cancer, aging spots, freckles	smoke

WILD PLANTS USED BY NATIVE AMERICANS

*denotes poison, narcotic, or abortifacient

Botanical	Part	How Prepared	Medicine Form	Remedy For	Foodstuff
REDROOT	leaf	dried/steeped	tea gargle	sore throat	
	root	raw/boiled	tea	sedative, headache, joint pain, muscle aches, convulsions	tea
ROCKY MOUNTAIN MAPLE	inner twig	raw/boiled	wash	eye sores, feminine douche, sties, cataracts	stew flavoring
	bark	raw/boiled	tea	worms	tea
	leaf	dried/steeped	tea	liver & spleen ailments, hepatitis, tonsillitis, swollen glands	tea
ROCKY MOUNTAIN RASPBERRY	leaf	raw/boiled	tea	eases childbirth, fevers, internal hemorrhaging, breath freshener, slows menstrual flow, eases menstrual cramps, constipation, croup	tea & salad
	berry	raw/steeped	tea	miscarriage preventive	tea
	berry	raw	chew & ingest	vomiting, diarrhea, colitis	
SAGE	leaf	raw/boiled	strong tea	regulates menstrual cycle, reduces breast milk flow, deodorant	tea
	leaf	dried/steeped	tea	stomach calmative, nausea, flatulence, liver ailments, kidney stones, gallstones, gargle for mouth & gum lesions, swollen glands, tonsillitis, hepatitis, aging, antidepressant	tea
	leaf	raw/juice	drops	warts, skin cancer, tumors	

WILD PLANTS USED BY NATIVE AMERICANS

*denotes poison, narcotic, or abortifacient

Botanical	Part	How Prepared	Medicine Form	Remedy For	Foodstuff
SALSIFY	sap	boiled	tea	gallstones	salad (leaf)
	sap	dried	chewed		chewing gum
SARSAPARILLA	root	raw/boiled	tea	venereal diseases, blood purifier, appendicitis	tea
	root	raw/mashed	compress	infected sores, antidote for poisons	stew flavoring
SASSAFRAS	flower	raw/boiled	tea	fevers, chills, congestion, constipation	tea
	leaf	dried/powdered			stew thickener
	leaf	raw/crushed	compress	skin lesions, wounds, hives	smoke
	bark	raw/mashed	compress	sore eyes, ear infections	
	root	raw/mashed	compress	bruises, sprains, swellings	
	root bark	dried/steeped	tea	kidney ailments, bronchitis, high blood pressure, promotes profuse perspiration, bowel cleanser	tea

WILD PLANTS USED BY NATIVE AMERICANS

*denotes poison, narcotic, or abortifacient

Botanical	Part	How Prepared	Medicine Form	Remedy For	Foodstuff
SAXIFRAGE	leaf	raw/boiled	tea	kidney & bladder ailments	tea
	leaf	raw	wild greens	scurvy, anemia	salad
SCURVY GRASS	leaf & stem	raw	wild greens	scurvy, anemia	salad
	root	roasted			potato
SERVICEBERRY	inner bark	raw/boiled	wash	sore eyes	
	young berry	raw/steeped	tea	diarrhea	tea
	mature berry	raw/mashed	fruit	scurvy, anemia	pemmican additive
SHEPHERD'S PURSE	leaf	raw/crushed	compress	wounds, bruises, ear infection	
	leaf	raw/boiled	tea	internal hemorrhaging, childbirth hemorrhaging, ulcers	tea
	leaf	raw	wild greens	scurvy	salad
	seed	raw	spice	vitamin deficiency, anemia	seeds, stew flavoring, bread flour
	pod	roasted	wild food	vitamin deficiency, anemia	vegetable
	sap	soaked in moss	compress	nosebleeds	

WILD PLANTS USED BY NATIVE AMERICANS

*denotes poison, narcotic, or abortifacient

Botanical	Part	How Prepared	Medicine Form	Remedy For	Foodstuff
SKULLCAP	leaf	dried/steeped	tea	sedative, headaches, fever, abdominal cramps, insomnia, high blood pressure, coughs, heart palpitations, allergies	tea
SLIPPERY ELM	inner bark	raw/mashed	paste	ulcerated wounds, boils, skin cancer, burns	
	inner bark	raw/boiled	tea	laxative, antitoxin, bursitis	tea
	inner bark	raw/boiled	wash	chapped skin, rashes	
	root	raw/boiled	tea	eases childbirth, ulcers	tea
SOLOMON'S SEAL	root	raw/boiled	tea	broken bones	tea & bread flour
	root	raw/boiled	wash	freckles, skin discoloration, bruises, hemorrhaging wounds	fruit (berry)

146

WILD PLANTS USED BY NATIVE AMERICANS

*denotes poison, narcotic, or abortifacient

Botanical	Part	How Prepared	Medicine Form	Remedy For	Foodstuff
SORREL	leaf	raw/boiled	drink	stomach hemorrhaging	lemonade & stew flavoring
	leaf	raw	wild greens	scurvy, anemia	salad
	leaf	raw/crushed	compress	skin tumors, boils, warts	
	root	raw/boiled	tea	slows profuse menstrual flow, nosebleeds	tea & soup
SPLEENWORT FERN	leaf	raw/boiled	tea	abdominal cramps, diarrhea, eases childbirth, spleen	tea
	leaf	raw		moth repellent	
	leaf	raw/boiled	wash	blisters, poison ivy, skin abrasions & sores, bites, ear infection	
SQUAWBERRY	berry	raw	food	diarrhea	fruit
	leaf	dried/steeped	tea	bleeding, miscarriage preventive, reduces menstrual flow & pain	tea
STARWORT	leaf	raw/crushed	compress	swellings, abscesses, boils, ulcerated wounds, infected sores, hemorrhoids	
	leaf	dried/steeped	tea	cancer, constipation, hepatitis, swollen glands, tonsillitis, appendicitis, blood purifier	tea
	leaf	raw	wild greens	vitamin deficiency, anemia	salad

WILD PLANTS USED BY NATIVE AMERICANS

*denotes poison, narcotic, or abortifacient

Botanical	Part	How Prepared	Medicine Form	Remedy For	Foodstuff
STILLINGIA	root	raw/boiled	tea	bronchitis, sore throat, swollen glands, tonsillitis, hepatitis, broken bones, blood purifier, sprains, rheumatism, spleen pain, bursitis, cancer	tea
STONECROP	leaf	raw/crushed	poultice	warts, skin tumors, skin cancer, gangrene	
	leaf	raw/boiled	tea	fever, ulcers, kidney stones, appendicitis	tea
	leaf	raw/crushed	juice wash	ulcerated sores, boils	
SUMAC	flower	raw/boiled	wash	sore & infected eyes, sties	
	bark	raw/boiled	wash	burns, sunburn, eczema, blisters, external bleeding, hives, itching rashes, wrinkles	
	inner bark	raw/boiled	wash	astringent	
	sap	raw	paste	toothache	
	juice	raw	salve	infected sores/wounds	
	berry	raw/boiled	gargle	sore throat, gum lesions	smoke
	root	raw/boiled	tea	internal hemorrhaging, ulcers	

148

WILD PLANTS USED BY NATIVE AMERICANS

*denotes poison, narcotic, or abortifacient

Botanical	Part	How Prepared	Medicine Form	Remedy For	Foodstuff
SUNFLOWER	flower	raw/boiled	wash	arthritis, rheumatism, bursitis	brussels sprouts, soup
	seed	raw	food	bronchitis, scurvy, chills, promotes perspiration	seeds & coffee substitute
	seed	raw/boiled	tea	prostate rejuvenator, diuretic	bread flour & tea
	root	raw/mashed	compress	bruises, blisters, snake bites, spider bites	smoke (leaf)
SWEET-RUSH ROOT	root	raw	chew & ingest	flatulence	
	root	raw/boiled	tea	colic, digestive upsets	tea
	rootstalk	raw	chew & ingest	pain reliever	

149

WILD PLANTS USED BY NATIVE AMERICANS

*denotes poison, narcotic, or abortifacient

Botanical	Part	How Prepared	Medicine Form	Remedy For	Foodstuff
*TANSY	whole	raw/boiled	strong tea	contraception	tea
	flower	raw/steeped	weak tea	fever, gall bladder ailments, worms, heart palpitations	tea
	leaf	raw/boiled	wash	lower-leg pains	
	leaf	raw/crushed	compress	sprains, headache	
	seed	raw/steeped	weak tea	laxative, promotes menstruation	tea
	seed	boiled/mashed	compress	bruises, sunburn, warts, freckles, lower-back pain, skin growths, cancer tumors	
	sap	boiled	wash	insect repellent	
THYME	leaf	raw/crushed	compress	antiseptic, cankers	spice
	leaf	dried/steeped	tea	colic, flatulence, colds, bronchitis, whooping cough, promotes profuse perspiration	tea
	leaf	raw/crushed	liniment	neuralgia, arthritis, rheumatism, toothache, swelling pain, deodorant	

WILD PLANTS USED BY NATIVE AMERICANS

*denotes poison, narcotic, or abortifacient

Botanical	Part	How Prepared	Medicine Form	Remedy For	Foodstuff
UVA-URSI (Kinnikinnick)	leaf	raw/steeped	tea	blood purifier, hepatitis, internal hemorrhaging, acne	tea & smoke
	berry	raw	food	diuretic, diabetes, prostate ailments, kidney stones	fruit
VALERIAN	root	dried/ground			bread flour
	root	raw/boiled	bath additive	exhaustion	
	root	dried/boiled	tea	sedative, abdominal cramps, headache, heart palpitations, insomnia, hypertension, anemia, convulsions	tea
WALNUT	leaf	raw/boiled	wash	eczema, hives, boils, ulcerated sores, astringent, external hemorrhaging	
	bark	raw/boiled	wash	arthritis, skin diseases, chicken pox, measles, itching rashes	
	inner bark	raw/boiled	tea	laxative, ulcers, diverticulitis	tea
	hull	raw/mashed	syrup	worms	syrup (sap)
	hull juice	raw/mashed	wash	head & body lice, dandruff	
	hull juice	raw with honey	syrup	bronchitis, coughs, asthma	
	nut	raw	food	vitamin deficiency, anemia	nuts, oil, bread flour

WILD PLANTS USED BY NATIVE AMERICANS

*denotes poison, narcotic, or abortifacient

Botanical	Part	How Prepared	Medicine Form	Remedy For	Foodstuff
WATERCRESS	leaf	raw	wild greens	high in vitamin E, acidity balancer	salad
	leaf	raw/boiled	tea	liver ailments, stamina, hepatitis, tonsillitis, swollen glands, heart strengthener, kidney stones, spleen pain, acidity balancer, aging, anemia, sedative	tea & soup
WHITE POND LILY	root	raw/boiled	tea	bladder ailments, diarrhea, prostate ailments, kidney ailments	tea
	root	raw/boiled	wash	feminine douche for all womb & uterine abrasions and inflammations	bread flour
	root	raw/mashed	poultice	gum lesions, tooth pain	vegetable (stem)
	root	raw juice	liniment	discolored skin areas	

WILD PLANTS USED BY NATIVE AMERICANS

*denotes poison, narcotic, or abortifacient

Botanical	Part	How Prepared	Medicine Form	Remedy For	Foodstuff
WILD LETTUCE	juice	raw	syrup	pain reliever, headaches, intestinal calmative, abdominal cramps, hypnotic, sedative	syrup
	sap	raw/boiled	paste	hives, toothache, poison ivy & oak	smoke & vegetable (leaf)
	sap	raw/boiled	syrup	bronchitis, coughs	
WILD LICORICE	root	raw/boiled	tea	laxative, fevers	tea
	root	raw/mashed	oil	earaches, neuralgia	
	root	raw	gum chew	coughs, bronchitis, inner ear pressure	chewing gum
WILD ONION	bulb	raw/mashed	compress	pneumonia, infected sores, congestion, sprains	vegetable
	bulb	raw/boiled	tea	scurvy, worms, flu, antibiotic, allergies, appendicitis, whooping cough	tea & soup
	bulb	raw/boiled	wash	hives, itching skin rashes, bites, frostbite	stew flavoring
	bulb	raw/mashed	juice	earache	

*denotes poison, narcotic, or abortifacient

Botanical	Part	How Prepared	Medicine Form	Remedy For	Foodstuff
WILD RICE	rice	raw/boiled	food	high blood pressure, heart palpitations	porridge, bread flour
WILLOW	leaf	raw/mashed	poultice	nosebleeds, toothache, hemorrhoids	
	bark	dried/powdered	wash	astringent, detergent, dandruff	
	inner bark	raw/boiled	tea	venereal disease	tea
	inner bark	raw/mashed	compress	infections, wounds, gangrene, antibiotic, bleeding	
WINTERGREEN	leaf	raw/boiled	gargle	sore throats	salad
	leaf	raw/mashed	compress	swellings, sore muscles, painful joints, pleurisy, sprains	oil
	leaf	dried/steeped	tea	ulcers, colic, gall bladder, internal hemorrhaging, liver & spleen ailments, flatulence, aging	tea
	berry	raw	food	promotes breast-milk flow	fruit & stew flavoring

WILD PLANTS USED BY NATIVE AMERICANS

*denotes poison, narcotic, or abortifacient

Botanical	Part	How Prepared	Medicine Form	Remedy For	Foodstuff
WITCH HAZEL	whole	raw/boiled	steam	bronchitis, flu, coughs	
	leaf	raw/crushed	compress	swellings, bruises, sprains	
	leaf	raw/boiled	tea	stomach ulcers, external hemorrhaging	tea
WORMWOOD	leaf	raw/boiled	tea	bladder, emphysema, tape- & roundworm, jaundice, tonsillitis, liver & spleen ailments, colitis, hepatitis, blood purifier, appendicitis	tea
	leaf	raw/crushed	liniment	sprains, bruises, swellings, rheumatism, arthritis, lower-back pain	
*YARROW	leaf	raw/mashed	poultice	toothache, gum lesions, ear infection	smoke
	leaf	raw/mashed	compress	anesthetic, external hemorrhaging	
	leaf	raw/boiled	wash	anesthetic, burns, sore breasts, irritated eyes, measles, chickenpox, hives, poison ivy & oak	
	root	raw/steeped	weak tea	internal hemorrhaging, colds, swollen glands, hepatitis, gall bladder, blood purifier, appetite, diabetes	tea
	root	raw/boiled	strong tea	contraceptive	tea

WILD PLANTS USED BY NATIVE AMERICANS

*denotes poison, narcotic, or abortifacient

Botanical	Part	How Prepared	Medicine Form	Remedy For	Foodstuff
YELLOW DOCK	leaf	raw	wild greens	scurvy, high in vitamins A & C	salad
	root	dried/steeped	tea	ulcers, swollen glands, tonsillitis, hepatitis, blood builder, liver & spleen ailments, anemia, coughing	tea
	root	raw/mashed	compress	swellings, ulcerated wounds, cysts, leg pain	
YERBA SANTA	leaf	raw/mashed	compress	rheumatism, skin pain, hemorrhoids, hives, swellings, skin sores	
	leaf	raw	gum	breath freshener	chewing gum
	leaf	dried	smoked	asthma, bronchitis, lung congestion	smoke
	leaf	raw/steeped	gargle	sore throats, gum lesions	
	leaf	raw/boiled	tea	vomiting, diarrhea, coughs, ulcers, bronchitis	tea

156

WILD PLANTS USED BY NATIVE AMERICANS

*denotes poison, narcotic, or abortifacient

Botanical	Part	How Prepared	Medicine Form	Remedy For	Foodstuff
YUCCA	flower	raw	food		snack
	leaf	dried/steeped	tea	arthritis, fever, headache, rheumatism, ulcers, appendicitis	tea & salad
	fruit	raw	food	laxative	fruit
	fruit	baked	food		bread flour
	root	raw/mashed	compress	ulcerated wounds & sores, hives, chickenpox, itching rashes, gangrene	
	root	dried/ground	detergent & shampoo	cleanliness	

157

THE DARK SIDE OF NATURE

There are many aspects of daily life that serve to verify the validity of the rules of polarity and duality: light versus darkness, warmth and cold, happiness versus sadness. So, too, do we see and experience the positive and negative aspects of tools such as fire, vehicles, and knives—all helpful to the careful and aware individual, all harmful if misused.

But in some cases, nature's negatives can be transformed into positives. While some plants are "poisonous" in their natural state, modern pharmaceutical firms extract and use these so-called poisons and formulate them into various compounds that are, in turn, used to heal. Thus the Earth Mother's negatives turn into positives.

However, if you are interested in using plants in their natural state for botanical healing, you must be keenly aware of the potential dangers. You must familiarize yourself with those plants that can be fatal if ingested or cause serious skin irritations if handled. Many of these are ordinary houseplants or common flowers. Some may be cultivated in your own yard. They're beautiful and lovely to look at, but can pose real health risks.

And that's where knowledge comes into play and takes over.

Nature, in all of its wonderful aspects, provides for balance and equilibrium. Thus some plants have poisonous components that cause serious side effects, and some can cause fatal reactions.

Any book that addresses botanical healing needs to discuss this darker side. This section lists those plants that have some type of negative-reaction ingredient or component. It's important to be aware of such agents when learning about the Earth Mother's natural medicines.

There are three types of poison terms used to clarify the following chart:

Oral: means biological symptoms affecting the lips, mouth tissue, tongue, and throat.

Systemic: means biological symptoms affecting one or more internal physiological systems—respiratory, circulatory, nervous, digestive, or reproductive.

Dermatitis: means biological symptoms affecting the skin.

THE DARK SIDE OF NATURE

Botanical	Common Names	Poisonous Part	Poison Type	Symptoms	Treatment
AGRIMONY (flowering plant)	Cocklebur	Stem	Dermatitis	May cause skin irritation on contact	Thorough washing Antihistamines
AMARYLLIS (flowering garden plant)	Belladonna lily	Bulb	Systemic	Vomiting & diarrhea Abdominal pain/spasms Respiratory paralysis MAY BE FATAL	Immediate hospitalization
APPLE (fruit tree)	Same	Seed/Leaf	Systemic	Headache, giddiness Rapid heart palpitations Respiratory distress Vomiting, convulsions Possible coma MAY BE FATAL	Immediate hospitalization
ARNICA (sunflower family)	Catbane	Flower/Root	Systemic	Vomiting Depressed respiration Muscle weakness Possible coma MAY BE FATAL	Immediate hospitalization
		Stem	Dermatitis	May cause skin irritation on contact	Thorough washing Antihistamines
ASPARAGUS (stalk plant)	Same	Berry	Systemic	Vomiting Diarrhea	Home treatment
		Stem	Dermatitis	May cause skin irritation on contact	Thorough washing Antihistamines

159

THE DARK SIDE OF NATURE

Botanical	Common Names	Poisonous Part	Poison Type	Symptoms	Treatment
AZALEA (flowering plant)	Rhododendron Rose laurel	Entire (including honey made from nectar)	Oral	Caustic to mouth tissue and throat	Immediate hospitalization
			Systemic	Vomiting, diarrhea Eye tearing Headache Impaired vision Muscle paralysis Convulsions Possible coma MAY BE FATAL	Immediate hospitalization
BANEBERRY (flowering herb)	Snakeberry	Entire	Oral	Ulceration of mouth tissue and throat	Immediate hospitalization
			Systemic	Bloody vomiting & diarrhea Mental disorientation Convulsions MAY BE FATAL	Immediate hospitalization
BITTERSWEET (berry shrub)	Redroot Fevertwig	Entire	Systemic	Severe vomiting & diarrhea Rapid heart rate Depression of nervous system may occur	Immediate hospitalization
BLACK LOCUST (flowering tree)	Acacia Silver chain	Entire	Systemic	Vomiting & diarrhea Muscle weakness Profuse sweating Depressed respiration Possible coma MAY BE FATAL	Immediate hospitalization

Botanical	Common Names	Poisonous Part	Poison Type	Symptoms	Treatment
BLACK MUSTARD (flowering herb)	Same	Root/Seed	Systemic	Vomiting & diarrhea Abdominal pain/cramping	Immediate hospitalization
BLEEDING HEART (flowering plant)	Same	Entire	Systemic	Depressed respiration Slowed heart rate Possible convulsions MAY BE FATAL	Immediate hospitalization
		Stem	Dermatitis	May cause skin irritation on contact	Thorough washing Antihistamines
BLOODROOT (flowering plant)	Same	Root/Sap	Systemic	Vomiting Muscle weakness Depressed heart rate MAY BE FATAL	Immediate hospitalization
BLUE COHOSH (flowering herb)	Squawroot Blue ginseng	Root/Berry	Systemic	Severe intestinal cramping with diarrhea	Home treatment with attention given to ingestion of fluids to prevent dehydration
BOXWOOD (berry shrub)	Same	Entire	Systemic	Vomiting Abdominal pain/cramping Possible convulsions MAY BE FATAL	Immediate hospitalization
		Leaf	Dermatitis	May cause skin irritation on contact	Thorough washing Antihistamines

THE DARK SIDE OF NATURE

Botanical	Common Names	Poisonous Part	Poison Type	Symptoms	Treatment
BUCKTHORN (berry shrub)	Coffeeberry	Entire	Systemic	Severe abdominal cramping Respiratory failure through paralysis MAY BE FATAL	Immediate hospitalization
BUTTERCUP (flowering herb)	Devil's claw Figwort Spearwort	Entire	Oral	Inflammation of mouth tissue and throat with blistering	Immediate hospitalization
		Leaf/Sap	Systemic	Vomiting & diarrhea Profuse sweating Increased salivation Dizziness Mental disorientation Convulsions Possible coma MAY BE FATAL	Immediate hospitalization
			Dermatitis	Severe skin irritation may develop from sap contact	Medical attention advised
CALADIUM (houseplant)	Elephant's ear	Entire	Oral	Severe irritation & swelling & pain in mouth & throat MAY BE FATAL if swelling blocks airways	Medical attention advised
CALLA (stalk plant)	Calla lily	Leaf	Oral	Caustic to mouth tissue and throat with possible swelling MAY BE FATAL if swelling blocks airways	Medical attention advised
			Dermatitis	May cause skin irritation on contact	Thorough washing Antihistamines

Botanical	Common Names	Poisonous Part	Poison Type	Symptoms	Treatment
CANDELABRA CACTUS (succulent plant)	Same	Entire	Oral	Caustic to mouth tissue and throat	Medical attention advised
			Systemic	Vomiting, diarrhea with severe abdominal pain and cramping Vision distortion	Immediate hospitalization
		Sap	Dermatitis	May cause skin irritation on contact	Thorough washing Antihistamines
CASTOR BEAN (ornamental shrub)	Palma christi	Entire	Oral	Caustic to mouth tissue and throat	Medical attention advised
			Systemic	Vomiting Severe abdominal cramping Severe diarrhea Vision distortion Respiratory distress Heart failure Convulsions MAY BE FATAL	Immediate hospitalization
		Seed	Dermatitis	May cause skin irritation on contact	Thorough washing Antihistamines
CHOKECHERRY (flowering shrub)	Western chokecherry	Entire	Systemic	Vomiting, diarrhea Abdominal pain with cramping Profuse sweating Depressed respiration Convulsions Possible coma MAY BE FATAL	Immediate hospitalization

163

THE DARK SIDE OF NATURE

Botanical	Common Names	Poisonous Part	Poison Type	Symptoms	Treatment
CLEMATIS (flowering vine)	Same	Entire	Oral	Severe inflammation and pain of mouth tissue and throat	Immediate hospitalization
			Systemic	Bloody vomiting & diarrhea Abdominal cramping Mental disorientation Convulsions MAY BE FATAL	Immediate hospitalization
		Leaf	Dermatitis	May cause skin irritation	Thorough washing Antihistamines
COLUMBINE (wildflower)	Same	Entire (in some species)	Systemic	Giddiness Depressed respiration Muscle paralysis Convulsions Possible coma MAY BE FATAL	Immediate hospitalization
COTTON ROOT (herb shrub)	Same	Root	Systemic	Abdominal pains and cramping Uterine cramping/ contractions POSSIBLE SPONTANEOUS ABORTION	Immediate hospitalization
COWSLIP (flowering herb)	Marsh marigold	Entire	Oral	Severe inflammation of mouth tissue and throat	Immediate hospitalization
			Systemic	Severe abdominal cramping with bloody vomiting and diarrhea	Immediate hospitalization

164

Botanical	Common Names	Poisonous Part	Poison Type	Symptoms	Treatment
CROWN OF THORNS (spiny houseplant)	Christ thorn	Entire	Oral	Caustic to mouth tissue and throat	Medical attention advised
			Systemic	Severe abdominal pain and cramping Depressed respiration Vomiting, diarrhea	Immediate hospitalization
		Sap	Dermatitis	May cause skin irritation on contact	Thorough washing Antihistamines
DAFFODIL (flowering plant)	Narcissus Jonquil	Bulb	Systemic	Vomiting, diarrhea Muscle spasms Convulsions MAY BE FATAL	Immediate hospitalization
		Leaf/Bulb	Dermatitis	May cause skin irritations	Thorough washing Antihistamines
DEATH CAMAS (flowering herb)	Soap plant	Entire	Oral	Caustic to mouth tissue and throat	Medical attention advised
			Systemic	Vomiting Headache Mental disorientation Depressed heart rate Convulsions Possible coma MAY BE FATAL	Immediate hospitalization

THE DARK SIDE OF NATURE

Botanical	Common Names	Poisonous Part	Poison Type	Symptoms	Treatment
DIEFFENBACHIA (houseplant)	Dumb plant Dumb cane	Leaf	Oral	Severe inflammation and swelling of mouth and throat causing impaired speech MAY BE FATAL if throat swells to block airway	Immediate hospitalization
		Sap	Dermatitis	May cause skin irritation on contact	Thorough washing Antihistamines
ELDERBERRY (flowering tree)	American elder	Entire	Systemic	Vomiting, diarrhea Severe abdominal pain and cramping	Medical attention advised
FALSE HELLEBORE (flowering shrub)	Same	Entire	Oral	Severe pain in mouth tissue	Immediate hospitalization
			Systemic	Vomiting, diarrhea Abdominal cramping Depressed respiration Possible coma MAY BE FATAL	Immediate hospitalization
FALSE PARSLEY (flowering plant)	Dog parsley Fool's parsley	Entire	Systemic	Headache Convulsive vomiting	Medical attention advised
FLAMING LILY (tropical houseplant)	Pigtail plant Flamingo plant	Leaf/Stem	Oral	Inflammation and blistering of mouth tissue and throat MAY BE FATAL if throat swells and blocks airway	Medical attention advised

Botanical	Common Names	Poisonous Part	Poison Type	Symptoms	Treatment
FLATSPINE RAGWEED	Same	Leaf	Systemic	Abdominal pain and cramping Uterine contractions POSSIBLE SPONTANEOUS ABORTION	Immediate hospitalization
FOXGLOVE (flowering plant)	Fairy thimble	Entire	Oral	Severe pain to mouth tissue and tongue	Immediate hospitalization
			Systemic	Vomiting, diarrhea Abdominal cramping Irregular heart rate Convulsions Possible coma MAY BE FATAL	Immediate hospitalization
GOLDEN CHAIN (flowering tree)	Bean tree	Entire	Systemic	Vomiting, diarrhea Severe abdominal pain Headache Mental disorientation Increased heart rate MAY BE FATAL	Immediate hospitalization
HENBANE (flowering weed)	Poison tobacco Black henbane	Leaf/Seed	Oral	Dry mouth	Immediate hospitalization
		Leaf/Stem	Dermatitis	Dry skin or severe rash	Thorough washing Antihistamines
		Entire	Systemic	Fever Impaired vision Headache Mental disorientation Increased heart rate Hallucinations	Immediate hospitalization

167

THE DARK SIDE OF NATURE

Botanical	Common Names	Poisonous Part	Poison Type	Symptoms	Treatment
HOLLY (evergreen bush)	English holly American holly	Berry	Systemic	Vomiting, diarrhea Severe abdominal pains MAY BE FATAL	Immediate hospitalization
HONEYSUCKLE (flowering vine)	Woodbine	Berry	Systemic	Vomiting, diarrhea Abdominal pain Increased heart rate Convulsions MAY BE FATAL due to respiratory failure	Immediate hospitalization
HORSE CHESTNUT (flowering plant)	Buckeye	Entire (including honey made from nectar)	Systemic	Abdominal cramping Mental disorientation Vertigo Severe uterine contractions Possible coma MAY CAUSE SPONTANEOUS ABORTION MAY BE FATAL	Immediate hospitalization
HYACINTH (flowering plant)	Same	Entire	Systemic	Vomiting, diarrhea Severe abdominal pain and cramping	Immediate hospitalization
		Bulb	Dermatitis	May cause skin irritation on contact	Thorough washing Antihistamines

Botanical	Common Names	Poisonous Part	Poison Type	Symptoms	Treatment
HYDRANGEA (flowering shrub)	Hills-of-snow	Entire	Systemic	Vomiting, diarrhea Abdominal pain Increased heart rate Profuse sweating Convulsions Possible coma MAY BE FATAL	Immediate hospitalization
INDIAN HEMP (flowering pod plant)	Dogbane Hemp dogbane	Entire	Systemic	Strong narcotic Vomiting Hallucinations MAY BE FATAL	Immediate hospitalization for overdose
IRIS (flowering plant)	Flag Fleur-de-lis	Root	Systemic	Vomiting, diarrhea Abdominal pain and cramping	Home treatment for symptoms unless they are extreme or persistent
IVY (climbing vine)	English ivy	Leaf/Berry	Oral Systemic	Irritation to mouth tissue and throat Vomiting, diarrhea Abdominal cramping Depressed respiration Possible coma MAY BE FATAL	Medical attention advised Immediate hospitalization

THE DARK SIDE OF NATURE

Botanical	Common Names	Poisonous Part	Poison Type	Symptoms	Treatment
JACK-IN-THE-PULPIT (flowering plant)	Memory root, Dragon tail, Pepper turnip	Entire	Oral	Inflammation of mouth tissue and throat with possible swelling, MAY BE FATAL if swelling of throat blocks airway	Medical attention advised
JASMINE (flowering vine)	Star jasmine, Yellow jasmine	Entire (including honey from nectar)	Systemic	Vomiting, Headache, Muscle weakness, Mental disorientation, Distortion of vision, Depressed respiration, Convulsions, MAY BE FATAL	Immediate hospitalization
		Stem	Dermatitis	May cause skin irritation on contact	Thorough washing, Antihistamines
JIMSONWEED (flowering plant)	Stinkweed, Thorn apple, Moonflower, Datura	Entire (including nectar)	Oral, Systemic	Dry mouth, Skin flushing, Increased blood pressure, Rapid heart rate, Headache, Mental disorientation, Hallucinations, Possible coma, MAY BE FATAL	Medical attention advised, Immediate hospitalization

170

Botanical	Common Names	Poisonous Part	Poison Type	Symptoms	Treatment
LAMB'S-QUARTER (flowering herb)	Goosefoot	Entire	Systemic	Vomiting Headache Vertigo Mental disorientation Depressed respiration Convulsions Possible coma MAY BE FATAL	Immediate hospitalization
LARKSPUR (flowering plant)	Delphinium	Entire	Oral	Caustic to mouth tissue	Medical attention advised
			Systemic	Vomiting Rapid heart rate Depressed respiration Convulsions Possible coma MAY BE FATAL	Immediate hospitalization
		Stem	Dermatitis	May cause skin irritation	Thorough washing Antihistamines
LILY OF THE VALLEY (flowering plant)	Muguet	Entire	Oral	Caustic to mouth tissue	Medical attention advised
			Systemic	Vomiting, diarrhea Headache Vertigo Abdominal cramping Rapid heart palpitations Muscle paralysis Possible coma MAY BE FATAL	Immediate hospitalization

171

THE DARK SIDE OF NATURE

Botanical	Common Names	Poisonous Part	Poison Type	Symptoms	Treatment
LOBELIA (flowering plant)	Indian tobacco Wild tobacco Cardinal flower	Entire	Systemic	Vomiting Headache Vertigo Abdominal pain and cramping Mental disorientation Depressed respiration Convulsions Possible coma MAY BE FATAL	Immediate hospitalization
LOCOWEED (flowering herb)	Crazyweed Rattleweed Loco	Leaf	Systemic	Vomiting, diarrhea Abdominal pain Vertigo Mental disorientation	Immediate hospitalization
LUPINE (flowering herb)	Bluebonnet	Entire	Systemic	Mental disorientation Depressed respiration Convulsions Possible coma MAY BE FATAL	Immediate hospitalization
MANDRAKE (flowering herb)	Mayapple Indian apple	Entire	Systemic	Vomiting, diarrhea Abdominal pains Muscle weakness Possible coma MAY BE FATAL	Immediate hospitalization

172

Botanical	Common Names	Poisonous Part	Poison Type	Symptoms	Treatment
MILKWEED (pod plant)	Same	Entire	Systemic	Vomiting, diarrhea Severe abdominal pains and cramping Muscle weakness Depressed respiration MAY BE FATAL	Immediate hospitalization
MISTLETOE (berry plant)	Same	Entire	Systemic	Vomiting, diarrhea Severe abdominal cramping Depressed heart rate Severe uterine contractions Convulsions Possible coma MAY CAUSE SPONTANEOUS ABORTION MAY BE FATAL	Immediate hospitalization
MONKSHOOD (flowering plant)	Wolfsbane	Entire	Oral Systemic	Severe mouth and throat irritation Vomiting Rapid heart palpitations Distorted vision Muscle paralysis MAY BE FATAL <u>WITHIN HOURS</u>	Medical attention advised Immediate Hospitalization
MORNING GLORY (flowering vine)	Blue star	Seeds	Systemic	Vomiting, diarrhea Severe abdominal pains Mental disorientation Hallucinations Possible coma MAY BE FATAL	Immediate hospitalization

THE DARK SIDE OF NATURE

Botanical	Common Names	Poisonous Part	Poison Type	Symptoms	Treatment
MOUNTAIN LAUREL (flowering bush)	Wood laurel Ivy bush	Leaf/Nectar	Oral	Severe irritation to mouth tissue	Medical attention advised
			Systemic	Vomiting, diarrhea Headache Distorted vision Depressed heart rate Eye tearing Convulsions Possible coma MAY BE FATAL	Immediate Hospitalization
MULBERRY (flowering fruit tree)	Same	Unripe fruit/ sap	Systemic	Vomiting Muscle paralysis Hallucinations Convulsions MAY BE FATAL	Immediate hospitalization
		Sap	Dermatitis	May cause skin irritations	Thorough washing Antihistamines
NIGHTSHADE (flowering berry plant)	Belladonna Poisonberry Black nightshade Deadly nightshade	Entire	Systemic	Severe abdominal pains Muscle paralysis Profuse perspiration Distorted vision Fever Hallucinations Rapid heart palpitations Possible coma MAY BE FATAL	Immediate hospitalization
			Dermatitis	Severe skin rash may occur	Medical attention advised

174

Botanical	Common Names	Poisonous Part	Poison Type	Symptoms	Treatment
OLEANDER (flowering shrub)	Same	Entire (including nectar, honey from nectar, & smoke from burning)	Oral	Severe pain in mouth tissue and throat	Immediate hospitalization
			Systemic	Vomitting, diarrhea Severe abdominal pain and cramping Depressed heart rate Respiratory distress Convulsions Coma DEATH WITHIN 24 HOURS	Immediate hospitalization
		Leaf	Dermatitis	May irritate skin on contact	Medical attention advised
PASQUEFLOWER (flowering herb)	Nightcaps Thimbleweed Wild crocus	Entire	Oral	Severe inflammation of mouth tissue and throat	Immediate hospitalization
			Systemic	Bloody vomiting & diarrhea Rapid heart palpitations Abdominal cramping MAY BE FATAL	Immediate hospitalization
		Leaf	Dermatitis	May cause skin blistering	Medical attention advised
PEACH (flowering fruit tree)	Peach	Pit/Leaf	Systemic	Vomiting Vertigo Headache Mental disorientation Respiratory distress Rapid heart palpitations Convulsions Possible coma MAY BE FATAL due to cyanide poisoning	Immediate hospitalization

THE DARK SIDE OF NATURE

Botanical	Common Names	Poisonous Part	Poison Type	Symptoms	Treatment
PEPPER BUSH (flowering bush)	Dog laurel Sweetbells	Leaf/Nectar	Oral	Severe caustic irritation to mouth tissue and tongue	Medical attention advised
			Systemic	Vomiting, diarrhea Headache Muscle weakness Distorted vision Possible coma MAY BE FATAL	Immediate hospitalization
PEYOTE (flowering cactus)	Mescal Mescal bean	Root buttons	Systemic	Vomiting Distorted vision Vertigo Hallucinations	Immediate hospitalization for overdose
PHILODENDRON (houseplant)	Same	Leaf	Oral	Caustic to lips, mouth tissue, tongue, and throat	Medical attention advised
			Dermatitis	May cause skin irritation to sensitive skin types	Thorough washing Antihistamines
POINSETTIA (flowering plant)	Christmas flower	Leaf/Stem/Sap	Oral	Caustic to lips, mouth tissue, tongue, and throat	Medical attention advised
			Systemic	Vomiting, diarrhea Mental disorientation	Immediate hospitalization
		Sap	Dermatitis	May cause skin irritation to sensitive skin types	Thorough washing Antihistamines

176

Botanical	Common Names	Poisonous Part	Poison Type	Symptoms	Treatment
POISON HEMLOCK (flowering plant)	Snakeweed Spotted hemlock Winter fern	Entire	Oral	Caustic irritation to lips, mouth tissue, tongue, and throat	Medical attention advised
			Systemic	Vomiting Severe abdominal cramping Headache Mental disorientation Possible coma MAY BE FATAL	Immediate hospitalization
POISON IVY/ OAK/SUMAC (low green plant)	Same	Entire	Dermatitis	Severe skin irritation on contact	Thorough washing Antihistamines
POKEWEED (flowering plant)	Indian poke Pokeberry Redweed	Entire	Oral	Caustic to lips, mouth tissue, tongue, and throat	Medical attention advised
			Systemic	Vomiting, diarrhea Severe abdominal cramping Profuse perspiration Depressed respiration Muscle spasms Stupor MAY BE FATAL	Immediate hospitalization

THE DARK SIDE OF NATURE

Botanical	Common Names	Poisonous Part	Poison Type	Symptoms	Treatment
POPPY (flowering plant)	Golden poppy	Entire	Systemic	Respiratory distress Mental disorientation Hallucinations Stupor Possible coma MAY BE FATAL	Immediate hospitalization
POTATO (underground tuber)	Irish potato White potato	*Green* potato/ sprouts/ unripe berry	Systemic	Vomiting, diarrhea Severe abdominal cramping Headache Depressed respiration Slowed heart rate Muscle paralysis Possible coma MAY BE FATAL	Immediate hospitalization
PRIVET HEDGE (flowering shrub)	Prim Waxleaf	Entire	Systemic	Vomiting, diarrhea Severe abdominal cramping Muscle weakness Convulsions MAY BE FATAL	Immediate hospitalization

Botanical	Common Names	Poisonous Part	Poison Type	Symptoms	Treatment
RHUBARB (stalk plant)	Wine plant Pieplant	Leaf/Root	Oral	Caustic to mouth tissue, tongue, and throat. May cause throat swelling. MAY BE FATAL due to throat swelling that blocks airway	Immediate hospitalization
			Systemic	Vomiting, diarrhea Severe abdominal cramping Headache Respiratory distress Possible coma MAY BE FATAL	Immediate hospitalization
SNAKEROOT (flowering shrub)	White snakeroot	Entire	Systemic	Severe vomiting Depressed respiration Mental disorientation Liver damage Possible coma MAY BE FATAL	Immediate hospitalization
SNOWBERRY (flowering bush)	Waxberry	Berry	Systemic	Vomiting & diarrhea	Medical attention advised
SNOW-ON-THE-MOUNTAIN (groundcover)	Ghostweed	Leaf/Stem/Sap (including honey from nectar)	Oral	Severe caustic irritation to lips, mouth tissue, tongue, and throat	Medical attention advised
			Systemic	Vomiting, diarrhea Lowered blood pressure Slowed heart rate Respiratory distress MAY BE FATAL	Immediate hospitalization

179

THE DARK SIDE OF NATURE

Botanical	Common Names	Poisonous Part	Poison Type	Symptoms	Treatment
STAR-OF-BETHLEHEM (stalk plant)	Wonder flower	Entire	Oral	Severe pain to lips, mouth tissue, tongue, and throat	Medical attention advised
			Systemic	Vomiting, diarrhea Severe abdominal cramping	Immediate hospitalization due to severity of symptoms
STINGING NETTLE (stalk plant)	Same	Hairs on leaf & stem	Dermatitis	Severe skin burning and skin irritation that may last 48 hours or more	Thorough washing Antihistamines
SWALLOWWORT (flowering plant)	Celandine Wort weed	Entire	Systemic	Vomiting, diarrhea Respiratory distress Headache Fever Possible coma MAY BE FATAL due to heart failure	Immediate hospitalization
SWAMPWOOD (flowering shrub)	Leather bush Moosewood Leatherwood	Entire	Oral	Severe caustic irritation to lips, mouth tissue, tongue, and throat	Medical attention advised
		Sap	Dermatitis	May cause skin irritations	Thorough washing Antihistamines

Botanical	Common Names	Poisonous Part	Poison Type	Symptoms	Treatment
SWEET PEA (flowering vine)	Everlasting pea	Entire	Systemic	Slowed heart rate Respiratory distress Muscle paralysis Possible coma MAY BE FATAL	Immediate hospitalization
TANSY (flowering plant)	Buttons Common tansy	Entire	Systemic	Severe abdominal pain and cramping Severe uterine contractions MAY CAUSE SPONTANEOUS ABORTION	Immediate hospitalization
WATER HEMLOCK (flowering plant)	Spotted cowbane Beaver poison	Entire	Systemic	Severe vomiting Convulsions USUALLY FATAL	Immediate hospitalization
WISTERIA (flowering tree)	Same	Entire	Systemic	Vomiting Severe abdominal pain	Immediate hospitalization
YARROW (flowering plant)	Achillea Sneezewort	Root	Systemic	Severe abdominal pain and cramping Severe uterine contractions MAY CAUSE SPONTANEOUS ABORTION	Immediate hospitalization

181

THE DARK SIDE OF NATURE

Botanical	Common Names	Poisonous Part	Poison Type	Symptoms	Treatment
YEW (evergreen shrub)	Ground hemlock	Entire	Systemic	Vomiting Severe abdominal cramping Muscle spasms Mental disorientation Rapid heart palpitations Possible coma MAY BE FATAL	Immediate hospitalization

THE EARTH MOTHER'S PHARMACY

While gathering together all of No-Eyes' health material, I noticed that there was something of great importance missing. She and I had never discussed verifying natural botanical healing by comparing its treatments to modern medicine and pharmaceutical preparations.

I sometimes feel that many modern physicians, in their great hostility to natural botanical cures, have altogether forgotten how many of their "wonder drugs" are made up of one or more natural plants or substances. Have they completely forgotten the importance of botanicals?

Most people depend solely on the physician's prescription slip for their medicines. Few patients are aware of the natural botanicals that were used as the prescription's base or main formula ingredient.

I decided to add the following section to No-Eyes' material as an informative look at the uses of natural botanicals in today's pharmaceutical medications.

A MEDICAL GLOSSARY

Abortifacient: induces abortion/labor
Alkaloid: organic formula base
Analgesic: stops pain
Anesthetic: producing no pain
Anodyne: relieves pain
Anthelmintic: destructive to worms/intestinal parasites
Antibiotic: destructive to internal bacteria
Antispasmodic: relieves spasms
Aperient: mild intestinal laxative
Astringent: stops secretions
Carminative: relieves intestinal gas
Cathartic: stimulates bowel evacuation
Cholagogue: stimulates gall bladder activity
Choleretic: stimulates bile excretion from liver
Coagulant: slows or stops bleeding
Demulcent: soothing to inflamed/irritated areas
Diaphoretic: stimulates perspiration output
Diuretic: stimulates urine output
Dyspepsia: indigestion
Emetic: produces vomiting reaction
Emmenagogue: stimulates menstrual flow
Expectorant: promotes ability to cough up mucus
Febrifuge: lowers fever
Galactagogue: stimulates milk flow
Hallucinogenic: produces hallucinations/neurological stimulant
Hemostatic: stops bleeding
Hepatic: stimulates normal liver functioning
Hydragogue: producing watery discharge

Narcotic: producing sleep/stupor
Resolvent: stops growth
Stimulant: promotes biological/neurological activity
Stomachic: promotes normal stomach functioning
Tranquilizer: soothes nervous system
Vulnerary: promotes wound healing

THE EARTH MOTHER'S PHARMACY

Natural Botanical or Source	Medicinal Function	Pharmaceutical Drug or Active Agent
AFRICAN ROOT	Dysentery Antidiarrheic	UZARA
AFRICAN SEEDPOD	Anthelmintic	WARAS
AFRICAN SHRUB	Heart disease Cortisone source	STROPHANTHIN SARMENTOGENIN
ALDER	Laxative Emetic	PHENOL GLYCOSIDES/ RHAMMOXANTHIN
ALMOND OIL	Hemorrhoid ointment	BENZALDEHYDE
ALUMROOT	Astringent Hemostatic	ALUMEN
AMARYLLIS	Cathartic	LYCORINE
AMERICAN CENTAURY	Febrifuge Stomachic Aperient	GLYCOSIDE BITTERS/ OLEANOLIC ACID
AMMI FRUIT	Heart disease Bronchitis	TANNINS
ANAMIRTA BERRY	Respiratory stimulant	PICROTOXIN
ANDIRA PLANT	Anthelmintic	CHRYSAROBIN
ANGELICA	Carminative Stomachic Diuretic Diaphoretic	PHELLANDRENE COUMARIN
ANISE OIL	Pharmaceutical ingredient Carminative	ANISUM ANETHOLE
ANTIMONY OIL	Resolvent Vulnerary	TRICHLORIDE
ARECA NUT	Anthelmintic	GUAVACINE
ARNICA	Heart disease Nervine Tranquilizer Liniment (sprains/ bruises)	TANNIN

THE EARTH MOTHER'S PHARMACY

Natural Botanical or Source	Medicinal Function	Pharmaceutical Drug or Active Agent
ARTICHOKE	Hepatic Choleretic	CYNARINE
ASCOMYCETE FUNGI	Antibiotic	PENICILLIN
ASIAN BALSAM	Skin diseases	STYRAX
ASIAN GERANIUM	Astringent Dysentery Vulnerary Diuretic Gum Poultice Hemostatic	TANNINS
ASPARAGUS	Diuretic	ASPARAGIN
ASPERGILLACEAE MOLD	Antibiotic	MYCOCIDIN
AUTUMN CROCUS	Gout	COLCHICINE
BALSAM	Antirheumatic Febrifuge Diuretic Anti-itch agent	BENZOIN
BAMBOO	Anthelmintic	ARECADINE
BARBADOS NUTS	Cathartic	CURCAS
BARBERRY	Boils Cathartic Choleretic	BERBERINE
BASIL	Carminative	METHYL CHAVICOL
BASSWOOD	Stimulant Demulcent Headache Burns Sedative baths	BENNE-OIL
BAYCURU ROOT	Astringent Hemostatic	CURU
BEARBERRY	Kidney diseases	ARBUTIN
BEAR'S-FOOT	Antimalarial Antispasmodic Anthelmintic Stomachic	ALDEHYDE/TANNIN
BEDSTRAW	Diuretic	SILICIC ACID
BEECH	Bronchitis Tuberculosis Respiratory diseases	TANNINS

THE EARTH MOTHER'S PHARMACY

Natural Botanical or Source	Medicinal Function	Pharmaceutical Drug or Active Agent
BEET	Menstrual aid	BETAINE
BETEL NUT	Astringent Anthelmintic	ARECADINE
BINDWEED	Diuretic Cathartic Hydragogue Choleretic Anthelmintic	CONVOLVULUS/ QUININE
BIRCH	Diuretic Antiseptic	SAPONINS
BITO TREE	Anthelmintic	ZACHUN OIL
BITTER APPLE	Cathartic	CITRULLIN
BITTER-BLAAR	Diabetes	BRADYCHYLAENA
BITTERSWEET	Narcotic Diuretic Diaphoretic	ALKALOIDS
BLACKBERRY	Tonic Astringent Antidiarrheic Stomachic Antinausea Emmenagogue	TANNINS
BLACK-BIRCH BARK	Rheumatism	METHYL SALICYLATE
BLACK CARAWAY	Bronchitis Cough suppressant	COUMARIN/SAPONIN
BLACK HAW	Antispasmodic Uterine sedative	SCOPOLETINE/ COUMARINS/ OLEANOLIC
BLACK MUSTARD	Stimulates skin circulation	SINAPINE
BLACK PEPPER	Carminative	PIPERINE
BLACK SNAKEROOT	Antispasmodic	CIMICIFUGIN
BLACK WALNUT	Anthelmintic	TANNINS
BLACK WALNUT LEAVES	Antibiotic	JUGLONE
BLESSED THISTLE	Dyspepsia Hepatic Choleretic Emmenagogue	TANNIN

THE EARTH MOTHER'S PHARMACY

Natural Botanical or Source	Medicinal Function	Pharmaceutical Drug or Active Agent
BLISTER BUG	Diuretic	CANTHARIDE
BLOODROOT	Emetic Cholagogue Skin diseases	ALKALOIDS
BLUE LUNGWORT	Diuretic Astringent Aperient	SILICIC ACID/ ALLANTOIN
BLUE VERVAIN	Epilepsy Antispasmodic	ALKALOIDS
BONESET	Diuretic Stomachic Diaphoretic Febrifuge Aperient Antispasmodic Choleretic	EUPARIN/TANNIN/ TRITERPENES
BORAGE	Heart disease	BORAGO
BOVISTA FUNGUS	Antiseptic Tranquilizer	HYCOPERDON
BOXWOOD	Febrifuge	BUXINE
BROOM PLANT	Emetic	SCOPARIN
BUCKBEAN	Tonic Febrifuge	MENYANTHINE/TANNIN/ BITTERS
BUCKTHORN	Antirheumatic	FRANGULIN
BUCKWHEAT	Heart disease Coagulant Vascular strengthener	QUININE
BUGLEWEED	Astringent Tranquilizer	TANNIN
BURDOCK ROOT	Diuretic Diaphoretic Antiseptic Laxative Emmenagogue	ASARONE/TANNIN
BUTEA TREE	Anthelmintic	MOODOOGA OIL
BUTTERNUT ROOT	Aperient	TANNINS
CABBAGE	Insulin	VEGULIN

THE EARTH MOTHER'S PHARMACY

Natural Botanical or Source	Medicinal Function	Pharmaceutical Drug or Active Agent
CACAO PLANT	Anodyne	THEOBROMINE
	Diuretic	
	Antiseptic	SODIOSALICYLATE
	Heart disease	
	Diuretic	SODIUM ACETATE
CACTUS	Cardiovascular and spinal stimulant	ANHALONIUM
CAJEPUT TREE	Dental anodyne	OIL OF CAJEPUT
	Rheumatism	(Cajeputol)
	Anthelmintic	CAJEPUTENE
	Antispasmodic	
CALABAR BEAN	Tetanus	CALABARINE
	Antispasmodic	ESERINE
	Emphysema	PHYSOSTIGMINE
CALAMUS ROOT	Carminative	ASARONE/TANNIN
	Digestive stimulant	
	Aperient	
CALEDULA (Marigold)	Vulnerary	SAPONIN
	Resolvent	
	Choleretic	
CALUMBA ROOT	Stomachic	SILICIC ACID
CAMBOGIA GUM	Cathartic	QUININE
	Hydragogue	
CANELLA BARK	Stomachic	CANELLICINE
	Tonic	
	Stimulant	
CARAWAY	Antispasmodic	COUMARIN/CARVENE
	Carminative	
	Stomachic	
	Galactagogue	
CARDAMOM SEED	Carminative	CARDAMONIUM
CARROT SEED	Diuretic	CAROTENE
	Stimulant	
CASCARA BARK	Cathartic	GLYCOSIDES
CASSAVA ROOT	Corneal ulcers	CASSARIPE
	Eye diseases	
	Conjunctivitis	
CASTOR BEAN	Cathartic	RICININE/RICIN
	Galactagogue	

THE EARTH MOTHER'S PHARMACY

Natural Botanical or Source	Medicinal Function	Pharmaceutical Drug or Active Agent
CATNIP LEAVES	Nerve Stimulant Carminative Colic Sedative Antispasmodic Diaphoretic Emmenagogue Headache Choleretic	PROTOPINE/SAPONIN
CAYENNE PEPPER	Carminative Stimulant Liniment	CAPSAICIN CAPCISUM CAPSICOL
CEDAR OIL	Microscopy surgery	CEDAROL
CEREAL FUNGUS	Narcotic Uterine stimulant	ERGOTAMINE
CHAMOMILE	Tonic Febrifuge	AZULENE
CHAULMOOGRA-SEED OIL	Skin diseases	TARAKTOGENES
CHAWSTICK	Dentifrice Tonic	GOUANIA
CHAYA	Resolvent	TRICHLORIDE
CHERVIL	Diuretic	CHAIROPHYUM
CHICKWEED	Demulcent Blood cleanser Ulcers/boils Hemorrhoidal poultice	SAPONINS
CHILE ORCHID	Diuretic	DIURETINE
CHOKECHERRY	Astringent Sedative	LAETRILE/ CYANOGENTIC GLYCOSIDES
CINCHONA BARK	Heart disease	QUINIDINE
CINNAMON OIL	Pharmaceutical ingredient Pharmaceutical ingredient Stomachic	CINNAMOL CINNAMALDEHYDE EUGENOL
CITRUS PECTIN	Antispasmodic Antidiarrheic	KAOPECTATE

THE EARTH MOTHER'S PHARMACY

Natural Botanical or Source	Medicinal Function	Pharmaceutical Drug or Active Agent
CLITOCYBE MUSHROOM	Antibiotic	CLITOCYBINE

CLOVE	Antiseptic
	Topical anesthetic
	Dental anodyne
	Carminative
	Antispasmodic
	Antinausea medication
		CARYPHYLLIN/
		  VOLATILE OIL/
		  TANNINS

COBWEBS (spiders')	Hemostatic	ARANEUM
COCA LEAVES	Narcotic Anesthetic	COCAINE

COCONUT OIL	Pharmaceutical
	  ingredient for
	  suppositories
		COPRAOL

COD LIVER	Diuretic Cathartic	BUTYLAMINE
COFFEE BEAN	Headaches Asthma Nerve stimulant Diuretic	TANNIN/CAFFEINE
CORALROOT	Diaphoretic Febrifuge Carminative Anthelmintic Cathartic Choleretic	PHYTOTOXIN (Toxalbumin curcin)
CORIANDER	Carminative	METHYL-CHAVICOL
CORIANDER OIL	Pharmaceutical ingredient	CORIANDRUM
CORYDALIS	Diuretic Anthelmintic Antispasmodic	CORYDALINE/ CANADINE
COTTON	Hemostatic Antiseptic dressing	BETAINE/SALICYLATE

COTTON BARK	Diuretic
	Emmenagogue
		PHENOLCARBONIC
		  ACID
		  TANNINS

COUCHGRASS ROOT	Diuretic Cystitis Antibiotic	MANNITOL/TRITICIN

THE EARTH MOTHER'S PHARMACY

Natural Botanical or Source	Medicinal Function	Pharmaceutical Drug or Active Agent

CRANBERRY BARK	Antispasmodic
	Diuretic
	Uterine sedative
	Blood purifier
	Cholagogue
		ALKALOIDS/
		  FLAVINOIDS/
		  TANNINS

CROCUS	Stimulant Emmenagogue	COLCHICHINE
CUMIN SEED	Carminative	CYMINUM
CYCLAMEN ROOT	Emetic Cathartic	PHENOL GLYCOSIDES
CYPRESS OIL	Whooping Cough	CUPRESSIN
DAMIANA	Diuretic Tonic Nervine	PINENE/CINEOL
DAMMAR SAP	Microscopy surgery Orthopedic plaster ingredient	DAMMAROL
DAPHNE TREE	Cathartic Stimulant	MEZEREON
DELPHINIUM	Diuretic Emmenagogue Lice/parasites	AJACINE/DELPHININE
DERRIS ROOT	External parasite insecticide	ROTENONE
DEVIL'S BIT	Blood cleanser	SCABIOSA
DEVIL'S CLAW	Diabetes	INSULIN
DITA BARK	Anesthetic Skeletal muscle relaxant	DITAINE
DOGBANE	Diuretic Heart disease	CYMARIN
DOGWOOD	Astringent	CORNINE/TANNIN
DRAGON'S BLOOD	Astringent	RAPHIDES
EARTH BOLE	Dental powders Skin poultice	FERRIC OXIDE CLAY BOLE
ELDERBERRY	Cathartic Emetic	CYANOGENIC GLYCOSIDES
ELEMI SAP	Skin ulceration ointment	CANARIUM

THE EARTH MOTHER'S PHARMACY

Natural Botanical or Source	Medicinal Function	Pharmaceutical Drug or Active Agent
ELM BARK	Demulcent	MUCILAGE/TANNINS
ENGLISH WALNUT	Anti-inflammatory	TANNINS
EUCALYPTUS	Muscle liniment	PIPERITOL
EUROPEAN SNAKEROOT	Antibiotic	ALLANTOIN/SAPONIN
EVERLASTING	Choleretic Pancreatitis Stomachic	PHYTOSTERIN/ COUMARIN
EYEBRIGHT	Eye diseases Conjunctivitis Eyewash	MANNITE/TANNIN
FENNEL	Expectorant Carminative Antispasmodic Stomachic	TENCHONE/ANETHOLE/ TOCOPHEROL/ LINOLEIC ACID
FENNEL OIL	Pharmaceutical ingredient	FENNOLE
FENUGREEK	Poultices	TRYPTOPHANE/LYSINE/ ALKALOIDS
FIG	Narcotic Cathartic	ASIMININE DOLIARIIN
FIG FRUIT	Laxative Stomachic	ALBUMIN
FIG SAP	Anthelmintic	PROTEINASE
FIGWORT	Diuretic Cathartic	SAPONINS
FLAXSEED	Demulcent Analgesic Aperient	LINOLENIC ACID/ MUCINS
FOSSIL FAUNA	Skin disease ointment Hemorrhoidal/vaginal suppositories	SAUROL
FOXGLOVE	Heart disease Diuretic	DIGITALIS GITALIN/GITOXIN/ DIGITOXIN
GALIUM	Urine suppressant	APERINE
GARLIC	Chemical balance stabilizer Antibiotic	ALLIUM

THE EARTH MOTHER'S PHARMACY

Natural Botanical or Source	Medicinal Function	Pharmaceutical Drug or Active Agent
GARLIC (continued)	Choleretic Antispasmodic Cholagogue Digestive stimulant	
GENTIAN ROOT	Digestive stimulant	GENTIOPICRIN
GENTIAN VIOLET	Athlete's foot Stomachic Laboratory slide stain	GENTIANIN GENTIOPICRIN GENTIANOPHIL
GERANIUM	Astringent Antidiarrheic	GERANION
GOLDTHREAD	Astringent	TANNIN
GOLDENROD	Diuretic Vulnerary Anti-inflammatory Hydragogue	CATECHIN/SAPONINS
GORSE SEED	Diuretic Tonic	ULEXINE
GREENHEART TREE	Antimalarial tonic	BEBURU
GREEN HELLEBORE	Heart disease	VERATRUM ALKALOIDS
GUACO	Asthma Gout Rheumatism	GUAIACOL
GYMNEMA LEAVES	Medicinal flavoring	FUNGICIDE/TANNINS
HEDGE HYSSOP	Emetic Diuretic Cathartic	GLYCOSIDES
HELLEBORE	Hydragogue Cathartic Emmenagogue	HELLEBORIN/SAPONINS
HEMLOCK OIL	Expectorant Diuretic	TEREBINTHINATE
HEMP	Tranquilizer Anticonvulsant	CANNABIS (Hashish)
HOLLY	Astringent Sedative Febrifuge Tonic	RUTIN/ILICIN
HONEY	Antihistamine Pharmaceutical ingredient	MELLITE

THE EARTH MOTHER'S PHARMACY

Natural Botanical or Source	Medicinal Function	Pharmaceutical Drug or Active Agent
HOPS	Sedative Tonic Stomachic	PICRIC ACID/TANNINS
HOREHOUND	Asthma Cough suppressant Anthelmintic Vulnerary Cholagogue	MARRUBIUM/TANNIN
HORSE CHESTNUT	Heart disease Hemostatic	PURINE/ALBUMIN
HORSEMINT	Diaphoretic	MENTHONE
HORSERADISH	Diaphoretic Antiseptic Aperient	ASPARAGINE/BENNE-OIL
HORSETAIL	Diuretic Astringent Stomachic Eye diseases Tonic Dyspepsia	SILICIC ACID/ SAPPONIN/ AMINO ACIDS
HUCKLEBERRY	Intestinal astringent	VACCINIUM
ICELAND MOSS	Demulcent Stomachic Digestive stimulant	CETRARIN/ ISOLICHENIN/ LICHENIN/FUMARIC ACID
INDIAN MYRTLE	Cathartic Anthelmintic	TANNINS
INDIAN RUBBER PLANT	Chloroform Ether	HYDROCARBON
IPECAC	Dysentery Emetic	IPECAC
IRISH MOSS	Demulcent Antidiarrheic Bronchitis Obesity	BROMINE
IVORY NUT	Heart disease Antibiotic	HEXANITRIN MANNOSIDOSTREP- TOMYCIN
JABORANDI	Diaphoretic	PILOCARPINE
JACK BEAN	Globulin	CONCANAVALLIN

THE EARTH MOTHER'S PHARMACY

Natural Botanical or Source	Medicinal Function	Pharmaceutical Drug or Active Agent
JACOB'S LADDER	Ulcer treatment	POLEMONIUM
JALAP	Cathartic	JALAPIN
JAMBOLANA BARK	Stomachic Diaphoretic	PILOCARPINE
JAVA COCA	Local anesthetic	TROPACOCAINE
JAVA PLANT	Stomachic	SAPONIN
JESUITS' BARK	Antimalarial Analgesic	GLYCOSIDES/TANNINS
JIMSONWEED	Narcotic Antispasmodic Parkinson's disease Asthma (smoke) Hemorrhoids (ointment)	STRAMONIUM
JOB'S TEARS	Anodyne Diuretic	METHYL SALICYLATE
JUNIPER	Antiseptic Carminative Stomachic Diuretic	GALLATANNINS/LIGRIN/ GLUCURONIC ACID
JUNIPER OIL	Gout Rheumatism Skin/gum ulcer ointment	SAVIN
KAVA SHRUB	Cystitis Gonorrhea	BLENNOPHROSIN
KOSAM SEEDS	Dysentery	TANNINS
KOTYLE HERB	Leprosy Skin diseases Syphilis	HYDROCOTYLE
KURCHI ROOT	Dysentery Febrifuge	TANNINS
LADY'S-MANTLE	Anti-inflammatory Antispasmodic Astringent Tranquilizer	SALICYLIC ACID
LARCH BARK	Diuretic Emmenagogue Laxative Skin disease astringent	LARICIC ACID

THE EARTH MOTHER'S PHARMACY

Natural Botanical or Source	Medicinal Function	Pharmaceutical Drug or Active Agent
LARCH OIL	Antibiotic Antiseptic Gout Rheumatism	LARICOL
LAVENDER	Stomachic Carminative Choleretic Vulnerary	COUMARIN/TANNIN
LAVENDER OIL	Pharmaceutical perfuming agent	LAVANDULA
LEMON BALM	Antispasmodic Diaphoretic Stimulant	CITROL/LIMONENE
LEMON OIL	Pharmaceutical flavoring agent	CITRUS LIMON
LEOPARD'S-BANE	Cardiac stimulant Cathartic Emetic	ACETYLENE
LETTUCE	Sedative	LACTUCIN
LICHENS	Pharmaceutical colorant	CUDBEAR

LILY OF THE VALLEY	Diuretic
	Heart disease
		CONVALLAMARIN/
		  TANNIN
		  CONVALLARIN

LIVERWORT	Hepatic Choleretic	HEPATICA
MAGNOLIA BARK	Diaphoretic Dysentery Febrifuge Rheumatism	GLAUCA
MAIDALOKRI BARK	Antidiarrheic Dysentery	TELRANTHERA
MAIDENHAIR FERN	Demulcent syrup Heart disease Hepatic Vascular diseases	TANNINS
MAIZE (corn)	Antiseptic Cystitis Demulcent Diuretic Gonorrhea	MAIZENIC ACID/ MUCILAGE

THE EARTH MOTHER'S PHARMACY

Natural Botanical or Source	Medicinal Function	Pharmaceutical Drug or Active Agent
MANACA	Gout Rheumatism	HOPEANA
MANDRAKE	Narcotic Sedative	MANDRAGORINE
MANSA ROOT	Antimalarial Dysentery	GLYCOSIDES/TANNIN
MAQUI LILAC	Febrifuge	GLYCOSIDE BITTERS
MARJORAM	Astringent Cholagogue Expectorant	TANNIN
MATICO	Hemostatic	SALICYLATE/TANNIN
MEXICAN YAM	Cortisonelike agent	BOTOGENIN
MILK THISTLE	Cholagogue	TUMARIC ACID/ ALBUMIN
MINT	Arthritis Carminative Counterirritant Joint anodyne Stomachic	MENTHOL
MISTLETOE	Asthma Diuretic Heart disease Uterine stimulant Whooping cough	VISCIN
MONKSHOOD	Analgesic Febrifuge Topical anesthetic	ACONITINE

MOONSEED
(curare)
	Skeletal muscle relaxant
	Anticonvulsant
	Antispasmodic
	Muscle relaxant
	   administered along
	   with general
	   anesthesia
	Snakebite
		TUBOCURARINE
		TINOSPORA

MUAWE BARK	Heart disease	HYDROBROMIDE
MULBERRY	Anthelmintic Aperient Febrifuge Narcotic Sedative	ALKALOIDS

THE EARTH MOTHER'S PHARMACY

Natural Botanical or Source	Medicinal Function	Pharmaceutical Drug or Active Agent
MULLEIN	Bronchitis Demulcent Systemic alkalizer	HESPERIDINE/SAPONINS
MUSHROOM	Antibiotic	POLYSPORIN
MYRRH	Dentifrice (whitener) Gum disease wash Stomachic	EUGENOL/LIMONENE/ MYRRHIN
NIGHTSHADE	Tranquilizer	BELLADONNA
NORTH AMERICAN CYPRESS	Rheumatism	TAXODIUM RESIN
NUTMEG OIL	Pharmaceutical ingredient	MYRISTICA
OAK	Astringent Hemostatic	TANNINS
OLEANDER	Aperient Diuretic	NERIIN/OLEANDRIN
OLIVE	Antispasmodic Aperient Astringent Choleretic Heart disease Stomachic	OLEIC/LINOLEIC ACIDS OLEUROPIN/TANNIN
OLIVE OIL	Laxative Wound/bruise poultice	PHYTOSTERIN/ LECITHIN
ONION	Blood purifier Cathartic Diuretic Expectorant Stimulant Whooping cough	VOLATILE OILS
OPIUM POPPY	Analgesic Narcotic	MORPHINE
ORANGE OIL	Pharmaceutical flavoring agent	ORANGE OIL
ORCHID ROOT	Antispasmodic Nervine	LACTONES/QUINONES
ORMOSINE SEED	Narcotic Sedative	HYDROCHLORIDE
OUROUPARIA LEAF	Antidiarrheic Sore throat topical	CATECHU

THE EARTH MOTHER'S PHARMACY

Natural Botanical or Source	Medicinal Function	Pharmaceutical Drug or Active Agent
OYSTER SHELL	Rickets	CARBONICA
PANSY	Tonic	VIOLAQUERCITRIN/ VIOLINE
	Emetic	TANNIN/SAPONINS
PAPAYA	Herniated disks	PAPAIN ENZYME
PAWPAW BARK	Cathartic Emetic Anthelmintic Lice	ALKALOIDS/BITTERS
PEAT	Absorbent dressings	PEAT
PENCIL FLOWER	Uterine sedative	STYLOSANTHES
PENNYROYAL LEAVES	Anthelmintic Carminative Diaphoretic Emmenagogue Headaches	FUNGICIDE/TANNINS
PEPPERMINT	Antispasmodic Carminative Cathartic	MENTHONE
PEPPERMINT OIL	Arthritis Carminative Headache Sinusitis Rheumatism Joint-pain anodyne	MENTHOL
PERIWINKLE	Tonic (cancer) Stomachic	ALKALOIDS
PEYOTE CACTUS	Anodyne Febrifuge Tranquilizer	MESCALINE
PHEASANT'S-EYE	Heart disease Local anesthetic	ADOMITOL/ADONIN
PIG EMBRYOS	Hemoglobin preparation	SANGUINOFORM
PIG BILE	Liver disorders	BILIRUBIN
PINEAPPLE	Digestive enzyme	BROMELIN
PINE RESIN	Medical adhesive	ROSIN
PIPSISSEWA	Astringent Diaphoretic Diuretic Rheumatism	LIGNIN/SALINE

THE EARTH MOTHER'S PHARMACY

Natural Botanical or Source	Medicinal Function	Pharmaceutical Drug or Active Agent
PISTACHIO TREE	Microscopy surgery Dentistry substance Hemostatic Stomachic	MASTIC
PLANTAIN	Anodyne Dysentery Hemorrhoids Insect bites/stings Vulnerary Skin irritations	MUCILAGE
POKEWEED	Rheumatism Purgative Cathartic	SAPONIN/TANNIN
PRICKLY ASH	Tonic Stomachic Diaphoretic Nervine	XANTHOXYLINE
PUMPKIN SEED	Anthelmintic Diuretic	PEPO
PURPLE CONEFLOWER	Vulnerary	BETAINE/PHENOLIC ACID
QUACK GRASS	Antibiotic Rheumatism	SILICIC ACID
QUEBRACHO BARK	Emetic Asthma	ASPIDOSAMIN ASPIDOSPERMA
RANDIA NUT	Emetic	GLYCOSIDES
RASPBERRY LEAVES	Diuretic Choleretic Uterine muscle relaxant	SILICIC ACID/TANNINS
RED RASPBERRY	Pharmaceutical flavoring agent	RASPBERRY
REINDEER MOSS	Stomachic Cleansing wash	RANGIFIDE
RHUBARB	Astringent Cathartic Gastric tonic Aperient Cholagogue	TETRARIN RHEUM/TANNINS CATECHIN/ GLUCOGALLIN
ROSEMARY	Antiseptic Carminative Stomachic	TANNIN/ALKALOID
ROSEMARY OIL	Pharmaceutical perfuming agent	VOLATILE OILS

THE EARTH MOTHER'S PHARMACY

Natural Botanical or Source	Medicinal Function	Pharmaceutical Drug or Active Agent
ROSE OIL	Pharmaceutical perfuming agent	ROSA
ROSE TREE	Vulnerary Intestinal parasites	BRAYERA
RUE LEAF OIL	Emmenagogue Abortifacient Eye diseases Antispasmodic Sedative	RUTIN RUTARELINE
RUSBYI BARK	Cathartic Emetic	TANNINS
SABADILLA SEED	Emetic Cathartic	CEVADINE
SAFFLOWER	Diaphoretic Diuretic	TINCTORIUS
SAINT JOHN'S WORT	Aperient Astringent Snakebite Vulnerary	TUTSAN
SAJINA	Dyspepsia Rheumatism	BENNE-OIL
SALVIA OIL	Astringent Carminative	SAVIOL
SANDALWOOD OIL	Mucous membrane antiseptic	SANDALOL
SANDARAC	Dental impression varnish	SANDARACING
SARSAPARILLA ROOT	Diuretic Diaphoretic	SARSAPONIN PARILLIN
SASSAFRAS OIL	Antinarcotic	SAFROL
SASSAFRAS ROOT	Carminative Diaphoretic Diuretic Skin diseases	TANNIN
SASSAFRAS SAP	Eye disease balm Demulcent	RESINS
SAW PALMETTO	Diuretic Expectorant	CAROTENE/TANNIN
SAXIFRAGE BARK	Astringent Choleretic Diuretic	ASCORBIC ACID

THE EARTH MOTHER'S PHARMACY

Natural Botanical or Source	Medicinal Function	Pharmaceutical Drug or Active Agent
SCABWORT	Bronchitis Diaphoretic Diuretic	ELECAMPANE
SCAPOLIA ROOT	Narcotic Sedative	ATROPA
SCOTCH PINE	Antiseptic Bronchitis Diuretic	PINIPICIN/TANNIN
SEA ONION	Heart disease Diuretic	RUBELLIN/TANNIN/ CARDIAC GLYCOSIDES
SENECA SNAKEROOT	Asthma Bronchitis Laryngitis Pneumonia	SAPONINS
SENNA	Cathartic	MUCIN
SERPENT TREE	Cathartic Emetic Heart disease	RETAMINE
SESAME SEED	Demulcent Dysentery	BENNE-OIL
SHEEP ADRENALS	Heart stimulant Hemostatic	SANGRENAL
SHEPHERD'S PURSE	Astringent Coagulant Rheumatism Uterine stimulant	BURSINE
SILKWORM	Silk used in surgery	SERICUM
SILKWORM CHRYSALIS	Solid alcohol steroid	BOMBICESTEROL
SIMARUBA BARK	Astringent Tonic	TANNIN
SKULLCAP	Antispasmodic Tranquilizer	ALKALOIDS
SLIPPERY-ELM BARK	Abortifacient Demulcent Vaginal tumors Vulnerary	MUCILAGE/TANNINS
SNAKEHEAD	Aperient Tonic Anthelmintic	CHELONE CHELANIN

THE EARTH MOTHER'S PHARMACY

Natural Botanical or Source	Medicinal Function	Pharmaceutical Drug or Active Agent
SNAKEROOT	Tranquilizer Sedative	RESERPINE
SNAKE VENOM	Epilepsy	CROTALIN
SNOWFLAKE PLANT	Emetic	LEUCOIUM
SNOWFLOWER	Aperient Diuretic	CHIONANTHIN
SOAPWORT	Aperient Blood purifier Diuretic Skin diseases	SAPONETIN
SOIL BACTERIA	Antibiotic	BACITRACIN/NEOMYCIN
SOUTH AMERICAN IRIS	Cathartic Diuretic	GALAXIOIDES
SOYBEAN	Antibiotic	CANAVALIN
SOYMIDA BARK	Astringent Febrifuge	GLYCOSIDES/TANNIN
SPICE TREE	Antidiarrheic Carminative Headache	METHYL SALICYLATE
SPRUCE OIL	Muscle liniment	PINEOL
SQUILL	Heart disease	SCILLARIEN
STILLINGIA	Cathartic Cholagogue Diaphoretic Diuretic	GLYCOSIDES/TANNIN
STONECROP	Astringent Vulnerary	ALKALOIDS/TANNIN
STONEROOT	Diuretic Heart disease Hemorrhoids	GLYCOSIDES/TANNIN
STONESEED	Contraceptive	LITHOSPERMA
SUMAC	Antidiarrheic Astringent Headache Skin diseases Vulnerary	TANNINS
SWEET CLOVER	Anodyne Sedative Tranquilizer	MELILOTIC ACID/ ORTHO- OXYCINNAMIC ACID
SWEET COLTSFOOT	Antispasmodic	PETASITE

THE EARTH MOTHER'S PHARMACY

Natural Botanical or Source	Medicinal Function	Pharmaceutical Drug or Active Agent
SWEET-GUM TREE	Antidiarrheic Cough suppressant	LIQUIDAMBAR
TAMANO TREE OIL	Leprosy Skin diseases	ETHYL ESTER
TAMARISK GALL	Astringent	TANNINS
TANSY	Abortifacient Anthelmintic Diuretic Emmenagogue	TANACETIN/ TANACETONE
THIMBLEWEED	Diuretic Tonic	TANNINS
THYME	Anthelmintic Antineuralgic Antirheumatic Carminative Intestinal antiseptic Surgery antiseptic	THYMOL/CARVACROL
TOAD PAROTID GLANDS	Heart disease	BUFAGIN
TOAD-SKIN SECRETIONS	Pharmaceutical ingredient	METHYL BETAINE
TOBACCO	Anodyne Antispasmodic Diuretic Emetic Heart depressant Juice destroys parasites Poultice ingredient Relaxant Smoke inhaled for asthma/laryngitis Tetanus treatment Strychnine poisoning treatment Vulnerary	ANABASINE/ ALKALOIDS/ NICOTINE
TRILLIUM	Antidiarrheic Astringent Dysentery Emmenagogue Expectorant Hemostatic Uterine hemorrhaging	TRILLARIN/TANNINS

THE EARTH MOTHER'S PHARMACY

Natural Botanical or Source	Medicinal Function	Pharmaceutical Drug or Active Agent
VALERIAN ROOT	Anticonvulsive Anodyne Antispasmodic Carminative Epilepsy Tranquilizer	VALERIANIC ACID/ ALKALOIDS
VANILLA BEAN	Stimulant Gastric stimulant Hypnotic Hemostatic	KOAMIN VANILLIN PARAPHENETIDIN
VERONA	Aperient Cholagogue	LEPTANDRIN
VERONICA	Heart disease Anthelmintic	VERNONIN
VIPER VENOM (copperhead, rattlesnake, water moccasin)	Hemostatic	VIPERINE
VIRGINIA SNAKEROOT	Emetic Snakebite antidote	BITTERS
WABA ROOT	Local anesthetic	OUABAIN
WATERCRESS	Choleretic Systemic tonic	GLYCOSIDE
WATERMELON SEED	Solid alcohol steroid	CUCURBITOL
WHITE-BIRCH BARK	Pharmaceutical preparation	TAR OIL
WHITE CEDAR	Diuretic Emmenagogue	TETRANORTRITERPENE
WHITE DEAD NETTLE	Hemostatic	LAMINE/TANNIN
WHITE HELLEBORE	Cathartic Emetic	JERVINE/ PROTOVERATRINES
WILD MARJORAM	Astringent Choleretic Liniment	THYMOL
WILD MORNING GLORY	Carminative Febrifuge Gout	GLYCOSIDES/BITTERS
WILD TAMARIND	Emmenagogue	LUCAENA

THE EARTH MOTHER'S PHARMACY

Natural Botanical or Source	Medicinal Function	Pharmaceutical Drug or Active Agent
WINTERBERRY BARK	Andoyne Antiseptic Astringent Diuretic Rheumatism Tonic	METHYL SALICYLATE/ ALDEHYDE/TANNIN
WITCH HAZEL	Astringent Bruises/sprains liniment Complexion conditioner Hemostatic	GALLIC ACIDS/ SAPONINS/TANNINS
WOOD BETONY	Astringent Cathartic Emetic	BETONY
WOOD TAR	Expectorant Pulmonary tuberculosis	CREOSOTE
WORMSEED	Carminative Cathartic Choleretic Anthelmintic	SANTONIN THUJONE/ABSINTHIN
YARROW	Anti-inflammatory Antiseptic Antispasmodic Cholagogue	CINEOLINE/TANNINS
YELLOWROOT	Stomachic	ALKALOIDS
YERBA BUENA	Anthelmintic Carminative Febrifuge Antiseptic	THYMOL/VOLATILE OILS
YERBA DE LA GOLONDRINA	Snakebite	BITTERS/TANNINS
YERBA REUMA	Astringent	TANNINS
YERBA SANTA	Bronchitis	COUMARIN/SAPONIN

THE HEALING WAY
The Application of Gateway Healing

THE OPENED GATE

My talks with No-Eyes regarding Earthway living were far more involved than I could ever have anticipated. Because of the scope of her botanicals, I had at first thought that they were the extent of the lessons on health she planned on sharing with me.

But at the time, after we had discussed man's relationships with the sky and earth and all the botanicals, I foolishly thought it might be a nice gesture on my part to share with No-Eyes what was presently transpiring with the so-called New Age healers. Little did I suspect what her reaction would be, or more amazingly, how much more she had to teach me.

"No-Eyes," I began, "did you know that there are people who specialize in healing with stones?"

"Nope."

"That's good, isn't it?"

She just shrugged the narrow shoulders. "Could be . . . maybe."

Her reaction was difficult to read.

"And others are using crystals."

"What so."

"Well, I think that's good. I mean, we have this beautiful bond with the earth, and using earth's products is a big healing advancement."

"Could be," came her clipped reply.

I wasn't sure if I should continue or just choose another topic altogether. I tried one more time.

"Some are even using color."

207

"What else?" she asked.

"And something called aromatherapy or essence healing. It's based on the scents of flowers."

"Humph! Just flowers? What else they usin'?"

"Massage therapy."

"What else?"

I hesitated as I tried to recall more types of healing I'd heard of. "That's all I can think of."

Silence.

"I can't remember if there's any more or not, No-Eyes."

"No-Eyes hear Summer first time. I not got broken ear."

"We've come a long way with this healing, huh, No-Eyes?"

Silence.

"No-Eyes?"

"That be baby stuff."

"What?"

"Now Summer got broken ears. No-Eyes say that that stuff be only first baby-step stuff."

"Why?"

"'Cause it be all in so many pieces, that why. How healin' gonna be good if it be in pieces all over place?"

"I'm not following you."

Her eyes softened. "What totems they usin'?"

"Totems?"

The wise eyes closed, then gently opened to peer over at me.

"Tell No-Eyes what time of day each healin' be. What special sound be used? What day of week each healin' be given?"

I had no idea what she was talking about and I didn't pretend that I did. "I've never heard of those aspects being brought into healing. Is this something new?"

A wry smile tipped the corners of her thin lips. Above the smile a sparkling twinkle lighted the depths of her all-seeing eyes.

"No-Eyes gonna share some great thing with Summer this day. Yup, all those things got plenty to do with right human healing."

Just the way she spoke her words and how she held herself gave the room an aura of a mystery about to unfold.

"You mean healings should only be done at a certain time of day?"

She smiled. *"Six* times of day."

"They can be done *all* day?"

"Nope."

"Well you just said . . ."

A cautioning finger rose to snake before my nose.

"Watch what Summer gonna say now. No-Eyes say there be six times of day for healing—not for *all* healing."

How odd that was to me. I thought a bit on it. "There're special times for different healings?"

She simply beamed.

"But I've never heard of that. Is that like the special time that surgeries should be avoided—during the full moon?"

"What so." She shrugged. "That be somethin' like what No-Eyes be talkin' 'bout."

"But how does one know what time's right for which healing?"

The eyes sparkled, glinted. "Sun be at different power. Different power make different vibration. Each vibration gotta match reason for healing. See?"

She'd left me way behind. I screwed up my brows.

And she laughed. "We gone too far. We gonna go back an' talk 'bout beginning."

I sighed. "That'd be nice."

Creak-thud. Creak-thud.

"Where'd all these new aspects come from?" I asked, anxious to get into her material.

"New?"

"Well I've never *seen* any health books that talk about time!"

Silence.

"Or are there?"

She shrugged. "No-Eyes don't read."

"But *you'd* know."

Only the rocker spoke.

"So?" I pushed.

"What so?"

I sighed and waited until my wise one was ready to stop playing with me. I waited for quite some time.

"Summer?" came the long-awaited opening.

"Yes."

"What No-Eyes gonna talk 'bout not be in books."

"Somehow I knew you were going to say that."

She didn't smile. She was very serious. "This stuff not be new stuff, either. It been done long, long ago."

Silence.

Creak-thud. Creak-thud.

"No-Eyes?"

"Yup."

"Can I ask some questions about this material?"

"Summer always been free to ask. That how Summer learn."

"How long ago?"

"Long, *long* ago."

"Did the Indians practice this type of healing?"

"Only at first."

"Well, was this widely practiced before or after them?"

She squinted a peculiar look over at me. "Summer, Indian peoples always been here."

"Well, yes. . . ." Pinning down historical dates had never been easy with No-Eyes. "Was this healing done by a race that worked with crystals and had flying machines?"

Her grin then widened. She leaned far forward. "Still *is,*" she whispered.

My eyes bugged.

She twittered behind her hand.

And her elfin mirth was contagious. I smiled at her pixie amusement.

"Are you saying that . . . that you got this information from a . . . vision?"

The light twittering now exploded into a full-blown, gum-exposing laugh.

I grinned wide at her. "I made a joke, huh, No-Eyes?"

Her head bobbed.

Grinning silence.

Creak-thud.

Our eyes locked as my mind raced for an answer that wouldn't be funny. Then I made a wild stab at it.

"Your special friends. *They* told you these things, didn't they, No-Eyes?"

The noisy rocker stilled. She wasn't laughing, twittering, or even smiling. Now we were into the serious stuff—the *very* serious stuff.

I now treaded gently. "How do *they* use this method? They're different."

"They use it to *share*—not for them—for *us.*"

I thought on that. So her special friends gave her the age-old healing methods for humankind to begin using once again, just as they had so long, long ago. Now my head swam and swirled with a zillion questions.

"Have they shared this with others? Why haven't we heard about it? Does this special healing have a name? Do healers have to study it for a long time? Is that why it isn't known yet?"

"SUMMER!"

"I'm sorry, but I'm so excited!"

Her wrinkled hands gestured for me to slow down. She said we'd get everything covered one step at a time. Everything was always one step at a time.

"Now, we gonna get questions answered, then we gonna go back to beginning an' see how it all be so connected. No-Eyes' friends say it be time now to talk 'bout this Healing Way. They talk to No-Eyes 'bout it 'cause we been so close. They say peoples now gonna need to lift up bodies to new level. Healing Way help to do that."

"So this *is* new."

"Nope. It be done long, long—"

"No-Eyes, I meant new to *us—now.*"

"Yup. It be new *old* stuff."

"Does it have a name or something?"

"Yup."

"Well?"

"They always call it Gateway Healing."

I silently rolled that term over my tongue a few times to get the feel of it. "I like the sound of that, but why 'gateway'?"

"Easy. It come from them gates."

That really told me a lot. My silence also told her a lot.

"Summer," she began gently, "Earth Mother got Power Points in her body. We got Power Points, too. We be her children. We be just like her." She then pointed to the areas of her body to show me where the Power Points were. They coincided with the chakra centers . . . almost.

"You pointed to six," I said.

"Yup."

"Isn't there one more?"

She was emphatic. "Six."

I certainly didn't want to contradict her wisdom nor, for that matter, the high knowledge of her friends. But we were definitely at a standstill until she explained.

"No-Eyes," I began respectfully, "people today believe there're seven."

"Peoples today believe plenty dumb stuff. Six."

"Well, okay, but let me just show you where they think these seven are." Slowly I touched each part of myself and named them. Raising my hand to my forehead, I began the test. "Pituitary."

"Yup."

The hand went to the back of my head at the base of my skull. "Pineal." Nod.

"Thyroid," I said, indicating the throat area.

Another nod.

So far so good. Hand now over heart, I whispered, "Thymus or heart."

"Go on," she urged.

Now I was around my waist. "Adrenals."

"Yup."

The hand slightly lowered. "Cells of Ley . . ."

Her head was vigorously shaking back and forth. "Nope."

My hand lowered further. "Gonads."

"Yup."

Silence.

Creak-thud. Creak-thud.

"There's no cells of Leydig?"

"Yup, but they not be a Power *Point.* Friends say they not be point at all! They be somethin' different. Them cells be called the *Force.*"

Force? Force . . . Kundalini?

"Is this force like a current through the body?"

"Yup. They tell No-Eyes to tell Summer somethin'. They say to look up your cell word an' understand real meaning. It not be special power gland at all, it be cells that 'move' *after* gland up here an' gland down here wake up!" She'd indicated her forehead and between her legs. The pituitary and gonads . . . hormones . . . kundalini force. *The* Force.

"So they say there's six Power Points and that what people think of as the seventh is really the moving force?"

"Now Summer got it."

I was silent while I let this new idea sink in. I wanted to remember to check this out after I went home later that day. Then another thought struck me. "No-Eyes, have you ever heard of something called the solar plexus? Some folks think that's a Power Point, too."

"Nope. That all-mixed-up thinkin'. That not be any gland. No-Eyes know that word from friends. That plexus place just be connector, that all."

"Connector? You mean where the silver cord is attached. That would explain the sensitivity of the area. Psychic impressions stimulate that area sometimes."

"That right. But Summer no get too stuck on that cord business. Summer been 'out' without it."

"Yes," I said, remembering some of our other work together. But I didn't want to change the subject. Instead, I said, "Those Power Points, people call them chakras, No-Eyes."

"No-Eyes know. But that be race word."

"There's another one?"

"Friends say they be called Gates. They be Gates 'cause Force go through each one. Gates closed and then they open for Force. See?"

"And you said the Healing Way is called Gateway, so the healing has something to do with the Gates."

"Healing Way got all to do with Gates, Summer. Healing got *all* to do with them Power Points called Gates.

"Each Gate control special organ an' sickness. Each Gate got own special vibration. Each sickness got own special vibration, too. So all sickness healing stuff gotta match main vibration of controlling Gate. See? That why that healin' stuff Summer been tellin' No-Eyes 'bout not been so good. It only be good if all be put together an' connected right with same vibration of Gate. See? Summer, we got to match vibrations if we gonna be ready to go to next level. See? Peoples gonna need to rise to next vibration level to survive what be comin'. See?"

Boy, was that a mouthful to see!

But the rest of what No-Eyes taught me that day is far too complicated for me to share with you verbatim. So instead, I'll attempt a straightforward explanation of No-Eyes' Gateway Healing and follow it up with two charts and a closer look at how some specific illnesses can be treated in this way.

Since the Gates are our human body's Power Points, they are also called Governing Gates because they actually do govern certain organs and, natu-

GOVERNING GATES

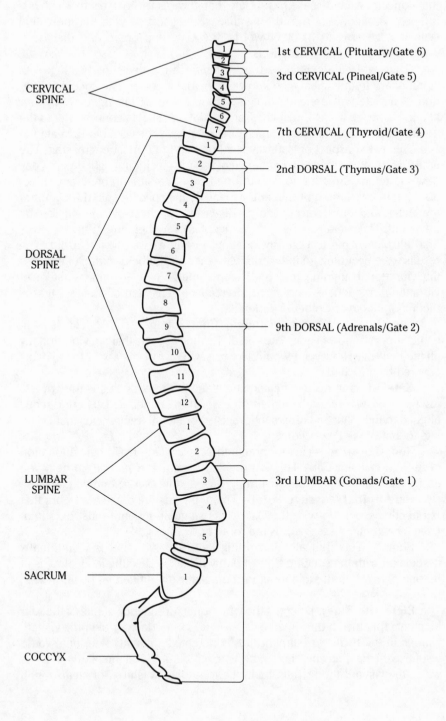

1st CERVICAL (Pituitary/Gate 6)

3rd CERVICAL (Pineal/Gate 5)

CERVICAL
SPINE

7th CERVICAL (Thyroid/Gate 4)

2nd DORSAL (Thymus/Gate 3)

DORSAL
SPINE

9th DORSAL (Adrenals/Gate 2)

LUMBAR
SPINE

3rd LUMBAR (Gonads/Gate 1)

SACRUM

COCCYX

rally, any illnesses that those organs can suffer from. Therefore, following that concept, each disease has a Gate that governs it. Since each Gate has a different vibration, so, too, do the diseases associated with the individual Gate that governs it. In other words, the Gate and organ and disease it governs have the same vibrations.

Gateway Healing is based on *aligning* all aspects of healing with vibrationary frequencies, also known as fields of power. The specific vibration of a Gate will perfectly match the vibrations of the right twenty-four healing aspects. In healing it is essential that *all* aspects contributing to the treatment possess the exact same vibratory rate as the Gate being treated.

This is the aspect of Gateway Healing that I find most engrossing. The entire treatment is made up of a range of aspects, including light density, day of week, totem, direction to face during healing treatment, breathing direction, treatment duration time, and especially the specific spinal location of the Gates and their corresponding diseases. All must be aligned for the treatment. The overall scope of the concept is overwhelming. When No-Eyes first introduced me to Gateway Healing, I couldn't wait to test it out. The results were beautiful; an indescribable sense of well-being came of it due to the vibrational aligning that had been done. When an entire system of vibrational frequencies is aligned, it creates a sensation of oneness that is incomparable to any other experience.

The Gate Alignment Treatment Chart on pages 222–223 is self-explanatory. It shows each Gate and all healing aspects that are vibrationally aligned with it. However, I would like to say a few words about the aspects covered by the chart.

Gate—This indicates the specific gland of the body that is the governing Power Point of the concerned illness. All treatment aspects are directly aligned to this Gate and represent precise vibrational frequencies that correlate to that of the Power Point.

Body Location—This pinpoints the associated physiological location of the Power Point Gate. This is provided for quick reference, to help you easily locate the area of the governing Gate and its corresponding gland.

Gate Spinal Massage Point—This indicates the precise vertebra that is directly associated with the Gate. This singular vertebra must be stimulated by a gentle massage. It is the root of the illness.

Planet—This indicates the ruling celestial body that is vibrationally associated with the specific Gate and any diseases affecting it. Healing is at its optimum when this planet is in a magnetically influential position with the earth.

Element—This represents the vibrational frequency of one of the four elements that match the specific Gate. This is important for aligning visualizations in the healing treatment. If the indicated element is air, one would visualize the healing energies to "blow" over the Gate and the ill organ. If it is water, the visualization would be in the form of a "washing" or cleansing. If fire is indicated, a visualization of "burning away" is intended. When earth is shown as the element to visualize, the patient envisions a "grounding" type of action being done whereby the Gate, affected organ, and illness are covered with "earth packs" and then cleansed away. This represents the earth's power to "draw out" impurities and negatives within the system.

Ruling Totem—This is directly connected to the visualizations done for healing. Each animal signifies the type of aggressiveness or gentleness needed to approach the treatment. The totem is also used to envision the animal devouring the diseased cells or carrying away the unwanted condition. You should envision the totem animal fighting the disease—and winning.

Detrimental Wind—This indicates the atmospheric wind current and air temperature that will serve to worsen the illness or ailment. These vary according to the illness and this aspect is included to help the patient be better aware of atmospheric conditions that will negatively affect an ailment.

Aggravating Weather—Like the detrimental wind above, this important aspect will assist in determining which atmospheric conditions will worsen an illness or chronic ailment. This is a variable aspect that directly corresponds to specific illnesses or physiological conditions.

Day of Week—This aspect is based on the routine of man and his inner time clock. For most people, the week is a cycle of time that affects certain physiological conditions. Some of these are best treated at the beginning of the cycle, and others at the end. The time of the week to treat an illness most effectively depends upon which Gate governs it. Cycles of time have vibratory rates that connect them to the Gates.

Moon Phase—This simply means that each bodily disease corresponds to a specific moon phase vibrational frequency due to the varying degrees of the moon's magnetic pull. Healing is best done when the specific disease is aligned to the corresponding moon phase. This aspect is a variable and is associated with the vibrations of the specific ailment rather than with a singular Gate.

Light Density—This aspect is like the day of week and moon phases. Gates are sensitive to celestial influences because we are comprised not only of earth stuff, but also sky stuff and starstuff, as No-Eyes would aptly put it. Our Power Point sensors are finely tuned to operate at their optimum when they are in alignment with the vibrational light density from the sun. The sun's light has a specific density at each time of day, whether it is cloudy or clear. Each such density corresponds to a specific Gate's vibrational receptivity.

Direction to Face—The directional points have vibrational frequencies that can be aligned to the Gates. Direction has power. This is important to understand. There are specific vibrations associated with each direction, which relates them to the Gates. This is a major aspect of our close connection to the earth.

To use this aspect during healing, position the body so that it is in direct alignment with the given direction. This will best be explained in the color-breathing-direction aspect.

Treatment Duration—Because of the sensitivity levels of the different Gates, the length of treatment is different for each. The pituitary Gate is the most sensitive; therefore, treatment duration in this area cannot be lengthy. It's important to realize that because Gateway Healing aligns all aspects to like vibratory frequencies, it greatly intensifies the power of such healing treatments. It would be similar to the importance of timing the radioactive exposure of X rays. The more sensitive Gates cannot be exposed to more treatment than is necessary. The ten-minute exposure time for the pituitary Gate is equal in power to the sixty minutes of duration for the gonads, which are so much denser. This is essential to effective and safe treatments.

Color—This indicates the visual spectrum aspect that directly correlates to the Gate's vibrational frequency. Each Gate has an associated color. This specific color is an important aspect in healing treatments because its inclusion soothes the Gate and brings a protective aura that attracts healing energies while, at the same time, it repels negative ones.

Color Breathing Direction—No-Eyes stressed the importance of color breathing. As indicated in the color aspect above, each color has a vibration that should be aligned to the specific Gate. Visualize the corresponding color being drawn in, either through the head or feet, depending on the "heat" of the color. Hot colors are brought up through the soles of the feet, while the cool colors are brought down through the head and directed to bathe the Gate and ill organ.

In order to use this aspect properly, you must bring in the direction aspect that was previously outlined. If a *cool* color needs to be brought down through the head, the *head* is presented to the given direction. If a *hot* color is brought up through the soles of the feet, the *feet* need to be presented to the given direction. *Remember: Hot colors mean that the feet point to the directional coordinate. Cool colors mean that the head points to the directional coordinate.* This is important for maximum effect. (For green, it's optional which way one faces, for the color is brought in through the center of being.)

Musical Note—Music represents the tone scale of sound. As such, music is composed of a wide range of vibrational frequencies. Because of this, certain notes are associated with the corresponding frequencies of the Gates. This provides an important healing aspect that is applied to Gateway Healing.

Instrument Sound—Just as music has vibrational frequencies according to the notes, various musical instruments produce a variety of frequencies according to their overall type of sound. By using specific musical instruments in healing, the vibrational frequencies can be consistently maintained.

Nature Sound—Nature is a harmonizing symphony of sounds. Sounds have tonal vibrations. The inclusion of nature sounds is important in Gateway Healing because these natural earth frequencies can directly be matched with the specific Gate vibrations. By using these natural sounds the healing qualities of nature itself are applied to the treatment, thereby incorporating the earth aspect of nature.

Illness Spinal Massage Point—This indicates the precise vertebra to stimulate when treating a specific ailment. Since various ailments are associated with individual vertebrae within a Gate spread, this aspect is a variable according to the disease. Depending on which vertebra is indicated, the disease can be treated by gently massaging its specific associated location. Just as the Gate vertebra is massaged, so too is the disease or ailment vertebra stimulated in a like manner.

Essential Oil—This aspect is similar to the aromatherapy or essence healing that is being done today, but it takes the concept a step further. The essential oil needs to be massaged very gently over and around the specific Gate's vertebra location *and* the precise vertebra location of the illness (they may be different because of the Gate spread along the vertebrae). This essential oil may also be used to scent the patient's home for additional effectiveness. Each oil has an associated vibrational frequency that matches the Gates.

Wood Scent—This is one of the direct vibrational earth connections. Like the nature sound, nature scents also vibrate to varying rates of frequency. Specific scents in nature are directly aligned to the Gates. The specific wood scent is burned as incense during treatment or within the patient's home. The point is to surround the patient with as many vibrational alignments as possible so that the affected Gate can continuously be stimulated with like frequencies.

Solarized-Water Glass Color—Solarized water is pure (distilled) water that has been exposed to sunlight for twenty-four hours over the course of two to three days. The specific color comes from the clear glass container it was exposed in. By sipping (not drinking) the solarized water, the entire system can absorb the vibrational frequency needed for the specific Gate being treated. Solarized water can only be *sipped*. It will lose its potency after eighteen hours, so more than one bottle should be used and rotated so there is a constant supply during the complete length of the treatment.

Crystallite, Stone, Metal—These are capable of precise vibratory alignments to the Gates. Although some of these alignments may, at first, appear incongruous, they have perfect vibrationary frequencies. An example would be Gate two, the adrenals. The crystallite is citrine quartz; the metal, pyrite; and the stone, obsidian. To some of you, that might appear rather odd, yet they are perfectly aligned. Please do not let the color of the object interfere with this concept. Color matching is not the issue; only the perfection of the vibrationary frequencies is.

The stones, crystallites, and metals are placed over the Gate spinal point and over the affected disease spinal point during healing. They can also be placed over the specific organ in question. It's a good point to stress that these stones, crystallites, and metals should also be carried about on the person until wellness has been achieved.

No-Eyes expressed concern regarding how "gemstones" are presently being used for healing and other spiritual purposes. No-Eyes said that only the purest gemstones could be used for such purposes. Most of those used by people today are ineffective and even harmful. No-Eyes did not recommend the use of any gemstones in Gateway Healing. She felt mankind should leave them alone until their qualities were better understood.

Botanicals—This healing aspect is another variable that is directly associated with the specific disease rather than the individual Gate affected. Therefore these will be different according to their healing properties and how they vibrationally associate to the individual ailment rather than the Gate.

In the "Ailments and Their Gateway Treatment" section that follows the Gateway Alignment Healing Chart, wherever botanicals are listed, they should be taken in the form of capsules (two capsules twice per day), or in the form of loose tea (one teaspoon steeped in a cup of hot water three times per day) unless otherwise indicated.

If salves or ointments are suggested, these can be applied on the skin, unless otherwise indicated. All recommended botanical ingredients can be obtained through your local health food stores or those listed in the Appendix.

Please also note that the botanicals listed in the "Ailments and Their Gateway Treatment" section are only those that are most preferred. For a more inclusive listing of botanical remedies, see the preceding sections entitled "Ailments and Their Botanical Treatments" and "Wild Plants Used by Native Americans."

Because Gateway Healing is a completely new method of healing treatment, I want to give you an example of how an individual patient can use this information. The example I've chosen is the Gateway treatment for abscesses. All healing treatments will vibrationally be aligned to the frequency of the Gate that governs this ailment.

Gate: The Gate that governs abscesses is the sixth, the pituitary. Once the Gate is known, all other associated healing aspects can be determined by following across the chart and by referring to the specific ailment in the section called "Ailments and Their Gateway Treatment."

Body Location: This indicates where the actual Gate is located on your body. This is important so that you know what area of your body to target in your visualizations. In this case, visualizations will be done around the area between the eyebrows.

Gate Spinal Massage Point: The precise vertebra that governs abscesses is the first cervical. You should gently massage this point with the essential oil discussed below.

Planet: The planet associated with the sixth Gate (the pituitary) is Naa-yu (Moon). Healing treatment will be at its optimum when this celestial body is aligned so it magnetically influences the ailment of abscesses. In this case, because the moon is the associated planet, you should practice healing during the recommended moon phase (see below).

Element: The patient afflicted with abscesses should use the element of water in the visualizations. Water is a wonderful healing element. Visualize the abscesses being soaked in water and then being completely washed away. Visualize water bathing the Gate vertebra (first cervical) and the illness vertebra (second cervical).

Ruling Totem: The owl is the ruling totem for the sixth Gate. The patient should visualize an owl at night as it swoops down and takes away the abscessed condition. The owl will be swift and clean in its performance. It will completely devour the offending abscess.

Detrimental Wind: For abscesses the detrimental wind is a warm southerly. More intense healing efforts must be applied during this atmospheric time. A chronic susceptibility toward abscesses will be increased during this time.

Aggravating Weather: As with the above, the healing technique must be intensified during this time of low pressure, low altitude, high humidity, and warm/hot temperatures. This specific atmospheric condition may increase the susceptibility toward abscesses.

Day of Week: Treatment for abscesses will be most effective on Monday. Monday is the day that most frequently produces increased stress; therefore it is this day that is best for treatment in order to stave off the affecting negatives that worsen this condition. Monday is the vibrationally aligned day for the sixth Gate. Monday is the most effective day to treat this Gate.

Moon Phase: Treat abscesses when the moon is waning. This is because the magnetic influence of the moon during this time creates a pulling-away effect on the system. You want the abscesses to pull away and wane.

Light Density: Dawn is the light density that will be most effective for treating abscesses because it is in direct vibrational alignment with the sixth Gate.

Direction to Face: In relation to the above, east is the direction that is directly associated with the sixth Gate and will be the direction to place your head during treatment.

Treatment Duration: For abscesses, the duration of treatment will not be more than ten minutes because of the extreme sensitivity of the sixth Gate (pituitary).

Color: The color that is vibrationally aligned with the sixth Gate is white. All color-associated treatments should use white. Visualizations will be a brilliant white as the patient envisions this color bathing the abscesses, the first cervical of the Gate, the second cervical of the illness, and the area between the eyebrows. A square of white flannel cloth is placed over these areas during treatment.

Color Breathing Direction: For the sixth Gate, the patient visualizes a brilliant white being pulled *down through the head* with each breath inhaled. As the color is envisioned as a current flowing down through the head, it passes over the associated vertebrae and abscesses. As it passes over these areas, it settles in pools and bathes the areas with its healing color.

Musical Note: The musical note for the treatment of abscesses and the sixth Gate is ti. This note is silently hummed as a mantra by the patient for the duration of the treatment. This aspect brings the entire body in tune with the corresponding vibrational frequency required for correct alignment.

Instrument Sound: During treatment for abscesses music of the pan flute should be heard. This instrument is in direct frequency with the sixth Gate.

Nature Sound: The patient should be exposed to the sound of the wind (or gentle breezes) while listening to pan flute music. The nature sound is best used as the background accompaniment to the instrument sound. They are to be heard simultaneously as a harmonious blend of sound frequencies.

Illness Spinal Massage Point: For an abscess, the second cervical is the specific vertebra that must be attended to. A small square of white cloth is placed over the vertebra and then gently massaged with the corresponding essential oil.

Essential Oil: For the sixth Gate, patchouli is the essential oil that is its corresponding frequency. This oil will be massaged into the white cloth placed over both vertebra areas of the Gate and illness spinal points.

Wood Scent: In treating abscesses, the wood scent that is vibrationally aligned to the sixth Gate is all pines. Therefore, during treatment, pine incense is burned to create the aligned frequency to the surrounding atmosphere.

Solarized-Water Glass Color: Since the associated color for abscesses and the sixth Gate is white, the corresponding solarized-water glass color is milkglass. Place distilled water in a milkglass container and leave it in the sunlight for twenty-four hours over the course of two to three days. This is to be *sipped* during the day in addition to normal water intake. Four juice glasses of the solarized water should be consumed each day of treatment.

Crystallite: Milky quartz is the crystallite that possesses the same vibrational frequency as the sixth Gate and, therefore, abscesses. The crystallite is placed over the two spinal vertebra points after they've been massaged. The milky quartz crystallite should be alternated with the stone of white marble and the metal of cerussite. Each ten-minute treatment will alternately use the above three aspects. They should *not* be combined in one treatment.

Stone: As explained above, white marble is vibrationally aligned with the sixth Gate and used in the treatment of abscesses.

Metal: Cerussite contains the same frequency as the sixth Gate and is used in the treatment of all illnesses governed by that Power Point. Thus, cerussite is the metal used for abscesses.

Botanical: The healing botanical's alumroot, cabbage, onion, pine, puffball, and red clover should be taken in capsule form or as loose tea. Two capsules should be taken twice per day, or for tea, one teaspoon steeped in a cup of hot water three times per day.

Gateway Healing has been given by those of our brothers and friends who have loved us from the beginning of time. And although I'm not supposed to say this . . . I'm honored that they have shared their ancient knowledge. They have stressed the importance for the human biological form to rise up into a higher vibrationary frequency for our civilization's future existence. Now they have given a Healing Way to assist that rise to the future. We have been given the Rite of Passage.

AILMENTS AND THEIR GATEWAY TREATMENT

ABSCESSES

Gate: 6/Pituitary
Body Location: Between eyebrows
Gate Spinal Massage Point: 1st cervical
Planet: Moon
Element: Water
Ruling Totem: Owl
Detrimental Wind: Warm southerly
Aggravating Weather: Low pressure, low altitude, high humidity, warm/hot
   temperatures
Day of Week: Monday
Moon Phase: Waning
Light Density: Dawn
Direction to Face: East
Treatment Duration: 10 minutes
Color: White
Color Breathing Direction: Down through head
Musical Note: Ti
Instrument Sound: Pan flute
Nature Sound: Wind
Illness Spinal Massage Point: 2nd cervical
Essential Oil: Patchouli
Wood Scent: All pines

GATE ALIGNMENT TREATMENT CHART

	1	2	3	4	5	6	7	8	9	10	11	12	13
Gate	Body Location	Gate Spinal Massage Point	Planet	Element	Ruling Totem	Detrimental Wind	Aggravating Weather	Day of Week	Moon Phase	Light Density	Direction to Face	Treatment Duration	Treatment Color
Pituitary	Between Eye Brows	1st Cervical	Naa-Yu (Moon)	Water	Owl	Variable	Variable	Monday	Variable	Dawn	East	10 Min.	White
Pineal	Base of Brain	3rd Cervical	Mee-Yaa-nu (Venus)	Air	Wolf	Variable	Variable	Friday	Variable	Morning	East	20 min.	Purple
Thyroid	Throat	7th Cervical	Quaa-Qu (Jupiter)	Air	Buffalo	Variable	Variable	Thursday	Variable	Noon	West	30 min.	Blue
Thymus	Heart	2nd Dorsal	Saa-Qu-Ya (Saturn)	Earth	Turtle	Variable	Variable	Saturday	Variable	Afternoon	South	40 min.	Green
Adrenals	Kidneys	9th Dorsal	Waa-Pu (Mercury)	Fire	Horse	Variable	Variable	Wednesday	Variable	Dusk	North	50 min.	Yellow
Gonads	Pelvis	3rd Lumbar	Qu-Say-u (Mars)	Fire	Snake	Variable	Variable	Tuesday	Variable	Night	North	60 min.	Red

NOTE: Variables correspond with specific ailments and are detailed in the following section.

222

GATE ALIGNMENT TREATMENT CHART (continued)

14	15	16	17	18	19	20	21	22	23	24	25
Color Breathing Direction	Musical Note	Instrument Sound	Nature Sound	Illness Spinal Massage Point	Essential Oil	Wood Scent	Solarized Water Glass Color	Crystallite	Stone	Metal	Botanical
Down through head	Ti	Pan Flute	Wind	Variable	Patchouli	All Pines	Milkglass	Milky Quartz	White Marble	Cerussite	Variable
Down Through Head	La	Violin	Rain	Variable	Lavender	Piñon	Purple	Amethyst	Open Geode	Compact Hematite	Variable
Down Through Head	Sol	Flute	Birdsong	Variable	Cedar	Cedar	Blue	Blue Quartz	Basalt	Azurite	Variable
Horizontally in through Naval	Fa	Drums	Surf	Variable	Eucalyptus	Eucalyptus	Green	Green Tourmaline	Feldspar	Malachite	Variable
Up Through Soles of Feet	Mi	Cello	Stream	Variable	Juniper	Juniper	Yellow	Citrine Quartz	Obsidian	Pyrite	Variable
Up Through Soles of Feet	Do	Piano	Forest	Variable	Sandalwood	Mesquite	Red	Rose Quartz	Rose Stone	Cinnabar	Variable

223

Solarized-Water Glass Color: Milkglass
Crystallite: Milky quartz
Stone: White marble
Metal: Cerussite
Botanical: Alumroot, cabbage, onion, pine, puffball, red clover

Abscess Generalities

Most all abscesses result directly from an unbalanced condition within the physical system. Maintain a level *emotional* balance. Refrain from allowing others to upset you. Do not dwell on personal failures or disappointments, but rather plan out positive and active steps toward improvement.

Refrain from ingesting red meats, pork, and organ meat. No fried foods. Eat more raw apples and include raw onions in your diet.

ACNE

Gate: 5/Pineal
Body Location: Base of brain
Gate Spinal Massage Point: 3rd cervical
Planet: Venus
Element: Air
Ruling Totem: Wolf
Detrimental Wind: Warm southerly
Aggravating Weather: Low pressure, high humidity, low altitude, warm/hot temperatures
Day of Week: Friday
Moon Phase: Waxing
Light Density: Morning
Direction to Face: East
Treatment Duration: 20 minutes
Color: Purple
Color Breathing Direction: Down through head
Musical Note: La
Instrument Sound: Violin
Nature Sound: Rain
Illness Spinal Massage Point: 3rd cervical
Essential Oil: Lavender
Wood Scent: Piñon
Solarized-Water Glass Color: Purple
Crystallite: Amethyst
Stone: Open geode
Metal: Compact hematite
Botanical: Chaparral, dandelion, garlic, mullein, palma christi, pine tea, red clover

Acne Generalities

Although acne is most frequently seen in adolescents, outbreaks can flare up in adults as well. Acne is a form of internal abscess. It is the direct result of an emotionally and/or chemically unbalanced system. Don't ever underrate the effects of emotions such as anger, depression, anxiety, and stress, for these are the harmful negative agents that generate so much of the body's unbalanced condition.

Limit sugars, food additives (such as the nitrates and artificial flavorings and colorings), and preservatives. Ingest plenty of raw apples and include raw onion in your diet wherever possible. Drink mullein tea at least twice a day, for this will help make your system more alkaline and negate the acidic condition that the abscess must have to thrive. Omit all corn products, including snack foods, for corn will stimulate an acne condition. Omit all red meats, pork, and organ parts. Omit all fried foods. Broil, bake, braise, or poach. Drink at least eight glasses of water per day. Avoid alcoholic beverages, for these will tend to create a congested system whereby the cleansing action of other ingested treatments will be hampered.

Maintain a faithful hygienic regimen. Gently clean affected surfaces thoroughly with a natural vitamin-E soap. Vitamin E with pure glycerine is excellent. Follow this up with a gentle patting of witch hazel, as this is a wonderful natural skin conditioner and toner for the complexion. Even after the acne is cleared up, you should maintain this daily routine to keep your skin healthy.

ADENOIDS

Gate: 5/Pineal
Body Location: Base of brain
Gate Spinal Massage Point: 3rd cervical
Planet: Venus
Element: Air
Ruling Totem: Wolf
Detrimental Wind: Cold northerly
Aggravating Weather: Low pressure, low altitude, high humidity, cool/cold temperatures
Day of Week: Friday
Moon Phase: Waxing
Light Density: Morning
Direction to Face: East
Treatment Duration: 20 minutes
Color: Purple
Color Breathing Direction: Down through head
Musical Note: La
Instrument Sound: Violin

Nature Sound: Rain
Illness Spinal Massage Point: 4th cervical
Essential Oil: Lavender
Wood Scent: Piñon
Solarized-Water Glass Color: Purple
Crystallite: Amethyst
Stone: Open geode
Metal: Compact hematite
Botanical: Alfalfa, horehound, mullein, oak, red clover, Rocky Mountain
    maple, starwort, yellow dock

ALCOHOLISM

Gate: 5/Pineal
Body Location: Base of brain
Gate Spinal Massage Point: 3rd cervical
Planet: Venus
Element: Air
Ruling Totem: Wolf
Detrimental Wind: Warm southerly
Aggravating Weather: Low pressure, high altitude, high humidity, warm/hot
    temperatures
Day of Week: Friday
Moon Phase: Waning
Light Density: Morning
Direction to Face: East
Treatment Duration: 20 minutes
Color: Purple
Color Breathing Direction: Down through head
Musical Note: La
Instrument Sound: Violin
Nature Sound: Rain
Illness Spinal Massage Point: 4th cervical
Essential Oil: Lavender
Wood Scent: Piñon
Solarized-Water Glass Color: Purple
Crystallite: Amethyst
Stone: Open geode
Metal: Compact hematite
Botanical: Angelica, elecampane, mullein, plantain, red clover, Rocky
    Mountain maple, wormwood

Alcoholism Generalities

Alcoholism is finally being recognized as a disease and not the condition of a derelict. An ingestion of warm tea consisting of the combined herbs of angelica, elecampane, mullein, red clover, and Rocky Mountain maple will greatly abate the sufferer's urge toward alcohol. Allow sufficient time in the daily schedule for exercise and sweat baths as well.

ALLERGIES

Gate: 2/Adrenals
Body Location: Kidneys
Gate Spinal Massage Point: 9th dorsal
Planet: Mercury
Element: Fire
Ruling Totem: Horse
Detrimental Wind: Warm southerly
Aggravating Weather: Low pressure, low altitude, high humidity, warm/hot
    temperatures
Day of Week: Wednesday
Moon Phase: Waning
Light Density: Dusk
Direction to Face: North
Treatment Duration: 50 minutes
Color: Yellow
Color Breathing Direction: Up through soles
Musical Note: Mi
Instrument Sound: Cello
Nature Sound: Stream
Illness Spinal Massage Point: 9th dorsal and 4th cervical
Essential Oil: Juniper
Wood Scent: Juniper
Solarized-Water Glass Color: Yellow
Crystallite: Citrine quartz
Stone: Obsidian
Metal: Pyrite
Botanical: Aspen, blessed thistle, fireweed, goldenseal, lichen, lobelia,
    pleurisy root, skullcap, valerian root

Allergy Generalities

Not all allergies show up early in life. They can become evident at any time. Allergies are usually a direct result of an overabundance of specific negative emotions, but they can also result from an influence from a previous lifetime. In any case, they can most definitely be alleviated or eased through emotional stability and the ingestion of plantain, almonds, and mullein tea. The botanicals offered earlier should be beneficial to you. It's also important to ingest only honey processed in your own geographical locale, for the bees have gathered the pollen from plants in your region that may be affecting your condition. By ingesting locally produced honey, you are in effect partaking in an immunity buildup treatment.

ANEMIA

Gate: 2/Adrenals
Body Location: Kidneys
Gate Spinal Massage Point: 9th dorsal
Planet: Mercury
Element: Fire
Ruling Totem: Horse
Detrimental Wind: Warm westerly
Aggravating Weather: Low pressure, low altitude, high humidity, warm/hot temperatures
Day of Week: Wednesday
Moon Phase: Waxing
Light Density: Dusk
Direction to Face: North
Treatment Duration: 50 minutes
Color: Yellow
Color Breathing Direction: Up through soles
Musical Note: Mi
Instrument Sound: Cello
Nature Sound: Stream
Illness Spinal Massage Point: 5th dorsal
Essential Oil: Juniper
Wood Scent: Juniper
Solarized-Water Glass Color: Yellow
Crystallite: Citrine quartz
Stone: Obsidian
Metal: Pyrite
Botanical: Alfalfa, aspen, chicory, dandelion, fireweed, lobelia, mullein, pine, purslane, red clover, scurvy grass

Anemia Generalities

Anemia is the absence of important nutrients that contribute to rich and healthy blood. The ingestion of foods such as alfalfa, almonds, chaparral, crisp and fresh greens (which include purslane, plantain, and dandelion), egg yolks, pine tea, and fowl will most certainly help to alleviate this condition. Rest is most important in curing this ailment. The addition of gelatin will increase the absorption of the vitamins and minerals. Foods high in iron are recommended.

APPENDICITIS

Gate: 1/Gonads
Body Location: Pelvis
Gate Spinal Massage Point: 3rd lumbar
Planet: Mars
Element: Fire
Ruling Totem: Snake
Detrimental Wind: Warm southerly
Aggravating Weather: Low pressure, low altitude, high humidity, warm/hot
    temperatures
Day of Week: Tuesday
Moon Phase: Waning
Light Density: Night
Direction to Face: North
Treatment Duration: 60 minutes
Color: Red
Color Breathing Direction: Up through soles
Musical Note: Do
Instrument Sound: Piano
Nature Sound: Forest
Illness Spinal Massage Point: 2nd lumbar
Essential Oil: Sandalwood
Wood Scent: Mesquite
Solarized-Water Glass Color: Red
Crystallite: Rose quartz
Stone: Rose stone
Metal: Cinnabar
Botanical: Birch, chamomile, chicory, dandelion, goldenseal, mullein, oak,
    parsley, prickly pear, red clover, wild onion

Appendicitis Generalities

Acute appendicitis requires immediate professional evaluation and attention. Chronic appendicitis is a condition that can be eased by adequate rest, maintaining a moderate exercise program (rather than an excessively strenuous one), and the ingestion of such foods as chamomile and mullein tea, alfalfa, onions, garlic, cabbage, honey, almonds, plantain, and purslane.

ARTHRITIS

Gate: 2/Adrenals
Body Location: Kidneys
Gate Spinal Massage Point: 9th dorsal
Planet: Mercury
Element: Fire

Ruling Totem: Horse
Detrimental Wind: Cold westerly
Aggravating Weather: Low pressure, low altitude, high humidity, cool/cold
    temperatures
Day of Week: Wednesday
Moon Phase: Waning
Light Density: Dusk
Direction to Face: North
Treatment Duration: 50 minutes
Color: Yellow
Color Breathing Direction: Up through soles
Musical Note: Mi
Instrument Sound: Cello
Nature Sound: Stream
Illness Spinal Massage Point: 5th dorsal
Essential Oil: Juniper
Wood Scent: Juniper
Solarized-Water Glass Color: Yellow
Crystallite: Citrine quartz
Stone: Obsidian
Metal: Pyrite
Botanical: Alfalfa, black cohosh, burdock, chaparral, hawthorn, nettle,
    peppermint, sunflower, wild licorice, wintergreen, yucca

Arthritis Generalities

Arthritis does not have to be debilitating. By following simple steps, it
can be eased to an extent that allows the sufferer to maintain a near-to-
normal lifestyle.

Massage affected areas with a mixture of castor oil and peppermint oil.
Limit caffeine, sugars, salt, and fried foods in your diet. Omit all red meats,
pork, organ meats, and chemical food additives. Maintain a regular exercise
routine. Avoid humid climates (a very important aspect in the treatment of
arthritis).

Arthritis is also a condition connected to excessive metals and radon
within the earth. You should have the radon level checked in your home and
take immediate steps if you get more than trace readings. Residential areas
that have been established over or near old mines, tailing sites, or dump
sites are definitely a danger to those who suffer from this joint condition.

ASTHMA

Gate: 4/Thyroid
Body Location: Throat
Gate Spinal Massage Point: 7th cervical
Planet: Jupiter

Element: Air
Ruling Totem: Buffalo
Detrimental Wind: Warm southerly
Aggravating Weather: Low pressure, low altitude, high humidity, warm/hot
     temperatures, high pollution
Day of Week: Thursday
Moon Phase: Waning
Light Density: Noon
Direction to Face: West
Treatment Duration: 30 minutes
Color: Blue
Color Breathing Direction: Down through head
Musical Note: Sol
Instrument Sound: Flute
Nature Sound: Birdsong
Illness Spinal Massage Point: 1st dorsal
Essential Oil: Cedar
Wood Scent: Cedar
Solarized-Water Glass Color: Blue
Crystallite: Blue quartz
Stone: Basalt
Metal: Azurite
Botanical: Angelica, birch, chokecherry, comfrey, eucalyptus, garlic,
     horehound, hyssop, lungwort, mullein, purslane, rosemary

Asthma Generalities

Asthma can be a frightening condition. It can greatly be eased by avoiding humid climates. High altitudes and dry areas are recommended. Avoid emotionally disturbing or irritating situations. Meditation in restful surroundings helps to maintain a balanced emotional state of mind. Eat broiled seafood, fowl, celery, grapefruit, grape juice, spinach, and peaches. Avoid oranges and all food additives. Stay indoors during high pollution days if you live in a city.

ATHLETE'S FOOT

Gate: 1/Gonads
Body Location: Pelvis
Gate Spinal Massage Point: 3rd lumbar
Planet: Mars
Element: Fire
Ruling Totem: Snake
Detrimental Wind: Warm southerly
Aggravating Weather: Low pressure, low altitude, high humidity, warm/hot
     temperatures

Day of Week: Tuesday
Moon Phase: New
Light Density: Night
Direction to Face: North
Treatment Duration: 60 minutes
Color: Red
Color Breathing Direction: Up through soles
Musical Note: Do
Instrument Sound: Piano
Nature Sound: Forest
Illness Spinal Massage Point: 5th lumbar
Essential Oil: Sandalwood
Wood Scent: Mesquite
Solarized-Water Glass Color: Red
Crystallite: Rose quartz
Stone: Rose stone
Metal: Cinnabar
Botanical: Black walnut, castor bean, elder, gentian violet, goldenrod,
   juniper, uva-ursi

Athlete's Foot Generalities

Avoid conditions that keep the feet in a moist/warm condition. Bathe regularly, even twice a day. Wash affected areas thoroughly with castile soap, pat dry, and apply gentian violet around entire areas. At night, wash areas again and massage a mixture of vitamin-E oil and castor oil into them. Wear clean white socks to bed. Powder inside of shoes with baby talc. Change socks often. Eat almonds, figs, dates, apricots, fish and fowl, pumpkin, and prunes. Drink at least eight glasses of water per day. When at leisure, sit with feet elevated and exposed to the air.

BACK PAIN

Gate: 1/Gonads
Body Location: Pelvis
Gate Spinal Massage Point: 3rd lumbar
Planet: Mars
Element: Fire
Ruling Totem: Snake
Detrimental Wind: Cold northerly
Aggravating Weather: Low pressure, low altitude, high humidity, cool/cold
   temperatures
Day of Week: Tuesday
Moon Phase: Waning
Light Density: Night
Direction to Face: North

Treatment Duration: 60 minutes
Color: Red
Color Breathing Direction: Up through soles
Musical Note: Do
Instrument Sound: Piano
Nature Sound: Forest
Illness Spinal Massage Point: 4th lumbar
Essential Oil: Sandalwood
Wood Scent: Mesquite
Solarized-Water Glass Color: Red
Crystallite: Rose quartz
Stone: Rose stone
Metal: Cinnabar
Botanical: Alder bark, black cohosh, black mustard, clove, elecampane,
    gentian, mullein, peppermint, thyme, yellow dock

Back Pain Generalities

Back pain can be a warning symptom signaling a serious internal-organ malfunction. Be sure to seek a professional evaluation to establish that the organs are normal. If they are, you can then treat lower-back pain with proper diet and exercise combined with herbal massages and compresses. Retire with a compress soaked with mullein and peppermint wrapped with a white flannel cloth, applied to the problem area of your back. Stretching exercises are most beneficial. It's also extremely helpful to see a chiropractor routinely, for once the entire spinal column is properly aligned, you will experience enhanced overall health and well-being.

BLADDER AILMENTS

Gate: 1/Gonads
Body Location: Pelvis
Gate Spinal Massage Point: 3rd lumbar
Planet: Mars
Element: Fire
Ruling Totem: Snake
Detrimental Wind: Cold northerly
Aggravating Weather: Low pressure, low altitude, high humidity, cool/cold
    temperatures
Day of Week: Tuesday
Moon Phase: Waning
Light Density: Night
Direction to Face: North
Treatment Duration: 60 minutes
Color: Red
Color Breathing Direction: Up through soles

Musical Note: Do
Instrument Sound: Piano
Nature Sound: Forest
Illness Spinal Massage Point: 3rd lumbar
Essential Oil: Sandalwood
Wood Scent: Mesquite
Solarized-Water Glass Color: Red
Crystallite: Rose quartz
Stone: Rose stone
Metal: Cinnabar
Botanical: Birch, black cohosh, gingerroot, goldenseal, horsetail, juniper,
      lobelia, marshmallow, parsley, pipsissewa

Bladder Ailment Generalities

As with any organ complaint, you should first have the condition evaluated by a professional. Generally, plenty of exercise is vital here. Get adequate rest at night. Drink at least eight glasses of water per day (or more). Eat fresh and crisp vegetables and fruits including parsley and alfalfa, grapefruit, raspberries, onions, and radishes. Many bladder ailments stem directly from an emotional imbalance or mental disturbances such as nerves and anxieties. Chamomile tea will settle the nerves and calm the system. Avoid all alcoholic beverages.

BLOOD PRESSURE (to stabilize)

Gate: 2/Adrenals
Body Location: Kidneys
Gate Spinal Massage Point: 9th dorsal
Planet: Mercury
Element: Fire
Ruling Totem: Horse
Detrimental Wind: Warm westerly
Aggravating Weather: Low pressure, low altitude, high humidity, warm/hot
      temperatures
Day of Week: Wednesday
Moon Phase: Waning
Light Density: Dusk
Direction to Face: North
Treatment Duration: 50 minutes
Color: Yellow
Color Breathing Direction: Up through soles
Musical Note: Mi
Instrument Sound: Cello
Nature Sound: Stream
Illness Spinal Massage Point: 5th dorsal

Essential Oil: Juniper
Wood Scent: Juniper
Solarized-Water Glass Color: Yellow
Crystallite: Citrine quartz
Stone: Obsidian
Metal: Pyrite
Botanical: Blue vervain, clove, garlic, gentian, hyssop, onion, parsley, strawberry leaves, watercress

Blood Pressure Generalities

You should find moderate exercise in the form of quiet evening walks most helpful. Eat such foods as almonds, fresh greens, garlic, fish and fowl, onions, dandelions, plantain, whole grains, and wild rice. Avoid all alcoholic and caffeine drinks. Absolutely *no* red or organ meats. No pork. And keep the urge to judge others under tight control. Watch those emotions!

BOILS

Gate: 2/Adrenals
Body Location: Kidneys
Gate Spinal Massage Point: 9th dorsal
Planet: Mercury
Element: Fire
Ruling Totem: Horse
Detrimental Wind: Warm southerly
Aggravating Weather: Low pressure, low altitude, high humidity, warm/hot temperatures
Day of Week: Wednesday
Moon Phase: Waxing
Light Density: Dusk
Direction to Face: North
Treatment Duration: 50 minutes
Color: Yellow
Color Breathing Direction: Up through soles
Musical Note: Mi
Instrument Sound: Cello
Nature Sound: Stream
Illness Spinal Massage Point: 11th dorsal
Essential Oil: Juniper
Wood Scent: Juniper
Solarized-Water Glass Color: Yellow
Crystallite: Citrine quartz
Stone: Obsidian
Metal: Pyrite

Botanical: Chaparral, echinacea, garlic, goldenseal, myrrh, onion, pine, plantain, red clover, slippery-elm bark, walnut

Boils Generalities

You need to balance the chemicals within your body to bring the acid/alkaline ratio back into balance. Take sweat baths with baking soda in the water. Ingest freely of celery, egg yolks, cabbage, garlic, pine tea, dandelion greens, onion, and mullein tea. Avoid oranges. Drink a small glass of grape juice before each meal. Limit sugars, salts, and avoid food additives. *Contain that temper!*

BOWEL CLEANSER (for constipation and toxins)

Gate: 2/Adrenals
Body Location: Kidneys
Gate Spinal Massage Point: 9th dorsal
Planet: Mercury
Element: Fire
Ruling Totem: Horse
Detrimental Wind: Warm westerly
Aggravating Weather: Low pressure, low altitude, high humidity, warm/hot temperatures
Day of Week: Wednesday
Moon Phase: Waning
Light Density: Dusk
Direction to Face: North
Treatment Duration: 50 minutes
Color: Yellow
Color Breathing Direction: Up through soles
Musical Note: Mi
Instrument Sound: Cello
Nature Sound: Stream
Illness Spinal Massage Point: 1st lumbar
Essential Oil: Juniper
Wood Scent: Juniper
Solarized-Water Glass Color: Yellow
Crystallite: Citrine quartz
Stone: Obsidian
Metal: Pyrite
Botanical: Birch, buckthorn, cascara sagrada, cotton root, elder, fennel, onion, peppermint, plantain, red clover, wild licorice, yucca

Bowel Generalities

Exercise is most important to maintain regular movement of waste through the lower intestines and colon. If the waste is not kept moist enough, it will not move freely. Thus, you must drink at least eight glasses of water per day. Add generous portions of fresh plantain to salads. Drink fennel tea, as this is a wonderful natural carminative (gas reliever). Eat raw apples (with skins), figs, rhubarb, and whole grains. Omit all white-flour products, including pasta, from diet.

BRONCHITIS

Gate: 3/Thymus
Body Location: Heart
Gate Spinal Massage Point: 2nd dorsal
Planet: Saturn
Element: Earth
Ruling Totem: Turtle
Detrimental Wind: Warm southerly
Aggravating Weather: Low pressure, low altitude, high humidity, warm/hot temperatures
Day of Week: Saturday
Moon Phase: Waning
Light Density: Afternoon
Direction to Face: South
Treatment Duration: 40 minutes
Color: Green
Color Breathing Direction: Horizontally in through navel
Musical Note: Fa
Instrument Sound: Drums
Nature Sound: Surf
Illness Spinal Massage Point: 3rd dorsal
Essential Oil: Eucalyptus
Wood Scent: Eucalyptus
Solarized-Water Glass Color: Green
Crystallite: Green tourmaline
Stone: Feldspar
Metal: Malachite
Botanical: Angelica, coltsfoot, comfrey, eucalyptus, garlic, honey, lungwort, mullein, wild lettuce, wild licorice

Bronchitis Generalities

Severe bronchitis requires professional evaluation. Chronic, mild cases can be eased by never overexerting yourself with exercise. Adequate rest periods are important. Foods to include in the daily diet are seafood, celery, garlic, grapefruit, fowl, mullein tea, and grape juice taken before each meal. Rest with chest elevated. Provide a humidifier, as extremely dry air will tend to aggravate the condition within the home. Lightly apply eucalyptus oil to chest area (caution—may be an irritant to those with sensitive skin). Inhale eucalyptus or thyme steam.

BURSITIS

Gate: 4/Thyroid
Body Location: Throat
Gate Spinal Massage Point: 7th cervical
Planet: Jupiter
Element: Air
Ruling Totem: Buffalo
Detrimental Wind: Cold westerly
Aggravating Weather: Low pressure, low altitude, high humidity, cool/cold temperatures
Day of Week: Thursday
Moon Phase: Waning
Light Density: Noon
Direction to Face: West
Treatment Duration: 30 minutes
Color: Blue
Color Breathing Direction: Down through head
Musical Note: Sol
Instrument Sound: Flute
Nature Sound: Birdsong
Illness Spinal Massage Point: 7th cervical
Essential Oil: Cedar
Wood Scent: Cedar
Solarized-Water Glass Color: Blue
Crystallite: Blue quartz
Stone: Basalt
Metal: Azurite
Botanical: Black cohosh, black mustard, chaparral, gentian, nettle, peppermint, wintergreen, yucca

Bursitis Generalities

Apply a paste made up of black mustard, chaparral, nettle, and peppermint and bind it with white flannel around the affected area. Include such foods as alfalfa, chicory, dandelion, plantain, oranges, grapefruit, seafood, and crisp salads in the daily diet. Avoid *all* fried foods and those with chemical additives. A tea with valerian, skullcap, hops, and lady's-slipper root would be a good idea during the day and just prior to retiring.

CANCER

Gate: 6/Pituitary
Body Location: Between eyebrows
Gate Spinal Massage Point: 1st cervical
Planet: Moon
Element: Water
Ruling Totem: Owl
Detrimental Wind: Warm westerly
Aggravating Weather: Low pressure, low altitude, high humidity, warm/hot
    temperatures
Day of Week: Monday
Moon Phase: Waning
Light Density: Dawn
Direction to Face: East
Treatment Duration: 10 minutes
Color: White
Color Breathing Direction: Down through head
Musical Note: Ti
Instrument Sound: Pan flute
Nature Sound: Wind
Illness Spinal Massage Point: 1st and 2nd cervical
Essential Oil: Patchouli
Wood Scent: All pines
Solarized-Water Glass Color: Milkglass
Crystallite: Milky quartz
Stone: White marble
Metal: Cerussite
Botanical: Bayberry bark, buckthorn, chaparral, echinacea, garlic, grape-
    root, Norwegian kelp, onion, peach bark, red clover

Cancer Generalities

Cancer can be completely obliterated from within the system only by having the diseased cells destroyed. One way this may be achieved is by routine concentrated visualization. You should visualize antibodies (the T cells) voraciously consuming the cancer cells and annihilating them completely. Follow the Gateway instructions and listen to the wind through the trees while you visualize that white wind sweeping the cancer cells out of your body. Or visualize the water sweeping them away. Eat plenty of figs, peaches, grapefruit, and nuts and seeds. Daily, take garlic, chaparral, peach bark, red clover, stillingia, echinacea, and Norwegian kelp. And always, think beautiful thoughts and remember that the mind is the computer of the body that controls *all* its systems and cells. *Use* the mind to direct the cells to fight off the invaders within the system. And do it *often* (four times a day, at least).

CANKERS

Gate: 5/Pineal
Body Location: Base of brain
Gate Spinal Massage Point: 3rd cervical
Planet: Venus
Element: Air
Ruling Totem: Wolf
Detrimental Wind: Warm southerly
Aggravating Weather: Low pressure, high altitude, high humidity, warm/hot
   temperatures
Day of Week: Friday
Moon Phase: Waning
Light Density: Morning
Direction to Face: East
Treatment Duration: 20 minutes
Color: Purple
Color Breathing Direction: Down through head
Musical Note: La
Instrument Sound: Violin
Nature Sound: Rain
Illness Spinal Massage Point: 4th cervical
Essential Oil: Lavender
Wood Scent: Piñon
Solarized-Water Glass Color: Purple
Crystallite: Amethyst
Stone: Open geode
Metal: Compact hematite
Botanical: Camphor, comfrey, eucalyptus, goldenseal root, myrrh, palma
   christi, plantain

Cankers Generalities

Make a paste of goldenseal root, comfrey, plantain, and myrrh. Apply this with a cotton swab to the affected area several times a day. Foods to avoid are sugars, oranges, food additives, and caffeine. Ingest plenty of almonds, plantain, grapes, fresh greens, and wheat germ. Onions (raw) and garlic are especially helpful because they act as a natural antibiotic. Keep a tight control on excessive energies. Direct them in a positive manner!

CHEST CONGESTION

Gate: 3/Thymus
Body Location: Heart
Gate Spinal Massage Point: 2nd dorsal
Planet: Saturn
Element: Earth

Ruling Totem: Turtle
Detrimental Wind: Warm southerly
Aggravating Weather: Low pressure, low altitude, high humidity, warm/hot
  temperatures
Day of Week: Saturday
Moon Phase: Waxing
Light Density: Afternoon
Direction to Face: South
Treatment Duration: 40 minutes
Color: Green
Color Breathing Direction: Horizontally in through navel
Musical Note: Fa
Instrument Sound: Drums
Nature Sound: Surf
Illness Spinal Massage Point: 3rd dorsal
Essential Oil: Eucalyptus
Wood Scent: Eucalyptus
Solarized-Water Glass Color: Green
Crystallite: Green tourmaline
Stone: Feldspar
Metal: Malachite
Botanical: Bayberry, black mustard, capsicum, clove, echinacea, fennel,
  fenugreek, garlic, lobelia, mullein, onion, pine

CHICKEN POX

Gate: 2/Adrenals
Body Location: Kidneys
Gate Spinal Massage Point: 9th dorsal
Planet: Mercury
Element: Fire
Ruling Totem: Horse
Detrimental Wind: Warm southerly
Aggravating Weather: Low pressure, low altitude, high humidity, warm/hot
  temperatures
Day of Week: Wednesday
Moon Phase: Waning
Light Density: Dusk
Direction to Face: North
Treatment Duration: 50 minutes
Color: Yellow
Color Breathing Direction: Up through soles
Musical Note: Mi
Instrument Sound: Cello
Nature Sound: Stream

Illness Spinal Massage Point: 11th dorsal
Essential Oil: Juniper
Wood Scent: Juniper
Solarized-Water Glass Color: Yellow
Crystallite: Citrine quartz
Stone: Obsidian
Metal: Pyrite
Botanical: Aloe, aspen, chamomile, cinquefoil, dandelion, elecampane,
      goldenseal, oak, pine, plantain, wild lettuce

Chicken Pox Generalities

Once chicken pox has taken hold within the system, there is not much left to do but try to alleviate the symptoms. Apply a paste made up of a mixture of aspen, dandelion, goldenseal, pine, and vitamin-E oil to the eruptions. This will not only supply needed antibiotic action to the eruptions, but it will also aid in the soothing of the itching. Foods to include in the daily diet are buttermilk, black cherries, cabbage, egg yolks, and plenty of salad consisting of plantain, dandelion leaves, and spinach. Chamomile tea with pine needles steeped in it would be an additional internal healing aid.

CIRCULATION (to improve)

Gate: 2/Adrenals
Body Location: Kidneys
Gate Spinal Massage Point: 9th dorsal
Planet: Mercury
Element: Fire
Ruling Totem: Horse
Detrimental Wind: Warm westerly
Aggravating Weather: Low pressure, low altitude, high humidity, warm/hot
      temperatures
Day of Week: Wednesday
Moon Phase: Waning
Light Density: Dusk
Direction to Face: North
Treatment Duration: 50 minutes
Color: Yellow
Color Breathing Direction: Up through soles
Musical Note: Mi
Instrument Sound: Cello
Nature Sound: Stream
Illness Spinal Massage Point: 5th dorsal
Essential Oil: Juniper
Wood Scent: Juniper

Solarized-Water Glass Color: Yellow
Crystallite: Citrine quartz
Stone: Obsidian
Metal: Pyrite
Botanical: Bayberry bark, black haw, capsicum, cloves, dandelion, garlic, ginseng, mullein, onion, parsley, peppermint

Circulation Generalities

Take time in the daily schedule for moderate exercise; walking is by far the best form. Avoid sitting in one position for too long. Avoid standing for too long. Get out into the fresh air and sunshine. Daily ingest such foods as broccoli, carrots, grapes, dates, figs, peaches, radishes, and onions. Keep to light foods such as broiled fish and fowl. Avoid *all* fried foods. Avoid *all* red meats. Avoid *all* forms of pork. All these are taboo for the circulatory system as they create a sluggish and fatty condition. Limit the intake of sugars, salts, and all food additives. Think more positively about your life! People with poor circulation tend to put down themselves and their abilities and are usually comparing themselves to others who they believe are superior to themselves. Think *positively* and get enough exercise.

COLITIS

Gate: 2/Adrenals
Body Location: Kidneys
Gate Spinal Massage Point: 9th dorsal
Planet: Mercury
Element: Fire
Ruling Totem: Horse
Detrimental Wind: Warm westerly
Aggravating Weather: Low pressure, low altitude, high humidity, warm/hot temperatures
Day of Week: Wednesday
Moon Phase: Waning
Light Density: Dusk
Direction to Face: North
Treatment Duration: 50 minutes
Color: Yellow
Color Breathing Direction: Up through soles
Musical Note: Mi
Instrument Sound: Cello
Nature Sound: Stream
Illness Spinal Massage Point: 1st lumbar
Essential Oil: Juniper
Wood Scent: Juniper
Solarized-Water Glass Color: Yellow

Crystallite: Citrine quartz
Stone: Obsidian
Metal: Pyrite
Botanical: Barberry, blackberry, capsicum, cascara sagrada, fennel, garlic,
    goldenseal root, red raspberry leaves

Colitis Generalities

Colitis is most often caused by mental attitudes that negatively affect the physical digestive system. Such a condition indicates a serious need to examine any adverse emotional situations in your life. Remove and eliminate the upsetting condition and the colitis will ease itself into a more healthful and regular operation. Until such time occurs, ingest a tea made from a mixture of lobelia, fennel, and red raspberry leaves with a pinch of capsicum. This formula will most often alleviate the distress. However, generally, the root of the cause will be at issue here. Keep the energies from exploding through the emotions! An additional tea made from valerian, lady's slipper, skullcap, and hops will bring improvement if taken twice daily. Valerian alone will not produce the desired results. But watch those emotions! Your mind is hurting you. Watch the nerves. Calm yourself and learn to deal with anxiety, and correct situations that are causing it.

CONJUNCTIVITIS

Gate: 6/Pituitary
Body Location: Between eyebrows
Gate Spinal Massage Point: 1st cervical
Planet: Moon
Element: Water
Ruling Totem: Owl
Detrimental Wind: Warm westerly
Aggravating Weather: Low pressure, low altitude, high humidity, warm/hot
    temperatures
Day of Week: Monday
Moon Phase: Waning
Light Density: Dawn
Direction to Face: East
Treatment Duration: 10 minutes
Color: White
Color Breathing Direction: Down through head
Musical Note: Ti
Instrument Sound: Pan flute
Nature Sound: Wind
Illness Spinal Massage Point: 2nd cervical
Essential Oil: Patchouli

Wood Scent: All pines
Solarized-Water Glass Color: Milkglass
Crystallite: Milky quartz
Stone: White marble
Metal: Cerussite
Botanical: Aspen, borage, eyebright, oak, Rocky Mountain maple, Rocky
    Mountain raspberry, rosemary, yarrow

Conjunctivitis Generalities

Any infectious condition within the system can be alleviated by bringing that system back into a more balanced condition. Include such foods as brussels sprouts, figs, carrots, squash, wild rice, whole grains, almonds, and mullein tea in the daily diet. Take aspen bark, oak bark, and eyebright steeped in a tea and use this liquid as a gentle eyewash several times a day (this is used on the skin around the eye *only*). Wash the eyes themselves in warm water only. Get plenty of rest and visualize the eyes in a clear and normal state. Take time out for silent meditative activities.

NOTE: Severe conjunctivitis (pinkeye) can quickly become a serious sight-threatening condition that is highly contagious. If white or greenish sticky matter is in evidence in conjunction with red eyes, seek immediate professional treatment. Most often, antibiotic ophthalmic solutions such as Cortisporin or sulfacetamide sodium suspensions will be prescribed. Follow the instructions to the letter.

CRAMPS (Menstrual)

Gate: 1/Gonads
Body Location: Pelvis
Gate Spinal Massage Point: 3rd lumbar
Planet: Mars
Element: Fire
Ruling Totem: Snake
Detrimental Wind: Warm westerly
Aggravating Weather: Low pressure, low altitude, high humidity, warm/hot
    temperatures
Day of Week: Tuesday
Moon Phase: Waxing
Light Density: Night
Direction to Face: North
Treatment Duration: 60 minutes
Color: Red
Color Breathing Direction: Up through soles
Musical Note: Do

Instrument Sound: Piano
Nature Sound: Forest
Illness Spinal Massage Point: 3rd lumbar
Essential Oil: Sandalwood
Wood Scent: Mesquite
Solarized-Water Glass Color: Red
Crystallite: Rose quartz
Stone: Rose stone
Metal: Cinnabar
Botanical: Blessed thistle, blue cohosh, capsicum, cramp bark, false
     unicorn root, lady's-slipper root, squaw vine, uva-ursi

Menstrual Cramp Generalities

In the case of severe cramping or bleeding, professional advice should be sought as there are several serious conditions that may cause this. However, if they are caused because of regular menstruation each month, then the condition can completely be avoided by taking the following herbs two days prior to the onset of the menstrual time through to its conclusion: blessed thistle, capsicum, cramp bark, false unicorn root, lady's-slipper root, marshmallow root, squawvine, and uva-ursi. These are combined in a tea. Also, drink chamomile tea with a pinch of capsicum. Eat watercress, raspberries, and salads with raw yellow onion. Learn to ignore more! Many times when the mind perceives the forthcoming menstrual time, it will automatically anticipate the onslaught of pain; therefore, the pain becomes an actuality. Pain does not necessarily have to accompany the menstrual time. But for those women who experience actual organically induced pain rather than the mentally induced type, the above-mentioned tea formula will give great relief.

CROUP

Gate: 4/Thyroid
Body Location: Throat
Gate Spinal Massage Point: 7th cervical
Planet: Jupiter
Element: Air
Ruling Totem: Buffalo
Detrimental Wind: Warm southerly
Aggravating Weather: Low pressure, low altitude, high humidity, warm/hot
     temperatures
Day of Week: Thursday
Moon Phase: Waxing
Light Density: Noon
Direction to Face: West
Treatment Duration: 30 minutes

Color: Blue
Color Breathing Direction: Down through head
Musical Note: Sol
Instrument Sound: Flute
Nature Sound: Birdsong
Illness Spinal Massage Point: 6th cervical
Essential Oil: Cedar
Wood Scent: Cedar
Solarized-Water Glass Color: Blue
Crystallite: Blue quartz
Stone: Basalt
Metal: Azurite
Botanical: Angelica, aspen, barberry bark, capsicum, chokecherry,
     eucalyptus, fennel, garlic, honey, lobelia, wild onion

Croup Generalities

Fresh air is most important with any type of chest congestion, cough, or head cold. However, too many people forget the all-important part of keeping the head covered whenever out in cold weather. A large percentage of the body's heat is lost through the top of the head, just as steam escapes from a thermos when the cap is removed. Hold on to that body heat! Eat such foods as figs, almonds, grapes, blueberries, oranges, and grapefruit. Onions and garlic are wonderful for such conditions. A hot tea with fennel, aspen bark, and lobelia with a pinch of capsicum and honey will calm the system. Inhale eucalyptus steam.

DANDRUFF

Gate: 6/Pituitary
Body Location: Between eyebrows
Gate Spinal Massage Point: 1st cervical
Planet: Moon
Element: Water
Ruling Totem: Owl
Detrimental Wind: Cold northerly
Aggravating Weather: Low pressure, high altitude, low humidity, cool/cold
     temperatures
Day of Week: Monday
Moon Phase: Waning
Light Density: Dawn
Direction to Face: East
Treatment Duration: 10 minutes
Color: White
Color Breathing Direction: Down through head
Musical Note: Ti

Instrument Sound: Pan flute
Nature Sound: Wind
Illness Spinal Massage Point: 1st cervical
Essential Oil: Patchouli
Wood Scent: All pines
Solarized-Water Glass Color: Milkglass
Crystallite: Milky quartz
Stone: White marble
Metal: Cerussite
Botanical: Birch, chicory, cucumber root, dandelion, fireweed, goldenseal
    root, juniper, nettle, peanut oil, pine, willow

Dandruff Generalities

A good shampoo with natural moisturizers in it should be used. Frequent washings do not cause dryness. Work peanut oil into the scalp each
evening, massage gently for ten minutes, and wrap the head with a white
flannel cloth overnight. Avoid drying agents such as hairsprays, perfume,
and the like. Avoid holding the hair dryer too close to the head. Never spray
perfume onto the hair. Eat molasses, whole grains, plantain, wheat germ,
and grapes. Use honey instead of pure sugar or any artificial sweeteners.
Brush hair daily before each shampooing. And, watch those negative
thoughts!

DIABETES

Gate: 3/Thymus
Body Location: Heart
Gate Spinal Massage Point: 2nd dorsal
Planet: Saturn
Element: Earth
Ruling Totem: Turtle
Detrimental Wind: Cold northerly
Aggravating Weather: Low pressure, low altitude, high humidity, cool/cold
    temperatures
Day of Week: Saturday
Moon Phase: Waning
Light Density: Afternoon
Direction to Face: South
Treatment Duration: 40 minutes
Color: Green
Color Breathing Direction: Horizontally in through navel
Musical Note: Fa
Instrument Sound: Drums
Nature Sound: Surf

Illness Spinal Massage Point: 2nd dorsal
Essential Oil: Eucalyptus
Wood Scent: Eucalyptus
Solarized-Water Glass Color: Green
Crystallite: Green tourmaline
Stone: Feldspar
Metal: Malachite
Botanical: Dandelion, fennel, garlic, goldenseal, horsetail, pipsissewa, red clover, uva-ursi, yarrow

Diabetes Generalities

People born between December 22 and January 19 are most susceptible to diabetes, often in conjunction with heart disease. Regular moderate exercise such as enjoyable walks in the fresh air and sunshine are highly beneficial. Avoid all fried foods and all artificial food additives and sweeteners. Never eat pork in any form. Never eat red meats. Instead, eat plenty of broiled seafood, fowl, peaches, dates, crisp greens with dandelion, and whole-grain breads (only), and drink plenty of water. Also, watch those emotions! Accept life!

DIVERTICULITIS

Gate: 2/Adrenals
Body Location: Kidneys
Gate Spinal Massage Point: 9th dorsal
Planet: Mercury
Element: Fire
Ruling Totem: Horse
Detrimental Wind: Warm westerly
Aggravating Weather: Low pressure, low altitude, high humidity, warm/hot temperatures
Day of Week: Wednesday
Moon Phase: Waning
Light Density: Dusk
Direction to Face: North
Treatment Duration: 50 minutes
Color: Yellow
Color Breathing Direction: Up through soles
Musical Note: Mi
Instrument Sound: Cello
Nature Sound: Stream
Illness Spinal Massage Point: 1st lumbar
Essential Oil: Juniper
Wood Scent: Juniper

Solarized-Water Glass Color: Yellow
Crystallite: Citrine quartz
Stone: Obsidian
Metal: Pyrite
Botanical: Black haw, black walnut, cascara sagrada, fennel, garlic, Rocky
   Mountain raspberry, wormwood

Diverticulitis Generalities

As with colitis, this disease indicates a need to keep careful watch over negative emotions and a tendency toward overexcitability and/or anxiety. Channel the negative energies into constructive outlets instead of harboring them deep within your body. Avoid spicy seasonings. Avoid all red meats and all forms of pork. Drink at least eight glasses of water per day. Eat almonds, whole-grain breads, cottage cheese, and yogurt. Avoid acidic fruits completely. Think good thoughts and stop dwelling upon the negative aspects of your life. Life is what *you* make it, *how* you look at it. Change your perspective and alter your angle of sight. Stop judging others. Let life *be.*

DRY SKIN

Gate: 2/Adrenals
Body Location: Kidneys
Gate Spinal Massage Point: 9th dorsal
Planet: Mercury
Element: Fire
Ruling Totem: Horse
Detrimental Wind: Cold northerly
Aggravating Weather: Low pressure, high altitude, low humidity, cool/cold
   temperatures
Day of Week: Wednesday
Moon Phase: Waxing to full
Light Density: Dusk
Direction to Face: North
Treatment Duration: 50 minutes
Color: Yellow
Color Breathing Direction: Up through soles
Musical Note: Mi
Instrument Sound: Cello
Nature Sound: Stream
Illness Spinal Massage Point: 11th dorsal
Essential Oil: Juniper
Wood Scent: Juniper
Solarized-Water Glass Color: Yellow
Crystallite: Citrine quartz
Stone: Obsidian

Metal: Pyrite
Botanical: Black mustard, comfrey, olive oil, palma christi, peanut oil, plantain, slippery-elm bark

Dry Skin Generalities

Apply a mixture of olive oil, palma christi, peanut oil, and vitamin-E oil to the dry areas. Foods to include in the diet are olives, broiled seafood and fowl, strawberries, and a salad consisting of plantain, cabbage, spinach, and onions (raw). Avoid wearing jewelry, both the costume variety and excessive amounts of expensive jewelry. Massage a cream made from beeswax and plantain over the dry area prior to retiring. If the area is the hands, cover this salve with gloves.

If the entire body is dry, change the body soap you're using. As suggested previously, a natural vitamin-E and glycerine mix is best. It is cleansing but not drying to the skin surfaces.

ECZEMA

Gate: 5/Pineal
Body Location: Base of brain
Gate Spinal Massage Point: 3rd cervical
Planet: Venus
Element: Air
Ruling Totem: Wolf
Detrimental Wind: Warm southerly
Aggravating Weather: Low pressure, low altitude, high humidity, warm/hot temperatures
Day of Week: Friday
Moon Phase: Waning
Light Density: Morning
Direction to Face: East
Treatment Duration: 20 minutes
Color: Purple
Color Breathing Direction: Down through head
Musical Note: La
Instrument Sound: Violin
Nature Sound: Rain
Illness Spinal Massage Point: 3rd cervical
Essential Oil: Lavender
Wood Scent: Piñon
Solarized-Water Glass Color: Purple
Crystallite: Amethyst
Stone: Open geode
Metal: Compact hematite
Botanical: Aspen, dandelion, garlic, goldenseal, onion, puffball, slippery-elm bark, sumac, walnut, yarrow

Eczema Generalities

This condition is often directly related to dry, cold weather conditions, especially affecting the skin of the face—areas around the eyebrows, nose, and chin. This does not have to be permanent, however. A salve made up of vitamin-E oil, goldenseal, myrrh, and castor oil will heal the affected areas, and if the applications are maintained on a nightly basis routinely, they will eliminate future occurrences.

EMOTIONAL STRESS EFFECTS

Gate: 6/Pituitary
Body Location: Between eyebrows
Gate Spinal Massage Point: 1st cervical
Planet: Moon
Element: Water
Ruling Totem: Owl
Detrimental Wind: Warm westerly
Aggravating Weather: Low pressure, low altitude, high humidity, warm/hot temperatures
Day of Week: Monday
Moon Phase: Waning
Light Density: Dawn
Direction to Face: East
Treatment Duration: 10 minutes
Color: White
Color Breathing Direction: Down through head
Musical Note: Ti
Instrument Sound: Pan flute
Nature Sound: Wind
Illness Spinal Massage Point: 1st cervical
Essential Oil: Patchouli
Wood Scent: All pines
Solarized-Water Glass Color: Milkglass
Crystallite: Milky quartz
Stone: White marble
Metal: Cerussite
Botanical: Blue vervain, cotton root, ginseng, hops, lady's slipper, lobelia, skullcap, valerian root

Emotional Stress Generalities

Severe emotional stress requires immediate evaluation and treatment by a qualified physician. Minor distress can be calmed by ingesting a tea from the combined herbs of ginseng, hops, lobelia, skullcap, lady's slipper, and valerian root. Remember that valerian root alone will not have any significant effect until it is combined with the other herbs. Chamomile tea during the day has a calming effect upon a mildly nervous system. Learn to love life and, most important, love yourself. Avoid meddling and prejudgments! Use routine meditation to control anxiety attacks or nervousness.

EMPHYSEMA

Gate: 3/Thymus
Body Location: Heart
Gate Spinal Massage Point: 2nd dorsal
Planet: Saturn
Element: Earth
Ruling Totem: Turtle
Detrimental Wind: Warm southerly
Aggravating Weather: Low pressure, low altitude, high humidity, warm/hot temperatures
Day of Week: Saturday
Moon Phase: Waning
Light Density: Afternoon
Direction to Face: South
Treatment Duration: 40 minutes
Color: Green
Color Breathing Direction: Horizontally in through navel
Musical Note: Fa
Instrument Sound: Drums
Nature Sound: Surf
Illness Spinal Massage Point: 3rd dorsal
Essential Oil: Eucalyptus
Wood Scent: Eucalyptus
Solarized-Water Glass Color: Green
Crystallite: Green tourmaline
Stone: Feldspar
Metal: Malachite
Botanical: Angelica, bergamot, coltsfoot, comfrey, garlic, honey, lobelia, lungwort, mullein, nettle, pleurisy root

Emphysema Generalities

Mild emphysema can effectively be eased through several simply applied methods of visualization, tea ingestion, abstinence from various substances, and avoidance of pollutants. Visualize pure alpine air circulating through your respiratory system at every breath. Practice this diligently. Drink a tea mixture of mullein, angelica, and lobelia sweetened with a few drops of unfiltered honey. Avoid polluted air, dry indoor air, and strong scents of any kind. Eucalyptus steam will help clear the bronchial passages. Rest and sleep with the chest region elevated.

EXHAUSTION

Gate: 6/Pituitary
Body Location: Between eyebrows
Gate Spinal Massage Point: 1st cervical
Planet: Moon
Element: Water
Ruling Totem: Owl
Detrimental Wind: Warm westerly
Aggravating Weather: Low pressure, low altitude, high humidity, warm/hot
    temperatures
Day of Week: Monday
Moon Phase: Waxing
Light Density: Dawn
Direction to Face: East
Treatment Duration: 10 minutes
Color: White
Color Breathing Direction: Down through head
Musical Note: Ti
Instrument Sound: Pan flute
Nature Sound: Wind
Illness Spinal Massage Point: 1st cervical
Essential Oil: Patchouli
Wood Scent: All pines
Solarized-Water Glass Color: Milkglass
Crystallite: Milky quartz
Stone: White marble
Metal: Cerussite
Botanical: Bee pollen, bitterroot, ginseng, gotu kola, watercress

Exhaustion Generalities

Exhaustion is a bona fide physiological condition, but its causes are not always of a physical nature. In fact, most cases of exhaustion are caused by mental or emotional problems. Both causes can be alleviated with adequate rest and a tea made from ginseng, gotu kola, bee pollen, and watercress. This tea must have all these herbs combined to be effective.

Examine your life! Are you lonely? Are you in need of attention? Are you just plain tired of certain situations or even of life itself? Many times exhaustion is a symptomatic warning of a more grave emotional disease that is manifesting itself through the physical in order to receive attention from others. Seek the proper help here! And remember, life is truly only as good as you *see* it.

EYE AILMENTS

Gate: 6/Pituitary
Body Location: Between eyebrows
Gate Spinal Massage Point: 1st cervical
Planet: Moon
Element: Water
Ruling Totem: Owl
Detrimental Wind: Warm westerly
Aggravating Weather: Low pressure, low altitude, high humidity, warm/hot temperatures
Day of Week: Monday
Moon Phase: Waxing
Light Density: Dawn
Direction to Face: East
Treatment Duration: 10 minutes
Color: White
Color Breathing Direction: Down through head
Musical Note: Ti
Instrument Sound: Pan flute
Nature Sound: Wind
Illness Spinal Massage Point: 2nd cervical
Essential Oil: Patchouli
Wood Scent: All pines
Solarized-Water Glass Color: Milkglass
Crystallite: Milky quartz
Stone: White marble
Metal: Cerussite
Botanical: Bayberry bark, borage, eyebright, Rocky Mountain maple, sassafras, sumac, yarrow

Eye Ailment Generalities

Eyesight can be strengthened. Tired eyes can be rested and refreshed. Red and sore eyes can be brightened and cleared. Severe infection requires immediate medical attention by a qualified professional. Minor irritations can be alleviated through an application of bayberry bark, eyebright, and yarrow swabbed *around* the affected eye. Eat carrots, oranges, plantain, wheat germ, whole grains, and seafood.

FLATULENCE

Gate: 2/Adrenals
Body Location: Kidneys
Gate Spinal Massage Point: 9th dorsal
Planet: Mercury

Element: Fire
Ruling Totem: Horse
Detrimental Wind: Warm southerly
Aggravating Weather: Low pressure, low altitude, high humidity, warm/hot
    temperatures
Day of Week: Wednesday
Moon Phase: Waning/new
Light Density: Dusk
Direction to Face: North
Treatment Duration: 50 minutes
Color: Yellow
Color Breathing Direction: Up through soles
Musical Note: Mi
Instrument Sound: Cello
Nature Sound: Stream
Illness Spinal Massage Point: 12th dorsal
Essential Oil: Juniper
Wood Scent: Juniper
Solarized-Water Glass Color: Yellow
Crystallite: Citrine quartz
Stone: Obsidian
Metal: Pyrite
Botanical: Bayberry bark, dandelion, fennel, gingerroot, peppermint, red
    clover, rhubarb

Flatulence Generalities

Flatulence is most frequently caused by a poor lifestyle. Oftentimes you eat too fast, are too hurried through life to take an all-important relaxing hour for lunch or dinner. Overactive mental activities and overreactive emotions also contribute to this uncomfortable and often painful condition. Slow down the pace! Eat slowly in peaceful surroundings. Stop eating too fast. Relief comes quickly from a tea made from fennel, peppermint, and red clover. Avoid spicy seasonings, pork, and heavy red meats, as these greatly contribute to this uncomfortable condition.

FLU

Gate: 3/Thymus
Body Location: Heart
Gate Spinal Massage Point: 2nd dorsal
Planet: Saturn
Element: Earth
Ruling Totem: Turtle
Detrimental Wind: Warm southerly

Aggravating Weather: Low pressure, low altitude, high humidity, warm/hot
    temperatures
Day of Week: Saturday
Moon Phase: Waning
Light Density: Afternoon
Direction to Face: South
Treatment Duration: 40 minutes
Color: Green
Color Breathing Direction: Horizontally in through navel
Musical Note: Fa
Instrument Sound: Drums
Nature Sound: Surf
Illness Spinal Massage Point: 3rd dorsal
Essential Oil: Eucalyptus
Wood Scent: Eucalyptus
Solarized-Water Glass Color: Green
Crystallite: Green tourmaline
Stone: Feldspar
Metal: Malachite
Botanical: Aspen, black haw, capsicum, clove, eucalyptus, fennel, garlic,
    honey, mullein, sassafras, thyme, white pine

Flu Generalities

Having a bout with the flu can be very debilitating and uncomfortable, but it doesn't have to be that way. In the first place, you wouldn't have gotten it if you'd maintained a proper alkaline level in your system. Stop eating sugars and meats and drinking alcoholic beverages. Eat oranges, almonds, apples, figs, and grapefruits. Drink plenty of mullein tea with honey and a pinch of capsicum. Take sweat baths, taking extra precautions against getting a chill afterward. Slow down your lifestyle pace long enough to care for yourself in the proper way. Pay more attention to what you eat! A light coating of camphor oil over the chest, neck, and soles of the feet will aid in breathing and clearing congestion. Inhale eucalyptus steam to clear the sinus cavities.

Frame of mind and the emotions play a key role in opening up the system for the flu. Anxiety, anger, continual hate, or envy and jealousy are all blockers of alkalinity. And when the body is out of alkalinity and into acidity . . . anything can enter to hurt your system.

GALL BLADDER AILMENTS

Gate: 2/Adrenals
Body Location: Kidneys
Gate Spinal Massage Point: 9th dorsal

Planet: Mercury
Element: Fire
Ruling Totem: Horse
Detrimental Wind: Cold northerly
Aggravating Weather: Low pressure, low altitude, high humidity, cool/cold
    temperatures
Day of Week: Wednesday
Moon Phase: Waning
Light Density: Dusk
Direction to Face: North
Treatment Duration: 50 minutes
Color: Yellow
Color Breathing Direction: Up through soles
Musical Note: Mi
Instrument Sound: Cello
Nature Sound: Stream
Illness Spinal Massage Point: 4th dorsal
Essential Oil: Juniper
Wood Scent: Juniper
Solarized-Water Glass Color: Yellow
Crystallite: Citrine quartz
Stone: Obsidian
Metal: Pyrite
Botanical: Blue vervain, dandelion, goldenseal, graperoot, hops, lobelia,
    papaya, red clover, rhubarb, tansy, wintergreen

Gall Bladder Generalities

Exercise and balanced emotions are needed here. Keep negative
thoughts and emotional energies well under control. Stop eating pork and
red meats. These will be found to irritate this condition. Eat plenty of fresh
and crisp greens including dandelion leaves, plantain, and celery. Also eat
broiled seafood, radishes, strawberries, and almonds. Avoid spicy seasonings. Use no artificial sweeteners under any circumstances.

GASTRITIS

Gate: 2/Adrenals
Body Location: Kidneys
Gate Spinal Massage Point: 9th dorsal
Planet: Mercury
Element: Fire
Ruling Totem: Horse
Detrimental Wind: Warm southerly
Aggravating Weather: Low pressure, low altitude, high humidity, warm/hot
    temperatures

Day of Week: Wednesday
Moon Phase: Waning/new
Light Density: Dusk
Direction to Face: North
Treatment Duration: 50 minutes
Color: Yellow
Color Breathing Direction: Up through soles
Musical Note: Mi
Instrument Sound: Cello
Nature Sound: Stream
Illness Spinal Massage Point: 7th dorsal
Essential Oil: Juniper
Wood Scent: Juniper
Solarized-Water Glass Color: Yellow
Crystallite: Citrine quartz
Stone: Obsidian
Metal: Pyrite
Botanical: Blackberry, fennel, goldenseal root, mullein

GENERAL RESPIRATORY AILMENTS

Gate: 4/Thyroid
Body Location: Throat
Gate Spinal Massage Point: 7th cervical
Planet: Jupiter
Element: Air
Ruling Totem: Buffalo
Detrimental Wind: Warm southerly
Aggravating Weather: Low pressure, low altitude, high humidity, warm/hot
     temperatures
Day of Week: Thursday
Moon Phase: Waxing/full
Light Density: Noon
Direction to Face: West
Treatment Duration: 30 minutes
Color: Blue
Color Breathing Direction: Down through head
Musical Note: Sol
Instrument Sound: Flute
Nature Sound: Birdsong
Illness Spinal Massage Point: 1st dorsal
Essential Oil: Cedar
Wood Scent: Cedar
Solarized-Water Glass Color: Blue
Crystallite: Blue quartz

Stone: Basalt

Metal: Azurite

Botanical: Angelica, black mustard, chokecherry, elecampane, eucalyptus, feverbush, garlic, hyssop, lobelia, mullein, pine, thyme

General Respiratory Generalities

Common respiratory ailments are often the result of poor lifestyle habits such as being careless about how you dress in inclement weather, not maintaining an alkaline balance within your body, overexertion during exercise, and eating the wrong foods. Drink mullein tea three times per day to get the system back into a healthful alkaline state. Stop eating red meats and pork. Inhale eucalyptus steam to clear airways. Drink a tea with the combined ingredients of peppermint, lobelia, pine, and thyme.

Watch those emotions! Frequently respiratory ailments can be directly traced back to these negative attitudes. They hurt you! Accept life! Love yourself!

If you reside in a city that is frequently on a high-pollution alert . . . then move!

GUM AILMENTS

Gate: 5/Pineal

Body Location: Base of brain

Gate Spinal Massage Point: 3rd cervical

Planet: Venus

Element: Air

Ruling Totem: Wolf

Detrimental Wind: Warm southerly

Aggravating Weather: Low pressure, low altitude, high humidity, warm/hot temperatures

Day of Week: Friday

Moon Phase: Waning

Light Density: Morning

Direction to Face: East

Treatment Duration: 20 minutes

Color: Purple

Color Breathing Direction: Down through head

Musical Note: La

Instrument Sound: Violin

Nature Sound: Rain

Illness Spinal Massage Point: 4th cervical

Essential Oil: Lavender

Wood Scent: Piñon

Solarized-Water Glass Color: Purple

Crystallite: Amethyst

Stone: Open geode
Metal: Compact hematite
Botanical: Comfrey, frostwort, goldenseal, horsetail, myrrh, thyme, white
   pond lily

Gum Ailment Generalities

Most gum problems can be remedied with good habitual hygienic procedures such as brushing three times per day (more if needed), careful and unrushed flossing, and close scrutiny of the teeth and surrounding gums. Most commercial toothpastes are virtually useless. Instead, use a paste made from baking soda, hydrogen peroxide, salt, and myrrh. This mixture will keep the teeth white and heal most any gum problems that are beginning. A paste of goldenseal and myrrh will heal gum cankers, too. Conclude your nightly brushing and flossing with a swabbing of myrrh around gums and over teeth. Myrrh is a whitener and has also been effective in treating mouth-tissue lesions.

As has been previously stated: more is not better. It has been advised by No-Eyes' friends that the current concept of human ingestion of fluoride is not as healthful as we believe it to be. Fluorinated water is quite enough for our physiological systems; to increase the intake by ingesting it in our dentifrices and also having the teeth themselves treated in the dental office is not recommended. No-Eyes often commented on the human penchant to go overboard once a good thing is discovered.

HEADACHE

Gate: 6/Pituitary
Body Location: Between eyebrows
Gate Spinal Massage Point: 1st cervical
Planet: Moon
Element: Water
Ruling Totem: Owl
Detrimental Wind: Warm westerly
Aggravating Weather: Low pressure, high altitude, high humidity, warm/hot
   temperatures
Day of Week: Monday
Moon Phase: Waxing
Light Density: Dawn
Direction to Face: East
Treatment Duration: 10 minutes
Color: White
Color Breathing Direction: Down through head
Musical Note: Ti
Instrument Sound: Pan flute
Nature Sound: Wind

Illness Spinal Massage Point: 1st cervical
Essential Oil: Patchouli
Wood Scent: All pines
Solarized-Water Glass Color: Milkglass
Crystallite: Milky quartz
Stone: White marble
Metal: Cerussite
Botanical: Blue vervain, cotton root, dandelion, lady's slipper, lobelia, mullein, peppermint, red clover, skullcap, valerian

Headache Generalities

Like many other physical ailments, headaches are most frequently caused by an imbalance in mental and emotional states. In this instance, a tight rein kept on the overemotionalism and negative thinking will prevent the onslaught. Some severe headaches emanate from the sinus area. These can be alleviated by inhaling eucalyptus steam and drinking mullein tea with a sprig of peppermint in it. A light layer of camphorated oil applied over the nose bridge will also help. Rub it in using a gentle massage motion along the forehead and beneath the eyes. Avoid rooms with stale air. Avoid strong odors and loud noises. Get enough exercise. Keep those negative thoughts under control!

Severe headaches can also be alleviated by placing two moistened peppermint tea bags side by side on the back of the neck. Wrap in place and rest for twenty to forty minutes—longer if needed.

Frequently chronic headaches in conjunction with neckaches are generated by an unaligned vertebra. You may need a visit to your local chiropractor.

HEART AILMENTS

Gate: 3/Thymus
Body Location: Heart
Gate Spinal Massage Point: 2nd dorsal
Planet: Saturn
Element: Earth
Ruling Totem: Turtle
Detrimental Wind: Warm southerly
Aggravating Weather: Low pressure, low altitude, high humidity, warm/hot temperatures
Day of Week: Saturday
Moon Phase: Waning
Light Density: Afternoon
Direction to Face: South
Treatment Duration: 40 minutes
Color: Green

Color Breathing Direction: Horizontally in through navel
Musical Note: Fa
Instrument Sound: Drums
Nature Sound: Surf
Illness Spinal Massage Point: 2nd dorsal
Essential Oil: Eucalyptus
Wood Scent: Eucalyptus
Solarized-Water Glass Color: Green
Crystallite: Green tourmaline
Stone: Feldspar
Metal: Malachite
Botanical: Black haw, blue vervain, digitalis, garlic, horehound, onion, parsley, pokeroot, skullcap, valerian, wild rice

Heart Ailment Generalities

Heart palpitations are not uncommon among normally healthy people. However, if they occur often and with intense regularity, professional evaluation is advised. For occasional bouts, analyze your regular diet. Avoid spicy seasonings, pork, red meats, caffeine, and all artificial food additives and artificial sweeteners. Control your emotions (especially that temper). Eat plenty of almonds daily, broiled seafood, apples, figs, plantain, dandelion greens, parsley, wild lettuce, and whole grains. Avoid white bread like the plague. And an aspirin taken every other day helps to keep the blood thinned.

HEMORRHAGING (Menstrual)

Gate: 1/Gonads
Body Location: Pelvis
Gate Spinal Massage Point: 3rd lumbar
Planet: Mars
Element: Fire
Ruling Totem: Snake
Detrimental Wind: Warm westerly
Aggravating Weather: Low pressure, low altitude, high humidity, warm/hot temperatures
Day of Week: Tuesday
Moon Phase: Waning/new
Light Density: Night
Direction to Face: North
Treatment Duration: 60 minutes
Color: Red
Color Breathing Direction: Up through soles
Musical Note: Do
Instrument Sound: Piano

Nature Sound: Forest
Illness Spinal Massage Point: 3rd lumbar
Essential Oil: Sandalwood
Wood Scent: Mesquite
Solarized-Water Glass Color: Red
Crystallite: Rose quartz
Stone: Rose stone
Metal: Cinnabar
Botanical: Black haw, capsicum, cotton root, cramp bark, marshmallow
    root, plantain, Rocky Mountain raspberry, sorrel, squawberry

Hemorrhaging Generalities

This condition does not have to be a continual problem. The rate of menstrual flow can markedly be reduced by simply ingesting an herbal formula three times per day. This is begun two days before the onset of the menstrual flow and should be taken through to its conclusion. Combine the black haw, capsicum, cotton root, cramp bark, marshmallow root, plantain, Rocky Mountain raspberry, sorrel, and squawberry plus blessed thistle in a hot tea. You will find that not only is the flow slowed to a more normal degree, but your accompanying discomfort complaints will also have disappeared. As always, if the condition persists, your body is telling you that a more serious condition is present and that you need to seek professional advice. These recommendations are made as suggestions to be followed only after your condition has been evaluated by a professional.

HEMORRHOIDS

Gate: 1/Gonads
Body Location: Pelvis
Gate Spinal Massage Point: 3rd lumbar
Planet: Mars
Element: Fire
Ruling Totem: Snake
Detrimental Wind: Warm westerly
Aggravating Weather: Low pressure, low altitude, high humidity, warm/hot
    temperatures
Day of Week: Tuesday
Moon Phase: Waxing
Light Density: Night
Direction to Face: North
Treatment Duration: 60 minutes
Color: Red
Color Breathing Direction: Up through soles
Musical Note: Do

Instrument Sound: Piano
Nature Sound: Forest
Illness Spinal Massage Point: Sacrum
Essential Oil: Sandalwood
Wood Scent: Mesquite
Solarized-Water Glass Color: Red
Crystallite: Rose quartz
Stone: Rose stone
Metal: Cinnabar
Botanical: Alder bark, almond oil, goldenseal, lobelia, palma christi,
    starwort, white oak, willow

Hemmorhoid Generalities

Hemorrhoids need not be a problem. If the proper foods are ingested, the digestive system will have no trouble voiding its waste products. Constipation and/or childbirth contributes to this problem. Apply a salve made from castor oil, vitamin-E oil, sweet almond oil, and goldenseal to the area after each bowel movement or whenever needed. Avoid white-flour products, sugar, red meats, pork, and excessive pasta. Eat liberally of the whole grains, seeds and nuts, and fresh and crisp greens including alfalfa, grapefruit, almonds, and apples. Also, stand erect and reach your arms to the ceiling, slowly stretch forward, and bend to reach hands as far to the floor as possible. This exercise pulls up the intestines and aids in reducing the complaint. This should be a daily exercise; you should stretch and touch toward your toes about ten times.

HORMONE IMBALANCE

Gate: 6/Pituitary
Body Location: Between eyebrows
Gate Spinal Massage Point: 1st cervical
Planet: Moon
Element: Water
Ruling Totem: Owl
Detrimental Wind: Warm southerly
Aggravating Weather: Low pressure, low altitude, high humidity, warm/hot
    temperatures
Day of Week: Monday
Moon Phase: Full
Light Density: Dawn
Direction to Face: East
Treatment Duration: 10 minutes
Color: White
Color Breathing Direction: Down through head
Musical Note: Ti

Instrument Sound: Pan flute
Nature Sound: Wind
Illness Spinal Massage Point: 1st cervical
Essential Oil: Patchouli
Wood Scent: All pines
Solarized-Water Glass Color: Milkglass
Crystallite: Milky quartz
Stone: White marble
Metal: Cerussite
Botanical: Alfalfa, black cohosh, echinacea, fennel, ginseng, mullein, Norwegian kelp, papaya, red clover, sarsaparilla

Hormone Imbalance Generalities

A tea formulated with the alfalfa, black cohosh, echinacea, fennel, ginseng, mullein, Norwegian kelp, papaya, red clover, and sarsaparilla will bring the hormone balance more in line. Eat fresh and crisp salads including such greens as Norwegian kelp, alfalfa, spinach, and plantain; also eat egg yolks, grapes, grapefruit, apples, and almonds. Avoid the heavy red meats and all forms of pork. Food additives affect the system's delicate balance and vibrations. Avoid alcohol and caffeine. Avoid excessive sugars and sugar substitutes. Drink at least eight glasses of water per day. Get enough moderate exercise; walking in the fresh air and sunshine would be an excellent way to meet this last requirement.

HYPERACTIVITY

Gate: 6/Pituitary
Body Location: Between eyebrows
Gate Spinal Massage Point: 1st cervical
Planet: Moon
Element: Water
Ruling Totem: Owl
Detrimental Wind: Warm westerly
Aggravating Weather: Low pressure, low altitude, high humidity, warm/hot temperatures
Day of Week: Monday
Moon Phase: Full
Light Density: Dawn
Direction to Face: East
Treatment Duration: 10 minutes
Color: White
Color Breathing Direction: Down through head
Musical Note: Ti
Instrument Sound: Pan flute
Nature Sound: Wind

Illness Spinal Massage Point: 1st cervical
Essential Oil: Patchouli
Wood Scent: All pines
Solarized-Water Glass Color: Milkglass
Crystallite: Milky quartz
Stone: White marble
Metal: Cerussite
Botanical: Bitterroot, black cohosh, blue vervain, hops, lady's-slipper root,
      lobelia, skullcap, valerian

Hyperactivity Generalities

Hyperactivity is usually a problem in childhood; however, it occurs in adults as well. The most damaging culprit in creating the condition is food additives, such as artificial coloring, flavors, and preservatives like nitrates and sugar. You won't escape the effects of hyperactivity by using sugar substitutes either, for they in themselves create different and more severe effects within the physical and mental systems. Eat wholesome, high-protein foods. Avoid red meats and pork and all fried foods. Replace them with broiled, steamed, and baked foods. Yogurt is excellent! Almonds (eight per day) are wonderful for this condition.

IMPETIGO

Gate: 6/Pituitary
Body Location: Between eyebrows
Gate Spinal Massage Point: 1st cervical
Planet: Moon
Element: Water
Ruling Totem: Owl
Detrimental Wind: Warm southerly
Aggravating Weather: Low pressure, low altitude, high humidity, warm/hot
      temperatures
Day of Week: Monday
Moon Phase: Full
Light Density: Dawn
Direction to Face: East
Treatment Duration: 10 minutes
Color: White
Color Breathing Direction: Down through head
Musical Note: Ti
Instrument Sound: Pan flute
Nature Sound: Wind
Illness Spinal Massage Point: 1st cervical
Essential Oil: Patchouli
Wood Scent: All pines

Solarized-Water Glass Color: Milkglass
Crystallite: Milky quartz
Stone: White marble
Metal: Cerussite
Botanical: Black mustard, dandelion, fireweed, goldenseal, juniper, nettle,
    peanut oil, pine, slippery-elm bark, vitamin E, willow

Impetigo Generalities

Daily washing with vitamin E and glycerine soap followed by a gentle massage of castor oil mixed with peanut oil has been most effective for this condition.

KIDNEY AILMENTS

Gate: 2/Adrenals
Body Location: Kidneys
Gate Spinal Massage Point: 9th dorsal
Planet: Mercury
Element: Fire
Ruling Totem: Horse
Detrimental Wind: Cold northerly
Aggravating Weather: Low pressure, low altitude, high humidity, cool/cold
    temperatures
Day of Week: Wednesday
Moon Phase: Waning
Light Density: Dusk
Direction to Face: North
Treatment Duration: 50 minutes
Color: Yellow
Color Breathing Direction: Up through soles
Musical Note: Mi
Instrument Sound: Cello
Nature Sound: Stream
Illness Spinal Massage Point: 10th dorsal
Essential Oil: Juniper
Wood Scent: Juniper
Solarized-Water Glass Color: Yellow
Crystallite: Citrine quartz
Stone: Obsidian
Metal: Pyrite
Botanical: Alder bark, almonds, black cohosh, chaparral, marshmallow
    root, mullein, red clover, uva-ursi

LEG CIRCULATION

Gate: 1/Gonads
Body Location: Pelvis
Gate Spinal Massage Point: 3rd lumbar
Planet: Mars
Element: Fire
Ruling Totem: Snake
Detrimental Wind: Warm westerly
Aggravating Weather: Low pressure, low altitude, high humidity, warm/hot temperatures
Day of Week: Tuesday
Moon Phase: Waning
Light Density: Night
Direction to Face: North
Treatment Duration: 60 minutes
Color: Red
Color Breathing Direction: Up through soles
Musical Note: Do
Instrument Sound: Piano
Nature Sound: Forest
Illness Spinal Massage Point: 5th lumbar
Essential Oil: Sandalwood
Wood Scent: Mesquite
Solarized-Water Glass Color: Red
Crystallite: Rose quartz
Stone: Rose stone
Metal: Cinnabar
Botanical: Amaranth, aspen bark, birch bark, capsicum, chicory, dandelion, fireweed, lobelia, purslane, wintergreen

Leg Circulation Generalities

Lifestyle often is the cause of this condition. Culprits include certain occupations that require standing for long periods of time, jobs that include a great deal of walking, or even worse, work that has the employee sitting all day. Moderate exercise is necessary to correct the condition. Stretches are most helpful. Often leg pain is caused from lack of proper circulation or constricted blood vessels. Massage painful areas with a salve made from boiled aspen bark, dandelion leaves, lobelia, wintergreen, and olive oil mixed with castor oil. Once you've massaged this into the leg, wrap your limb with a white flannel cloth and leave overnight. Drink dandelion tea with a pinch of capsicum added. Avoid sitting with legs crossed. Avoid knee-high stockings that constrict the blood vessels on the leg just beneath the knee.

LIVER AILMENTS

Gate: 2/Adrenals
Body Location: Kidneys
Gate Spinal Massage Point: 9th dorsal
Planet: Mercury
Element: Fire
Ruling Totem: Horse
Detrimental Wind: Warm westerly
Aggravating Weather: Low pressure, low altitude, high humidity, warm/hot
    temperatures
Day of Week: Wednesday
Moon Phase: Waning/new
Light Density: Dusk
Direction to Face: North
Treatment Duration: 50 minutes
Color: Yellow
Color Breathing Direction: Up through soles
Musical Note: Mi
Instrument Sound: Cello
Nature Sound: Stream
Illness Spinal Massage Point: 5th dorsal
Essential Oil: Juniper
Wood Scent: Juniper
Solarized-Water Glass Color: Yellow
Crystallite: Citrine quartz
Stone: Obsidian
Metal: Pyrite
Botanical: Alder bark, almonds, black cohosh, chaparral, marshmallow
    root, red clover, uva-ursi

MEASLES

Gate: 2/Adrenals
Body Location: Kidneys
Gate Spinal Massage Point: 9th dorsal
Planet: Mercury
Element: Fire
Ruling Totem: Horse
Detrimental Wind: Warm southerly
Aggravating Weather: Low pressure, low altitude, high humidity, warm/hot
    temperatures
Day of Week: Wednesday
Moon Phase: Waning
Light Density: Dusk
Direction to Face: North

Treatment Duration: 50 minutes
Color: Yellow
Color Breathing Direction: Up through soles
Musical Note: Mi
Instrument Sound: Cello
Nature Sound: Stream
Illness Spinal Massage Point: 11th dorsal
Essential Oil: Juniper
Wood Scent: Juniper
Solarized-Water Glass Color: Yellow
Crystallite: Citrine quartz
Stone: Obsidian
Metal: Pyrite
Botanical: Aloe, aspen, chamomile, cinquefoil, dandelion, elecampane, goldenseal root, oak, pine, plantain, wild lettuce

MEMORY

Gate: 6/Pituitary
Body Location: Between eyebrows
Gate Spinal Massage Point: 1st cervical
Planet: Moon
Element: Water
Ruling Totem: Owl
Detrimental Wind: Warm westerly
Aggravating Weather: Low pressure, low altitude, high humidity, warm/hot temperatures
Day of Week: Monday
Moon Phase: Full
Light Density: Dawn
Direction to Face: East
Treatment Duration: 10 minutes
Color: White
Color Breathing Direction: Down through head
Musical Note: Ti
Instrument Sound: Pan flute
Nature Sound: Wind
Illness Spinal Massage Point: 1st cervical
Essential Oil: Patchouli
Wood Scent: All pines
Solarized-Water Glass Color: Milkglass
Crystallite: Milky quartz
Stone: White marble
Metal: Cerussite
Botanical: Bee pollen, blessed thistle, blue vervain, capsicum, ginseng, gotu kola, lobelia, rosemary

Memory Generalities

Most memory problems, if not the result of severe trauma to the head, are karmic. Vitamins will stimulate this ability, as will certain amino acids. A tea formulated from bee pollen, blessed thistle, blue vervain, ginseng, gotu kola, lobelia, and rosemary with the addition of a pinch of capsicum will immediately stimulate the memory. This is especially helpful to students who must do intensive studying in preparation for exams. This same formula will aid a mentally disabled child, especially when given daily in conjunction with a proper diet.

NERVOUS TENSION

Gate: 6/Pituitary
Body Location: Between eyebrows
Gate Spinal Massage Point: 1st cervical
Planet: Moon
Element: Water
Ruling Totem: Owl
Detrimental Wind: Warm southerly
Aggravating Weather: Low pressure, low altitude, high humidity, warm/hot
    temperatures
Day of Week: Monday
Moon Phase: Waxing
Light Density: Dawn
Direction to Face: East
Treatment Duration: 10 minutes
Color: White
Color Breathing Direction: Down through head
Musical Note: Ti
Instrument Sound: Pan flute
Nature Sound: Wind
Illness Spinal Massage Point: 1st cervical
Essential Oil: Patchouli
Wood Scent: All pines
Solarized-Water Glass Color: Milkglass
Crystallite: Milky quartz
Stone: White marble
Metal: Cerussite
Botanical: Black cohosh, hops, lady's-slipper root, lobelia, skullcap,
    valerian

Nervous Tension Generalities

Most nervous tension is the result of mental and emotional causes. You must first address the emotions and mental disease before the symptomatic effects can be alleviated. Calm yourself. Analyze each situation before allowing it to affect you so adversely. Live your life for each new beautiful day. Don't worry about tomorrow or about situations over which you have no control. Acceptance is the *rule!* A tea made from black cohosh, hops, lady's-slipper root, lobelia, skullcap, and valerian will help. Chamomile with rosemary can also calm the nervous system. However, address the root of the problem!

OBESITY

Gate: 6/Pituitary
Body Location: Between eyebrows
Gate Spinal Massage Point: 1st cervical
Planet: Moon
Element: Water
Ruling Totem: Owl
Detrimental Wind: Cold northerly
Aggravating Weather: Low pressure, low altitude, low humidity, cool/cold temperatures
Day of Week: Monday
Moon Phase: Waning
Light Density: Dawn
Direction to Face: East
Treatment Duration: 10 minutes
Color: White
Color Breathing Direction: Down through head
Musical Note: Ti
Instrument Sound: Pan flute
Nature Sound: Wind
Illness Spinal Massage Point: 1st cervical
Essential Oil: Patchouli
Wood Scent: All pines
Solarized-Water Glass Color: Milkglass
Crystallite: Milky quartz
Stone: White marble
Metal: Cerussite
Botanical: Alfalfa, capsicum, chaparral, echinacea, fennel, ginseng, gotu kola, licorice root, Norwegian kelp, papaya, red clover, rhubarb

Obesity Generalities

Obesity can be caused by a glandular dysfunction, your genetic heritage, your karmic legacy, or your own poor eating habits. If your problem is a self-induced condition, you need to adjust your daily lifestyle. Your diet should exclude all red meats, pork, and organ meats. Absolutely no fried foods, sugars, sugar substitutes, or artificial food additives of any kind (because of their tendency to create a hyperactive condition). Drink at least eight glasses of water per day. Drink a small juice glass of grape juice before each meal. Never skip a meal, especially breakfast. Eat figs, almonds, grapefruit, grapes, yogurt, egg yolks, broiled seafood, baked chicken, and generous portions of crisp and fresh greens that include chopped, fresh, raw white onions. An herbal complex of red clover, echinacea, fennel, Norwegian kelp, garlic, ginseng, and gotu kola should be taken twice per day in the form of a hot tea. Don't make the weather an excuse for not getting out and walking and walking and walking and walking some more. Walking is the very best form of exercise there is.

PLEURISY

Gate: 3/Thymus
Body Location: Heart
Gate Spinal Massage Point: 2nd dorsal
Planet: Saturn
Element: Earth
Ruling Totem: Turtle
Detrimental Wind: Warm southerly
Aggravating Weather: Low pressure, low altitude, high humidity, warm/hot temperatures
Day of Week: Saturday
Moon Phase: Waning
Light Density: Afternoon
Direction to Face: South
Treatment Duration: 40 minutes
Color: Green
Color Breathing Direction: Horizontally in through navel
Musical Note: Fa
Instrument Sound: Drums
Nature Sound: Surf
Illness Spinal Massage Point: 3rd dorsal
Essential Oil: Eucalyptus
Wood Scent: Eucalyptus
Solarized-Water Glass Color: Green
Crystallite: Green tourmaline
Stone: Feldspar
Metal: Malachite
Botanical: Angelica, aspen bark, birch bark, black cohosh, chokecherry, eucalyptus, lobelia, mullein, pine, pleurisy root

POISON IVY/OAK

Gate: 2/Adrenals
Body Location: Kidneys

Gate Spinal Massage Point: 9th dorsal
Planet: Mercury
Element: Fire
Ruling Totem: Horse
Detrimental Wind: Warm southerly
Aggravating Weather: Low pressure, low altitude, high humidity, warm/hot temperatures
Day of Week: Wednesday
Moon Phase: Waning
Light Density: Dusk
Direction to Face: North
Treatment Duration: 50 minutes
Color: Yellow
Color Breathing Direction: Up through soles
Musical Note: Mi
Instrument Sound: Cello
Nature Sound: Stream
Illness Spinal Massage Point: 11th dorsal
Essential Oil: Juniper
Wood Scent: Juniper
Solarized-Water Glass Color: Yellow
Crystallite: Citrine quartz
Stone: Obsidian
Metal: Pyrite
Botanical: Blue vervain, mandrake root, plantain, sarsaparilla

Poison Ivy/Oak Generalities

Mother Nature fools us with plants that are seriously irritating to the skin (plants that cause what is called contact dermatitis). However, she wouldn't do that without also providing us with an "antidote" plant, one that counteracts the irritation. In the case of poison ivy/oak, that "antidote" plant is plantain. Wash the affected area thoroughly with a castile soap. Make a salve of plantain, castor oil, and blue vervain and apply it liberally over the area. Drink mullein tea to clear your internal system, and learn to recognize the dangerous botanicals *before* venturing out into the woods!

RHEUMATISM

Gate: 2/Adrenals
Body Location: Kidneys
Gate Spinal Massage Point: 9th dorsal
Planet: Mercury
Element: Fire
Ruling Totem: Horse

Detrimental Wind: Cold westerly
Aggravating Weather: Low pressure, low altitude, high humidity, cool/cold
     temperatures
Day of Week: Wednesday
Moon Phase: Waning/New
Light Density: Dusk
Direction to Face: North
Treatment Duration: 50 minutes
Color: Yellow
Color Breathing Direction: Up through soles
Musical Note: Mi
Instrument Sound: Cello
Nature Sound: Stream
Illness Spinal Massage Point: 12th dorsal
Essential Oil: Juniper
Wood Scent: Juniper
Solarized-Water Glass Color: Yellow
Crystallite: Citrine quartz
Stone: Obsidian
Metal: Pyrite
Botanical: Birch bark, black cohosh, dandelion, eucalyptus, licorice root,
     magnolia, nettle, peppermint, sunflower, wintergreen, yerba santa,
     yucca

Rheumatism Generalities

Rheumatism does not have to be as painful or debilitating as it is with
some sufferers. This condition can greatly be relieved by making a salve out
of steamed dandelion leaves, eucalyptus oil, magnolia leaves, peppermint
oil, and wintergreen oil. This formula gently massaged over the painful areas
will ease your discomfort and will allow you to enjoy a better lifestyle. Drink
mullein tea with peppermint leaves steeped in the cup. Get daily exercise in
the form of morning and evening walks. Be active.

SINUS PROBLEMS

Gate: 6/Pituitary
Body Location: Between eyebrows
Gate Spinal Massage Point: 1st cervical
Planet: Moon
Element: Water
Ruling Totem: Owl
Detrimental Wind: Warm westerly
Aggravating Weather: Low pressure, low altitude, high humidity, warm/hot
     temperatures
Day of Week: Monday

Moon Phase: Waning/New
Light Density: Dawn
Direction to Face: East
Treatment Duration: 10 minutes
Color: White
Color Breathing Direction: Down through head
Musical Note: Ti
Instrument Sound: Pan flute
Nature Sound: Wind
Illness Spinal Massage Point: 2nd cervical
Essential Oil: Patchouli
Wood Scent: All pines
Solarized-Water Glass Color: Milkglass
Crystallite: Milky quartz
Stone: White marble
Metal: Cerussite
Botanical: Aspen, camphor, cherry bark, eucalyptus, fennel, ginger,
    goldenseal root, mullein, nettle, Rocky Mountain raspberry

Sinus Generalities

This condition is most often the result of eating the wrong foods, including the ingestion of the heavy red meats and pork. The problem can also oftentimes have a karmic cause or be the result of a physical obstruction. In any case, eating right is the paramount recommendation here. Drink mullein tea with crushed fennel seeds steeped in the cup. Inhale eucalyptus steam. Make a salve out of castor oil, wintergreen oil, and steeped aspen bark. Massage this salve gently over chest, neck, bridge of nose, temples, forehead, and soles of feet. Rest quietly while the vapors are clearing the sinus cavities. Think positive thoughts! If you own a hand massage, use this over the forehead and upper cheeks beneath the eyes.

TEETH

Gate: 5/Pineal
Body Location: Base of brain
Gate Spinal Massage Point: 3rd cervical
Planet: Venus
Element: Air
Ruling Totem: Wolf
Detrimental Wind: Cold northerly
Aggravating Weather: Low pressure, low altitude, high humidity, cool/cold
    temperatures
Day of Week: Friday
Moon Phase: Waning/New
Light Density: Morning

Direction to Face: East
Treatment Duration: 20 minutes
Color: Purple
Color Breathing Direction: Down through head
Musical Note: La
Instrument Sound: Violin
Nature Sound: Rain
Illness Spinal Massage Point: 3rd cervical
Essential Oil: Lavender
Wood Scent: Piñon
Solarized-Water Glass Color: Purple
Crystallite: Amethyst
Stone: Open geode
Metal: Compact hematite
Botanical: Goldenseal, myrrh

Teeth Generalities

Please refer to "gum ailments" for this aspect of the mouth. Teeth can be kept whiter by swabbing them after the nightly brushing and flossing with myrrh tincture. This can be ordered from your local pharmacist. It's made by Lilly Pharmaceuticals.

The New Age dentist will have his office decorated in shades of purple and will play recordings of soft violin music alternating with gentle rain sounds. All his patient chairs will face east and an essence-of-piñon-wood incense will fill the air. All his major surgery will be scheduled around the new moon to avoid excessive bleeding. The time for major surgery will be Friday morning.

TONSILLITIS (post-op)

Gate: 4/Thyroid
Body Location: Throat
Gate Spinal Massage Point: 7th cervical
Planet: Jupiter
Element: Air
Ruling Totem: Buffalo
Detrimental Wind: Cold northerly
Aggravating Weather: Low pressure, low altitude, high humidity, cool/cold
    temperatures
Day of Week: Thursday
Moon Phase: Waning/new
Light Density: Noon
Direction to Face: West
Treatment Duration: 30 minutes
Color: Blue

Color Breathing Direction: Down through head
Musical Note: Sol
Instrument Sound: Flute
Nature Sound: Birdsong
Illness Spinal Massage Point: 6th cervical
Essential Oil: Cedar
Wood Scent: Cedar
Solarized-Water Glass Color: Blue
Crystallite: Blue quartz
Stone: Basalt
Metal: Azurite
Botanical: Alfalfa, chicory, horehound, mullein, nettle, oak, plantain, red
    clover, Rocky Mountain maple, starwort, yellow dock

Tonsillitis Generalities

Severe tonsillitis, when a fever is evident, should be evaluated by a qualified professional. However, severe sore throats can be relieved by drinking a tea made from the combined ingredients of feverbush, horehound, mullein, plantain, red clover, and starwort. A salve made from eucalyptus oil, castor oil, and steeped oak bark gently massaged over the upper neck will alleviate the swollen glands.

When sore throats are evident, examine the tonsils for infected sacs. Such sacs look like a cluster of white seeds. These can be removed with a cotton swab. By removing these clusters, you remove the infection and almost immediately the sore throat leaves. However, these clusters are a sign of positive infection, and if they persist in returning (becoming a chronic condition), a tonsillectomy is most often indicated.

SECTION
TWO

THE
M·I·N·D

The Seed of
Fruitful Knowledge

1

THE TOXIN

Contaminating Negative Attitudes

In the warm company of my wise visionary, I was constantly gaining fulfilling knowledge; in that wondrous knowledge, I was becoming an entirely alive person. I felt as though I was truly whole. I was stretching my God-given senses as far as I could, and the expanded awareness I gained was indeed breathtaking.

It was summer. And one late afternoon I decided to climb one of the thickly wooded hills surrounding our small log cabin. I crossed over its sun-drenched ridge and settled myself down to watch the tourists as they traveled through my vast backyard of mountains.

I was virtually invisible amid the dense woodland growth, and I remained for hours watching the unending line of cars, trucks, and motor homes that snaked their adventurous way along the narrow ridge road that eventually leads them into the famous gold-mining town of Cripple Creek.

I watched them move along the road across my fertile mountain valley. I watched them come and I watched them go. What a pity they don't realize where to find the real wealth of tourist attractions they seek. Why don't they stop along the way to smell the wild sage that grows so profusely by the rims of the narrow road? Don't they see the deep, lush valleys separating them and me? Don't they sense the majestic hand that fashioned all the glorious beauty around them? The road to Cripple Creek twists through some of the most magnificent mountain scenery in all of Colorado, yet so few seem to stop even to notice or to smell its wayside wildflowers.

At such times people's lack of awareness irritated me. I repositioned myself so that I could no longer view the longer bumper-to-bumper procession of vehicles. Instead, I reclined among a clump of columbine and gazed up through the green pine branches into my ocean of blue.

A brilliant stellar jay cawed loudly from a nearby treetop, and the stream below sent up a mesmerizing song of peacefulness.

I closed my eyes. I could lie there all day letting my tired body absorb the rejuvenating energies of the warm and kindly Sun Spirit while the sage-scented breeze placed gentle kisses upon my face. Nature was my healer. It was my loyal friend.

Suddenly, I found myself to be the center of some raucous attention. Incessant wild bantering between playful chipmunks strongly challenged the constant chattering of the mountain kaibab squirrels. They were vying for my attention again, for they knew I had brought my usual bag of sunflower seeds along. They chattered and clucked as they scampered about in the thick underbrush.

When I slowly stretched out my hand and uncurled my fingers, they skittered for cover behind the nearest sun-baked rocks and thorny bushes. I remained statue still and spoke to them in a low, soft tone. Soon they cautiously peered over and through their natural shields, ears quivering, tails flicking, nose whiskers twitching, and wee hearts wildly beating within tiny rib cages.

Eventually, one dared another, and soon my hand was being bravely picked at by little, rough tongues and needle-sharp paws. My meager offerings miraculously vanished within the blink of an owl's eye, disappearing into my tiny, furry friends' bulging cheeks. They returned again and again until I had no more to offer them.

After my little friends left, I got up, stretched, and walked over to a grouping of large rocks. I sat on a wind-worn boulder and silently allowed my entire being to expand with the enormity of space that tried to enter into my humble understanding. The valley below was littered with deep ravines that were now darkly shadowed by the harsh angle of the sun's retreating golden light. I had been on the mountainside for a long while, and I knew my surroundings would soon flare up with the flash of fiery alpenglow.

Then it began.

The late-afternoon sun released her mighty bowstring. I perceived the nuance of air rushing past me, the sound of the sun's flaming orange arrows whistling down from the western ridge. And as the rays struck their target, the great expansive valley ignited in a raging inferno of orange light. It blazed for a mere few seconds before fading to a soft pink glow of embers that quickly cooled to steel gray, then black. Absolute blackness enveloped me as the dark-hooded figure of Night regally spread his Cloak of Eternity and boldly exposed the dancing firmament.

I continued to sit alone and feel the immediate surge of Night's chilling breath upon my cheeks. I raised my head and absorbed the infinite sight of billions of twinkling beacons in the heavens. I reveled in their fireworks, the celebration of life, and I was thankful I had gained the awareness of life.

The following morning was to be one of my days of learning. I found my wisened teacher to be in an exceptionally good humor. I couldn't claim the same, and she was quick to spot my dark mood.

"Summer need to talk 'bout what upsetting head. No-Eyes see a dark enemy crouching there."

I plopped down onto her sagging couch. "Not really."

She scooted her old rocker up to me and settled herself. "What so!" she exclaimed. "Summer gonna let it fester into some sickness maybe?"

I merely shrugged as I stared at the worn braided rug. "There's no solution to my personal problems, so what's the use of talking about them?"

The Old One rocked as if she hadn't heard me. Then she spoke with compassion. "There always be solution to all problems, just got to look harder, deeper. Some solutions hide behind bushes, some in hollow of big tree, some even hide in own head."

I appreciated her attempt to help, but I remained certain I was backed against a wall this time. "No-Eyes, this is a problem that I have no control over. I just have no say in its solution."

Her eyes narrowed as she leaned forward and peered through them. "This problem upset Summer?"

"Yeah, it's very upsetting."

"Then if there be a cause, there be solution, too!"

I shook my head. "Look, why don't we just forget it and—"

"No!" She stamped her foot. "We *not* gonna ignore stuff here! We gonna get to bottom of this upsetting stuff that bother Summer."

I was definitely locked in. I sulked.

She calmed as the rocker's steady movement began. "Now, that be much better. Tell No-Eyes 'bout this problem that got no solution."

I had my head down but managed to raise my eyes just enough to peer up at her and get a quick fix on her mood. She was patiently waiting. It was no good, just as I had expected. She was determined to get through this no matter what.

I sighed deeply. "Well," I began slowly, "it's nothing to do with my own family, I mean within my own house. It's my friend's relatives."

"Go on," she prodded.

"They're not speaking to each other."

"Who not speakin' to each other?"

If that's the way she wanted it, that's the way she was going to get it. "Her mother and her sister Beth aren't talking to her other sister, Erica, because of something Erica did to upset them. They have practically disowned her. And her father has disowned my friend because when she first came to Colorado, she lived in an apartment building that had blacks and Hispanics living there, too. He said that she was trash and that she wouldn't ever amount to anything. My friend hasn't heard from her father in nine years."

No-Eyes thought before speaking. "What Summer's friend Erica do that be so bad? What she do that make mother not speak to her?"

"She fell in love with the wrong man; at least in the others' eyes he was wrong."

No-Eyes thought on that. "He be of different race then?"

"No."

"He be some bad guy, a criminal?"

"No."

"He treat Erica right?"

"Yes."

Silence.

Waiting.

"Her father not like other races, huh?"

"He despises them."

The old woman sent the rocker into a frantic commotion of creaks and thuds.

"I told you it couldn't be solved," I added before letting her comment.

She merely shook her head. "What be solved here is how friend gonna look at stuff. Friend no have control over others' awareness or lack of it, their ignorance. But friend can have control over self—how it affect self. See?"

"She's tried to make each side understand the others' and—"

Her tongue began clicking furiously. "Tsk-tsk, that be no good. That only bring friend into middle! It be bad medicine to be in middle of family problems."

"She found that out already," I said sadly. "I was going to say that it's very hard being aware. The living of spiritual attitudes is very difficult when you're dealing with narrow-minded ignorance."

She was thinking. "They go to church? These ones that shut out friend and her sister, they go to church?"

"Every week," I answered with disgust. I knew where her line of questioning was leading.

"They be big hypocrites! Summer, you no can do anything with these kind of peoples. All friend can do is lead good life, life of awareness. Friend have to let others alone, especially the spiritually unaware ones. Friend never gonna convince these others of right way of forgiveness, right way of acceptance of others' frailties."

"I know that. So what's her solution?"

"Acceptance, that all there be left. Accept family with their negative attitudes and bad emotions. They gonna get plenty sick with them. If they no make bodies sick, then Summer can be sure that their spirits be sick. They gonna die someday and then they gonna see how sick they make their spirits."

I felt ill with it all. "I realize that. That's what bothers me so—my friend couldn't make them see that. She feels very bad."

The Old One leaned forward and patted my knee. "Friend done what had to be done. It in *their* yard now. Beside, what friend's father think of all this stuff between her mother and sisters?"

I sighed heavily. "Who knows? He left her when she was only ten. He lives in the South somewhere and nobody's heard from him. That's the way he wants it, I guess."

"Friend heard from him though."

"Yeah, only because she wanted to forgive, patch things up and begin again. Fathers and daughters should have a bond of love that survives the pettiness of life's temporary troubles between them. But he didn't like where she was living at the time, remember? He said she was trash because she was living in that apartment where minorities lived, too."

"No-Eyes remember. But friend have to also remember that she did right thing anyway. No can help other's attitudes and unawareness, right?" Then she hesitated. "Summer been up on ridge watching tourists again, huh?"

I nodded.

"They be just like friend's family; they not be aware of nature's beauty, of the innocence to life. They got heads too full of wants, personal opinions, judgments, personal desires."

"I guess."

"So, friend must accept these bad feelings of others. It be too bad, but it be all part of life. Everybody be different. All peoples gonna pay someday for bad attitudes toward others. They not be thankful for families they got. Someday family members gonna die and then those others gonna be alone—so sorry for how they acted, what they said, how they shunned. But it gonna be too, too late then. It just gonna be too, too late for everybody then."

My head was down while I thought on her words about the sad situation.

The Old One called, "Summer?"

"Mmmm."

Her voice softened to a baby's breath. "What your friend's name be?"

Creak—thud.

Creak—thud.

My silence confirmed her suspicions. She closed her eyes and rocked.

No-Eyes and I talked long into that late afternoon about people's different attitudes and negative emotions. She spent a great deal of time detailing exactly how these adverse thoughts toward others were actually a deadly cancerous contaminant that negatively affected an individual's health by invading the body and eating away at one's mental well-being. She spoke of the emotions of envy and jealousy. She extolled the virtue of acceptance, and No-Eyes spent considerable time discussing family relationships.

The following material is taken from that sensitive discussion.

* * *

Within each respective religion are holy days during which the people contemplate their erring ways. They repent and seek God's forgiveness.

No-Eyes expressed shock that people reserve certain days for this activity. For the glorious way of Indian life was based upon daily thanksgiving for the Great Spirit's bounties and upon daily deep reflection, meditation, and vision quests that brought the Indian in touch with himself, his purpose upon the earth, and his union with the Great Spirit.

The world has become decayed with the stinking and rotting emotions of envy, blind ambition, jealousy, ridicule, judgments, and strife. Granted, social and economic conditions can prove to be extremely trying on the most honest and upright of men; however, the ill feelings of greed and selfish wants create harmful and destructive vibrational forces around and within you.

If you could only actually *see* the negative effects that your adverse emotions and thoughts have upon your immediate surroundings, you would promptly change—reverse—your ways. Be *aware* that every unspoken thought, whether it be for good or for ill, carries with it an effect upon your physical, mental, and spiritual being. If you truly comprehended this single law, you would *not* waste your days wanting and wishing for better times; you would *not* criticize the actions of others; you would *not* be envious or pompous. Instead, you would center your consciousness on the constructive positive thoughts of daily life and concentrate your individual efforts on attempting to accomplish the best you can according to your given talents.

Each daybreak, when you awake, offer your entire day to God. Talk to Him; He hears your every utterance. Tell Him that your day and all of its problems are in His hands and that you will not worry or fret because you know He will take care of things. This is not blaming God for your troubles. Every individual is personally responsible for his own life and decisions and, correspondingly, has the obligation to face those responsibilities. However, the burden can always be lessened.

Perhaps you're an atheist. That's fine. It's your prerogative to believe as you wish. My point is that negative emotions don't have to be retained within the self. An atheist can awake to a bright new day, appreciating each moment of life at a time. You are the sum total of your own thoughts and deeds.

Now, if you honestly examine your motives for your emotions of envy and hate, judgments and punishments, you will discover that they stem from your own feelings of repressed superiority. And if you are to rid yourself of these negative attitudes, you must first realize that all people are equal in the eyes of God. All people are on the same level; there simply are no superior people. Everyone makes mistakes, nobody's perfect. Know that you alone are in charge of your own life. You must answer for your outwardly displayed superiority, for your envious feelings, for hate-filled emotions, for judgments that are not yours to make.

It is so important to see others as that shining essence of God that dwells within everyone. Please, listen and comprehend this.

Many of mankind's problems and continual discords stem directly from people's superior attitudes, whether it be that they feel themselves superior racially, socially, morally, politically, or religiously. Some people have the tendency to view themselves as the epitome of excellence; they place themselves on the high throne of untouchability as they sit in absolute judgment on those who would be less perfect. They are as the Queen of Hearts from *Alice's Adventures in Wonderland,* randomly pointing their fingers and bellowing, "Off with her head!" Please understand that only God can do that. Are you so perfect that you put yourself with God to judge the erring ways of others? That you can pass judgment, punishment, and abandonment? Examine yourself! Examine the gross and irreverent imperfection you find there! If you must judge as a god, then please, balance yourself out with godly forgiveness also.

Forgiveness means total acceptance. Think upon this. *Total acceptance.* The proof of total acceptance is the erasure of all evidence of withheld grudges and ill feelings. Examine yourself! You are but a minute segment of mankind. Leave the supreme judgments and the almighty attributes to the lone Entity who deserves to possess them. Come and return amid your fellow men, who are just as imperfect as you are. Love one another. There's no time left for anything else.

Family relationships depend on the openness of the family's members; love, selfless unconditional love coupled with acceptance, is what bonds a family together. Our children are our most precious commodity. Their endless faith and boundless love are the hope and salvation of the future of our planet Earth. Their imaginative abilities can bring our world to new and enlightened heights that we have yet to envision. The time has come for adults to open their minds as little children and take delighted joy in the new discoveries they find there.

The time has come for innocent faith, for childlike blindness to the frailties of others, for no-strings-attached forgiveness, for trust, and for love finally to be unconditional.

The time has come for all people to unite in a warm brotherhood of love and acceptance—now, before the hourglass empties. Stop contaminating your systems with the toxins of negative emotions, prejudices, personal superiority, bigotry, and hatred. Accept your fellow men as the equals they are. See your negative attitudes and emotions for what they are. These emotions will contaminate your physical body, causing ulcers, heart irregularities, digestive dysfunctions, and chronic problems. These negative attitudes and emotions will cause mental aberrations such as paranoia, depression, schizophrenia, and eventual suicidal tendencies. These emotions will contaminate and poison the spiritual system, causing an inability to relate well to your fellow men and bringing about serious repercussions upon the spirit of self in the afterlife. The most damaging environmental contaminant is negative attitudes that destroy and eat away the natural loving relationships between men.

History has proven this fact and the time has come to learn from history so its cyclical repetitions will be broken once and for all. Know that our remaining time is short. Our days are now numbered. Let it be known that those who have read these words have been given the knowledge. The Forgivers in life shall stand tall, while the Arrogant in life shall cower. Now is the time to do the final editing of the Life Book you open before God.

THE ANTIDOTE
The Curative Therapy of
Dream Interpretation

One late-autumn day, when the aspens had given up their golden jewels, the teasing wind howled like a wild banshee as it whipped a glaze of snow against our schoolhouse windows. It would cleverly retreat, and then, with renewed confidence, forcefully advance for another whipping assault upon the old, time-worn cabin on the hill.

We remained undaunted by this fierce Warrior of Nature, for inside, we were filled with the physical warmth of our crackling fire, we were consumed with the loving glow of our shared friendship.

I lay on my back in front of the dancing fire that kicked its energetic heels and tossed its fiery tresses in reflective gaiety over the low ceiling rafters. I was content.

No-Eyes sat cross-legged next to me. She, too, was basking in the soothing rays of the warm fire. She, too, absorbed the soft serenity of our friendship.

The sharp contrast between the within and the without of this blustery day was beautiful. The fierce and powerful mood of Nature wailed and ranted about outside in the bitterness. It was one of the Earth Mother's more glorious spectacles to behold. Yet, the soft peacefulness of the cabin that joined with the gentleness of our special companionship was also truly beautiful. Our silence was almost a sacred thing. The snapping of the fire soothed and bathed us in a sound that is synonymous with pleasing soul comfort. We lovingly drifted upon the gentle, warm waves of our awareness of each other.

A whisper, soft as butterfly breath, rode upon the waves of warmth. "Summer gonna fall asleep," the Old One gently cautioned.

"No way," I crooned with a smile. "I'm enjoying this too much."

She was grinning with shared satisfaction. "This feel good to No-Eyes, too."

I snuggled down closer to the fire. "I could lie here all day and not say one word."

Silence.

I looked up to her. "Well . . . couldn't *you?*"

A wispy gray brow rose. "Summer no learn that way."

"Come on, No-Eyes," I urged hopefully, "let's just be lazy, just this once." I watched her expression. It remained unchanged.

Silence.

My eyes rounded in anticipation. "That must mean you're thinking about it," I hinted.

Silence.

I listened in on the well-oiled gears of her mind. She wasn't buying my idea.

"Humph! No-Eyes no buy today."

"Humph!" I teased back.

She grinned from ear to ear, exposing the healthy pink gums.

I rolled over to face the fire. I waited.

"Summer no worry. Summer gonna stay here today, just listen."

I perked up. "I don't have anything special to do? No hard journeys?"

"Nope. Summer just gonna listen. No-Eyes gonna do all talk stuff."

That sounded good to me. I settled down more with my chin on my hands. It was very restful within the cozy cabin.

"Summer no *sleep!*" came her soft bark.

I laughed. "Are you kidding? My ears are wide open."

A thin, bony finger came snaking toward me. "Summer make sure *eyes* stay that way."

"They will. I promise. Your talks are far from boring."

The Old One patted my shoulder. "No-Eyes gonna talk 'bout dream stuff now. Summer gonna get lot dream stuff here. Summer be aware."

"I am, No-Eyes, I am. Shoot."

The old Visionary spoke long into the early evening. She often excitedly animated her words with comical expressions and flung arms. Her day-long lecture held my undivided attention. She gave invaluable insights into the methods of properly interpreting dreams. She outlined the accurate meanings of the specific symbols, signs, colors, and activities of dreams. I often interrupted her in order to clarify a certain point. We discussed several important facets of her entire dream-interpretation system.

The Visionary stressed that man's negative attitudes and emotions were a cancerous contaminant for his body and mind, but that through correct dream interpretation, he could find renewed hope for solving problems. Dreams could show him the subconscious sources for damaging negative attitudes and thereby give him the tools to correct them. She also stressed that the *antidote* for the contaminant was to make corrections based on the direction given by dream interpretation.

No-Eyes' lecture on what she called dream stuff follows.

People need to realize that there is not a single night that passes without at least one complete dream coursing through their subconscious minds. You dream *every* night. "I never have dreams," some of you contend earnestly. Oh, yes, you *do!* You just don't recall them. How utterly unfortunate that is.

Dreams expose the dreamer to a thriving universe of new realities. Dreams reveal invaluable information by which we can, by the proper methods, solve our daily problems and receive guidance that leads to a more aware and contented life.

Your dreams are a clear expression of your daily life, and they offer plausible and simple solutions to the troubles assailing your waking hours.

Today's science now recognizes the therapeutic aspects of sleep and dreaming. Scientific researchers have conclusively verified the fact that dreams are an essential aspect of man's mental and physical health.

It is a fact that *everyone* dreams *every* night. Many dreams may not be remembered upon awakening, though. All dreams occur during the period of sleep called the rapid eye movement or the REM state, and they may continue for several hours.

Frequently, dreams are clear representations of the dreamer's actual life, but most are wholly symbolic and require analytical interpretation by someone who can accurately read the bewildering symbols for their respective true meanings.

When an individual begins to understand his personal actions, thoughts, and unique situations through dream scrutiny, he becomes more aware of his negative attitudes and is consequently forced to take a more critical look at himself. Once you can correctly decipher your dreams, you may have no more need for that monthly visit to the psychiatrist or counselor.

There are four main types of dreams:

Symbol	*Realm of Meaning*
Earth	Physical
Air	Mental
Fire	Emotional
Water	Spiritual

These designate the four facets of man's nature. For example, a dream that depicts a devastating wind, such as a tornado, relates directly to your own mental activities and cautions you to calm your destructive thoughts. (Only you can determine the highly specific meaning of such messages of caution.)

A dream of any type of water always refers to your spiritual self, your awareness or advancement. All other details of the dream would then relate directly to your spirituality and, therefore, provide you with clear-cut clues as to its precise meaning.

Dreams may be initiated from several sources within the mind. There are three levels of the subconscious. First, there is the immediate level, which functions just above the conscious mind. From this level come dreams that are affected by various outside stimuli. Dreams that originate from here are frequently frivolous and disjointed.

Second, there is a still higher plane of the subconscious that initiates the dreams relating directly to specific physiological functions of the dreamer. Pay close attention to these, as they are intended to warn of an immediate harmful physical condition.

Third, there is the highest level of the subconscious mind, which originates dreams relating to your mental condition.

Dreams may clearly be shown to you from the subconscious mind of another. You may, in sleep, mentally or emotionally "connect" with a close relative or friend, whereby you experience the sleep-state visions and thoughts of that person.

Dreams can also come from the superconscious level of your mind. From this deepest level comes the evidence of heightened awareness. The superconscious mind prepares precognitive visions and supplies you with the spiritual guidance you so desperately need to fulfill your purpose on earth.

Many times, you may awake from an especially peaceful and sound slumber with an expanded feeling of euphoric wholeness. This usually happens when, during your sleep state, your spirit went out and spent time with God.

Sleep enables your higher spirit to be released from its cumbersome physical confines, freeing it to accomplish its intended work while your body is at complete rest. The spirit may go out to aid others, it may enter into a place of higher learning, it may simply rest, or it may be called to claim witness to God's presence. If this is what has occurred during your sleep, you will awaken with a wonderfully fulfilled feeling. You will lie in bed for a while wondering why you feel so good about yourself and about life in general. Some of you will recall partial fragments of the spirit's experiences, but most often your conscious memory will forget unless you work diligently on opening up your meditative faculties. Such dreams are directly from God and remembrance of them is usually only rewarded to those who can recognize the Source upon awakening.

You may contend that you can recall your dreams only in fragmented bits and pieces, and that they are too jumbled for you to be able to make any reasonable sense out of. If your dreams are this illogical, you have either remembered only small segments of them, your conscious blocks have barred the major message, or the dream itself is trying to tell you that there is some aspect of your life that is abnormally "out-of-tune" or "illogical." Please attempt to stick with it and unravel the vital messages that come to you during sleep. If you can bring yourselves to face consciously the problems of life, you will also discover yourselves receiving invaluable and simple solutions to them.

Dreams that recur frequently are signs of the dreamer's stern nature. You, in your physical wakeful state, are not being openly receptive to ideas, and you are unyielding about making adjustments that interrupt your present lifestyle. Also, this may allude to your continually withheld emotions.

Dreams that frighten you and cause you to awaken in a cold sweat are cautioning you to pay more serious attention to your mental or physical condition. They are counseling you that your present situation is a "horror" and to make the recommended adjustments.

Dreams not only give warnings and depictions of the dreamer's wrong-doings, they also serve to reward and to commend your daily conscious achievements, your right thinking and living. Dreams that encourage often include brilliantly vivid designs, called meanders. If you are ever fortunate enough to experience an undulating design in exquisite Technicolor just before awakening, you are being acknowledged for your spiritual perseverance. A dream concluding with a meander is the highest form of acknowledgment from the otherside.

Now that you have a general background on the importance of dreams, let's discuss the precise symbology of them.

Please, dispose of any popular dream interpretation material you may have. If you are to benefit from the efforts of interpreting the symbolic fragments of your dreams, you must use the following listing. Although it is far from complete, it is correct and comprehensive enough to provide the dreamer with enough explicit interpretations. If you read and study the following listing, you will find that the hidden meanings of many symbols are quite logical, and you will find it is not so difficult to find yourself looking with clarity upon your nightly dreamscapes.

A DREAM SYMBOL DICTIONARY

A

Abbreviations denote the need for the dreamer to *cut short* certain aspects in the daily life. They may also refer to specific factors the dreamer will recognize by the individual letters of the abbreviation. Remember these.

Abyss signifies the dreamer's tendency toward following paths that will lead nowhere. This cautions the dreamer to take more of a broad overview of his or her life and where he or she is going.

Accelerators refer to the rate of action taken. Do you frequently procrastinate? This would be represented by a *slow-moving vehicle*. Do you completely ignore situations that require action? This would then be symbolized by a *stuck accelerator*. Perhaps you react too quickly to situations, which would be indicated by a *speeding vehicle*.

Accidents in dreams come as warnings. They are almost always a premonition and may refer to the dreamer or another individual known to the dreamer. This dream symbol is very important; respect it by taking great care.

Accusations signify wrongdoing directed at either the dreamer or someone connected with him/her. Carefully note what the accusations were and who they were directed to.

Aces, as in a deck of cards, designate a winning situation for the dreamer.

Aches within the dreamer's body while dreaming signify an unwell condition that is being evidenced within the aura field. Take special note of these, for they signify a real physical condition that needs to be corrected.

Acid denotes a burning condition. This dream fragment can refer to an individual, situation, or belief system that may end up "burning" the dreamer in some way. Acid may also indicate drugs.

Acne is a symbol that may have a dual meaning. It may be a sign that you need to take better care of your complexion. Or it may denote an infectious condition relating to how the dreamer presents him- or herself. Since the face contains most of the perceiving senses, this symbol might be a negative indication about how one sees, hears, or speaks. Only you, the dreamer, can accurately analyze this condition . . . if you are completely honest with yourself.

Acorns signify the beginnings or seeds of a stern and unyielding personality. A great mature oak can't bend in the wind and be resilient. Take this symbol as a warning to correct yourself. Be more open to ideas and be more giving in your nature.

Acronyms indicate the dreamer's strong need to give special attention to his current path and daily life. These vivid symbols can actually spell out those aspects of your life that need attention.

Activities and Positions of people in the dreamscape are extremely important to take note of and recall. They shed invaluable light on the dream's overall intent and serve to clarify other questionable symbols. (See specific activities such as BATHING, CAMPING, FALLING, etc. for further information.)

Adapters signify the dreamer's ability to adapt to changing conditions and/or situations in daily life.

Addicts represent an aspect in the dreamer's life that he/she is addicted to. This may not be a question of substance abuse, but could rather be indicating another individual, an activity, a place, or a way of interacting with others. Addictions can also refer to personality aberrations such as egotism, selfishness, aloofness, etc. Only you, the dreamer, can pinpoint what this dream symbol means . . . if you're honest with yourself.

Adding Machines represent the need for the dreamer to calculate properly the accuracy or inaccuracy of the various aspects of his or her daily life. Do they add up? Are they making any kind of logical sense? Do they make emotional sense?

Address Books exemplify the quality of friends. Check its color and condition. This aspect may also refer to the need to contact someone. If it means this, a specific name will appear within the dreamscape.

Adhesive Tape denotes the need for bringing a connectedness into the dreamer's life. This may refer to specific conditions or may indicate a general situation. Check closely for areas that require an adhesiveness.

Ad Libs signify the dreamer's penchant to make up excuses for his/her actions while never taking on the responsibility for any errors in judgment or reasoning. This dream fragment cautions the dreamer to own up to the truth of things instead of always making excuses.

Advertisers represent something the dreamer needs to look into. What is being advertised? This symbol may be a prompting for the dreamer to look into the matter or to temper his/her obsession with it. The dreamer will know which is intended here.

Afterburners denote the dreamer's need for additional physical or mental energy. This important dream symbol can also refer to the dreamer's habit of quitting just before the finish line or completion of a project or goal. Extra energy needs to be burned to spur the dreamer on to the finish line.

Air is the natural element that signifies the mental activities and conditions of man. Our thought waves are carried through the air just as effectively as those waves that are sent out by radio transmitters. The air carries our thought waves in diverse speeds and directions unless we have intentionally patterned them to do otherwise. In dreamscapes, the specific force of the air's energy will denote the individual's specific condition, the dreamer's mental health and well-being. (See specific air elements such as BREEZES, TORNADOES, WIND, etc. for further information.)

Airfields represent how the dreamer processes his/her thoughts. What specific condition is the dream airfield in? Is it overgrown with weeds? Remote? Busy? Desolate?

Airplanes represent the highest ideals, attitudes, and spiritual belief systems of the individual. In a premonition dream, they may also indicate a physical airplane. Be always watchful of any dream aspect that may be cautionary, and pay close heed to warnings concerning airplanes for the dreamer or for someone close to him or her.

Airport Terminals symbolize a spiritual search. What condition is the airport terminal in? Are you driving or walking *toward* it or *away* from it? Are you being directed to *another* terminal? This last would connote a different direction to follow with respect to your spiritual belief systems.

Airport terminals may also represent a real warning or premonition of impending disaster. Use extreme caution with this type of dream fragment and take preventive measures if the inner feeling from the dream is very strong.

Air Raids denote an actual raiding of your airwaves (thoughts). Are you letting someone talk you into things? Are you allowing someone else's belief system to take over your own? Are you still somewhat unwilling to accept their ideas? This is a serious dream symbol, for it literally means that someone is brainwashing you. Your Higher Self is sounding the alarm!

Air Traffic Controllers indicate a need to control your incoming spiritual data. Are you taking *every* spiritual concept as being God's truth? Please watch this, for there are many false prophets afoot. The assimilation of spiritual concepts needs to be steady and controlled. You should absorb one at a time. They need to be stacked up just as planes preparing for landing are, so that each can glide into the dreamer's consciousness and be safely stored with complete understanding before another concept is introduced. Fine logic and reason must be used before any single concept is accepted.

Alarms symbolize a severe warning. They may be referring to any one of the four aspects of our nature; physical, mental, emotional, or spiritual. Only the dreamer will be able to discern the appropriate application. Most often surrounding factors of the dreamscape assist in this clarification.

Albatrosses signify burdens. Usually the dreamer has created these him- or herself. This dream symbol cautions the dreamer to become less dependent upon those close to him. It may also be referring to another individual who is being an unnecessary burden to the dreamer. (This would, of course, not apply to a valid dependent, but rather to someone who could very well function on his or her own.)

Albums (photo) signify the importance of good family relationships and those of friends. It indicates a need not to forget such people. This dream symbol frequently is prompting you, the dreamer, to look back on your life to realize the value of people close to you. This symbol doesn't usually come unless you have lost sight of the worth of certain people close to you.

Alchemists represent a situation wherein you or someone else is trying to create something that cannot be or was never meant to be. This refers to such New Age concepts as "creating your own reality." We are all given certain aspects to work with, and to try to create something different just because that's what we want is not ethically or spiritually possible. The appearance of alchemists in our dreamscapes cautions us to gain personal acceptance instead of fighting fruitlessly to change things. This is a serious symbol and needs to be heeded.

Algae symbolize those aspects in our lives that are acting as spiritual foundations. A healthy pond cannot survive unless there are algae for the fish to feed upon. A barren pond supports no life.

Alley Cats signify a degenerate lifestyle. This dream symbol represents base aspects of an individual's life and indicates the need to rectify them. An extremely unspiritual lifestyle is indicated with this symbol.

Alligators represent those spiritual aspects of an individual's life that are self-serving. Water represents the spiritual aspect and the alligators live there; however, they strike out to prey on victims. This is an extremely serious warning for any dreamer.

Alligators may also refer to the actual representation and may symbolize a caution to be watchful of them, especially if the dreamer is in a position to be exposed to them (such as those in Florida).

Almanacs indicate the need to check your facts and to do more in-depth research. This dreamscape fragment would suggest that the dreamer tends to accept concepts or the word of others without being discriminatory.

Almonds represent the dreamer's urgent need to get his or her physical condition in check. Almonds are an active agent against certain forms of cancer.

Altimeters denote a need for the dreamer to be always watchful of his or her spiritual advancement and the speed of same. Altimeters record altitude, and, correspondingly, such a symbol within a dream would caution one either to proceed with caution or to slow down while taking one's spiritual journey. Too much information too fast will result in overload and confusion. Going too slow can result in stagnation.

Ambrosia denotes a false elixir the dreamer has taken. This important dream symbol suggests that the dreamer has found a quick fix to a problem or spiritual path. This comes as a warning.

Ambulances mean that immediate medical attention is required. This dream symbol indicates an individual's need to seek the professional advice of a qualified physician. Perhaps the person feels fine; then again, perhaps there is an underlying illness or dysfunction that is hidden from the dreamer's conscious view. Only a complete physical can accurately determine this. Ambulances also can refer to the need to see an MD instead of depending on faith healers or other healing methods the dreamer has been drawn to.

Amulets connote the dreamer's false belief system and tendency to be superstitious. It signifies that the dreamer is placing his or her faith in objects rather than in God.

Anchors symbolize the need for spiritual stability in the dreamer's life. This dream symbol represents a drifting spirituality, one that floats from one belief system to another. This tendency needs to be securely grounded, so that you can properly assimilate each specific concept on an individualized basis. You, the dreamer, are drifting from one spiritual concept to another, and you will never find the inner truths unless you drop anchor.

Anesthetists represent the dreamer's mental, emotional, or spiritual numbness. This is a serious dream symbol and strongly warns the dreamer to wake up and *feel*—to become sensitive to others.

Angelfish denote spiritual activities. Visually note the physical appearance and condition of these dream fish. Are they active? Or unmoving? Maybe sleeping? If an individual has healthy spiritual activities in his or her daily life, he or she will generate a dream with very active angelfish.

Angels symbolize the integration of man-made spiritual dogma with the Universal Truths of the Collective Wisdom. On a superficial level, angels denote a highly spiritually evolved entity in the dreamer's life.

Animal Breeders/Caretakers represent the dreamer's current sense of compassion and ability to use it. What physical condition is the animal caretaker in? Is he abusing his innocent charges? Is he caring for them with love and compassion? Compassion for others is a strong prerequisite for all those surviving the earth changes, for compassion and caring for others will be a natural and inherent trait for those who will carry on in the Age of Peace.

Animal Trainers denote how the dreamer manipulates friends. Is the trainer abusive? Or is the trainer gentle?

Announcers symbolize serious warnings. Recall what was being announced. This dream fragment is synonymous with the voice of the Higher Self or your personal Guide.

Answering Machines refer to the dreamer's tendency to not listen well and to avoid communication with others. Since good communication is so vital to quality relationships, this dream fragment comes as a warning to alter the dreamer's ways.

Antennas refer to the need for solid awareness and the complete reception of spiritual knowledge. This symbol may also denote a serious need for the dreamer to be more receptive to the ideas of those around him and to sharpen his or her own personal awareness level.

Anthropologists signify revelations of past life experiences, or the necessity for the dreamer to be regressed so he or she can resolve present conflicts or afflictions.

Antidotes symbolize those aspects in the dreamer's life that can well serve as solutions to current problems or problematic situations or relationships. This dreamscape segment is a direct answer to a troubling problem and evidences itself through your Higher Self.

Antique Dealers indicate those who would place a high value on their own talents or services. It may also represent the dreamer's tendency to value material possessions over spiritual aspects of life. This is a serious warning to alter the dreamer's ways.

Antique Shops represent antiquated thoughts or concepts. This may refer to the positive aspect of needing to look deeper into ancient ideas, or it may denote the negativity of antiquated and outdated ideals.

Antlers refer to the dreamer's emotional awareness of those around him or her. Are you being sensitive? Noncommittal? Heartless? Check or recall the condition of the antlers. Were they new and healthy? Ragged and hanging? Large? Small? Budding?

Ants indicate life's irritations. But ants can also denote an individual's good organizational skills and the ability to be a productive and contributing community member.

Aprons signify the covering up of an aspect of one's personality. This dream symbol shows that the dreamer doesn't like getting involved in another's situation or problem. He or she doesn't like getting dirty or marked in any way that would produce evidence of their personal involvement.

Aquariums symbolize the dreamer's spiritual arrogance. They indicate an individual who likes to show off spiritual talents and knowledge.

Archaeologists symbolize digging up the past in a negative sense, using it for unproductive purposes. They represent those who would expose the past transgressions of others.

Archers are messengers. This dream symbol refers to those individuals who would be carriers of spiritual wisdom; their purpose is to enlighten as many as possible.

Arches denote the roundness and curving nature of a spiritual individual. Arches indicate a need to pass gently through the openings in an individual's life. They serve as signposts marking the individual's spiritual passage.

Architects denote the planning of one's life course. This is most often a negative aspect, for our spirits have a life plan and we mess it up by trying to create our own realities. We have to be careful not to force on ourselves personal goals and outcomes that our spirits had no plans for.

Archives represent the purity and totality of the Universal Truths of the Collective Wisdom. Archives symbolize the spirit and letter of the pure wisdom set down by God. This may also refer to the Akashic Records, where all such knowledge is kept.

Armadas signify an aspect of the dreamer's life that enforces. This is a negative dream symbol because it suggests that the dreamer is being overbearing and manipulative in some way. Only the dreamer can discern the precise meaning of this . . . if he or she is honest enough.

Armageddon indicates that a final conflict is in the dreamer's near future. This dreamscape fragment may also refer to the actual prophesied final conflict between good and evil. The symbol may have come to help prepare the dreamer for his or her part in the final battle.

Armored Car/Truck denotes the dreamer's tendency to be emotionally untouchable. This dream symbol refers directly to the dreamer's self-created shell, the wall you have built around yourself. This is a dream of serious warning: Set aside the armor.

Arsenic symbolizes a poison the dreamer is either taking or is involved with. This symbol can refer to a situation, condition, other person, or belief system.

Art Gallery represents the objects of the dreamer's appreciation and admiration. Look carefully at the paintings. What are they representing? What condition are they in? Do they need restora-tion? Are the paintings portraits? Scenery? Impressionistic? Surrealistic? Fantasy? Depending upon the condition of the paintings and what they depict, the dreamer will be able to discern whether or not this particular fragment is negative or positive.

Artists symbolize the outward creativity of an individual that stems from that which is within the self.

Ashes denote the insignificance of the physical in comparison to the spiritual. It refers to the ending of all things and is a warning for the dreamer to realize it, so that he or she can readjust his or her priorities.

Ashtrays refer to the need for the dreamer to keep his or her perspective on situations and beliefs. Ashtrays remind the dreamer to realize that the past is gone, the bridges burned.

Aspirators symbolize the dreamer's need to clear out his or her congestion of information from the mind. This dream fragment directly refers to the dreamer's cluttered mind and the urgent need to suck out the unimportant concepts before he or she suffocates or chokes.

Assassins represent those individuals in the dreamer's life who may ultimately prove to be fatal. This may also refer to the specific path the dreamer is taking and the negative aspects that await him or her on it.

Assay Offices signify the dreamer's need to analyze his or her life. Ideally, an individual is searching for the golden friend, the golden spiritual belief system, the golden occupation and purpose. This specific dream symbol comes to caution the dreamer to analyze carefully his or her relationships and path.

Astrologers remind us that we are indeed made of sky stuff and that we have an ancient heritage that connects and bonds us to all living intelligences. Astrology symbology may also come in a dream to remind the dreamer that one is the way one is because of one's birth heritage under the heavens.

Astronauts denote our inherent ability to expand ourselves to far and finer dimensions. Astronauts are presented as a comfort to alleviate the dreamer's fear of stretching his or her consciousness and spirit's journeying abilities.

Astronomers signify the need to extend our awareness of ourselves in relation to other highly intelligent beings elsewhere. Astronomers urge us to come into a greater understanding of a Unified Brotherhood of Intelligent Life.

Atomizers exemplify a cover-up of some type. This refers to the perfuming or deodorizing of a bad or problematic situation, condition, or individual.

Atriums symbolize the openness of the dreamer's outwardly displayed attitudes and emotions. Check the condition of the dreamscape atrium. What was its color? Was it airy? Dark? Open to the light? Or enclosed with blinds?

Attics represent the conscious mind of the dreamer. They signify the dreamer's conscious thoughts during his or her waking hours. Is the attic dusty and filled with cobwebs? Is it orderly? Is it cluttered with memorabilia and old-fashioned articles? Is it dark and musty? Is it clean and bright?

Attorneys symbolize the forthright and zealous personality. This dream symbol emphasizes the need for complete honesty and justice in the dreamer's daily activities.

Auctioneers represent a sell-out personality. This is a caution for the dreamer to stop his underhanded activities. If the auctioneer is someone other than the dreamer, the dreamer is being warned that another is acting in a sell-out manner.

Augers denote that an intense, in-depth search is required. You need to dig down deeper for the truths behind a matter or belief.

Auras appear in dreamscapes to enlighten dreamers of their own or another's condition. What is the condition of the aura? Color? Rate of activity? Any aberrations?

Authority Figures usually represent the Higher Self. They are symbols of the highest ideals and attitudes to be followed. Attention must be given to the words, orders, or suggestions of any authority figure in the dreamscape.

Autobiographies signify the need for the dreamer to recall the overall experiences of his or her life. This dream segment comes when the dreamer has forgotten major events of great importance. Sometimes we forget the things we ourselves went through, and we need to recall these so we can better help others in similar situations.

Auto Mechanics designate professional medical people. Since the car/vehicle symbolizes our body, the auto mechanic is the one to repair and fix it. This dream symbol is important; the specific component of the vehicle that the mechanic is working on will clue the dreamer to which aspect of his or her own body is in need of medical attention. (See specific vehicle components such as BRAKES, HEADLIGHTS, WINDSHIELDS, etc. for further information.)

Autumn Season denotes a time for the dreamer to sit back and gather up his or her spiritual knowledge in preparation for resting with it and absorbing it for absolute comprehension.

Avatars are represented as those spiritual individuals in the current time frame who are sharing the highest form and purity of the Universal Truths. Avatars signify the True Teachers who've completed their Cycle of Return but have volunteered to reincarnate for the high purpose of enlightening the masses.

Aviaries symbolize the confinement of the dreamer's spiritual gifts or talents. This dream symbol seriously cautions the dreamer to set free these spiritual abilities, to use them for the betterment and enlightenment of others.

Axes signify trouble ahead on the dreamer's path. The dreamer is in a situation or relationship that will get the ax sooner or later. This dream symbol is a clear warning from the Higher Self to alter one's path and to be aware and watchful.

B

Babies denote immaturity or a feigned innocence. Babies may also refer to the dreamer's attitudes and emotions. It signifies a serious lack of maturity.

Baby Bonnets represent an immature or undeveloped thought process. It denotes a tendency to appear to think like a mature adult, while you are really thinking like a small child.

Baby Shoes represent an immature attitude toward your true path. They signify those who cannot accept the higher aspects of the spiritual truths. They are still in the baby stage of development.

   Baby shoes may also indicate the baby steps the dreamer is taking as he or she journeys along his or her life's path or spiritual development.

Baby-sitters connote compassion and nurturing. This may also have another interpretation: A baby-sitter may also represent an individual who has to deal with an immature individual in his or her daily relationships.

Backpacks symbolize those attitudes, ideals, and concepts that one must always carry along one's path. These would be one's own spiritual aspects and moral character.

Backspacing indicates the need for the dreamer to backtrack in life in order to gain a missed but necessary experience.

Badgers symbolize a nagging nature. They designate one who badgers others incessantly. Oftentimes this symbol indicates an individual who is dominating and in the continual habit of interfering in the lives of others.

Badges represent commendable deeds performed by the dreamer. This dream symbol serves as a commendation from the high spiritual forces and encourages the dreamer to continue along the right path.

Bags denote interference. If you, the dreamer, are interfering in another's affairs, you are being told to bag it and mind your own business.

Bakeries connote the ingestion of sugar and sweets. The surrounding circumstances of the dream will clarify the meaning of this for you in conjunction with the recalled condition of the sweets presented.

Bakers indicate growing spirituality. This dream symbol reflects the individual's manner of relating to his fellow men spiritually. It is not about his specific belief system, but rather how he treats others. A baker makes the bread of life for others.

Ballet Slippers indicate a path that is danced through. This is not a good omen, for it refers to one who does not have the seriousness a spiritual journey requires. The prancing, dancing, and flitting of ballet signifies an individual who is merely skimming the surface of the spiritual realm.

Bandages signify the dreamer's need to cover up a wound so it can heal. This translates into the suggestion to forget an emotional hurt so that the healing can begin.

Bandits represent a user type of personality. This may refer to one who uses spiritually, or one who is a status seeker who takes advantage of others to get higher on the social ladder.

Bandwagons are a negative symbol warning the dreamer to stop preaching to others. This doesn't necessarily refer to spiritual life, but can symbolize emotional, mental, and physical life instead. Are you always telling others how to do something? What to say? How to act?

Banks represent riches. These riches may be monetary or spiritual. Gold nuggets/bars/bullion imply physical or financial wealth. Silver coins/bars suggest spiritual wealth. Are you depositing or making a withdrawal? Is the bank empty? Is a robbery in progress? Are you the teller or banker? What are you doing? I hope you're not fixing the books!

Bank Transactions indicate how well the dreamer manages riches.

Banshees are a death harbinger. This may not mean a physical death, but may reflect a spiritual one or even a mental breakdown. This dream symbol is definitely a warning to be taken seriously.

Baptisms represent a spiritual awakening or development. They indicate a spiritual rebirth for the dreamer.

Barbarians symbolize the dreamer's tendency to be of a barbaric nature. This symbol refers to rudeness, insensitivity, lack of compassion, and general crudeness of character.

Barbecues signify anger or a burning situation that sizzles and cooks within the individual.

Barbershops indicate the need for the dreamer to adjust his or her thoughts. Are you *getting a haircut?* Then you need to cut out some superfluous or damaging thoughts or beliefs. A restyling would indicate that the dreamer requires a re-

arrangement of thought. A dye job signifies a change in thinking is required. What are the old and new colors?

Barefoot represents an individual who walks his path with full knowledge of what each important step means.

Bareheaded indicates an individual who openly shows how and what they think. This dream symbol represents an honest individual.

Bar Mitzvahs or Bat Mitzvahs signify the point in the dreamer's path where he or she has reached the stage of responsibility. This means that he or she is now in charge of his or her own development and should take the initiative to comprehend all spiritual concepts studied before reaching for more complex ones.

Barnacles connote all the extraneous aspects that weigh down our life and, in turn, slow development or progress.

Barns denote the corrupt and ignoble qualities of man's nature. Rarely can anyone but the dreamer him- or herself accurately analyze this dream fragment. The baser aspects of an individual are naturally very well concealed. Occasionally another person will be provided with enough background information to interpret this symbol for the dreamer. Barns represent an individual's most private thoughts and actions. These are usually obscene, heinous, or extremely negative aspects kept hidden from public view.

Barricades symbolize those self-imposed blocks that an individual sets up in the middle of the life path. These can be taken down at will, for they are mobile. Once the dreamer sees them for what they are, it's easier to move them aside so progress can continue.

Barrier Reefs denote the natural spiritual barriers that present themselves to everyone during their development. Some of these are generated by the individual's own spirit, some are presented by a personal Guide, and some are simply in place until the individual advances enough in comprehension and spiritual maturity to be able to handle further advancement properly. Barrier reefs are never self-imposed by the conscious or subconscious mind, but rather are set in place by higher forces to safeguard against spiritual overload or misuse.

Bartenders indicate the serving of negatives. This would refer to any individual who tends to pull those around him into negativity.

Basements denote the subconscious mind. Examine your dreamscape basement for activities and conditions. Also note the amount of light in the basement. Surrounding dream fragments will help to clarify what this symbol means to you regarding your own subconscious mind.

Baskets denote the need to give special attention to something. What is in the basket? What color is it? What is its condition? Baskets are for gathering material. What is it you need to gather in and save?

Bathhouses represent the serious need to cleanse a specific aspect of yourself. This dream symbol may refer to your emotional, mental, physical, or spiritual self. Check the condition and correct it.

Bathing means that a cleansing is needed by the individual represented in the dream.

Bathing Suits indicate that more spirituality is required. Get into the water!

Bath Mats represent spiritual protection. Check the condition and color of the mat. This will clarify the nature of the protection.

Bathrooms represent the need for cleansing. Again, check the other aspects of the dream to determine whether the intended message is for the physical, mental, or spiritual self.

Bats (animals) designate the dreamer's tendency to use his spiritual gifts of intuition in all situations. Although a bat is nearly blind, it uses its finely tuned faculties for guidance. Depending upon the dream's surroundings, bats may also suggest that the dreamer needs to make better use of his or her inner feelings—give them more credence.

Bats (sport) indicate how an individual is progressing. Are you batting zero? Batting your head against a wall? Are you batting one hundred?

Batteries connote a need for the dreamer to retain energy instead of expending it all uselessly. This is an important caution that comes from the Higher Self.

Battle-axes symbolize an angry and stern personality. The word in itself says this. Don't be a battle-ax in your relationships!

Bazaars represent the varied sources of learning that are available to the dreamer. Bazaars are a suggestion that the dreamer look around and be aware of the many opportunities for learning.

Beacons indicate sources of enlightenment that will enhance the dreamer's spiritual development. These dream symbols should always be given a high priority, for they literally light the way for the individual's spiritual path.

Bears signify an overbearing personality. This dream angle counsels the dreamer to examine his own personal method of dealing with others in relationships. Are you egotistical? Demanding? Also, bears may indicate that someone else in your life is oppressing you.

Beauticians/Barbers represent those individuals who would alter thoughts. But be careful in interpreting this symbol, for it can mean an individual who attempts to bring truth or one who alters it.

Beavers allude to the dreamer's attitude toward efficiency. Is the dreamscape beaver being industrious? Napping?

Bedbugs symbolize a negative factor connected with an individual's sleeping arrangements or patterns. Bedbugs signify a bugging condition in regard to the dreamer's bed.

Beds indicate more rest is recommended for the dreamer.

Bedspreads denote the type of rest the dreamer is receiving. What material was the dreamscape bedspread? What was its condition? Color? All these factors come together to create the message.

Beekeepers signify a draining personality. This implies an individual who takes and takes but never gives back.

Bees represent an individual's manner or organization. Bees are industrious and cooperative, giving workers. They exemplify the perfect harmony that is vital to any effort of effective and unselfish teamwork.

Beetles indicate harmful interferences in an individual's life, path, or belief systems. Watch for this, as this comes as a grave warning.

Belching denotes the need to bring up negative attitudes and get them out of the system.

Bellows symbolize the dreamer's need for more air. This dreamscape segment suggests that the dreamer is suffocating in some aspect of his or her life. You need to stop to take a breath!

Bells signify a call to spiritual duty and purpose.

Belt Buckles represent an individual's excuse for his self-created restraints. What does the buckle look like? Does it depict something in particular? A belt buckle clarifies why the restraining is done.

Belts symbolize restraints that are self-created.

Benches refer to the need for the individual to take occasional pauses along his or her path. The dreamer is being benched for a while.

Bibles symbolize truths that are reworked according to various slanted viewpoints. This is important because it cautions the dreamer to straighten out his spiritual perspectives and to be discriminating in what he or she accepts as truth.

Bicycles denote a mental, physical, or spiritual balance.

Billboards are always warnings or reminders for the dreamer. Pay special attention to what is displayed on the billboard, especially the words or numbers. What color was it?

Bills represent karma that comes due in an individual's life. They must be paid in order for advancement to take place.

Binders (notebook) refer to the need to collect and retain recently attained knowledge or information.

Binoculars represent the need for more detailed knowledge. This dream symbol suggests that the dreamer had better open up his eyes and take a closer look at something. Surrounding aspects will clarify what this something is.

Biofeedback Machines symbolize a severe warning to listen to yourself! This usually refers to the Higher Self or one's spiritual Guide.

Biographies denote the need for the dreamer to stop viewing others on a surface level, but rather to look deeper into the individual for a better understanding.

Bird Feeders indicate an individual's unique understanding of nature. Is the feeder full? Empty? Broken? Fallen?

Birdhouses symbolize an individual's noble and high ideals. Check the condition and color of the dreamscape birdhouse. Are there any occupants? Is it empty? Are there eggs or fledglings?

Birds (See specific bird types such as BLUEBIRDS, SWANS, VULTURES, etc.)

Birth Certificates signify an individual's spiritual heritage—not their ethnic one. This dream fragment will frequently inform the dreamer of his or her last-life experience, especially if the carryover soul tendencies are strong and indicate a need to draw on that information to perform current life tasks or complete the spirit's purpose.

Birthing signifies the bestowing of new life upon someone through the dreamer's awareness and knowledge or spiritual enlightenment.

Black Clothing is a forewarning of death. This may refer to the mental, physical, emotional, or spiritual changes.

Blackjacks exemplify an arm-twisting toughness of character either for the dreamer or the individual appearing in the dream.

Black Magic denotes the use of negatives or the dark side to attain one's individual goals. This dream fragment is a serious warning, for clearly either the dreamer or someone he or she knows is dabbling in danger.

Black Market signifies ill-achieved goals. It represents an underhanded manner of dealing with problems or fulfilling desires.

Black Sheep represent individuals who dare to be different. This dream symbol indicates one who follows his or her own path regardless of others.

Blacksmiths symbolize rejuvenations or reformations either being done or being required.

Blankets represent warmth of character. Check carefully for any telltale aspects such as color, design, or the condition of the fabric.

Bleach indicates the dreamer's tendency to whitewash many aspects of life.

Bleachers denote the dreamer's desire to sit back and watch others do the work. This may also represent a tendency to be fearful of making individual moves or using personal initiative before seeing others go first. This is a serious cautionary warning.

Bleeding represents a forthcoming sorrow. This, of course, may also indicate a physiological dysfunction that requires medical attention.

Blinders indicate self-imposed ignorance. Take these off!

Blindfolds refer to those aspects in the dreamer's life that keep one from seeing the light on a subject. These most often indicate another individual who keeps these on the dreamer's eyes.

Blindness denotes strengths. Although blind people cannot see, they are strong and maintain a near-normal lifestyle. This dream fragment refers to the adversities that may hamper one's path, but can be overcome with the individual's inner strength and perseverance.

Blindness may also indicate that the individual is blind to the facts or truths.

Blockades refer to those blocks in an individual's life that are put up by *others*. These must be seen for what they are. They can then be overcome.

Blood signifies the life force of an individual or situation. This may refer to the physical, mental, emotional, or spiritual nature of the dreamer.

Bloodhounds represent the ability to search out and pinpoint the causal factor(s) of any problem or negative condition.

Blotters indicate that a cleanup is needed. What has the dreamer allowed to overspill? Hurting or damaging words? Actions? Oftentimes this dream fragment will be suggesting that the dreamer needs to make apologies.

Blowing a Whistle designates an informer. This may be negative, but it might also refer to someone higher up cautioning you to stop something. Examine yourself, for the whistle-blower may very well be your own Higher Self!

Blowpipes symbolize a poisonous individual, belief system, or situation. This is a direct and clear warning for the dreamer to be cautious.

Blowtorches exemplify the dreamer's need to cut or burn through a block that is hampering advancement or development. This block may be physical, mental, emotional, or spiritual.

Bluebirds symbolize joyfulness, happy and stable relationships, and contented acceptance of life's conditions and situations.

Blueprints refer to plans the individual has for his or her life path, both physical and spiritual. It's important to remember that, although we can make our own desired plans, God and our spirits have their own ideas for us—and their plans take priority over ours.

Blue Ribbons indicate high praise from the highest source.

Boarders/Renters represent opportunities to balance karma. This dream symbol refers to those needy people who cross our paths who can be helped by our generosity or personal attention.

Boars represent a boarish character. Stop being so egotistical and haughty.

Boat Captains denote spiritual egotism. We are all captains of our own spiritual ships and cannot let others take our place.

Boats represent spiritual paths and their quality. Take heed of the boat's condition. What is the temperament of the waters? What color is the water? The sky? The boat?

Bobsleds signify a path that is not properly traveled upon, for the individual is attempting to speedily slide over it. The individual is taking the easiest route.

Bogs indicate a serious negative condition for the dreamer. Bogs represent those aspects that bog down the individual and hamper clear advancement along the life path. Notice how the bog is connected to other surrounding aspects of the dreamscape and you'll have a clearer view of exactly what it is that's bogging you down.

Boilers represent explosive conditions in the dreamer's life. These refer to those situations that will shortly boil over and create much upheaval in the dreamer's life. Take steps now to ease the situation.

Bolts indicate a need to make secure connections. This refers to a solid understanding in terms of the dreamer's relationships.

Bombs symbolize an explosive situation or condition that will prove to be detrimental to the dreamer. Are you bombing out on something? Is another individual holding the bomb or in control of it? What color is it?

Bones denote the foundation of one's attitudes and beliefs. This dreamscape segment directly refers to getting down to the bare bones of an issue.

Bookends symbolize a need for the dreamer to end his or her study on a particular subject. The dreamer will be clear on this aspect. This specific dreamscape symbol comes when the dreamer is not comprehending what he or she is reading.

Bookkeepers symbolize the Spirit Record. This dream image represents how the dreamer's Life Book is kept. Is the dreamer attempting to alter it? Keep two sets? This aspect is a warning, a reminder that all thoughts, words, and deeds are being recorded.

Bookmarks symbolize a need for the dreamer to take a much-needed pause in his or her current study or research in order to assimilate and fully comprehend the subject matter before going on. The bookmark suggests a return to the subject, but only after careful introspection.

Bookmobiles indicate the studying should be done in respect to the physical system. Does the dreamer need to study healing methods and ways? Look into a bothersome physical condition? Research a specific disease?

Books indicate a need for knowledge and more in-depth study in order for the dreamer to comprehend fully an issue or concept.

Bookstores suggest the acquisition of new knowledge. Are you purchasing books? What type? Are you walking out empty-handed? What section of the store are you browsing through? What is the condition of the bookstore? What kind of bookstore is it? Metaphysical? Adult? Children's?

Bookworms suggest that the dreamer get his face out from between the book pages and start applying his knowledge in life.

Boomerangs signify reversals or situations that will rebound with severe ramifications. Tread carefully here.

Boots refer to the outward aspects of one's walk along his or her path.

Cowboy Boots denote an individual direction and a wearer who is maintaining freedom to do the searching required.

Firemen's Boots indicate a determined seeker who strides forward, confident of his or her protection from any lurking dangers.

Hiking Boots connote one who takes his spiritual path at a metered pace in order to assimilate properly all varying aspects encountered along the way.

Jackboots represent a tramping through the path at a headlong pace irrespective of the values trodden upon.

Oversize Boots symbolize one who would shuffle along the path without making cautious steps. This individual is not fitting him- or herself to that which needs experiencing.

Rain Boots represent a pathwalker who does not allow any conditions of ill climate to interfere with his or her advancement.

Riding Boots symbolize one who desires to be carried along his or her life or spiritual path.

Rubber Boots refer to an individual who wants to insulate him- or herself eternally from any negatives along the path. This just cannot be so if one wishes to gain spiritual strength and endurance.

Ski Boots indicate an individual who desires to slide over his or her path to its end. This refers to one who is ignorant of life's realities.

Snow Boots connote one who walks his or her path confident that he or she will never be spiritually snowed by anyone.

Steel-Toed Boots denote one who is prepared for the unexpected along his or her pathways.

Undersized Boots symbolize a pathwalker who is forcing him- or herself along paths he or she is not prepared to approach yet.

Botanicals are living aspects of nature. All forms of growing things represent the dreamer's present state of spirituality. Healthy botanicals denote a healthy and true spiritual state, while diseased botanicals relate to an error or personal omission of that state. (See specific botanicals such as FLOWERS, FORESTS, GRASS, etc. for further information.)

Bottles represent something that is bottled up within the dreamer. Release this before damage occurs. The dreamer will know what this important dream symbol refers to, for only the dreamer can bottle something up inside him- or herself.

Boulders connote life's major problems. It is difficult to continue on your path without first removing the blocking boulder or obstacle. This dream image does not indicate the need to move around the boulder, but rather to deal squarely with it. This action will eliminate the physical problem and again clear your way. Never skirt an issue!

Bowls represent the need to contain or retain an aspect in the dreamer's life.

Boxcars symbolize those extraneous aspects one carries along one's path.

Boxers represent an argumentative personality. They refer to an individual who would make an outward display of confrontation or aggressive questioning throughout life. This clearly indicates a contrary personality.

Boxes indicate confinement. This refers to those aspects in the dreamer's life or along the spiritual path that the dreamer allows to box him or her in.

Bracelets represent subjugation.

Braces signify support systems. Look to see where the braces are. On the legs? Then the manner of one's path-walk needs supporting. On the teeth? Then the individual's speech needs more support; you need to back up the claims you make.

Brakes denote an immediate need to stop something the dreamer is doing. They can refer to an occupation, a spiritual path, a belief system, or interactions with others. Only the dreamer will automatically know which aspect this symbol applies to.

Breast Feeding indicates the bestowing of spiritual guidance and nurturing.

Breezes designate low mental activity. This dream fragment alludes to the fact that the dreamer has not been using his or her intelligence to its optimum capacity. However, depending on other aspects of the dream, a gentle breeze may be indicating the dreamer's need to slow down his mental activities. Perhaps a mental breakdown is in the offing and a rest is in order so that the foreseen event can be circumvented.

Brews indicate formulations. They can refer to the physical aspect of how one blends spirituality within one's daily life, or they can refer to the formulation of one's spiritual belief systems. Check ingredients if they're represented. Is the brew hot or cold? Is it a type of tea? Or an intoxicating mixture?

Bricklayers/Stone Masons are symbols of life's building blocks. This image stresses the importance of laying a solid foundation in all aspects of the dreamer's life.

Brides signify a new path in life. What color is her dress? Where was the ceremony held? Inside? Outside? What was the weather, rainy or sunny?

Briefcases are a reminder to be thoroughly briefed before presenting truths, concepts, or ideas to others.

Brooms suggest the dreamer needs to make a closer inspection of surface conditions or appearances. Clearly something needs sweeping away in order to obtain a better view.

Brushes denote the action of brushing things aside before proper attention has been given to them.

Bubbles indicate poisons to the life force, either physical, mental, or spiritual. Bubbles in the bloodstream are dangerous, just as negative conditions in life and along one's path present danger.

Buccaneers symbolize those individuals who would attempt to harm the dreamer's spiritual belief systems.

Buckets symbolize highly important aspects of spiritual truths that must be retained and used. Buckets most often are for the retaining of water (a spirit aspect); therefore this dream symbol is most important for the dreamer. It comes as a caution to save and comprehend spiritual truths.

Buffalos symbolize the dreamer's level of gullibility. Are you being charged by a herd of buffaloes? Then you are being buffaloed by someone. Are you the buffalo? Then this fragment of the dream is suggesting that you refrain from embellishing yourself or your situations.
The buffalo can also indicate the powerful driving forces of determination and perseverance. In this sense, it can have a positive aspect.

Bugles denote a call to be more aware in life. They represent a loud and clear call to action.

Buildings are usually the most prominent feature of a dreamscape. They are, therefore, highly significant and require careful consideration by the dreamer. Specific types of buildings possess unique implications. Every dream structure is presented for a specific reason. This purpose is to counsel the dreamer in regard to the condition of any of the four facets of human nature. (See specific building types such as FORTS, SHOPPING CENTERS, SILOS, etc. for further information.)

Building Something denotes the act of adding aspects to the dreamer's life. What is being constructed here?

Bullets signify the negative aspects of yourself that are hurting others.

Bulls denote narrow-mindedness, a bullish personality.

Bull's-eyes represent a right-on position, or a direct hit regarding one's current spiritual search.

Bumpers signify an individual's psychological tenacity and the strength of his or her defenses—how they bounce back. If the bumper is dented, this indicates an emotional hurt that is not permanent. If the bumper is like new, it means that the dreamer's defenses are completely and effectively insulating. If the bumper is missing altogether, this indicates emotional vulnerability.

Bunkhouses denote the nature of casual relationships. This dream fragment will emphasize how well the dreamer interacts with those he or she spends leisure time with.

Bunsen Burners indicate the dreamer needs to do some intense self-analysis. After the analysis is done, a change in perspective may result.

Buoys exemplify markers that serve as directional signs along the dreamer's spiritual path. Be mindful of these markers; they will stand out in your waking state.

Burglars indicate a stealthful personality.

Burying Something exemplifies the hiding of secrets or the covering up of a wrongdoing.

Bus/Cab Drivers represent a helpful personality.

Buses symbolize obesity. This need not refer to a present condition. This dream symbol may be cautioning you, the dreamer, to watch your diet to avoid loading yourself into a pre-obese condition.

Bus Stations represent a need for weight reduction. These may also indicate a need for the dreamer to travel. Are you purchasing a ticket? Do you have luggage? Check for the surrounding details of the dream to clarify the meaning of this symbol.

Butchers refer to a scathing personality.

Butter Churns indicate a richer and deeper understanding will be forthcoming for the dreamer.

Butterflies designate the dreamer's unique ability to rebound after setbacks. Butterflies symbolize rejuvenation and renewal.

Buttons indicate that a connection is needed by the dreamer. This usually refers to a physical linkup. Also, it may be the reverse—a need to unfasten or disconnect yourself from something or someone.

Buzzers exemplify the dreamer's need to make a quiet or discreet communication.

C

Cadavers symbolize learning opportunities in the dreamer's life. This may seem a bit odd, but remember that medical schools use cadavers—the products of physical death—as learning tools. Death is evidence both of the past and of change in the future. Thus, in your dream, cadavers indicate further learning.

Caddies represent indecision. This dream symbol denotes an individual who closely follows an idol figure and,

in so doing, is one who cannot make up his or her own mind.

Caged Birds indicate that the dreamer's emotions are continually suppressed. Are you not verbalizing your true feelings? Are you allowing them to fester and be caged within yourself? Please, set them free!

Cages denote a caged individual, mental attitude, or belief.

Calculators represent complex planning. This may have both positive and negative connotations. Are you a calculating individual? Conniving? Or do you need to apply more thought to your plans?

Calendars signify the passing of dates. Calendars frequently reveal a premonition in the form of an important date for the dreamer. Always note these.

Calipers exemplify the dreamer's need to be exact. This dream symbol suggests that the dreamer is in the habit of estimating things or too often assumes in error.

Cameramen connote the knowledge gained from life experiences and the ability to draw from them.

Cameras are a caution for the dreamer to remember something that is being explained through the dream symbols. In essence, a camera says: "Take a picture of this so you won't forget!"

Camera Shops symbolize the dreamer's need to analyze concepts or adjust perspectives for a clearer view.

Campers represent a free spirit.

Camping signifies a comforting respite from responsibilities or a situation. This may also refer to the pauses one takes along one's path. Many of these are needed for proper assimilation of truths and spiritual concepts.

Candles indicate a manner of spiritual sharing. Is the candle flame sputtering? Is it flickering? Is the flame strong? Is the candle burning at both ends? Is it quiet and soft and steady?

Candlesticks denote the individual's mode and quality of spiritual receptivity. What is the candlestick's condition? Style? Is it silver or gold? Wooden? Antique or modern?

Candy Shops represent the dreamer's material desires.

Canes symbolize God's truths—His staff.

Cannons speak of the dreamer's explosive personality. The need for calm is cautioned here.

Canoes symbolize a slow, steady, and tranquil spiritual search.

Can Openers represent the tools an individual uses to open up preserved ideas and concepts.

Canteens connote the spiritual reserves you need to carry with you for reinforcement along your path.

Capes indicate temporary protective measures taken by the dreamer.

Capstones indicate the finalization of an individual's current path or purpose.

Carbon Copies indicate a loss of individuality and the ability to think for oneself. This is a serious dream fragment that warns the dreamer to start taking the initiative.

Car Dealerships indicate that the dreamer needs to tend to the physical aspects of life—usually the body. What condition are the cars on the lot in? What color of vehicle was the dreamer looking at?

Cards (playing) symbolize the manner in which an individual plays his hand in life. Are you playing with a full deck? Are you holding any back? Are the cards all one color? Are they jokers? Aces? Full houses?

Card Shops indicate that communication is needed. What kind of card is the dreamer looking at? Get-well? Sympathy? For a relative? Friend? This dream fragment can be extremely revealing and frequently ends up being a premonition. If the dreamer is looking at a get-well card for a sister, that indicates that the sister may soon be ill. A black birthday card for a friend would be a premonition of that friend's possible death on or around his birthday.

Caretakers denote efficiency and organization in life.

Caricatures are signs of distorted perceptions. They usually indicate that the dreamer only sees the obvious exteriors of people or situations, rather than the true, inner aspects.

Carpenters symbolize the dreamer's freedom of choice to build on knowledge and talents for the betterment of mankind.

Carriages refer to the outdated health practices the dreamer might still use or believe in. They also indicate an inactive system that is low in energy.

Cars (large) indicate physical or mental excesses.

Cars (small) refer to the dreamer's need to take more conscientious care of his or her physical body. You are not giving your body the room or space in your life that it needs for proper attention.

Cartographers symbolize the ability to map out one's own life and the routes one can take to best meet all spiritual opportunities.

Carvings indicate that fine detail and the intricacies of life need to be perceived by the dreamer. Look more closely. This may refer to an individual, situation, or belief system.

Cash Registers connote possessiveness of material objects in the dreamer's life. This dream fragment is warning the dreamer to shift and correct priorities.

Caskets represent the precariousness of the physical as compared to the spiritual aspect of man.

Cassettes refer to listening. This dream symbol has both positive and negative meanings. The color and condition of the tape cassette are important. Sometimes we are advised to listen better to someone, and other times we're cautioned to *not* listen to them. The additional details of the dream surrounding this fragment will clarify its meaning for you.

Castaways are symbols of spiritual independence. This does not mean you, the dreamer, are stranded, but rather that you have been able to find your own way without following the crowd and feeling the need for a support system.

Castles are signs of the emptiness of the dreamer's life or extravagant goals. It can also refer to living in a fantasy world.

Catalogs symbolize life choices for the dreamer.

Caterpillars indicate a transitional stage. This dream fragment is a sign that the dreamer is presently in a temporary situation and that conditions will soon change.

Catfish allude to a cruel and pretentious spiritual nature. This symbol often indicates a cattiness connected to one's own spiritual beliefs. Watch this!

Cats represent the dreamer's casual independence.
> A *cheetah* signifies an independence that is reckless and fast paced,

one that may be somewhat mindless in its forward momentum. This animal may also suggest an independence that is too aggressive to others.
> A *Cheshire cat* indicates an independence that is haughty in nature. Watch that arrogance!
> A *panther* represents an independence that would be underhanded and sneaky.

Cattle symbolize the dreamer's lack of independence. Cattle imply that the dreamer needs to become less dependent on the norms and dictates of society. He is afraid to strike out on his own and be different, and is thereby sacrificing the uniqueness of the self.

Cavemen allude to an individual's antiquated attitudes, outdated ideas, or unawareness. It means the dreamer is clinging to Neanderthal concepts and should strive to leave behind the darkness to find enlightening knowledge.

Celestial Objects are another facet of nature. As with all sky objects, they symbolize aspects of pure spirituality. (See specific celestial objects such as COMETS, MOON, SUN, etc. for further information.)

Cellars represent the deep recesses of the subconscious mind. Are you fearful of the cellar? Is it forbidding and dark? Are secrets hidden down there? Fearsome things? Bring in the light!

Centipedes suggest an individual's ability to overcome irritations. Centipedes may be creepy to see as they suddenly skiddle across a floor or scramble down a wall, but remember, they are a friendly household insect that feeds upon the unwanted and irritating ones.

Certificates refer to commendations given from higher spiritual sources. What *type* of certificate was presented? What condition was it in? Are you striving for further excellence?

Chains denote dependencies. These must be broken in order to free oneself from the bindings that are holding one back.

Chalices exemplify the life force of spiritual truths and of God Himself. They empower one to continue striving for spiritual excellence.

Chalk connotes peripheral information or knowledge that can lead one into more complex and in-depth wisdom.

Chameleons illustrate the changeability of the dreamer's personality. Do you frequently change your mind? Do you find yourself constantly reversing decisions? Do you frequently vacillate between negative and positive emotions, decisions, or belief systems? Are you always the yes-man—never allowing yourself the freedom to express your own ideas or beliefs?

Channelers represent spiritual insecurities and self-created blocks. This is because people don't look within themselves for their own answers, but find it easier to pay someone else for their searching information. Channelers represent a spiritual deevolution for the individual because he or she is not stretching to grow spiritually. This represents an atrophied spiritual functioning and a stagnation of advancement.

Chanting signifies the dreamer's personal way to inner enlightenment and advancement.

Chaps represent the dreamer's need to protect him- or herself along the path of life. This is a temporary condition and will refer to a current situation.

Charge Cards symbolize the dreamer's impatience in attaining goals and the inability to place proper priorities on possessions.

Chariots represent a hyperactive system. The dreamer is charging here and there and creating a condition of anxiety.

Charms signify the dreamer's illogical superstitions.

Charts refer to the dreamer's overall perceptions.
> A *chart of the heavens* indicates one's awakening interest in spiritual realities.
> A *chart of the seas* represents one's overall perception of the spiritual Collective Wisdom.

Checkbooks connote the distribution of the dreamer's material or spiritual wealth. Check for the color of the checks. Are there many left in the book? Few? None?

Checklists symbolize the dreamer's need for awareness. Checklists are for those who are in the habit of forgetting to do things. This dreamscape fragment cautions the dreamer to be more aware of his hour-by-hour activities in life and to be more responsible.

Cheerleaders always indicate encouragement.

Chef Hats represent an individual who is always cooking up schemes in life.

Chefs represent a method of food preparation. In what condition is the dream chef's clothing? What is he doing? Is he dirty? Clean?

Chemists speak of the many formulas for spiritual advancement and attainment of truth. Beware of those who would claim there is but one.

Chess Games symbolize life participation. Check to see what the figures are made of. How are they represented? Historical figures? Mythical figures? Are you always being checkmated? Are you always checkmating others? Are the pieces used correctly, according to the rules? What colors are the playing field?

Chicken Coops indicate the confinements of insecurity.

Chickens signify an undue reluctance to face life.

Children allude to man's innocence and acceptance.

Chimney Sweeps represent the dreamer's need to maintain a clean and pure attitude for spiritual enlightenment.

Chiropractors symbolize the strength and power of integrity. This dream fragment refers to the ability to stand tall amid adversity.

Chisels represent the slow and careful advancement of an individual and his or her step-by-step self-discoveries.

Chock Blocks signify the dreamer's need for additional protection against moving too fast along his or her path. This dream facet refers to the need to pause and use caution against backsliding.

Chopsticks caution the dreamer against using the wrong means to gain an end.

Churches signify a specific spiritual belief system. Is the building in disrepair? Are you approaching it? Walking away? What denomination is it?

Circuit Breakers indicate the dreamer's need to stop and take a rest before he or she overloads. They usually refer to the mental system and would suggest that the dreamer is studying too hard or going at a furious pace and becoming oversaturated with information.

Circus Tents signify a distorted perspective of life. This facet clearly represents the dreamer's view of society as being a circus.

City Halls symbolize the letter of the law and the correct way of doing things.

Clams symbolize a quiet individual. Warning! Still waters run surprisingly deep. A quiet person usually denotes an analytic mind.

This dream symbol may also be a caution for the dreamer to clam up and use restraint when pushing his spiritual ideals onto others.

Clay represents the tenacity and malleability needed for a proper life or spiritual search.

Clerks/Salespeople signify the selling of oneself. Watch this important aspect for specific indicators as to precise meanings.

Climbing Stairs denotes spiritual ascent. Remember, note the stairs' condition and color for further insights.

Clockmakers represent those who would place limits. Remember that there is a precise time for all things.

Clocks represent warnings.
>   An *alarm clock ringing* signifies a sharp warning to wake up and correct your ways.
>   *Clock hands racing* are a sign that time is running out.
>   *Clocks on a kitchen wall/table* indicate that more time is required for a healthful digestion at mealtimes.
>   *Clocks in a rubbish receptacle* are a sign that the dreamer is wasting time.
>   *Broken Clocks* signify no time left or a death.
>   *Pointing to a Clock* symbolizes a caution for the dreamer to be aware of the passing of time. Is a finger pointing? What is its condition? Is it pudgy or is it a skeletal one? This directly refers to how much time you have. What number is the finger pointing to?

Clock Towers represent the proper time for certain events in the dreamer's life to occur.

Closets designate the dreamer's hidden self. This dream fragment refers to that which the dreamer keeps hidden from others. Some of these inner aspects may be fears, inhibitions, negative emotions, insecurities, damaging attitudes, injustices done, and the like.

Clothing, from headgear down to gloves and shoes, represents a valuable clue to the wearer's personality, spirituality, or physical condition. Each article lends additional clarity to the intention of the individual's appearance within the dream. Remember the details, for they are important signposts pointing the way to explicit insight. (See specific clothing articles such as APRONS, BELTS, COATS, etc. for further information.)

Clouds symbolize the dreamer's thought patterns.

> *Elongated clouds* denote the dreamer's penchant to scatter thoughts. It indicates a tendency to spread out single concepts, ideas, and notions until there is nothing of substance remaining.
>
> *Slow-moving clouds* represent the dreamer's inability to reach decisions or to comprehend conceptual or innovative ideas.
>
> *Fast-moving clouds* symbolize the dreamer's tendency to jump ahead mentally. This means a habit of thinking too fast (often placing the cart before the horse) and reaching conclusions that are in error or are not there to make.
>
> *Rectangular clouds* represent the dreamer's tendency to stay strictly within the confines or boundaries of his or her own preconceived notions. The dreamer is not open to new theories or any ideas that are not already personally stamped with his or her seal of approval.
>
> *Thunderheads* denote a prejudiced mind. The dreamer tends toward verbal or physical explosions after he or she has been subjected to new attitudes, ideas, or concepts. This clearly symbolizes a dangerously closed mind.

Clown fish represent a foolhardy individual. Humor has its valuable and therapeutic place within the framework of everyday life. However, a consistently jovial person who is compulsively funny is clearly displaying his or her false face. It is foolhardy to disguise oneself compulsively in this manner.

Clowns denote the foolish aspects of the dreamer's beliefs.

Clown suits connote feigned happiness. They indicate an immature attitude.

Coaches always represent those we listen to. Pay strict attention to these for clarity of intention. Those we listen to may not know of what they speak and discrimination is needed.

Coal connotes negative attitudes or conceptual ideas held by the dreamer.

Coasting indicates that the dreamer has a lazy attitude. You're too nonchalant about life or your spiritual path.

Coats denote an individual's need to cover up aspects of self.

Cobblestones symbolize a rough and rugged road that the dreamer has chosen to take.

Cobwebs represent the dreamer's lack of logic or deep reasoning thought.

Cockroaches indicate major problems that interfere with the health of one or more of the four aspects of man's nature. Examine *where* these insects appear in the dream. In a restaurant? In your own home? Which room? In a church?

Coffeepots indicate that something's brewing in the dreamer's life. This "something" might be a situation or the dreamer's thoughts. But note that a *coffeepot overflowing* specifically indicates that the dreamer is ingesting too much caffeine.

Coffee Shops refer to rests or breaks in the dreamer's life. This is usually a cautionary dream fragment, indicating that the dreamer had better start taking a break in his or her workaholic lifestyle.

This dream symbol may also have a spiritual aspect. The dreamer may need to take a break in his or her spiritual search, or risk missing some important concepts.

Coins are symbols of riches. Are they gold (material) or silver (spiritual)? What condition are they in? Are they old? New?

Colors play a unique role in the interpretation of any dream. Not only is the individual color important, but also its specific condition must be taken into account. Is it bright and clear? Or is it dull, mottled, or indistinct? Does it have a pattern?

Dream colors are not singular in significance. They can have either positive or negative connotations. Therefore, before the dreamer can analyze a color's true meaning, all the surrounding details of the dream must be considered.

The condition of a color is the most obvious clue as to its positive or negative character. All *clear and sharp colors* symbolize the positive and predominant aspect, while the *dull, mottled, or indistinct colors* represent the negative and underlying facet.

The following listing will help you decipher the vivid Technicolor features of your dreams. They will serve to lend an additional dimension and clarification to the dream's meaning as a whole.

BLUE always represents spirituality. Blue is the color of great bodies of water, which, in themselves, also signify spirituality. All shades of blue symbolize this spirituality. What is important is to analyze the background and surrounding features and circumstances of the dream, for spirituality can refer to the dreamer's personal religious beliefs, how the dreamer relates those beliefs to his or her daily life, or how well the dreamer is incorporating those beliefs into his or her relationships with others.

Blue's positive aspect: The dreamer is spiritually aware and is effectively living a good life according to God's laws. He or she is taking active steps to develop his or her inner self and gain enlightenment through personal development.

Blue's negative aspect: The dreamer is spiritually confused or is searching down the wrong paths for enlightenment. This may also signify that the dreamer gives only lip service to God (or his- or herself), while forgetting or ignoring the spiritually humane treatment of his or her fellow men.

BROWN is an earthy color, and since soil is brown, this color designates the practical, down-to-earth side of the dreamer's personality. This color symbolizes the inner, base desires that are deeply buried within the hidden character of the dreamer. Brown may refer to negative emotions, material extravagance, or illogical thinking. Heed the background details that will pinpoint which aspect is intended.

Brown's positive aspect: The dreamer is being shown that he or she is practical and well balanced in financial affairs, is down-to-earth in daily dealings with others, or is true to him- or herself.

Brown's negative aspect: The dreamer is being shown that he or she is harboring ill thoughts of others, or that private views are depressive. A less egotistical attitude toward worldly desires may be intended, or it may symbolize a need to return to more logical and analytical thinking.

ORANGE symbolizes the system's energies, both physical and mental.

Orange's positive aspect: The dreamer possesses a high level of emotional, mental, and physical energies, and these are being used in a beneficial manner for the betterment of society.

Orange's negative aspect: The dreamer is being warned that although energies are being maintained at a high level, he or she is not effectively using them. This is a serious warning.

YELLOW is the bright and cheery color of sunshine. Therefore, it represents a bubbly, extroverted personality, a characteristic that is synonymous with a contented life.

Yellow's positive aspect: The dreamer is happy with his or her station in life and possesses a complete acceptance of his or her lot. He or she is instrumental in bringing a ray or two of happiness into the lives of those around the dreamer.

Yellow's negative aspect: The dreamer does not recognize the positive aspects of his or her life. You are continually looking for negatives to complain or be depressed about. The dreamer is being cautioned to stop looking at life's dark clouds and to see the bright sun that shines just behind them. You may also suffer from an unwillingness to face life's new experiences, a trait tending toward cowardice.

RED is most universally associated with intense anger; hence the popular saying, "I saw red." Red is also associated with "stop" signs. Red may represent anger, the need to stop something, or excessive sexual activities of the mind or body.

Red's positive aspect: It may appear on the surface that red has no positive side, but when the dreamer has an inability to display emotions or feelings adequately, this color can have a positive meaning. It is telling the dreamer that he or she must learn to get his or her feelings out before these harbored emotions adversely affect the dreamer's physiological systems. When emotions (be they positive or negative) are continually repressed, they soon begin to fester and putrefy. They invariably seek an avenue of release, which, in the end, most often is through physical disease. Anger, if displayed in a controlled manner and positively vented, is mentally and physically therapeutic. Hit that pillow and get it *out!*

Red's negative aspect: But if repression is not your problem, red can be a stern warning to control your frequent displays of explosive anger, or your excessive mental or physical obsession with sex, or some other compulsive type of negative thought or action.

DARK PINK/ROSY colors symbolize the dreamer's compassion, love, and sympathetic attitudes.

Dark pink's positive aspect: The dreamer is being encouraged to continue his or her God-like unselfish attitudes toward humanity.

Dark pink's negative aspect: The dreamer is being cautioned to exhibit outwardly a more humane and compassionate view of his or her fellow men and their circumstances. This would mean that the dreamer needs to be less apathetic.

LIGHT PINK indicates a mental or physical weakness.

Light pink's positive aspect: The dreamer is being shown that a specific weakness is *not* a harmful condition. Many times the dreamer will be overly concerned about an emotional deficiency that he or she believes should be corrected. This dream color would then indicate that the trait in question is not a harmful one, but rather a positive personality trait that is unique to the individual. Some examples of strengths often misinterpreted as alleged weaknesses are true humility, an analytical mind (cautiousness), practicality, empathy, and fairness.

Light pink's negative aspect: As opposed to the above, this is a warning to the dreamer to strengthen certain physical or emotional traits that are lacking. These often include self-esteem, individuality, and the ability to express love and compassion.

GREEN is the color worn by surgeons in hospitals and is often the color on the walls of sickrooms. Green is a mentally and physically soothing and healing color. It is symbolic of healthfulness and continued growth. Also, depending on the other details of a given dream, green may also indicate an unhealthy, deep-seated jealousy.

Green's positive aspect: To be shown green surrounding the overall periphery of a physical body (whether this body be that of the dreamer or someone else) means that the body is in a healthful state. To have the color green appear to be emanating from the forehead indicates an absence of envy in that person.

Green's negative aspect: To be shown green emanating from a specific bodily area indicates that the individual represented possesses a physiological dysfunction in that part of the body. If a *clouded* green is emitting from the forehead area, the dreamer is being cautioned to avoid frequent jealousy in themselves or others. (Remember, the *condition* of the color will help you determine whether its meaning is positive or negative.)

GRAY most frequently indicates the physical brain or the mind that functions within it.

Gray's positive aspect: A clear and pure gray color around the dreamer's head or crown indicates clear and logical thinking.

Gray's negative aspect: An indistinct and dirty gray around the dreamer's head or crown indicates unclear or negative thinking. You need to shift your general viewpoint or possibly bring more logic and fewer preconceived judgments into your daily thought processes. A *muddy gray* may also warn of a physical dysfunction within the brain itself. Have you been experiencing frequent and unexplainable headaches, moments of forgetfulness, or bouts of dizziness or disorientation? Consult your physician if these symptoms accompany a dreamscape with muddy gray features.

BLACK represents mystery, darkness, wrongdoing, or evil. Black *always* accompanies a premonition dream of a forthcoming death.

Black's positive aspect: Black can have a positive meaning in a dream, but only when it comes to you as an explicit warning regarding other people. Unless the dreamer is an extremely aware individual during his or her waking hours, it is usually difficult to detect the hidden negative thoughts of those around him or her. Therefore, to dream of someone with an aura of black surrounding his or her head or crown symbolizes a warning for the dreamer to avoid relationships with this individual as he or she possesses hidden, dark thoughts and beliefs. To dream of a person who has the color black emitting from the heart indicates the forthcoming physical death of that individual. Please do not confuse these two. Remember, black around the crown indicates an evil or dark mind, while black around the heart is a sign of physical death.

Black's negative aspect: Black is negative when it is directly associated with the dreamer. It is a warning for the dreamer to reverse mental patterns immediately, before they consume him or her. It is rare for the dreamer to be shown his or her own death date; however, it is not entirely unheard of.

WHITE signifies the opposite of black. White is the epitome of purity and goodness.

White's positive aspect: A clear and sparkling white signifies a true and heartfelt personality.

White's negative aspect: A dirty white indicates a personality that is outwardly beyond reproach, yet is inwardly and secretively in opposition—a two-faced personality.

WHITE AND BLACK in combination designate the good-and-evil, the right-and-wrong, the clear-and-esoteric, the life-and-death aspects of any given situation or human condition.

Black and white's positive aspect: Free will gives each of us the potential for good and evil; we each embody a polarity of the positive and negative. We make our own choice as to which type of life we're going to pursue. The presence of these two contrasting colors in a dream signifies man's duality of nature or the polarity of a specified situation.

Black and white's negative aspect: A *black-and-white hat* represents the dreamer's mental vacillations; *black and white clothing* denotes conflicting actions; and *black and white shoes* represent the dreamer's continued tendency to walk differing paths rather than persevering along one. Are you seeking the easiest way through life? Are you frequently wallowing in indecision?

TURQUOISE is a pleasing blend of blue and green. Therefore, turquoise always represents spiritual health and well-being.

Turquoise's positive aspect: A clear and bright turquoise color represents right beliefs and the dreamer's effective use of those beliefs in his or her daily interactions with his or her fellow men. If the turquoise is white-speckled, it indicates that the dreamer's spiritual beliefs are advancing toward more absolute truths. Your new spiritual information is indeed correct, and a good grasp of these new concepts will give you a pure and aware understanding of your beliefs as a whole.

Turquoise's negative aspect: A dirty or black-speckled turquoise is a severe warning for the dreamer not to allow foreign beliefs to contaminate his or her inherent true ones. A turquoise that is white-speckled can be negative if the dreamer is not paying attention to his or her beliefs or is not following his or her path.

PURPLE is synonymous with the comfort found within attained wisdom and high spiritual enlightenment.

Purple's positive aspect: A clear and vivid purple represents the emotional maturity that accompanies attained wisdom. It signifies the comfort gained in the richness of the Light of Awareness.

Purple's negative aspect: A dull or dusty purple represents unattained comfort in present beliefs. It signifies an unsettled mind in regard to the integrity or accuracy of the dreamer's beliefs.

VARIANTS OF COLOR (HUES AND SHADES) indicate additional interpretations of the above colors. Many dreams are painted in splashes of a multitude of hues and shades. The dreamer needs to interpret the base color and then combine the meaning of the color it is mixed with. For instance, a greenish yellow would symbolize a sunny disposition (yellow) with an underlying or hidden aspect of jealousy (green). The predominant color will represent the outward characteristic that people see, and the secondary color will represent the underlying characteristic that is kept hidden from view.

Variants' positive aspect: This dream aspect can give the dreamer valuable insights into the true personalities and attitudes of others.

Variants' negative aspect: This dream

aspect can caution the dreamer to exhibit true feelings rather than be two-faced and hypocritical in his or her own personal relationships.

SPECKLED COLORS are another version of variants. Decide what the predominant color is, then take into account the meanings of each color of the speckles. Again, the predominant color indicates the outward traits, while the speckles will symbolize the new or *hidden* meanings.

Combs indicate the need to straighten out something in the dreamer's life, usually his or her thoughts.

Comedians represent a personality that is never serious.

Comets indicate the dreamer's sudden spiritual awakening. This symbol can have a negative meaning, indicating that the dreamer has allowed opportunities for spiritual enlightenment to pass by or die out.

Compasses indicate a better direction is required in the dreamer's life or spiritual path. Is the compass pointing in a specific direction? Is it spinning?

Computer Programmers signify an individual who thinks he or she can create his or her own reality. This dream aspect is important because it is a strong warning to the dreamer to follow the voice of his or her own spirit instead of trying to program his or her destiny according to selfish wants.

Computers symbolize the need to analyze situations, ideas, belief systems, or the self in more depth.

Computer Stores signify a specific spiritual doctrine. Is the building in disrepair? Are you approaching it? Walking away? What individual programs are you looking at?

Constellations are a spiritual recogni-

tion of the dreamer's efforts and/or development.

Construction Trucks denote the physiological construction of the body. What condition is this truck in? Trucks can also represent work in an individual's life. Therefore, a construction truck is a sign of the work and effort an individual puts into constructing a healthy body. The kind of truck is important here. The following are examples of many of the trucks you might see on a residential construction site.

Air-conditioning trucks represent a cool work attitude and the dreamer's control of work pressure.

It may also refer to the dreamer's internal cooling system. Is the truck in good shape?

Alarm-systems trucks indicate a discerning and cautious perspective on work. The dreamer proceeds carefully in his or her work and has foresight in daily planning.

It may also be an alarm going off, indicating something physiological is about to go awry.

Carpenter/lumber trucks symbolize the worker as being the backbone of his or her job. It stresses the importance of his or her particular duties.

It may also represent the dreamer's physiological skeletal system. It could be cautioning the dreamer to be extra careful as there may be an upcoming accident involving the bones. It may also be indicative of the need to see a chiropractor.

Cement trucks represent the dreamer's need to maintain good relationships with his or her employees or coworkers.

It may also indicate an actual physiological need to keep the digestive system in better operation and to refrain from so many starches for a while.

Deck/patio trucks symbolize the extensions the dreamer makes use of in his or her workplace. They refer to how much he or she goes out of his or her way to be helpful to peers.

The physiological aspect of this symbol refers to the body's extensions—the extremities (arms and legs) and how well or ill they may be.

Drywall trucks indicate underlying attitudes at the workplace. Are they rough? Smooth? Incomplete?

Physiologically, drywall refers to matter just beneath the skin. Do you have an acne condition? Boils? The need for attention here is indicated.

Electrical trucks denote the power or force of the dreamer's job. Is it weak? Strong? Sparking? Ready to blow?

Physiologically, this symbol represents the brain and associated dysfunctions. Are you having headaches? Dizziness? Frequent moments of forgetfulness? Sudden bouts of unexplained anger or mood swings?

Fencing trucks represent disharmony in the workplace. The dreamer is frequently sparring or fencing with others.

This dream fragment may also refer to the dreamer's physiological defense system—the immune system. Caution is advised not to exhaust oneself and weaken the body's defenses against invading infections or viruses.

Gas-utility trucks symbolize the dreamer's energy levels at work.

Physiologically, it refers to the digestive system and usually means the dreamer is eating incorrectly. Too fast? In negative moods while eating? Eating the wrong foods?

Glass/window trucks are a sign of how the dreamer views his job and its conditions.

Physiologically, this symbol indicates the eyes.

Grading trucks indicate the manner in which the dreamer performs his or her occupation. Is it hilly with ups and downs? Is it kept on an even keel?

Physiologically, this symbol denotes the dreamer's actual routine diet. Are you frequently starving yourself and then going on an eating binge?

Heating-contractor trucks indicate the dreamer's temperament at the workplace.

Physiologically, this symbol refers to the heart/circulatory system.

Insulation trucks symbolize the dreamer's ability to insulate him- or herself from pressures and work problems.

It may also indicate the physical need to take better precautionary measures in regard to your health.

Painting trucks are a sign of how the dreamer's work is completed. Is it rushed through each day so that details are left hanging? Is it all covered by end of day?

Physiologically, this symbol refers to the skin. Do you have any dermatological problems? Dryness?

Roofing trucks denote how the dreamer thinks and plans during his or her working hours.

Physiologically, the dreamer might want to give particular attention to the head area.

Septic/plumbing trucks denote the dreamer's moral and ethical attitudes in the workplace.

Correspondingly, this is a sign directly referring to the dreamer's physical elimination/assimilation system.

Siding trucks symbolize the dreamer's exterior attitude and ethics at the workplace.

It may also denote skin problems. Siding, like paint, is the final finish—the exterior.

Well-drilling trucks denote how well

the dreamer digs down for details and attends to them in the workplace.

So, too, can it refer to the body's water ingestion and the need for more intake.

Convenience Stores represent a lackadaisical attitude. No excuse for laziness is considered acceptable. Correct this aspect in the self.

Convention Centers symbolize information-sharing gatherings. What is being discussed? What is the building's condition? What mood is the crowd in?

Convents indicate spiritual isolation that is self-generated.

Convicts denote a wrongdoer. Search your emotions, actions, inner thoughts, and ideals. Could any of these be ways you imprison yourself physically, mentally, or spiritually?

Cookbooks represent recipes of fulfillment that are specific to each individual. Consider the kind of recipe represented.
Meat recipes refer to the need for more assertiveness and energy in terms of your opportunities for advancement.
Holiday recipes indicate a light mood and attitude are required.
Dessert recipes mean a soft approach is needed.
Ethnic recipes indicate an emphasis should be placed on a certain traditional belief system.
Stew recipes caution the cook (dreamer) to pursue in-depth thought, to stew a little over situations or conceptual beliefs.

Cooking indicates planning is being done or is required of the dreamer.

Cooking Utensils almost always refer to the dreamer's manner of food preparation.
Aluminum cookware causes serious physical illnesses (never use these unless they're coated).

Aluminum foil represents the same type of warning.
Copper utensils symbolize a warning. *Never* use them.
Forks represent a repressed personality. You're always holding down yourself or others.
Knives indicate a cutting has been or needs to be done in one's life.
Ladles signify a generous personality always ready to pour out his or her talents.
Spoons refer to the need to temper the spooning or dishing out one does.

Cooks are a sign of the quality of food preparation. Cooks may also refer to the act of always cooking something up and are a warning to stop it.

Coonskin Caps indicate a backward thought process.

Coral represents spiritual talents hidden beneath the surface. What color is the coral? What is its condition? Is it alive? Or is it dying from polluted waters?

Corkscrews are signs of a twisted or involved situation. Who is using the corkscrew?

Cornucopias symbolize the many spiritual gifts of the self.

Coupsticks symbolize the dreamer's bravery in overcoming his or her adversities.

Couriers represent middlemen and how they are used in the dreamer's life. Since it's always best to take the initiative and be solely responsible for your own actions, the use of middlemen (couriers) is usually a negative symbol.

Courthouses are signs of justice. Are you the judge? The plaintiff? What condition is the courthouse in? Are you just in all aspects of your life?

Cowboys are symbols of individualism

and freedom. Follow the voice of the dreamer's spirit.

Cows represent the dreamer's level of compassion. Cows are the symbol of nourishment—the emotional nourishment of sympathy and compassion given to your fellow men.

Coyotes illustrate man's solitude. If the animal is howling, this represents an aloneness of the heart.

In the Native American Indian belief system, the coyote represents the trickster. He is the wise one who is known for his penchant to mislead others, the mischievous one who cares not for consequences.

Crabs suggest a negative temperament. This dream symbol may also literally refer to a sexually transmitted infestation.

Cradles represent self-styled immaturity and ignorance.

Crayons indicate a juvenile attitude.

Crazy People indicate aberrations. This may refer to any of the four aspects of man's nature.

Creosote denotes a buildup of negative and damaging attitudes or beliefs that may ignite and burn the individual.

Crickets represent life's soothing aspects. They tend to smooth out the rough edges of an individual's personality.

Critics are signs of an individual who is always finding fault. Such people are usually egotistical or unhappy with themselves.

Crocodiles symbolize underlying spiritual forces that are negative or dark. Examine recent circumstances to understand what these crocodiles are representing.

Crossing Bridges represents the transitional stages of life or of one's path.

Crossing Guards represent Spirit Advisors. This dreamscape fragment should reinforce the dreamer's confidence in his or her spiritual protection.

Crossroads always indicate a point of decision for the dreamer. Look to your lifestyle and spiritual path.

Crowns/Tiaras represent the dreamer's high-minded ideas.

Crutches are a warning for the dreamer to stand on his or her own two feet, to stand tall and stop using other people or situations as excuses for not taking responsibility.

Crying is a sign of remorse and regret.

Crypts symbolize secrets the dreamer hides.

Crystal Balls signify unnecessary tools used for spiritual advancement and enlightenment. This also refers to an individual's obsession with the future. The latter interpretation holds a serious warning for the dreamer, for he or she is not living in the present.

Crystals symbolize spiritual attunement. What color are they?

Cupcakes denote a giving personality—sometimes too giving, to the point of being what some call a pushover.

Cupids always signify love. However, please be aware of the object of this love. Is it material possessions? What color is cupid's arrow? What is he shooting it at? Love is often a misdirected emotion. Check all the surrounding aspects of the dream for clarity here.

Curbs are a caution for the dreamer to curb an action, speech, or thought. It may also indicate a need for the dreamer to curb an excess (physical, mental, emotional, or spiritual).

Curling Irons indicate the need for the dreamer to soften straitlaced attitudes and stiff ideas or beliefs.

Curtains signify denials—aspects that are curtained off.

> *Black curtains* symbolize a death. This death may be an actuality (premonition), a mental one (total breakdown), or it may refer to a spiritual death (a rejection of God or the Truths).
>
> *Lacy curtains* indicate a denial that is generated from a fanciful attitude. (Check the COLOR, FABRIC, and PATTERNS sections for more information.)

Cutting Down Trees denotes spiritual skepticism and a disregard for those spiritual opportunities that could lead to advancement and enlightenment.

Cuttlebones symbolize the need for the dreamer to sharpen his or her manner of speech. This does not refer to a cutting speech, but rather language that is spoken with clarity of meaning. This dream symbol suggests that the dreamer has a tendency to beat around the bush instead of cutting right to the point of an issue.

D

Dairies are symbols of physical or spiritual nourishment. Check the building's occupants and condition for this dreamscape fragment's significance.

Dams signify spiritual blocks. You, the dreamer, are either damming up free-flowing spiritual aspects in your life by not sharing your knowledge or talents, or you have dammed up your way for advancement by crowding too many concepts in your mind. A dam indicates an individual's need to allow spirituality to flow out at a steady and controlled rate. This refers to how you use your spirituality in your daily life.

Dance Instructors indicate emotional well-being and lightheartedness. This dreamscape fragment urges the dreamer to have a more upbeat perspective on life.

Dance Studios represent a carefree attitude, an ability to dance through adversity. However, if the studio is located near any water (which represents spirituality), it is a negative symbol, for the dreamer is dancing through spirituality itself.

Daredevils denote chances taken in life.

Darkrooms allude to man's negative or evil aspects. Examine surrounding activities and conditions in the dream. Also, depending upon the activities carried out within the dream darkroom, this fragment may allude to that which the dreamer exposes. This may mean that the dreamer has uncovered or will uncover and bring to light some of his or her confusions.

Darts represent the barbs that hamper one's growth. Who is throwing the darts? This clarifies whether or not the dreamer is the one responsible for the barbs.

Datebooks indicate dates special to the dreamer. Pay close attention to any marked date.

Dead Ends symbolize those paths that the dreamer may consider taking that will be fruitless. This dreamscape fragment is a direct message from the Higher Self or one's Guide and comes to prevent the dreamer from wasting valuable time.

Deadwood represents those aspects of the dreamer's life that are extraneous and unnecessary to the attainment of his or her life goal or spiritual purpose.

Debris/Rubbish exemplifies that which clutters up the dreamer's life or belief systems. This is usually a definitive dream symbol. Check to see what the debris is.

Deck Shoes are a sign that one is insulating him- or herself from the spiritual path.

Decoys indicate something that is not genuine, credible, or trustworthy in the dreamer's life. They are a message from the Higher Self or one's Guide and come as a warning when the dreamer is about to accept a concept or individual as being valid.

Deeds signify a finality or genuineness.

Deer symbolize the dreamer's use of caution in life. This dreamscape fragment is either recommending that the dreamer exhibit more awareness in life, or it is commending the dreamer for his or her acute senses and perceptions. Check surrounding details of the dream for clarity here.

Deformities denote opportunities for the dreamer. Note what is deformed about the people involved.

Delivery People represent how the dreamer relates to his or her fellow men. Do you deliver? Are you always expecting deliveries from others?

Delivery Trucks symbolize your physical interactions with others. What type of delivery truck is this vehicle?
A *fish market delivery truck* alludes to the dreamer's inner spirituality.
A *flower shop delivery truck* refers to spiritual attitudes toward others.
A *pizza delivery truck* (food) denotes a caution against too much of this type of nourishment in your diet.
A *UPS delivery truck* represents the need to make a speedy communication.

Dens signify the manner or frequency of the dreamer's rest time.

Dental Floss indicates the need for the dreamer to eliminate the tendency to make needless insinuations. Since teeth designate spoken words, the area between the teeth (between the spoken words) symbolizes often hurtful and harmful innuendoes.

Dentists represent the quality of speech—not how intelligently you speak, but rather how kind your words are. Dentists are the representatives who would correct any negative language condition.

Dentist's Offices symbolize the need to correct negative speech. What is being done here is the key to the precise meaning for the dreamer.
Having teeth extracted means the dreamer needs to remove damaging language from his or her speech.
Getting dentures refers to an entire new manner of beautiful speech.
Having caps or crowns symbolizes hypocrisy.
Teeth being cleaned represents the need to clean up the dreamer's speech or language.
Gum disease treatments mean the dreamer's foundation of speech (attitudes) need to be treated and healed.
A filling means that the dreamer is actively working to remove negative language from his speech.

Derbys (hats) signify old-fashioned ideas.

Derricks symbolize one's search for valuable resources. This may refer to physical materialism or spiritual enhancements.

Derringers symbolize hidden ill feelings.

Descending Stairs/Ramps indicate the lowering of spiritual ideals. Correct this tendency.

Deserts indicate the absence of lush botanicals that signify gifts and talents. Therefore, if you see yourself in a desert, it indicates that your God-given talents are becoming parched, or drying up from neglect.

Designer Shoes indicate an individual who must follow the guru or most notable spiritual leader at any one time. This symbol comes directly from the Higher Self or one's Guide to warn the individual not to design or stylize his or her own spiritual path after another's.

Desks indicate research and study needs to be done.

Despair alludes to an individual's remorse over opportunities not taken or acted upon.

Devils/Demons/Imps are symbols of life's temptations. Be cautious when these symbols arise, for thinking these beings are just symbolic of evil is a grave error in spiritual judgment and comprehension.

Diagrams indicate clarification is needed for the dreamer to understand or assimilate concepts properly.

Dials denote the need for the dreamer to watch something carefully. How is your energy level? Anger level?

Diapers represent one who is out of control in regard to his or her negative aspects.

Diaries denote record keeping. The specific condition of the diary will clue the dreamer as to the precise meaning here.
A *black or tattered diary* refers to the dreamer's own diary and is a sign that he or she should not be keeping it.
A *white or new diary* means the dreamer should be keeping one.

Dice are signs of the law of probabilities and how quickly things can change in one's life.

Dictaphones are signs of an individual's habit of relegating work to others around them. This dreamscape fragment is usually a warning to the dreamer to attend to these details him- or herself.

Dictionaries signify a need to clarify terminology or concepts that the dreamer is misinterpreting or misunderstanding.

Dieticians are representatives of a type of diet. This can refer to food, but also reading (knowledge), or it may be pointing to the type of spiritual diet the dreamer is following. Consider the other details of the dream to clarify the meaning of the symbol.

Dining Rooms denote the quality, quantity, and mode of consumption. If this dream segment reveals a fast-paced meal being consumed by angered participants amid quarrels, take it as a warning to avoid such situations.

Dirt Roads represent the dreamer's individuality. This symbol indicates your incredible ability to blaze your own path through life according to your own beliefs.

Dirty Clothing signifies impurity. Is it a hat? This refers to mental activities. Are they gloves? This refers to the hands.

Dirty Vehicles suggest the need to cleanse the self, either in the mind or body—perhaps both, depending on the details in the dream.

Ditches are a sign of a seriously off-course situation. The dreamer has strayed away from his or her path. Whether he or she has inadvertently lost control or intentionally jumped ship is irrelevant. Ditches are a warning to get back on course.

Doctors represent those who would heal the dreamer's mental, physical, or spiritual disease.

Dodos (birds) denote an ignorant attitude. This symbol indicates that the dreamer is being resistant to knowledge or enlightenment. It symbolizes self-created ignorance for the purpose of escaping responsibilities.

Dogcatchers allude to captured friendships. This is a warning about the dreamer's manner of gaining friends.

Doghouses literally symbolize trouble for the dreamer. This dream fragment warns the dreamer that he or she is, or will be, in the doghouse for something said or done.

Dogs always symbolize the dreamer's friends and the personal relationship between them.

Colored dogs indicate the state of a current relationship. (Please check the COLOR section for further information.)

Injured dogs are signs of a friendship that has been injured in some way. This is a direct warning for the dreamer.

Sad/droopy dogs signify a friendship that is in a sad condition. This exemplifies a friend who is clearly sad over recent rifts or disagreements.

Dollars always represent the materialistic aspects of life.

Door Knockers indicate the need to knock. This symbol refers to the dreamer's reluctance to go forth and actively approach closed doors in his or her life. This is an important symbol as it has a highly spiritual connotation.

Doormen always refer to one's level of spiritual advancement. The door to higher enlightenment will not be opened if the individual has not understood the foundations of the preceding level. Doormen represent those aspects that control the opening and closing of your spiritual doors. These would be your Higher Self, your personal Guide. Doormen signify the Gatekeepers of your Gates (internal spiritual Power Points or chakras).

Doors symbolize important opportunities. The positioning and condition of the doors in your dream will clarify whether they are positive or negative opportunities.

A cantilevered door denotes the dreamer's need for inner balance before he or she can pass through.

A door opening into darkness is a sign that the dreamer is embarking on an activity, direction, or belief system that will ultimately prove to be destructive.

A door opening into light represents the dreamer's right path.

A dutch door symbolizes the entrance to a life path that will only supply the dreamer with half or a portion of the knowledge sought.

A French door is a sign that the dreamer is at the threshold of a path that he or she can see clearly.

Garbage or refuse at one's door speaks of the baser thoughts or activities that accompany the dreamer on his or her path. Clean up your act!

An intricately carved door is the way to wisdom. Such a door indicates the beauty of the Truths.

A locked or jammed door is a sign that the dreamer lacks the awareness or knowledge necessary to open the doors of life or spiritual advancement.

A missing door symbolizes the openness of one's path or way.

A steel door signifies opportunities that require much work on the dreamer's part.

A stone door is the way to ancient knowledge. Often these appear as great stones that need to be rolled back, such as in a tomb or Egyptian burial chamber.

A swinging door represents doubts regarding decisions in life. The dreamer keeps vacillating back and forth regarding a direction or path. You need to learn to close the door behind you.

An unhinged door signifies mental laziness. This is a warning to the dreamer not to proceed until he or she has made a firm decision.

A warped door represents the act of getting one's way by using warped logic.

Dough signifies one's free will. This dream image represents the rising and expanding of the dreamer's opportunities.

Doves are signs of peace. They may also foreshadow situations of contentedness and a peaceful life.

This dream symbol may also be advising the dreamer to take a peaceful stand on a specific situation.

Dowsers represent spiritual searches and the use of one's spiritual gifts along the way.

Dracula Capes represent a delving into the darker side of the esoteric Truths. Watch this!

Dragonflies are a strong positive spiritual aspect and can be instrumental in eliminating the negative ones.

Drawbridges represent man's self-created barriers. They are often raised or lowered according to the situation. Watch these, for bridges must always remain open.

Drawing represents the outlining of one's life goals.

Dredges signify the dreamer's need to stop skimming the surface of situations or knowledge. This important dream fragment warns the dreamer to scrape the bottom so that he or she can obtain full knowledge.

Dress Shoes are a sign of a pathwalker who feels he or she must always put his

or her best foot forward without ever allowing the true self to show.

Dried Flowers symbolize the dreamer's need to preserve his or her spiritual gifts or talents. This dream symbol is a strong warning for the individual to stop wasting these valuable and beautiful gifts.

Drifting in a Boat signifies an absence of spiritual direction in life. You need spiritual goals and a definitive path.

Drills signify the need for further study. This dream fragment suggests that something needs to be drilled into one's consciousness.

Driving Backward is a sign of the dreamer's retreat into the old, easier ways—a retreat away from the more difficult path of advancement.

Drowning represents the dreamer's spiritual saturation. This is an important dream fragment, for the Higher Self is warning the individual to come up for air before you drown in your spiritual intake. It's a stern warning to take it slow and easy with spiritual learning instead of reading and studying everything you can get your hands on.

Drug Dealers indicate the negative aspects of spiritual development.

Drugs indicate a dependency in the dreamer's life.

Drugstores are references to an individual's intake of medication. If the dreamer is returning drugs, then a reduction in medication is being recommended. If the dreamer is being given drugs, then an increase or new prescription is being advised. However, always check the color of the drugs, as this may indicate an additional caution. Are they black? Then you need to discontinue their use.

Druids are symbols of esoteric spiritual aspects. They are positive symbols.

Drumbeats are a call to the native ways,

meaning the natural way. This may refer to an individual's own path in life or one's spiritual direction.

Drum Majorettes are a sign of boastfulness.

Drunks are symbols of overindulgences. This overindulgence may be taking place in any area of life—mental, emotional, physical, or spiritual. We can become intoxicated by many things.

Dry Cleaners signify the need to pay special attention to removing the negative from your life and thought processes.

Dry Docks are a warning for the dreamer to take a rest in his or her spiritual research for a while.

Ducks allude to the dreamer's present state of spiritual vulnerability. This dream symbol is literally a warning to not be a sitting duck. You are being warned of a forthcoming spiritual confrontation, possibly an attack from skeptics, or perhaps an attack of doubt from within yourself.

Duels symbolize conflicts. This important dream fragment may be referring to the dreamer's own inner conflict or it may signify a more physical type of confrontation with another individual or situation. It may also indicate serious indecision concerning the dreamer's own path in life.

Dugouts represent the act of hiding. This image may mean that the dreamer needs to lay low for a while or that he needs to come out of his place of seclusion. Consult the other details of the dream to illuminate the meaning of this symbol.

Dummies/Mannequins symbolize ignorance. Many times this will be a self-created condition.

Dump Trucks represent the act of unburdening that which is harmful to the system. You must analyze the details of the dream and your own behavior to determine whether this symbol refers to the discontinuance of harmful eating habits or negative attitudes. This symbol may also refer to a physiological dysfunction of the large intestinal tract and/or colon, or it may refer to an emotional unburdening.

Dunce Caps are signs of foolish thoughts and beliefs.

Dust represents mental atrophy. Check to see exactly what needs to be dusted off.

Dye represents misrepresentations. Is some aspect in the dreamer's life being whitewashed? Check the color for specifics.

Dying designates the death of high ideals. This may also be a literal forewarning of a physical or spiritual death.

Dynamite represents a sudden revelation. Something is going to be blown wide open. This symbol may refer to the physical or the spiritual.

E

Eagles are symbols of the dreamer's free spirit. They most often refer to spiritual searching and a breaking away from mainstream ideas.

Earaches are signs that the dreamer has overloaded listening to a redundant subject.

Earphones are symbols of inner perception. Is the Higher Self attempting to get through the consciousness and speak to you? Do you need to listen to your own intuitions more?

Earrings symbolize repeated words that have been embellished—a dressing of the facts.

Earth is a symbol of man's physical aspect. It is here on earth that we physically encounter life's diseases, paths, and obstacles. The earth can indicate the direction of the physical body; it can reveal whether the dreamer is remaining stationary or retreating onto safe and easy paths; or it indicates the condition of the dreamer's physical path. (See specific earth elements such as EARTHQUAKES, GEODES, MOUNTAINS, etc. for further information.)

Earthenware (pottery) is a sign that the dreamer needs to get more down-to-earth.

Earthquakes clearly illustrate how shaky the dreamer's foundations are. The dreamer needs to evaluate his or her basic values and goals. Many times an earthquake dream is a forewarning of an actual event in the future.

Easels speak of the foundation of one's life. Easels hold the clean canvases that are the beginnings of paintings. We paint visualizations of our life path. Is the easel stable?

Eating represents the consumption of food or the absorption of ideas.

Echoes symbolize the voice of the dreamer and those words that need to be listened to by the self. This dream fragment is often a warning that the dreamer is not listening to his or her own advice.

Editors are signs of excesses. There is something in the dreamer's life that needs to be trimmed down, deleted, or revised. Check surrounding details of the dream to get a clear picture of the meaning of this symbol.

Eggshells represent a precarious situation, condition, or belief. This symbol warns of a fragile or delicate situation.

Electricians symbolize thought processes. Is your thinking without creativity? Without the spark of understanding?

Elements (nature) represent the four distinct facets of man, his physical, mental, emotional, and spiritual sides. The precise meaning of a specific element can be illuminated by the conditions and colors in the dream. All details must be intertwined in order to arrive at the correct implication of the dream's elements. (See the specific elements of AIR, EARTH, FIRE, and WATER for further information.)

Elephants symbolize the dreamer's magnanimous nature. This is a positive dream fragment that implies that the dreamer is functioning at an optimum level with respect to his or her use of God's laws. If the animal is in an unhealthy condition, the reverse is implied.

Elevators are signs of laziness in regard to one's life path. The dreamer is trying to take the easiest way to enlightenment.

Elevator Shoes indicate an individual who presents him- or herself in a false light of exceptional attainment. This refers to a braggart or an egotist.

Elf Shoes signify an individual who recognizes the many varying aspects of spiritual wisdom. Such people walk their path with their eyes and ears open to all the realities that are presented to them.

Elixirs symbolize false conditions, concepts, or paths. There are no quick fixes to these.

Embers are symbols of the underlying spirituality that is always burning within the dreamer. Do you need to flame the embers into full life? Are they going out?

Emblems may indicate something that needs attention or something that needs to be omitted.

Embryos symbolize the beginnings of an awakening. This dream symbol may refer to the dreamer's mental, emotional, or spiritual self.

Emergency Brakes indicate an immediate need to put a stop to something. In other words, just slowing down is not enough!

Emery Boards (See NAIL FILES)

Emollients (lanolin, etc.) represent those aspects of life that the dreamer uses to soothe rough situations.

Encyclopedias indicate in-depth study is needed. This symbol suggests that the dreamer is not looking at an issue or subject carefully enough.

Engines symbolize the heart. Is not the engine the heart of a vehicle? Check the engine's condition, paying close attention to all aspects surrounding it, for they symbolize those aspects of your life that affect your living heart (physically or emotionally).

Epitaphs are a warning to the dreamer. What does the epitaph say about the deceased? Is the deceased someone you know? Is it you?

Epoxy indicates the need for a securing or reconnection. This may refer to the dreamer's spiritual beliefs or a relationship.

Equations represent balance. The dreamer needs to balance an aspect in his or her life. Often, the dreamer is being warned to examine whether his or her acts live up to his or her beliefs. Do you practice what you preach?

Erasers indicate that some aspect of the dreamer's life needs to be eradicated.

Erosion is a sign that some aspect of the dreamer's life is eroding. Check relationships, your spiritual path, attitudes, emotions, lifestyle, or belief systems.

Evening Gowns are a sign that the individual is drawn to extravagance in life. Frequently there is a warning here that the dreamer has an excess love of material possessions.

Evergreens signify the eternal spiritual aspects. In what condition were the evergreens in your dream? What color? Yellow? Dying? Vibrant?

Eviction Notices are a severe warning to get out of a situation, relationship, belief system, or direction. Check surrounding details of the dream for more clarity.

Evil Eye represents an individual's fears. The evil eye does not work on its own, but rather appears to be effective when the victim believes in its power. So then, the evil eye as a dream fragment represents those fears the dreamer believes in. These are not necessarily things that really could harm the dreamer in and of themselves.

Executioners indicate the dreamer has a paranoid personality. This dream symbol represents those individuals in the dreamer's life who appear threatening or out to get him or her. Watch this, for this symbol indicates you're tending toward a persecuted-type personality.

Explorers typify those individuals who are free spirits and have a tendency to want to be self-discoverers in life. This is a very positive dream symbol.

Extension Cords indicate the dreamer's need to extend his or her self. The dreamer will usually understand the precise meaning of this symbol for it may refer to anything from attitudes, talents, and compassion to spiritual gifts or skills.

Extraterrestrials represent man's totality. This dream fragment comes to enlighten the individual of his or her far-reaching heritage. Other intelligent beings are evidence of humankind's living bond with all of life . . . the Unified Brotherhood of the Universe.

Such a dream symbol may also be the result of an actual physical communication made while the dreamer was asleep.

Eyes represent an individual's mode of perception. These revealing aspects of one's personality may not be outwardly expressed or noticeably perceived by others, but when expressed in dreams, they clearly illuminate the truth to one's inner self.

Bleeding eyes represent a deeply empathetic personality. The individual's perceptions of life cause personal pain and sorrow.

Blinking eyes indicate flightiness in all phases of man's nature.

Colored eyes denote specific characteristics. Refer to the COLOR section for further information.

Darting eyes symbolize a shifting perspective, one that vacillates and never quite settles on a solid viewpoint.

Eyeglasses are signs of the magnification of an individual's perspective.

Bifocals signify an individual who tends to perceive both the surface and the deeper aspects of another individual, situation, or belief system.

Broken glasses signify a shattered perspective. This dream symbol indicates that an individual's viewpoint has been proven wrong and a new one needs to be formulated.

Lost glasses represent an individual who usually isn't sure what his or her perspective is.

Monocles signify a narrow perspective that rarely views more than one side of an issue.

Sunglasses symbolize an individual with an altered perspective that's distinctly colored. Check the lens color for specifics here.

Hooded eyes signify deceptions and a hypocritical nature.

Large eyes represent heightened awareness and perceptions.

Misted eyes reflect a highly compassionate individual.

Slanted eyes indicate viewpoints or perspectives that are slanted.

This dream fragment indicates an extremely opinionated individual who refuses to see the total scope of things. Rather, such an individual sees only his or her own perspective.

Small eyes are signs of ignorance. They also speak of a small personality.

Squinted eyes symbolize a narrow-mindedness and a self-imposed inability to perceive the entire scope of things.

Staring eyes indicate unexpressed accusations.

Starry eyes are signs of an individual who is an idealist and rarely perceives or understands the true realities of life. Such people are usually considered unrealistic optimists.

F

Fabric/Sewing Shops symbolize interrelationships, and how the dreamer relates to his or her fellow men as a whole. It speaks of how one weaves oneself in with others. The dreamer will find it especially revealing to look at what type of material is being looked at or purchased.

Calico is the sign of a highly open and friendly personality.

Flannel symbolizes a down-to-earth and logical mind.

Imitation leathers/furs are the sign of a hypocritical personality.

Silk indicates an egotistical attitude toward others.

Wool represents a warm personality.

(Also refer to the COLORS and PATTERNS sections for further information.)

Facades are signs of a false front. They are a serious warning from the Higher Self to stop being phony.

Faces are symbols of the underlying realities of an individual's personality.

Birthmarks on faces indicate those individuals who are marked by a high degree of spirituality.

Dimples on faces indicate a light and humorous side to one's nature.

Distorted faces are signs of mental aberrations.

Flushed faces represent an explosive personality.

Heavy facial makeup is a sign of a hypocritical character.

Indistinct/unremarkable faces indicate a conforming personality.

Large ears are signs of awareness.

No face symbolizes indifference and apathy.

Oversize faces indicate an egotistical and arrogant personality.

Pale faces are signs of an introverted personality.

Protruding noses indicate an interfering personality.

Red faces symbolize an easily embarrassed individual.

Reflected faces (as in a mirror) are warnings of an unscrupulous personality.

Round/fat faces indicate avarice or greediness.

Scarred faces are signs of a difficult life.

Square faces signify an adamant personality, one whose mind is squared and set.

Thin/angular faces represent a highly reserved individual.

Undersize faces signify an individual who thinks small or is an introverted personality.

Factories indicate how an individual organizes or puts together his life goals. Check the condition of the factory buildings.

Fairies are signs from the extreme reaches of conceptual reality. This dream symbol cautions the dreamer to extend his or her learning across new barriers, to advance with an open mind and discover the beautiful truths that exist just beyond skepticism.

Fairy Rings represent those spiritual truths that cannot be proven or explained by means of physical science.

Falcons symbolize man's personal relationship with God.

Falling is a sign of a fear of failing or fear of the unknown. Such fear is a completely unnecessary emotion, for the discovery of that which dwells within the unknown is uplifting and enlightening.

Falling also may be a sign of the actual sensation of the spirit (or consciousness) lifting up out of the body before sleep.

False Alarms signify life situations that an individual thinks he's fearful of. Once you experience such situations, you usually find out that what you feared was nothing at all.

Fangs symbolize vicious and cutting speech.

Fans indicate a cooling-off period is needed. Is the dreamer angered? Upset? Overexuberant? Pushing to accomplish something? Forcing goals or events?

Farmers allude to the cultivation of talents and spiritual gifts.

Farmhouses are symbols of the home and family life. Check the physical condition of the farmhouse to illuminate further details.

Farriers signify a calming personality.

Fathers represent the male energy in family life and within the individual.

Fault Lines indicate points of negativity caused by an individual. This symbol refers to those harmful actions or words that are directly generated by the dreamer; they are the dreamer's fault.

Fax Machines symbolize the need for a speedy communication that demands hard backup. This most often will refer to legal issues.

Fear speaks of an individual's insecurities and lack of self-confidence in his or her own talents or abilities.

Feathered Warbonnets represent justifiable attitudes toward injustices.

Feathers signify a free spirit. Their appearance may indicate the need to allow the spirit more freedom or they may refer to one's self-confinements of thoughts and emotions.

Fedoras are symbols of underhanded ideas, attitudes, or deeds.

Fences indicate an individual is maintaining distance. Do you put up a brick wall between yourself and others?
    Fences can also indicate indecision. Are you sitting on the fence?

Ferrets are symbols of man's qualities of humor. Ferrets are fun-loving creatures that easily warm up to man and are amusing to watch at play. As a dream symbol, ferrets speak of how you interject humor into your daily life. Do you take yourself too seriously? Do you overemphasize humor and fail to extend to certain situations or individuals the seriousness they deserve?

Ferries symbolize the spiritual aspects of an individual's life. This dream fragment refers to an individual's use of spiritual talents in his or her life journey. Is the ferry waiting? Are you riding it? Is it gone? Is it rickety? Solid? Sinking? Overloaded? Empty?

Ferris Wheels signify a circling. The dreamer's path is going in circles with many ups and downs. This dream image is a clear warning to get off, look at your life, and move in a more productive, linear direction.

Fertilizers indicate the need to improve a dying condition. They may refer to a

spiritual condition or a mental perspective that requires new and fresh input.

Fighting/Arguing indicate that the dreamer's personality is fraught with indecision and conflict.

Figurines are warnings, although their meaning may be positive or negative. The exact nature of the figurine will clarify the precise meaning that is intended for the dreamer.

File Cabinets symbolize stored information. If data is important enough for the dreamer to store away, it's important enough to remember and use. What condition and color are the cabinets? Is the information stored there being ignored?

Film (camera) signifies the need to capture something and remember it. This may refer to an event, a belief system, or a situation in the dreamer's life.

Filters symbolize discernment. The dreamer is being advised to filter through incoming information; use logic, reason, and introspection.

Finger Painting indicates the individual has a childish manner of expressing him- or herself.

Fingers (pointing) signify a warning that the dreamer should feel guilty about a wrong done to another.

Fiords symbolize the narrow rites of passage in one's spiritual life.

Fire is the natural element that designates the extreme and dangerous intensity of man's emotions. Just as fire burns, so, too, it symbolizes our burning emotions, those that are fed by the fuels of obsessions. Fire consumes its fuel before dying out. Dreams of fire warn you, the dreamer, to control your wants before you end up consumed by them.
    Automobile fires caution the dreamer to control physical excesses. An

automobile is a symbol—the physical body. Analyze your desires in order to benefit from this important warning.

Clothing fires are a sign that the dreamer's wardrobe is a dangerous, false representation of his or her personality. This may warn that the dreamer is dressing in an overly sexual manner. He or she may be attempting to appear as more than he or she is or the attire may be slovenly. Only the dreamer knows why his or her clothes are afire.

Forest fires symbolize the wanton and intentional destruction of the dreamer's talents and abilities. This dream fragment may appear to indicate an irreversible situation, but remember that a forest that has been totally burned over will soon produce new green shoots. Therefore, the forest fire does not come into one's dream as an omen of final devastation or destruction, but rather as a sign of hope—a reassurance that the dreamer is not lost.

House fires symbolize excesses and dangerous energy levels within the human body. Like the automobile, a house represents the physical body. When a house fire presents itself within a dream, the dreamer needs to notice where the fire began.

An attic fire symbolizes a consuming desire or obsession within the dreamer's waking conscious state of mind.

A basement fire indicates that the dreamer's subconscious attitudes will eventually consume his or her consciousness.

A den fire indicates the dreamer's laziness will take over his life.

A kitchen fire indicates an unhealthy diet.

Office fires indicate the dreamer is overworked in his or her job.

Truck fires also are signs of working too hard and being overly involved emotionally with one's job.

Fire Alarms warn of procrastination and the inevitable rush to get out or finish because of it.

Firebreaks indicate the dreamer needs to take a break or rest from his or her fired-up emotions.

Fire Escapes suggest exit routes for a problematic or seemingly dead-end situation.

Fire Fighters symbolize self-control. They caution the dreamer to put out the fires of negative emotions or burning desires.

Fireflies indicate moments of spiritual illumination that spark into consciousness. They may suggest resolutions to problems or paths to spiritual enlightenment.

Fireflies may also refer to the Entities of Light who occasionally visit aware individuals.

Fireplaces symbolize warmth in relationships—heart warmth. Is there a roaring fire? A cold hearth? A bricked-up fireplace? An artificial one?

Fire Stations indicate an emergency need to get going on a plan, project, or path. A fire needs to be lit beneath the dreamer.

Fireworks warn of an explosive situation or belief system for the dreamer.

First Aid Kits signify the need to patch up quickly an aspect of an individual's life. Usually the dreamer will immediately know exactly what this dream symbol means, for something this urgent will certainly be a major situation in the dreamer's life.

Fish/Marine Life (See specific fish and marine life types such as CORAL,

FLOUNDER, MORAY EELS, PIRANHA, etc. for further information.)

Fishermen are signs of spiritual awareness and high advancement.

Fish Hatcheries refer to the birthing of spiritual concepts. This dream fragment speaks of spiritual talents that are developing (as embryos) within the self. Check the condition of the hatchery. Are there many or few fingerlings? What color are they?

Fishhooks symbolize a faulty spiritual search. Fishhooks snag any fish (spiritual concepts) that happen by. The spiritual search must be discriminating—it's not a sport. Be careful of what you call your truth.

Fishing signifies a spiritual search.

Fishing Lures are signs of a lazy spiritual search. The dreamer is a spiritual groupie who is easily lured to false prophets. Be discriminating!

Fish Markets represent an individual's total spiritual belief system. Are the fish rotting? Are there few or many fish? What kinds are there? Are you purchasing or walking away empty-handed?

Fishnets symbolize an undisciplined spiritual search. The dreamer doesn't know what to call the truth. He or she believes all spiritual concepts that come along.

Flag Bearers indicate loyalties. Their meaning may not be positive. Examine surrounding details to clarify this symbol's meaning.

Flags represent loyalties. These are frequently misplaced ideals held by the dreamer. Check the condition of the flag(s). What color are they? What is depicted on them?

Flagships indicate precedent-setting events or happenings. This dream symbol may also represent innovative individuals who are setting new guidelines for attitudes, beliefs, or spiritual ways.

Flamingos indicate the dreamer's tendency to live life according to his or her own personal dreams. They indicate a dreamer, one who exists with his or her head in the clouds and fails ever to firmly place both feet on the ground. Everyone needs goals, but dreams can become a serious danger when they overshadow the everyday realities of life. Face the responsibilities of the present first!

Flannel Shirts are signs of a down-to-earth personality, one who is unpretentious in all ways.

Flappers indicate a flighty and frivolous personality.

Flashbacks represent important events in the past that the individual needs to keep alive in memory.

Flash Cards symbolize truths that must consistently be used in the daily life.

Also, flash cards may represent extremely important messages the Higher Self or Guide is trying to get through to the individual's conscious mind.

Flashlights signify a need for better illumination or knowledge to be shed on a specific situation, relationship, or belief system.

Fleas indicate transmittable diseases. This dream fragment can be taken literally or it can refer to an infestation of some type within the mind or spirit.

Flies/Maggots represent faulty or destructive aspects of a situation, condition, relationship, individual, or belief system. Maggots represent the negatives that are birthing within the self.

Floodlights indicate the immediate need to get bright light on a situation, relationship, attitude, individual, or belief system so that the dreamer can see everything clearly.

Floors represent the foundations of ideals and belief systems.

    Carpeted floors indicate a warm and compassionate perspective.

    Holes in floors represent ideals or belief systems in error. (There's a hole in them.)

    Old floors signify antiquated attitudes and beliefs.

    Painted floors indicate the dreamer's tendency to outwardly subscribe to new, innovative ideas and belief systems but inwardly hold on to outdated ones.

    Rotted floors represent negative attitudes and belief systems.

    Sunken floors symbolize the dreamer's lowered values.

    Tiled floors indicate a cold personality.

    Tilted floors suggest slanted thinking, attitudes, or beliefs.

    Unfinished floors symbolize the dreamer's need for more specific and in-depth knowledge.

Florists signify one with beautiful and helpful attitudes. What are the condition of the flowers? Wilted? Fresh? Colorful? Dull?

Flounder (fish) indicate helplessness or a loss of direction in an individual's life. A spiritual floundering may be indicated here.

Flour indicates additional efforts are required by the dreamer.

Flowers indicate the dreamer's beautiful attitudes toward others. Are these flowers vibrant and strong? Or are they wilting, with their colors washed out? What color are they?

Flumes symbolize a speedy journey through one's spiritual path to awareness and enlightenment.

Flying is a symbol of awareness and/or spiritual enlightenment. This dream activity is frequently associated with actual out-of-body experiences that often give the feeling of flying.

Fog represents spiritual confusion. The dreamer is in a fog regarding his or her own beliefs.

Foghorns represent a spiritual warning. Usually this dream fragment implies that the dreamer is approaching an off-course spiritual path or belief system. This dream symbol comes from your Higher Self or personal Guide to help you steer through the fog of confusion.

Food Service Trucks are a caution for the dreamer to increase or decrease a specific intake (represented by the truck). What food is presented? Is the truck damaged? Is it new? The condition will tell you if you need to include or omit the food in question.

Football Players represent aggressiveness.

Footlights symbolize arrogance. They usually indicate that the dreamer wants to be in the spotlight, to be the leader or the one with the most knowledge. This dream fragment comes to caution the dreamer to stop trying to be the center of attention.

Footnotes signify the dreamer's need to check his or her sources of information.

Footstools indicate a rest is needed from one's journey. There are points in everyone's life or spiritual path where it's vital to pause so that present aspects can properly be assimilated. These are important respites, so be sure to honor them.

Footwear designates the manner in which an individual walks his or her life path. (See specific footwear types such as BALLET SLIPPERS, BABY SHOES, etc. for further information.)

Forceps signify a forced spiritual

awakening. This is a definite warning, for enlightenment cannot be a forced birthing.

Forest Rangers are an individual's spiritual conscience. What is the ranger doing? Is he failing to protect the forest and allowing transgressions to pass unattended? What is the condition of the forest? The ranger's clothing?

Forests denote the dreamer's overall attitudes. This applies to your daily general feelings. Are you usually content and therefore kind to others? Or are you depressed and uncommunicative? Check the condition and color of the forest for further clarity of meaning.

Forgers indicate imitations. This symbol cautions the dreamer to be himself and not to imitate others. You must follow your own unique path in life in order to achieve your personal destiny.

Formulas are presented in dreams to show the dreamer the resolution to a problem or conflict.

Forts indicate a stern personality or an introvert. This dream fragment cautions the dreamer to open up with more outward demonstrations of consideration, sympathy, and understanding of others. Do not continue to wall yourself in.

The reverse may apply. Is there an aspect of your life or personality that requires fortification or protection? Consult the details of the dream to determine the positive or negative meaning of this image.

Fortune-tellers are a warning to seek within yourself. They are also a warning to avoid living for the future instead of for the moment.

Fossils are the preserved truths. Aspects of spirituality are unalterable, carved in stone. Fossils do not refer to "old" in respect to being outdated, but rather to that which is immutable and eternal.

Four-leaf Clovers are symbols of chance. They indicate a chancy situation, relationship, or belief system.

Foxes symbolize shrewdness. Use this ability selectively and avoid negatively affecting others.

Foxholes, like dugouts, indicate a tendency for the individual to hide rather than to face his or her responsibilities. Foxholes indicate a battle of some type; therefore, heed the warning to fight your own battles.

Fractions are portions, a part of the whole, and their appearance in a dream indicates that the dreamer is only seeing part of a situation, individual, or problem. This symbol may also refer to one's spiritual beliefs.

Frames (picture/painting) symbolize one's perception of the subject represented within. What is the picture or painting of? What is the color and condition of the frame itself? Gilded? Broken? Cracked?

Freefalls are a sign of absolute faith and confidence in yourself and your path.

Freeloaders indicate a burdensome person, someone who takes advantage of others and feels no moral responsibility.

French Berets (caps) are a sign of an individual who cares about others and maintains loving attitudes.

Friction Tape symbolizes the need to smooth over a situation, relationship, or inner conflict.

Frogs/Toads are signs of a diseased physical or mental condition within the dreamer.

Frontiers indicate a new and adventurous direction for the dreamer. This may be a path already begun or one about to be embarked upon.

Frost indicates a chilly or cold personality, situation, or relationship.

Frosting is a symbol of an ultimate action or finalization.

Fruitgrowers/Pickers symbolize the cultivation of one's talents.

Fruit Trees are symbols of the dreamer's spiritual talents. Have you been spiritually fruitful, sharing your talents, skills, and abilities? Are the fruits in your dream dying on the vine? Are they lying rotten on the ground? Are they being picked too soon?

Fugues (mental) represent states of unawareness. This is a strong warning for the dreamer to be aware and responsible for his or her actions.

Funeral Homes are a sign of a death or dying situation for the dreamer. This can refer to any of the aspects of man's nature.

Funnels represent a control of an individual's knowledge intake. This indicates the need to assimilate a little at a time for proper comprehension.

Fur Hats indicate unjust and selfish attitudes.

Furnace Rooms represent an excessive intensity of character. This dream fragment may be referring to specific emotions, actions, or intents of the dreamer. Examine yourself and try to temper this intensity.

Furniture Stores indicate that which an individual surrounds the self with. Check the style of furniture presented.

Furriers symbolize apathy and greed.

Fur Shops represent hypocrisy and injustices.

Fuse Boxes represent an individual's level of comprehension of desired knowledge or spiritual concepts. Are all the fuses there? Are they all in good shape? Are some burned out?

Fuses are a symbol of an individual's measure of patience. Are you impatient to learn and trying to absorb more than you are capable of?

G

Gales/Gale Force Winds signify a warning against mental overexertion.

Gamblers represent those who take chances in life.

Gambling indicates a reckless disregard for one's mature responsibilities, either physical or spiritual.

Gambling Casinos represent risks taken. This may refer to an obsession with money or the dreamer's habit of throwing away what he or she has in hopes of what may be gained. This dream symbol frequently cautions the dreamer to appreciate his or her present life, attainments, or condition.

Game Boards warn against perceiving life or one's paths as just a game. What game is being presented in the dream? Chess? A board game? Ouija?

Gangs are negative groups. This may refer to physical or spiritual aspects of the dreamer's life.

Garages represent the pauses or restful stages of life. Just as the car represents our bodies, so, too, does the car's place of rest represent our own restful periods.

Garbage Cans are signs of waste. The dreamer should be able to understand what is meant here. Something is either being wasted or something needs to be "pitched."

Garbage Collectors are symbols of the

waste that is brought into one's life. Who is collecting the garbage in the dream? What is being collected?

Garbage Trucks symbolize an individual's accumulation of offensive matter or "garbage." What are you cluttering up your life and mind with? What are you mentally or spiritually ingesting?

Garbled Speech indicates a bewildered or perplexed mind. This suggests an individual who doesn't quite know what he or she is talking about.

Gardeners symbolize the nurturing of positive attitudes and spiritual beliefs. Check the condition of the gardener. What color is his clothing? If the garden is depicted, what condition is it in? Healthy? Wilting? Dried out or dead?

Gardens represent spiritual beauty and the blossoming of one's spiritual attitudes. Check the garden's condition. Is the garden healthy? Wilting? Dried out and dead? Is it full of colorful blossoms?

Gargoyles are symbols of distortions in life. They may refer to any of the aspects of man's nature: mental, physical, emotional, or spiritual.

Garlic/Onions indicate a negative has invaded the dreamer's physical, mental, or spiritual body. Examine this very carefully. Garlic and onions are nature's antibiotics.

Garters signify an individual's need to hold up an image before others. This dream symbol is usually a warning. Each person is unique and should never be fearful of being free to express him- or herself.

Gas Chambers caution the dreamer against being drawn into negative situations, relationships, or belief systems that can end up gassing you. This symbol often occurs when the dreamer may already be on a road to self-destruction.

Remember, the gas is usually a suffocating element.

Gaskets represent the need to seal something. The dreamer will most often know what this refers to in his or her own life. It suggests that a finalization is needed in some way.

Gas Station Attendants signify the need for strength and endurance. This dream fragment may be referring to physical life or spiritual power.

Gas Stations symbolize energy levels within the self. Check the condition of the gas station. Is it busy? Deserted?

Gas Tanks symbolize your energy levels in physical or mental activities. If they are empty, you are not productive. If they are overspilling, you are overexerting yourself.

Gates represent the way, those entrances to advancement along an individual's path.

Gearshifts indicate an individual's capacity for self-control. Each day, without consciously realizing it, we are continually switching gears. We're highly energized for our work, we slow down to eat lunch, we gear up again to finish out the day, we downshift for supper, and then we put ourselves in neutral as we relax in the evening. This dream fragment represents an individual's ability to use the proper gear for each particular activity.

Geese symbolize the dreamer's desire to escape hardships, his or her desire to fly from responsibilities or difficulties. This symbol is usually a warning to stay and to face life head-on.

Geiger Counters refer to one's intuitions. This is a suggestion for the dreamer to listen carefully to his or her feelings.

Gemstones (See STONES.)

Generators symbolize an individual's inner energies. They do not refer to physical energy, but rather to your spiritual energy for perseverance, strength of character, and determination.

Genies symbolize a dreamer, an individual who does not desire to work to achieve goals. He or she wants everything to be reality in an instant. This suggests a severely impatient and unrealistic personality who is not living in acceptance of life.

Geodes are symbols of life's hidden values. Just as a book's worth can't be judged by its cover, people or situations cannot be judged according to surface impressions. This boils down to the fact that surface impressions are meaningless. Examine your recent life situations and relationships for an accurate interpretation here. If this symbol appeared in your dream, you have probably misjudged or misinterpreted something important.

Geologists symbolize those who comprehend humankind's earth connection.

Germs symbolize negative attitudes, ideals, situations, relationships, or beliefs that the dreamer has allowed to contaminate the self.

Geysers represent the dreamer's spiritual outpouring, an eruption of awareness and enlightenment. The dreamer is openly sharing his or her compassion and goodness with others.

Ghost Dancers signify the individual's attention to spiritual protection.

Ghosts represent an individual's inner fears of the spiritual. They may also represent an actual manifestation. It's important to analyze the surrounding details of the dream to clarify the meaning of this symbol.

Ghost Towns are a sign of living in the past. This is a serious warning for the dreamer.

Giants represent one who is idolized or perceived as a giant among men. Please, there are no giants; everyone is equal.

Gift Shops symbolize the need to share or gift others with your physical or spiritual talents, abilities, or wealth.

Gingerbread Houses indicate an individual's perception of life as fantasy. The dreamer feels insecure in public and views his or her own little world as a realm of perfection.

Giraffes represent the dreamer's annoying habit of interfering. Are you frequently meddling in the private affairs of others? This dream fragment warns the dreamer to stop sticking his or her neck out and to mind the matters of his or her own backyard!

Glaciers symbolize the dreamer's frozen spirituality. Are your spiritual possessions frozen and unused? Thaw them!

Glassblowers represent creativity.

Gliders signify unawareness that is self-generated. This may also indicate that the dreamer has allowed him- or herself to glide into a situation without adequate forethought.

Gloves/Hand Coverings signify how one serves others in life.
>   *Boxing gloves* indicate a tough personality who begrudgingly gives help to others.
>   *Driving gloves* represent one who desires to be the leader in service and assistance to others.
>   *Fireproof gloves* symbolize one who feels he can handle any difficult or dangerous situation without getting burned.
>   *Kid gloves* indicate a soft touch to one's service. This symbol refers to one of great compassion.

Lace gloves represent one who is capable of handling the more difficult and delicate details of a situation.

Leather/suede gloves signify an individual who has experience in handling life's situations and is eager to give service to others.

Mittens symbolize one who bumbles his or her attempts at service because of an inability to organize his or her own life.

Opera-length gloves indicate one who expects great appreciation for service done by them.

Rubber gloves refer to individuals who would help but do not desire to get really involved—an insulated personality.

Surgical gloves represent the giving of specialized assistance and a willingness to help in all conditions and circumstances.

Welding gloves indicate an individual who is expert at welding together relationships and situations that have fallen apart.

Wool gloves symbolize a helping individual who places his or her heart into the service done. This represents a person who serves with a warm heart.

Glowworms represent a light in the darkness of one's path or search.

Glue indicates a sticky situation or relationship. What is sticking like glue? Is it someone? A belief system? An attitude?

Gnomes signify those aspects of nature that serve to enhance one's relationship with the earth.

Goalposts symbolize our life or spiritual goals. These dream fragments can serve the dreamer as important indicators of how he or she is proceeding toward those goals. Are the goalposts being torn down? Is the goalpost far away? Close?

Goats urge the dreamer against uncontrolled consumption. This is important because your health is obviously in jeopardy. Examine present circumstances to see if this symbol represents an emotional or spiritual aspect of your life. Are you voraciously ingesting knowledge that is false or not germane to your intended purpose?

Goblins symbolize spiritual fears. When one is spiritually protected and confident in his or her beliefs, there is no need to have such fears. This dream fragment is an important warning from the Higher Self to become more aware of the spiritual powers of self.

Go-carts indicate the need to sit down and give your direction a long and hard look. You're probably going around and around and not getting anywhere.

Gold is a symbol of finances. It may also refer to goodness or something good as gold. Check the surrounding details of the dream for further clarity.

Goldbrickers denote an individual who shirks his or her responsibilities in life or spiritual advancement.

Golden Calves signify misplaced priorities and false goals.

Golden Rulers connote right living and morality.

Goldfish symbolize spiritual confinements and restrictions. Please, never forget there is nothing as free as one's spirit.

Gold Rushes signify attainments that are not in keeping with one's spiritual quest. This symbol suggests that the dreamer has misplaced goals.

Golf Caps symbolize lackadaisical attitudes and a lack of serious thought.

Golf Shoes represent an individual who does not give seriousness to his or her life path, but rather tries to discover whatever leisure he or she can find along the way.

Goose Eggs symbolize an individual's serious mistakes.

Gophers signify an individual's tendency to choose many paths instead of sticking to one. This dream symbol warns the dreamer to stop digging around here and there for a comfortable niche.

Gorillas indicate emotional and mental dysfunctions on the part of the dreamer. Only you can pinpoint the intended warning here.

Gourds indicate spiritual opportunities.

Graduation Caps signify thoughts and ideals obtained through study rather than life experiences.

Graduation Gowns signify the attainment of higher knowledge though life experiences.

Grapevines represent rumors. Watch these.

Grass symbolizes the foundation of new spiritual attitudes and concepts. Are you watering and fertilizing it? Are you mowing it before it can seed and flourish? Are you letting it dry out and die because you're ignoring it? What color is it?

Grasshoppers depict a destructive force. Analyze this dream fragment carefully, for the destructive force may refer to a specific situation, belief, relationship, or individual in the dreamer's life. It may even be the dreamer's self. Since grasshoppers consume and destroy living botanicals (spiritual talents and ideals), they represent a destructive force that eats away at its victim.

Grass Roots symbolize foundations and beginnings.

Gravediggers signify negative outcomes. This means that a negative aspect of one's life is causing the dreamer to dig his own grave.

Grease/Grease Guns symbolize bribes or untrustworthiness. This dream fragment can expose ulterior motives.

Green Horns represent neophytes. This is an important symbol because you may find someone you thought was knowledgeable and experienced represented with a green horn.

Greenhouses symbolize an individual's present state of spirituality as outwardly and inwardly exemplified through his or her actions. What condition is the greenhouse in? Are there many plants and flowers within? Is it empty?

Greeting Cards indicate unspoken inner sentiments. Watch what these are saying. What color are they? Who is holding, selling, or sending them?

Grenades signify an individual who is ready to explode. This may refer to contained negative emotions or situations that can no longer be tolerated. Heed this severe warning.

Grindstones indicate the need for getting down to basics.

Gristmills symbolize one's spiritual abilities and how they are used.

Grocery Markets symbolize nutrition and diet. Is your dream grocery cart filled with junk foods? Are you purchasing fruits and vegetables? What colors are the food items you're buying? A food that is specifically bad for your system might be black or covered with bugs or rot. What kind of food is being singled out? Is it a specialty food market?

Grubs/Maggots indicate destruction in the early stages of development.

Guidebooks are significant dream symbols that are most often presented by one's Higher Self or Guide to show the way to the dreamer.

Guillotines signify actions by the dreamer that will backfire. This constitutes a grave warning to stop sticking your neck out.

Guinea Pigs symbolize an individual who is reluctant to attempt anything without seeing someone else experience it first. This suggests the dreamer is without faith and self-confidence.

Guns designate mental aberrations that are serious. This dream symbol usually precedes an explosive situation.

Guns (shooting) symbolize intense emotional conflicts. This is a severe warning to bring these to a quick resolution in a dignified manner instead of giving in to your violent impulses.

Gurus are symbols of spiritual fads. The appearance of this symbol in your dream is a warning to refrain from following others. The spiritual path is unique for each of us and we must travel it according to our own pace.

Gutters can be positive or negative symbols. In a positive sense, gutters can indicate that the individual is collecting and preserving all his or her spiritual strengths. In a negative sense, gutters can indicate a serious lack of spirituality in one's life.

Gymnasts symbolize excessive conniving. This suggests one who twists and contorts the facts.

Gypsy Moths signify individuals who would destroy another's spiritual belief system.

H

Haberdasheries represent the manner in which the dreamer's thoughts are covered or displayed. (See specific head-

gear such as DERBYS, FEDORAS, HARD HATS, etc. for further information.)

Hail symbolizes a bombardment of spiritual dogma. Just as hail can be seriously destructive, so, too, can one be harmed by an overload of new spiritual information. Beware of those who preach confusing and complicated concepts. God gave Truth in simplicity for all men to understand.

Examine the details of this dream. Is the dreamer standing in hail? Are others standing in hail while the dreamer is untouched? This would indicate it is the dreamer who is hailing down dogma on others.

Also, remember that any dreams that contain any of the natural forces of nature may in fact be premonitions of actual events.

Hair symbolizes an individual's thoughts. This doesn't necessarily refer to those thoughts that are openly expressed, but rather those that are contained within the silent confines of the mind.

Baldness is a sign of flightiness. This physical characteristic frequently represents an individual who rarely has a deep or meaningful thought or original idea.

Black/dull hair is a sign of depression. It may also indicate an individual who dabbles in the darker aspects of magic and uses his or her spiritual abilities for negative purposes.

Black/shiny hair symbolizes an esoteric thinker and a truth seeker.

Braids relate to the twisted thought process of a mentally unbalanced individual.

Curlers in hair are a sign of an individual who is trying to change his or her thoughts on an idea, concept, individual, or situation. However, the resulting curls will generate confusion.

Curly hair signifies mental confusion. This relates to an individual whose thoughts curl back and create illogical thought patterns.

Dyed hair denotes hypocrisy within the self. This indicates individuals who wish to think differently from the way they do. They thus never reveal their real, hidden thoughts.

Greased/oiled hair indicates hypocrisy of the highest order. This refers to one who slicks over true thoughts.

Hair ornaments signify extraneous concepts added to personal thoughts.

Long/shining hair symbolizes a truthful and straightforward personality.

Matted hair signifies errors in thought. This most often refers to those who are not clear thinkers. The thoughts are all stuck together and confusing.

Ponytails signify the desire not to think about something, to ignore it by putting the thoughts behind oneself. This is either a voluntary act of denial or it exemplifies the individual's inability to face facts and think about them.

Stiff hair symbolizes prejudice and narrow-mindedness. The thoughts are stiff and unyielding to new ideas or concepts.

Upswept hair indicates an individual who likes to have all their thoughts organized and neatly tied up.

White hair signifies mature and logical thinking. This indicates one who is enlightened.

Wigs allude to an individual's false thinking. Whether or not it's consciously done can be clarified by the surrounding details of the dream.

Yellow hair signifies a reluctance to share personal beliefs. This means that the individual is content within his or her own thoughts and doesn't want to share them.

Hairbrushes allude to the need to clean and straighten out an individual's thoughts, attitudes, or belief systems.

Hair Nets indicate uncontrollable thoughts need to be contained.

Hairpin Road Curves designate the dreamer's consistent tendency to travel the roads that return him or her to the beginning point. These curves signify the continual backtracking of the dreamer.

Hallways suggest periods of transition. Check lighting and condition to clarify the meaning of this dream fragment.

Halos signify spiritual enlightenment. Do not confuse this aspect with an aura.

Hammers symbolize forced enlightenment. Since enlightenment cannot be forced, this is a warning to pull back and ease up. Nothing should have to be hammered in.

Handbooks are a sign of a regimented lifestyle or path. Be more flexible and don't be afraid to extend yourself beyond your self-imposed rules and boundaries.

Hand Coverings (See GLOVES)

Handcuffs refer to an individual's belief that his or her hands are tied. This represents a situation that the dreamer usually does not want to face.

Handles indicate the need to get a handle on something. This refers to a misunderstanding or an incomprehensible concept.

Hands represent the type and quality of service done. This not only refers to service that is done for others, but also service done for the self.

Clenched hands symbolize repressed anger or anxieties.

Dirty hands indicate continual underhandedness or dirty dealings.

Handshakes symbolize friendships.

No hands symbolize procrastination and laziness.

Praying hands indicate the need for self-searching.

Red hands represent being caught red-handed.

Rough hands signify a crude personality. This represents one who is rough in his or her relationships with others. Oftentimes this individual is frequently rough on him- or herself as well.

Soft/clean hands represent honest work done through personal longsuffering.

Upturned hands have a triple meaning. They may refer to a lack of understanding, a giving personality, or an individual who always has his hand out.

Hangers indicate the need to let something go. The dreamer needs to hang it up, either temporarily or permanently.

Hard Hats refer to those individuals who maintain a hard-headed attitude. This indicates one who is difficult to convince and to introduce to new concepts.

Hardware Stores represent hard work. This may indicate that the dreamer needs to fix up his or her physical, mental, emotional, or spiritual condition.

Harlequins symbolize an individual who takes life or his or her path too lightly.

Harpoons symbolize spiritual selectivity.

Hatchets indicate negatives that need burying.

Hauling Trailers designate excessive physical weight. This dream fragment refers directly to an individual's physical body and its content of superfluous elements. Are you ingesting too many fats? Megavitamins? Too much of one thing?

Head Coverings denote deception or concealment of mental attitudes or thoughts. The specific headgear worn will give clear evidence as to the true thoughts of the individual in question. (See specific head coverings such as DERBYS, FUR HATS, GOLF CAPS, etc. for further information.)

Headlights symbolize logic (light on the subject).

Broken headlights indicate a viewpoint that is in error.

Dirty headlights symbolize not being able to see the entire picture.

Missing headlights represent a tendency to proceed blindly.

Health Clubs/Spas indicate the need to shape up an aspect of the dreamer's life. Only the dreamer will know which aspect this refers to.

Hearing Aids represent an inability to listen well. This signifies an individual's serious lack of awareness.

Hearses represent a death. This may be indicating a death of a relationship, a spiritual decline, or a premonition of an actual physical death.

Hedges indicate an individual's tendency to hedge instead of being straightforward in all ways.

Heirlooms represent those aspects of an individual's life that need to be cherished.

Helmets indicate one who feels the need to protect his or her personal thoughts or beliefs.

Herbalists signify natural healing techniques and a return to the natural way.

Hermits symbolize withdrawal. In a positive sense, this dream fragment may be advising the dreamer to withdraw from a specific activity, individual, group, or belief system. If it is a negative symbol, it is warning the dreamer to open up.

Hex Signs are not negative symbols, for they refer to the methods individuals use to protect themselves from spiritual attacks.

Hieroglyphics symbolize Truths that have been discovered by a novice. The Truths are simple, logical, and clearly comprehensible for those who are advanced in their spiritual development, but for others the Truths seem darkly esoteric and mysteriously complex. Only an increased level of awareness can prove this misconception to be in error.

High Chairs/Barstools signify immaturity. This may refer to one's attitudes, actions, or spiritual life.

High Heels indicate an individual who separates the self from his or her journey. This is a warning; one can never achieve spiritual enlightenment when one chooses to raise oneself above others.

Historical Figures symbolize an individual's own ideals. Who are you fashioning your life after? Examine this aspect of yourself and realize your own individuality.

Historical Sites always mark an important aspect for the individual dreamer. Many times these are locations of a past-life experience and will give the dreamer insights into present conditions and relationships.

Hitchhikers refer to laziness and one who moves along a path on the backs of others.

Hobby Shops indicate a need to divert the dreamer's mind to more constructive attitudes and activities.

Holograms symbolize false reality. Initially, a hologram may appear real, but upon closer inspection it is discovered to be a simple representation. This

dream fragment cautions the dreamer against accepting false impressions or surface appearances as absolute reality.

Hoodlums represent the baser aspects of the self. Are you robbing others of their knowledge, talents, or wealth? Are you swindling others in any manner?

Hope Chests represent all our dreams. What condition is the hope chest in? What color? What's inside it? Or is it empty?

Hornets/Wasps are a sign of unpleasant situations, relationships, and experiences in life. They are a symbol of life's frequent and unexpected stings.

Horoscopes are a spiritual warning against the tendency of being led through life. This is a serious caution to listen to your own inner voice and to use your free will.

Horses indicate a wild nature. Do you throw caution to the wind? Have you retained an immature and childish outlook? Do you shirk your adult responsibilities?

Hospitals are a warning to rejuvenate. Check your condition. Do you have chronic physical complaints? Are you frequently exhausted? Short-tempered? Depressed? Somewhere in the dreamer's life, a healing needs to be done. Was a specific room or medical department of the hospital depicted?

Hotels indicate a temporary situation or one in transition.

Hourglasses indicate the measure of time left. What is the hourglass's condition? Color? Is time running out?

Housepainters signify a cover-up. Check surrounding details of the dream for clarity here.

Houseplants symbolize the dreamer's attitudes as they are openly displayed within the home. Check the condition of these botanicals for further meaning.

Houses (that is, a general overview of a house) always signify the mind.

Abandoned houses represent a thoughtless personality.

Aluminum-sided houses indicate a defensive personality.

Beautifully cared for houses represent logical and right thinking.

Caves/underground houses indicate a highly discerning personality.

Desert adobes signify practicality.

Dilapidated houses indicate a renewal of attitudes is required.

Glass houses indicate egotism.

Houseboats symbolize spirituality.

Lean-tos/shacks signify apathy about possessions.

Log houses represent warm personalities.

Mansions indicate misplaced priorities.

Mountain homes/cabins signify sincerity, awareness, and serenity.

Seashore houses represent a closeness with God and a spiritual contentedness.

Shell houses represent a shallow personality.

Stone houses signify an introvert.

Tepee houses indicate a free spirit.

Unfinished houses speak of an inability to think analytically.

Humane Societies/Animal Shelters symbolize compassion.

Hummingbirds indicate frequent vacillation. This may refer to any of the four facets of man's nature.

Hunters symbolize a killing of innocence. This means the smothering of spiritual truths or positive attitudes. It can also refer to a predatory nature.

Hygrometers indicate the degree of an individual's spiritual awareness. What does the measurement read? High? Low?

I

Ice symbolizes frozen spiritual truths. They are usually voluntarily frozen by the individual.

Icehouses represent frigidity. This dream fragment refers to an unrelentingly cold personality that usually suffers from irregularities deep within the subconscious of the individual. Dig down to find these and *thaw* yourself!

Ice Makers represent those who believe there is only one spiritual way to God. Beware of teachers or proponents of only one path.

Ice Skates are a sign of an individual who skims the surface of spiritual concepts and has no full comprehension of any of the real truths.

Icons symbolize misplaced adoration.

Ignition Keys symbolize proper nutrition and physical fitness methods.

Broken keys indicate an individual who is continually breaking away from a correct diet.

Lost keys indicate that no healthful diet is subscribed to.

Wrong keys indicate a wrong type of diet.

Illusionists are individuals who are always fooling others. The appearance of this symbol in your dreams is a warning; your Higher Self is pointing these people out to you.

Import Shops represent the value of foreign ideas and concepts. The idea of "foreign" is not necessarily in the sense of another country, but rather can mean those ideas and concepts that are different from those the dreamer holds as his or her truths.

Inanimate Objects are extremely important dreamscape symbols, and their individual connotations must be incorporated into the fine fabric of the total dreamscape; each object, thread by single thread, serves to weave the final image of your dream tapestry. By giving the inanimate objects serious consideration, you will soon comprehend the magnitude of implications they represent.

It's important to remember that, although the inanimates have a general meaning, they can also connote a unique and specific representation for the dreamer. If this is the case, the precise interpretation will be all too clear for the dreamer. (See specific inanimate objects such as ALARMS, INGOTS, TALMUD, etc.)

Incense symbolizes unnecessary and excessive spiritual dogma. Incense represents the embellishments man adds to God's Truths.

Incinerators symbolize the disposal of negative attitudes or spiritual beliefs that are a waste to the individual.

Incubators symbolize the nurturing of newborn relationships or belief systems.

Index Cards indicate the need to better organize one's life.

Indian Agents represent hypocrisy and underhandedness.

Indian Corn symbolizes the seed of life.

Ingots indicate a love of money and materialism. This symbol suggests misplaced values and priorities in life.

Initials are always a message. These can be deciphered only by the individual dreamer. But be aware that such messages are usually important and worthy of close attention.

Injections represent new attitudes or beliefs. This symbol can have a positive or negative meaning, depending on what is being injected. Antibiotics? Saline? Addictive drugs? Tranquilizers?

Inscriptions are warnings. Give serious attention to what the inscription says.

Insects (See specific insect types such as LADYBUGS, MOTHS, SCORPIONS, etc. for further information.)

Insulation represents protectiveness. This may be something the dreamer needs or it may be something he or she needs to get rid of. What is the condition of the insulation? The color?

Insurance Agents signify a predatory nature, one that takes undue advantage of others, situations, or conditions.

Intaglios are signs that verify and validate the connection of man to the Universal Brotherhood of all Intelligent Lifeforms.

Intelligence Agents symbolize an invasion of privacy. This dreamscape facet will caution the dreamer to be more careful in choosing friends, or to be more private in daily dealings.

Interior Decorators refer to those individuals who would change others. This is a warning to protect yourself.

Invalids advise the dreamer to proceed upon his or her path regardless of problems or seemingly adverse conditions.

Inventors symbolize creativity and intellectual individuality.

Ironing symbolizes the quelling of a turbulent situation or relationship. You're getting it ironed out, or you need to iron it out.

Irons indicate the need to straighten something out. This could be one's thoughts, attitudes, relationships, situation, or beliefs.

Ivory alludes to the value of relationships. Are you removing it from a dead animal? Are you carving it? Are you just standing back and admiring it? Selling it? Giving it away?

Ivory Towers represent those places of

seclusion one tends to escape to. This does not necessarily suggest egotism, but rather withdrawal.

J

Jackals symbolize an individual's predatory nature.

Jack-in-the-boxes symbolize an insensitive personality. This dream fragment relates to an individual who never perceives the seriousness of life.

Jackknives signify impatience.

Jack-o'-lanterns represent an individual's perspective of life. How is it carved? Happy? Sad? Cruel and mean? Scary? Scared?

Jade represents protection from negative influences.

Jalopies indicate an individual who is a freethinker.

Jams/Jellies symbolize troubling situations, relations, or attitudes. This image suggests one who gets in a jam.

Janitors refer to the need to clean up one's house!

Jeans are a sign of an individual who is a nonconformist and free spirit, often a nonchalant personality.

Jellyfish represent the dreamer's lack of firm convictions. Such people use their stinging defense mechanisms to maintain their air of free-floating irresponsibility.

Jewelers signify the extraneous aspects of one's life. Check to see what kind of metals the jeweler is working with. Silver? Gold?

Jewelry (excessive) indicates an individual who frequently exaggerates in order to convince others.

Jewelry Boxes indicate an individual's storehouse of riches. Are they gold? Silver? Gems? Are they used for the self only or shared with others? Is the box empty? Overflowing? Stolen?

Jewelry Stores represent exterior values. These may be distinct from those values held within the self.

Jigsaw Puzzles symbolize the problems in an individual's life. Frequently this dream fragment will actually show the dreamer how to put the puzzle together.

Jockeys represent an individual with a tendency to be conniving and always ready to jockey into an advantageous position.

Jokers (cards) symbolize humiliation. This dream fragment suggests that the dreamer has been ridiculed or made a joke of.

Jolly Rogers represent fatalistic relationships, situations, paths, or belief systems. The dreamer should take this as a warning.

Journals represent the dreamer's urgent need to record events.

Judges always represent justice. But be sure to recall the condition of the judge and what type and color of robe he or she wore.

Jugglers symbolize efficiency and organization. Take this symbol as a reassurance that you can juggle responsibilities in life without letting some fall by the wayside.

Jujus are a serious warning to believe in yourself instead of placing your faith and trust in objects of superstition.

Jumpseats symbolize gullibility and how an individual allows him- or herself to be taken for a ride.

Jungle Gyms symbolize an individual's twisted life-style or spiritual path.

Jungles represent spiritual confusion and a schizophrenic state of mind. A frequent dream involving yourself within a jungle suggests that you need to seek professional psychiatric counseling.

Junk Collectors symbolize hidden values.

Juries are synonymous with your Higher Self and all those entities that would have spiritual authority over your direction. In the best case, you will be one of the jury members. This means that you, yourself, can be trusted to analyze and judge your own actions.

K

Kabbala represents the higher esoteric aspects of the spiritual truths. Check to note the condition of this book in your dream to see if it is right for you to delve into. Is it tattered? Dusty? Torn? Like new? Does a light surround it? Is it in shadow?

Kaddish is a Jewish prayer said over a deceased relative. It symbolizes an individual's attitude toward death.

Kaleidoscopes refer to distorted perceptions of an individual that keep altering.

Kamikazes represent a self-destructive personality. This may refer to an individual's emotional, mental, physical, or spiritual state.

Kangaroos symbolize the dreamer's continual tendency to be overprotective. This dream fragment counsels the dreamer to loosen the ties that bind. This does not necessarily imply that the dreamer needs to cut those important ties, but do give more freedom so that those precious ties will not break.

Kayaks symbolize an extremely personal and individualized spiritual journey.

Keepsakes are a sign of an individual's recognition and cherishing of his or her memories.

Kennels represent a possessive friend or other close individual. This dream fragment suggests that someone is keeping another contained within a relationship.

Kernels/Seeds symbolize an individual's inner talents. These may need to be nourished and developed. What color and condition are the seeds?

Keyholes represent opportunities in life. Are you using the keyhole? Just looking at it? Is it plugged?

Keys symbolize solutions to problems. What color and condition is the key? Is it rusted? Bent? Broken? New and shiny? Their condition speaks of how the dreamer chooses to use them.

Kibbutz represents an individual's community involvement. Is the kibbutz deserted? Crowded? Resourceful?

Kilns represent work applied for advancement. This dream fragment will reveal how much energy the dreamer applies to his or her journey.

Kindergartens signify a beginning learning stage.

Kings (See QUEENS)

Kitchens indicate the manner of food preparation. Check the dream kitchen's condition and color.

Kites symbolize an individual's reaching for inner understanding of his or her own mental and emotional impulses.

Kivas represent an individual's personal choice for practicing spiritual meditation. This symbol is important because it can show you whether or not your special place is right or not. Check the kiva's condition and color. If it's crowded, your choice is not good.

Klieg Lights indicate that much more light must be shed on an issue or subject for the dreamer to comprehend it completely.

Kneeling is a sign of subjugation. Watch what or whom is being knelt *to*. No one should kneel to anyone except God Himself!

Knights signify those individuals who have a tendency to fight for the rights of another.

Knitting Needles represent a manipulative individual or situation. This symbol is often a warning to the dreamer that he or she is being manipulated. But perhaps you yourself are doing the needling and controlling?

Knobs signify self-motivation. What condition and color are the knobs? Are they loose? Falling off? Solid? Wood? Metal?

Knots symbolize life problems that entangle the individual.

Knuckles symbolize conflicts. Are you the angered one with white knuckles? Check the surrounding details of the dream and correct the situation before it gets out of control.

Kowtowing signifies humbleness and subjugation.

L

Labels are a specific warning. Read what the label says. If it is without words (blank), then it's a warning for the dreamer to stop labeling others.

Labyrinths symbolize a complex path. This dream fragment indicates that your life or spiritual path will take many twists and turns—it is not a straight road. But all labyrinths have an end. You will not become lost, but you will need patience and acceptance along the way.

Lacquers indicate how something is finalized. This symbol refers to a deed, situation, or specific condition and how it has been finished. Is the lacquer cracked? Dull? Shiny? Smooth or rough? What colors are involved?

Ladders signify upward progression. This symbol will often clue the dreamer in on his or her present level of development. Check the condition of the ladder. Is it falling? Leaning? Rungs missing? Are there broken rungs below you? If so, you've advanced to a stage you're not ready for. You need to step down and repair the broken rung.

Ladybugs represent positive forces that serve to nullify negative and irritating or damaging factors in one's life.

Lambs always symbolize God.

Lamplighters represent spiritual advisors and teachers, people who light the way.

Lamps suggest illumination, a light on a situation or concept.

Land Developers symbolize avarice and the destruction of spirituality.

Land Mines symbolize those pitfalls or dangers that are a part of all life and spiritual paths.

Landslides represent a backsliding on one's path.

Lather indicates a situation, attitude, or belief that is riled up. The dreamer needs to settle down, clear away the confusion, and see with clarity.

Lathes indicate the need to formulate beliefs for yourself.

Laughter suggests a vivacious and gregarious personality. Check surrounding details of the dream. Are others laughing at you? If so, this dream fragment is a warning to check your actions and reexamine how best to proceed. The laughter of others shouldn't hamper your own progress. Perhaps more discretion is required.

Laundromats indicate a need for cleansing. This symbol frequently refers to both your outward expressions and your inner self.

Lava represents an inner seething of the self. Vent these emotions and address the reason for them.

Lawn Mowers indicate an individual's continued complacency with his or her beliefs. The dreamer is not allowing any growth to be accomplished.

Layered Clothing signifies a personality that is prepared for any eventuality. This rarely indicates a street person.

Leases signify extensions of time. Note any dates.

Leashes signify self-generated limitations. This symbol refers to those limits you place on your ability to learn and accept new knowledge.

Ledgers symbolize the dreamer's spiritual record or balance sheet. How does the ledger look?

Lemmings represent the dreamer's negative and destructive tendency to follow blindly another individual or a crowd. This may also indicate that the dreamer needs to develop a more individualized personality or belief system.

Leotards signify a second skin and indicate an individual who is tough and has perseverance.

Leprechauns represent the hidden aspects of spiritual development and the attainment of deeper wisdom.

Letter Openers symbolize the need for an individual to open up communications.

Librarians signify those who cherish knowledge.

Libraries (public) symbolize old knowledge. Are you checking out books? What types? Are you returning them? What colors are the jackets? What is their condition?

Library/Study (home) indicates that research or additional knowledge is required. What is the activity in the home library? Who is there? Which books are emphasized?

Lice suggest an unclean and unhealthy condition. This symbol may refer to an individual's actual physical conditions, or if the lice are seen in the hair, it can instead indicate an unclean or negative thought process.

Licenses represent individual rights, those actions, attitudes, beliefs, and paths that the dreamer has the right to pursue. You do not, for instance, have the license to tell anyone else how to live.

Liens signify spiritual debts. This refers to those unbalanced spiritual debts that must be paid before further advancement can be made by the individual.

Lifeguards symbolize that which is lifesaving. This symbol may refer to your belief system, to individuals, groups, concepts, or any other facet of your life that may act as a savior.

Life Preservers represent opportunities to gain spiritual advancement. They represent second chances.

Lighters symbolize that which gives the

light of illumination or awareness. This symbol may refer to a "who" rather than a "what," depending upon how the lighter is being used.

Lighthouses represent spiritual wisdom. Check the condition of the house. Is the beacon bright and strong? Weak? Out? This symbol represents how well your own inner spiritual light shines out among your peers.

Lightning Rods indicate a deep personal desire for a connection with God.

Lilliputians symbolize inferiority complexes.

Limelights indicate a superiority complex on the part of whomever the light is shining on. They may also indicate someone who should be in this spotlight. Surrounding details of the dream will clarify this for you.

Limousines are a warning to the dreamer to watch his or her tendency toward egotism and excessive concern over personal appearances.

Liniments represent that which soothes life's rough times.

Lions symbolize a braggart.

Lip Reading indicates words with hidden meaning.

Liquor represents negative forces in life that will impede your progress on your life path.

Living Rooms refer to the quality of an individual's attitudes about daily life. What condition is the living room in? What is the style of furniture? Colors?

Loafers (shoes) symbolize an individual who loafs along his or her life or spiritual path.

Lobsters indicate spiritual vacillation. Are you reaching out and grabbing at any

doctrine that presents itself? This symbol is often a warning to search for spiritual truths more carefully.

Locksmiths symbolize life's problems and their ultimate solutions. Don't look to others to solve your personal problems. Your solutions will come from within yourself! You have the keys.

Lodestars represent the way. This is a beautiful symbol that refers to the dreamer's spiritual path and its correctness.

Longshoremen symbolize how one's spiritual talents are used. Are they stored? Are they shipped out?

Looms symbolize the foundations of the many spiritual concepts that are woven into the Collective Wisdom of the Universal Truths.

Loons always represent mental aberrations. Check details of the dream to analyze whom this important message refers to.

Loopholes signify an individual with a conniving personality who seeks ways to wrangle out of things in life.

Lotteries symbolize chances taken in life that have little possibility of success.

Lovers refer to man's loving nature. What are the lovers doing? Are they arguing? Fighting? Loving?

Luggage represents the extraneous attitudes and beliefs one carries with him or her on the life path.

Lumberjacks represent destructive forces applied to spirituality. This symbol is a warning that the dreamer is either already exposed to some negative spiritual force or soon will be. Be extremely aware!

Lumberyards represent construction or building. This most often refers to relationships and the need for building strength in them.

M

Mace represents an individual's personal defenses against an outside attack.

Machine Guns symbolize a constant mental state of anger.

Magicians symbolize false prophets and the sleight-of-mind used to mesmerize the masses.

Magic Shops represent the many types of trickery available to individuals who would claim to have spiritual talents.

Magnets signify compulsions and obsessions.

Magnifying Glasses indicate deeper understanding is needed by the dreamer.

Magpies indicate the intake of something negative. This could be gossip listened to or "garbage" eaten. This symbol is a warning. Magpies represent individuals who continually ingest garbage in the form of spiritual concepts.

Maids refer to service given.

Mail People indicate the need for communication or warn the dreamer to expect to receive a message.

Makeup (cosmetics) symbolizes false fronts generated from insecurities.

Manholes represent life's pitfalls, which sometimes specifically include certain spiritual belief systems.

Maps appear in dreams to help you realize your life's direction so that you can more quickly accomplish your purpose. This message comes from your Higher Self or Guide.

Martyrs symbolize individuals who believe they're being persecuted.

Masks signify an individual's hypocrisy.

Masquerade Costumes symbolize an individual's desires or fears. The character presented will help you determine the dream's specific meaning.

Mausoleums symbolize buried memories or thoughts.

Meatpacking Houses represent the body's assimilation of various meats. Pay honest and close attention to this symbol. What color are the meats? Are they clean? Are bugs on the floor or infesting the food?

Medals are commendations from above.

Medical Buildings always indicate a need for health care. This symbol may refer to your physical, mental, emotional, or spiritual health.

Medical People indicate the dreamer needs some physical attention. What type of medical practitioner appeared in your dream? A chiropractor? An internist? A dentist? A therapist?

Medicine Chests indicate the need to exercise caution regarding drugs. Check the condition and color of the chest. If it's open, what drugs are represented? Check their specific color and condition.

Medicine Pipes symbolize honesty, trustworthiness, and a sealed bond.

Medicine Women signify an individual who is a natural-health practitioner.

Men's Suits refer to the business side of the individual represented. This symbol may indicate that the individual is always business oriented. This is not a good sign, for everyone needs to relax and be themselves.

Menus refer to choices in life.

Mercenaries indicate an unconscionable and conniving personality, an individual who would do anything for material gain.

Mermaids symbolize spiritual indecision.

Meteors signify incoming spiritual illumination or awareness.

Meter Readers symbolize the rate of one's progress. Recall what kind of meter was being read in the dream.
> *Electric meters* indicate the need to regulate knowledge and do more introspection and analyzing.
> *Gas meters* indicate a need for the individual to monitor his or her energy levels better.
> *Water meters* indicate the need for more stability in the individual's spiritual journey.

Metronomes indicate the need for the dreamer to use his or her time in a more efficient manner, to pace him- or herself better.

Mice symbolize the little irritations of life that nibble away at one's patience and perseverance.

Microphones indicate a great need for the dreamer or individual represented to be heard.

Microscopes indicate the need to more closely analyze an aspect of the dreamer's life or belief system.

Mildew symbolizes inattention. This symbol usually refers to an aspect of the dreamer's life that must be given immediate attention.

Military Caps suggest a regimented thought process, one that is not prepared to extend itself toward new ideas.

Military Officers represent arrogance.

Military Posts indicate domination. Are you the general? A soldier who takes orders?

Milk represents immaturity. This symbol can also indicate a physical requirement for more dairy foods in your diet.

Milk Trucks suggest the individual's need for an increase or decrease in the amount of dairy products in his or her diet. Details of the dream may give a more explicit meaning. Is the dreamer driving the truck? Leaving it? Is the milk truck coming toward you or going away?

Mimes represent straightforwardness through one's actions. This dream fragment suggests an individual who is open and honest; you wear your heart on your sleeve.

Miners signify the spiritual search. This symbol refers to the digging one does for the truths that lie just beneath the surface.

Miner's Hats symbolize an individual who has a knack for shedding light on ideas, thoughts, or belief systems. This refers to one who does not seek knowledge or information in the dark, but rather gives careful consideration to all matters.

Mines symbolize the mother lode of spiritual truths that are waiting to be discovered.

Minnows signify an insecure and nervous personality in relation to spiritual truths.

Mirages symbolize illusions and conceptual beliefs that are in error.

Mirrors represent self-examination. The appearance of this image in your dream indicates that you are not looking honestly at yourself.
> *Clouded mirrors* are a warning that the dreamer has an unclear perspective on him- or herself.

Colored mirrors indicate a viewpoint associated with the meaning of the color in question. Check the COLOR section for a clarification of this unique aspect.

Cracked mirrors indicate a distorted view of yourself.

Magnifying mirrors signify an exaggerated view of your self-worth.

Pitted mirrors indicate irregularities within yourself that you might not be aware of.

Warped/slanted mirrors suggest that you have an unbalanced view of yourself.

Moaning represents a regretful realization of transgressions voluntarily committed.

Moccasins indicate an individual who proceeds cautiously while still being aware on his or her path.

Mockingbirds signify an inability to think for oneself, an absence of a sense of individuality.

Models represent vanity. This symbol may also refer to the dreamer's desire to have a model to emulate.

Molds (forms) symbolize those individuals who advocate one uniform way. Take this as a warning and remember that we all make our own life. No one is the same or a replica of another.

Moles (rodents) represent an uncommunicative personality. Take this symbol as advice to open up to your fellow men and to face life with acceptance and light. Stop hiding from life's situations, problems, or conditions.

Monasteries represent a religious confinement. This symbol indicates the dreamer's preference for maintaining spiritual anonymity.

Money (See TELLERS)

Mongeese represent a sharp intelligence and quick wit. They represent the dreamer's extraordinary mental ability to perceive deceptions. In life, mongeese catch and kill snakes; therefore, they are quick to perceive and overpower the sneaky and devious.

Monkeys represent the dreamer's lack of seriousness and maturity. The dreamer needs to stop being so nonchalant.

This symbol can also be a warning to stop aping others' actions, ideas, or personalities.

Monks symbolize spiritual reclusiveness. This is a serious warning for the dreamer to share more of his or her spirituality in life.

Monuments represent personal loyalties. This dream symbol may have a positive or negative meaning. The condition of the monument will clarify the matter.

Beautiful/whole monuments indicate the dreamer should place his or her loyalties there.

Crumbling/marred monuments signify a loyalty that is misplaced.

Moon represents an individual's spiritual gifts and the frequency with which they're used constructively.

Full moon symbolizes the dreamer's daily use of his or her gifts. This is a positive symbol, as it reaffirms the dreamer's consistent acts of goodness and compassion.

Moon sliver indicates that the dreamer is only partially using his or her talents for the benefit of others.

Moon eclipse represents the dreamer's consistent use of his or her abilities for the wrong end. This is a serious warning.

New moon indicates that, although the dreamer possesses many gifts, they are not being used.

Moonflowers signify spiritual talents that are never hidden or withheld from others. This indicates a spiritually giving individual.

Mops indicate a cleanup is required. The dreamer will know what this refers to in his or her life.

Moray Eels indicate spiritual aggressiveness. Do you frequently find yourself trying to defend your personal beliefs? Do you continually attempt to convert others? This is a warning to cease such negative behavior.

Morse Codes symbolize misunderstandings, possibly on the part of the dreamer himself.

Mortar signifies the need for the dreamer to cement a situation, relationship, or belief system.

Morticians symbolize spiritual misconceptions and misplaced values. Take this symbol as a warning that you may be acting according to concepts that are lifeless and useless to you.

Mosaics symbolize the many aspects that come together to create the beautiful whole. This symbol may be referring to any of man's natures. Check the condition and color of the mosaic. What does it create? Are pieces missing?

Mosquitoes represent the possible drawbacks and negative events that can mar enjoyable activities or situations.

Motels represent transitions in life, temporary conditions, situations, or beliefs.

Mothballs indicate an individual's need to preserve something from being destroyed.

Mother Goose symbolizes an individual's tendency to fantasize about life in a childish manner.

Mothers signify nurturing. Mothers also symbolize a vehicle of life-giving concepts or enlightenment.

Moths symbolize a destructive force within the home. They also can represent a self-destructive attitude or belief on the part of the dreamer.

Motor Homes represent a temporary or transitional physiological feeling of illness or well-being. This needs close examination.

Mountain Climbers represent work applied to attain a goal.

Mountains symbolize the obstacles a dreamer faces before he or she can attain a goal. Mountains may also personify the dreamer's success in conquering those same obstacles. The intent will be clear. Is the dreamer at the mountain's foothills? Or is he or she standing triumphantly atop its peak?

Movie Producers represent false perspectives and those who produce them.

Movie Stars represent hypocrisy. This symbol has to do with one's way of living and perspective on life. The individual referred to is probably fooling him- or herself by attempting to ignore reality and to create a world of his or her own. The dreamer wants to live in a self-created fantasy world based on contrived viewpoints and attitudes. Such people are incapable of seeing situations as they actually are. They tend to glamorize their efforts or situations.

Also, check which movie star was represented in the dream. This gives clearer meaning to this symbol's total intent.

Movie Theaters signify the dreamer's unrealistic viewpoints or beliefs. This symbol is a warning of a tendency to escape into a self-created fantasy instead of facing life.

Moving Vans symbolize the need for the dreamer to relocate his or her home to a more healthful climate, or to be about his or her spirit's purpose in another locale.

Mud Rooms are a sign of negative attitudes brought into the home.

Mulch/Compost indicates a nurturing need. Take this as a warning to seek out those aspects of your life that have not been used; they've been allowed to grow stale and unfertilized and you need to nurture them.

Mules symbolize stubbornness and narrow-mindedness. A deeply inflexible character is indicated here.

Mummies indicate a stubborn and unyielding personality.

Museums represent antiquated thoughts or beliefs.

Music represents harmony between men or within the self.

Musicians represent spiritual harmony within the individual.

Music Shops signify an individual's spiritual awareness. Examine what type of music is being purchased or listened to. Is it harmonious or cacophonous? What colors are the album jackets?

Mythical Characters indicate prevarications. Do you frequently tell falsehoods? Is your life a living lie?

In rare instances, the mythical characters may actually present themselves as a warning of future situations that may be entering the dreamer's life. Analyze the character presented for the precise message here, for not all of these characters were mythical.

N

Nail Files represent the need to learn acceptance and to file down anxieties and impatience.

Nails (finger) symbolize the level of acceptance one has.
Bitten nails signify an absence of acceptance.

Broken nails symbolize a clawing for goals and an impatience for results.
Manicured nails signify total acceptance.

Nails (metal) signify the need for attachments. The dreamer will understand the specific meaning of this symbol, for there is an obvious need for attachment somewhere in his or her life.

Nakedness represents the act of exposing the reality of one's true self. This is a sign of real honesty without any sense of needing to hide anything shameful.

Napkins indicate the level of preparedness and awareness. Check the condition and color of the napkins to evaluate the dreamer's state of awareness.

Native Americans signify the sacredness of man's bond with all of nature.

Nature Aspects. Nature is in itself often the very foundation of the scene of a dream. Nature, in all its diversity, must play an integral role in the accurate interpretation of a dream. (See specific nature aspects such as ELEMENTS, GEODES, SWAMPS, VALLEYS, etc.)

Nautilus (shell) symbolizes the multidimensional interconnections of the Collective Wisdom.

Navigators are a sign of the set course of an individual's path. If you are not the navigator, something is wrong. Is the navigator confused? Lost? Setting a direct course? A new one?

Neckties indicate a choking personality that smothers concepts and thoughts.

Nests are a product of insecurity. They represent those aspects of life that the individual uses to find comfort and security.

Nets symbolize entrapments.

Newspapers signify awareness.

Night-robes represent the individual's desire to cover up his or her darker thoughts.

Night Watchmen symbolize an individual's protective powers. If the watchman is not doing the job or is sleeping, take this as a warning to correct this fault in yourself. Each individual must be prepared to protect his or her spirit.

Nooses are warnings of wrong paths or beliefs.

Notary Publics signify approval of one's life on the part of your Higher Self or Guide. Their appearance in your dream is a sign that your Higher Self or Guide agrees with how you are progressing with your life or spiritual path.

Novels signify escapism. They represent the manner by which the individual withdraws from the realities of life. Check the type of novel. Is it a romance? A mystery? Is it gory? An X-rated adult novel? The subject of the novel in your dream can be very revealing.

Novocaine represents emotional distancing and numbness. It's important to check all aspects of this dream fragment, for it may be advising the dreamer of the necessity to distance or numb him- or herself to current emotional disturbances, or it may be warning the dreamer to stop numbing him- or herself to the same.

Nuclear Plants symbolize a destructive personality or situation that has the capacity to contaminate all those around the dreamer.

Numbers provide vitally important information in dreams. Precise numerical amounts reveal additional meanings to the dream's landscape.

Numbers may be presented in the literal form of actual numerals (such as the numbers of a year, a day circled on a calendar, or a lone visual numeral), or they may appear in the form of objects appearing in multiples (such as three windows, eight insects, etc.). Whatever form they take, pay close attention to the numbers, for they are there to extend the dream's meaning and are crucial to interpreting the dream accurately.

One always represents the Universal God, the unity of spiritual truths, a personal oneness with the Creator.

Two represents weakness (spiritual, mental, emotional, or physical), since it is the split of one. It represents mental vacillation, a tendency toward chronic indecision, or spiritual fluctuations. Are you always sitting on the fence, never truly making any solid commitments one way or the other?

Three symbolizes inner energy and strength. This, too, can refer to any of the four aspects of man's nature.

Four signifies the physical body of the dreamer or whomever the number is symbolically associated with.

Five represents changes in the dreamer's mental, emotional, physical, or spiritual situations.

Six symbolizes the ultimate strength of the double three. Most frequently, the number six refers to mental, emotional, or spiritual strengths rather than physical ones.

Seven always has to do with the six spiritual forces that function within the physical body in conjunction with the body's own force; hence the total of seven. Seven is a high spiritual number. Are you ignoring your personal spiritual obligations? Are you meditating regularly? Are you opening yourself for the wrong purposes? Or perhaps you are working hard toward advancement and are being given a nod of approval from a higher source. Only you can decipher the exact meaning of the number seven in your dream by looking at yourself openly and honestly.

Eight signifies the inability to analyze situations correctly. It symbolizes unclear thinking. Are your judgments tainted by your personal prejudices? Is your analytical ability handicapped by bigotry, personal attitudes, or negative feelings harbored deep within yourself? The number eight indicates the need to shed prejudices, which, in turn, frees the mind and allows room for just and right thinking.

Nine is the strength of three tripled. Nine represents completion. Nine is an indication that you are achieving your goals.

Ten is an end unit. It is the closing of a circle. Ten therefore represents a oneness; it is a number of the wholeness of mental, emotional, physical, and spiritual characteristics. Ten ultimately signifies a return to God.

Eleven represents misplaced values. Attitudes and viewpoints are out of line, and priorities are not justifiable.

Twelve always signifies the power of truth and the force of spirituality. Twelve symbolizes spiritual leaders and the Bringers of Truth, enlightenment, and the knowledge of the Higher Self.

Numbers on a house represent a present or future relationship between the dreamer and the occupant of the dwelling. It can also indicate numerical meaning for your own house.

Numbers on a telephone represent some present or future relationship. Since the telephone itself represents a forthcoming communication, try dialing your dream number to see if there is a specific significance to it. Numbers on a telephone can also refer to how and in what manner you are interrelating with others—how you talk to them.

Numbers/dates on a tombstone always signify a death date. This death may be the real thing or it may represent a possibility. Usually other surrounding details of the dream will clue you in on the individual involved. Never assume it refers to yourself unless the dream specifically points in that direction, for it is a rarity to be shown one's own time of demise.

Numbers on a license plate most always are a warning of a future vehicular accident involving the dreamer or someone close to the dreamer *and* the vehicle represented. Sometimes this aspect also refers to a future connection of some kind between the dreamer and the license owner.

Numbers out of sequence on a timepiece indicate that your day, perhaps your life, is out of order . . . your timing is off. Do you begin a project and then leave it before it's completed? Do you procrastinate too frequently? This indicates that your life requires more organization. Take one thing at a time and complete it before moving on to the next. Be more efficient with your time management.

Numbers all the same on a timepiece signify a need for the dreamer to slow down. Take particular note of what number appears on the timepiece. Is it twelve noon? Perhaps you need to give more attention to your midday meal. Or perhaps you need to give more thought to truth and your personal enlightenment. Is the number seven? Perhaps you need to direct more attention to spirituality in your daily life when interacting with your peers. You need to live your spiritual beliefs when dealing with others. Is the number five? Perhaps you need to stop working when the workday is over (you're obviously overworking). Or it may mean that changes are forthcoming. Only the dreamer can accurately decipher the meaning of the clock time.

Numbers in an airport terminal represent warnings. Perhaps you should refrain from boarding a specific flight, or the numbers may be indicating an alternative flight that you *should* take. As in all dreams, the surrounding circumstances and conditions will enable you to differentiate between these two meanings.

Also, since an airplane's medium is the air (which indicates the mental aspects of man's nature), the numbers in the airport terminal may well indicate a condition of the dreamer's mental state.

Numbers circled or outstanding on a calendar indicate that day's significance for the dreamer. Be particularly aware on that day. If the date is *surrounded in black,* it may symbolize a death date; such a date is not necessarily that of the dreamer's, but perhaps refers to someone near to him or her. On the other hand, if the date is *surrounded in white or appears to shimmer,* it is a sign that something wonderful will occur on that day.

Numbers in the sky represent a communication from the highest Source. If the number is higher than twelve, the individual digits must be interpreted in sequence.

Numbers under water always designate the dreamer's spirituality. These numbers refer to the dreamer's spiritual thoughts and his or her interactions with peers—or with God. Again, if the number seen is more than twelve, interpret each digit sequentially.

Numbers on medication are a warning that you might want to increase or decrease the dosage you're taking. For instance, if you are pres-

ently ingesting three pills per day and the dream depicted a pill with the number two on it, you should consider decreasing your intake to two. Similarly, if you're taking one pill a day and the dream depicts three, you might want to increase your dosage. (You should, of course, check with your physician before making any such changes in the dosages of your medication.)

Numbers on grocery items are a warning to increase or decrease the amount of that food in your diet. This dream is particularly significant for those people who require a major modification of diet in order to maintain a healthy physiological system. Diet dreams must never be taken lightly.

Numbers on foreheads of people indicate that specific individual's true mental or spiritual state. A dream of this kind affords the dreamer important insight into the true nature of the hidden personalities of the individual depicted. It can be a warning or a much-needed revelation.

Numbers over the hearts of people signify that individual's true emotional state.

Numbers on a lottery ticket suggest a forthcoming change in the dreamer's financial status. This is not necessarily a positive omen. Perhaps the lottery ticket is torn in half? Is it dirtied? Check all details for a proper interpretation.

Numbers on a bankbook indicate a forthcoming change in the dreamer's riches. Mind you, this may not refer to the dreamer's financial life, but rather to riches bestowed by God. What color is the bankbook? Is the bankbook oversize and the numerals minute by comparison? If so, you have a great ability to help your peers, but you are not being generous with your talent. Correct this!

Nurse Caps symbolize an individual whose thought processes are tightly intertwined with compassion and deep caring.

Nurse Shoes indicate an individual who gives any assistance he or she can to others while walking his or her own life or spiritual path.

Nuts almost never refer to food. It's important to understand that our Higher Self possesses a wry sense of humor (as you may already have seen in the very literal meanings of many of the dream symbols). The meaning of nuts is also quite literal in that they signify that the dreamer is nuts or crazy because of something he or she has done or *is* doing.

O

Oars symbolize hard work and long-suffering while on the spiritual path. They represent the dreamer's struggles and backbreaking labor.

Oases symbolize those aspects of the dreamer's life that serve as places of cool respite. This may also apply to someone in the dreamer's life.

Obis signify those cumbersome aspects one carries around with him or her. This symbol can refer to emotional facets that are extraneous, such as grudges, or spiritual issues that are not germane to the truth.

Obituaries are a serious warning of a forthcoming death—either physical, mental, or spiritual. Pay close attention to recalling the name and date mentioned in the obituary.

Observatories indicate a closer and deeper analysis is required. The dreamer will usually know whether this refers to a current life situation or a spiritual belief.

Or perhaps it is recommending a re-evaluation of a particular relationship the dreamer is in.

Obstetricians symbolize those who have the knowledge and wisdom to bring forth new life or spiritual awakening in the dreamer.

Octopuses indicate a spiritual flailing. This dream fragment represents an individual's subconscious call for spiritual guidance and assistance, for the person is randomly reaching out in all directions for whatever spiritual concept he or she can grab on to.

Odometers signify an individual's progress in life.
> *Low mileage numbers* indicate a need to get going.
> *High mileage numbers* indicate that the dreamer has covered a great deal of ground and is now nearly finished.

Office Supply Stores indicate more tools are needed to fulfill the dreamer's purpose.

Ogres denote a constantly grumpy personality.

Oil Cans signify the need for the dreamer to smooth over irritations in his or her relationships with others. Also, this may refer to the dreamer's attitudes of him- or herself. Do you frequently feel grated by the words or actions of others? Remember acceptance!

Oilcloths indicate the need for more healthful eating habits.

Oil Refineries indicate a refinement is needed in the dreamer's current plans, spiritual path, or beliefs. It means that these are still too crude to accomplish anything productive or valuable.

Old-fashioned Hats symbolize old-fashioned thought processes or belief systems.

Old-fashioned Shoes signify an old-fashioned path that will not provide the individual with the opportunities needed to reach his or her spiritual goals.

Old Folks always represent wisdom unless they are depicted as senile or forgetful.

Opera Houses indicate social activities that are counterproductive. This is because operas are a replay of former events or programs.

Operations (medical) signify an individual's urgent need to operate on him- or herself. This may refer to how one interacts in a relationship, one's emotional state, one's mental health, or one's physical condition. This can also indicate an individual's spiritual state, path, or belief system. Since operations are the last resort, a cutting out of a diseased condition, this is an extremely important warning, for something in the dreamer's life needs emergency attention!

Opossums symbolize the dreamer's backward or inverted views. This dream fragment warns the dreamer to stop turning things around to suit him- or herself!

Optical Stores symbolize the need for an individual to clarify his or her perspective.

Optics indicate the need to clarify sight or perspective.

Optometrists signify those who have the knowledge and wisdom to bring enlightenment to others. Sometimes this dreamscape component will extend itself into a full-fledged optometric examination of the dreamer. This is unusually revealing, for the result of that examination will clearly show the dreamer exactly how he or she has been perceiving things and show what changes might be needed.
  A farsighted diagnosis represents a need to look at issues more closely.

A nearsighted diagnosis indicates the need to extend one's perspectives and sights.
A "tunnel vision" diagnosis means the dreamer must work to view issues from all angles.
A cataracts diagnosis indicates the need to cut through the opinionated ideas that are clouding one's perspective.

Orange Sticks symbolize an individual's need to clean up his or her act. This symbol specifically refers to the dirt beneath your fingernails—your underhanded manner of operating.

Orbits signify an unproductive situation or relationship, something that's always going round and round without ever making progress.

Organ Grinders remind the dreamer to pause for contemplation along life's path.

Orthopedic Shoes indicate an individual who makes corrections as needed along his or her path. They are aware of what needs to be changed within themselves and take active steps to make the required adjustments. This symbol suggests one who accepts the detours and obstacles in life and compensates for them.

Ostriches refer to man's subconscious denials. Many times this symbol is a warning to the dreamer to be less apprehensive about life and new concepts. Are you a timid individual, or one who simply denies problems and hides from them? Do you shun the spiritual truths because it is easier to remain comfortably ensconced within accepted traditional dogmas?

Ouija Boards are a severe warning! Never use these. This dream fragment is an urgent caution from the Higher Self or one's Guide. It literally screams at the dreamer to seek *within*. Multitudes of wayward and lower-level spirits make a game of coming through on the Ouija boards, and it's never to your benefit.

Outhouses represent unnecessary aspects. This symbol suggests the need to eliminate wasteful ideas, beliefs, or assumptions. This symbol might instead, of course, indicate the physical need to improve your digestive system.

Outlines suggest a need for the dreamer to have a plan.

Ovens refer to completion. This symbol may refer to a spiritual search or a specific path. Check the condition and temperature of the oven. Has something been overcooked? Underdone? Is the oven even on?

Overcast (sky) symbolizes an individual's mental cloudiness.

Owls represent heightened observations and developed awareness and perceptions. This symbol indicates an acute level of spiritual enlightenment.

In the Native American tradition, owls symbolize a connection with the spirit world. Often, they indicate that a spirit message is imminent.

Oxen signify overwork. Are you the beast of burden? Or are you overworking others?

Oxford (shoes) indicate an individual who is living in the past. Such people cannot move ahead with the times and accept new concepts.

Oxygen Masks represent an individual who feels smothered by new ideas or concepts. Even the thought of change makes such people panic to the point of not being able to breathe.

Oysters indicate an individual with an introverted personality or one who tends to close him- or herself off from new ideas or relationships.

P

Pacemakers represent an individual's need to pace him- or herself. This may apply to any of the four aspects of man's nature.

Pacifiers symbolize substitutions. They refer to those choices made in life that are less than honest or than what is actually needed. Pacifiers represent the easier path.

Pack Rats represent those individuals who have a tendency to collect everything, even if it's not useful. This is important, for it may even refer to one's spiritual beliefs.

Pantries represent reserves of inner strengths. Is the pantry full or empty? What condition are the supplies in? Are they moldy or fresh?

Paper Clips symbolize the dreamer's need for attachments.

Parachutes represent mental rationalizations. What color and condition is the parachute? Is it old? Are there any holes in it? Did it even work?

Parades symbolize egotism or exhibitionism. Who is in the parade?

Parakeets symbolize a spiritual yes-man, an individual who accepts any doctrine without bothering to give it the scrutiny it requires. This symbol indicates that the individual in question does not practice careful analytical thinking. Such people tend to cage concepts up within themselves, denying their thoughts the freedom to stretch and grow.

Paralysis indicates an individual who has a tendency to numb him- or herself. Do you tend to immobilize yourself? This is a warning that you choose not to be responsive.

Parrots symbolize a verbose individual.

Passageways refer to those aspects of one's life or journey that offer opportunities to extend knowledge.

Passkeys indicate those opportunities in one's life that offer advancement.

Passports represent one's rite of passage. They symbolize an individual's readiness for further learning.

Pathologists appear in dreams to remind you that careful analysis is required along your path to enlightenment.

Patterns are an indication of the manner in which multicolors are expressed in one's life. The dominant color in a pattern does not represent the dominant characteristic in a personality. Rather, the colors represent what we *are* and the patterns represent how we express our true selves. In this sense, the specific color is an important part of the overall pattern, but not the only important factor. Be sure to look up the individual colors elsewhere in this dictionary to get an accurate and full interpretation of your dream. Below, I will explain the meaning of various patterns.

Chain/cable patterns indicate a personality that is resistant to change. This symbol represents an individual who requires all aspects of life to hinge or connect with established tradition. Any thought or idea contrary to these preconceived notions cannot be valid. The individual is bonded or chained to a certain self-created reality and will resist any contradictions that could threaten to break a link in his or her protective fencing.

Checked patterns indicate a balanced personality, one who weighs each side of an argument, considers opposing ideas, and seeks a resolution. They are a sign of a thinker. They symbolize fair judgment and consideration.

Floral patterns indicate an extrovert, an individual who is always at the forefront of the crowd. Such people have a need to know what's going on, down to every last detail of a situation. They are quick to offer advice and ideas. Pay special attention to the precise color or mix of colors to determine if the floral pattern's overall meaning is positive or negative.

Geometric patterns indicate an indifferent individual, one with a "Who cares?" attitude toward life. They may also indicate a disorderly personality, one whose indifference is carefree. This symbol usually points to a mental or emotional problem that the individual attempts to cover up. Suicide-prone personalities are frequently represented in dreams by a geometric pattern in their clothing. Again, observe the colors to determine which negative is causing the apparent disorder.

Herringbone patterns are a sign of a logical mind. This pattern symbolizes one who will not judge, but rather will weigh the facts before coming to a final conclusion.

Plaid patterns signify an easy manner. This symbol indicates a completely laid-back personality that doesn't fluster easily. Here is a reasoning and mature thinker. This symbol will reveal a free spirit who shuns traditional thought in order to explore new possibilities. Fairness and simplicity are indicated with plaid patterns.

Polka-dot patterns relate to an individual's outward, or false, personality. The larger the dot, the greater the proportion of the personality that is outwardly presented. The smaller the dot, the smaller the percentage of the self that is outwardly displayed.

Striped patterns represent a split personality. This includes those referred to as two-faced and underhanded. This pattern exposes cheaters and liars. *A bold stripe* symbolizes the boldness of the individual's audacity. *A narrow stripe,* such as a pinstripe, signals those who try to hide their ruthlessness.

Swirled patterns indicate a vacillating personality, one who easily slips into role playing. This pattern is a sign of a placating individual, a yes-man. This pattern indicates one who does not have solid beliefs or personal opinions.

Tweed patterns signify a highly reserved personality, one who frequently is arrogant. This pattern indicates an individual who considers him- or herself to be perfect. Such a person can never allow his or her defenses to lower or to be weakened before others. This personality is always the leader, the one with a plan or the answers.

Pawn Shops symbolize sacrifices made by an individual.

Peacocks refer to an individual's excessive pride and outward display of egotism. Remember, people are created equal. Do not see yourself as superior, for you are not!

Peanuts symbolize the lesser aspects of life.

Pedestals are a clear warning to avoid placing anything or anyone on a pedestal.

Peelers (kitchen utensil) symbolize an urgent need for an individual to peel back the skin (surface layer) of something in his or her life. This is a warning to perceive that which is hidden or within yourself.

Pelicans symbolize man's gluttonous traits. These birds are associated with water, so their meaning in your dreams usually refers to your spiritual life.

Pendulums signify the swinging momentum or ups and downs of life.

Pentagons represent secretive dealings that may be destructive.

Penthouses indicate an individual who places him- or herself above others in all aspects of life.

People are the complex human components of dreams. People supplement the dreamscape, bestowing a true intricacy of meaning. People, as dream symbols, are more diverse in meaning than any image and are, indeed, often impossible to decipher. To accurately analyze the human facets of your dreams, you need to consider a myriad of segments associated with the people represented. Even if just one person presents him- or herself within your dream, you will need to recall the following vital characteristics about them:

Who was the person? What occupation did they represent (an architect, a plumber, etc.)?

How old was the person?

What were the person's precise physiological features?

What was the condition and color of the person's clothing? Any jewelry?

Most important, what were the person's exact words and deeds?

Once all the above aspects have accurately been recalled and recorded, the dreamer will need to systematically analyze all the individual facets to get an accurate interpretation of the overall meaning of the people in his or her dreams.

Perfumes indicate a cover-up of a less than pleasant situation, attitude, or belief.

Periscopes symbolize the need to come up for air in one's spiritual search. It's important that we move along our spiritual path at a steady, measured pace, so that we are able to assimilate the lessons of our journey. The more we try to absorb all at once, the more we will suffocate and confuse ourselves.

Permits represent what we allow ourselves on a personal level. This symbol can be very revealing. Note what type of permit was involved in your dream. Was it being taken away?

Pet Shops indicate friends around the dreamer. Most often these friends are only fair-weather ones who may need to be bought. When this situation presents itself in dreams, the dreamer needs to realize that buying friends is, in truth, getting no friends at all.

Pharmacists symbolize substances that can help heal the dreamer. They always indicate that some type of medicine is needed, but note that it might not be for your physiological system.

Philanthropists represent generosity or the opportunities to be generous in your life.

Phoenixes symbolize a resurrection, a new life, or a reincarnation. Scrutinize other aspects of the dream to determine this symbol's precise meaning.

Photographers indicate the need to live for the moment and not pine for the future or the past.

Pickaxes signify an individual's need to dig down for more in-depth information.

Picket Lines represent an individual's support and readiness to stand up to injustices.

Pickups (truck) suggest that you need to eat a healthier diet and work in more exercise.

Pigeonholes symbolize fragmentations. They usually appear in your dreams as a warning to avoid pigeonholing people, truths, or concepts.

Pillars symbolize an individual's view of perfection. This symbol most often appears as a warning; watch whom you perceive as a pillar of this or that. Remember that nobody is perfect.

Pillories signify self-reproach. This is a warning to stop being so hard on yourself.

Pills symbolize agents of correction. They may refer to medicinal pills or may point to that which the dreamer sees as being a cure-all in his or her life.

Piloting a Plane represents one's total control over his or her spiritual path and destiny.

Pilot Lights represent one's living spirit.

Pilots symbolize those who control their life path.

Pinnacles signify high points in an individual's life or spiritual journey.

Pins (safety) indicate temporary corrective measures need to be taken.

Pins and Needles represent extreme anxiety that stems from one's inability to accept life. Your Higher Consciousness or Guide is warning you that you are a worrywart who is always impatient to see things resolved and, consequently, is always on pins and needles.

Pioneers symbolize those individuals who forge ahead without fear. This indicates those who blaze their own trails of self-discovery.

Pipe Carriers represent highly peaceful individuals.

Pipe Fitters represent individuals who have a knack for putting the pieces together in a manner that doesn't allow for misjudgment or errors.

Pipers (flute) symbolize the false prophets, teachers, or those who mislead others.

Pipes symbolize an individual's perception of the truths.

    Corncob pipes represent a nonchalant attitude.

    Indian pipes represent a highly sacred attitude.

    Meerschaum pipes represent a highly respectful attitude.

    Old-fashioned pipes indicate a distancing is taking place.

Pipestones denote the sacred manner in which a spiritual aspect is performed.

Piranha symbolize narrow-mindedness in spiritual matters. This may refer to an individual's behavior in daily life or to his or her spiritual beliefs. Do you find yourself viciously striking out at others who hold differing beliefs? Do you openly and aggressively criticize them for their beliefs? Control this!

Pitfalls represent those aspects of one's life that cause setbacks and dangers.

Plains/Prairies symbolize the dreamer's unproductive life. They allude to the fact that you have not produced and are a warning to correct your empty life.

Planting (seeds) symbolizes an individual's distribution of high ideals among his or her peers. Check what kind of seeds. Note their condition and color.

Pliers indicate that one is prying things out before they're ready to come naturally. This comes as a warning not to force any process along your spiritual path.

Plows represent determination and the perseverance to plow through difficulties encountered along your path.

Plumbers indicate a physical disease within the dreamer's body.

Poachers represent stealth and dishonesty. This symbol suggests an individual who capitalizes on the accomplishments of others.

Pods symbolize those aspects of life that contain the fruits of knowledge.

Poets symbolize the lyrical and positive side of life.

Police are a warning to police yourself better.

Police Hats indicate those individuals who think they need evidence to verify every new concept or belief. They cannot entertain the possible.

Police Stations represent restraints. A police station in your dream indicates that someone is always watching you. If you are in the station, what are you doing? Are you the captain? In jail? Reporting a crime? Being arrested?

Politicians represent hypocrisy.

Pollen represents those aspects in one's life that enhance the positives.

Poltergeists indicate misunderstood spiritual concepts and an individual's self-created fears because of them.

Ponchos/Serapes indicate an individual who relates well to nature and the spiritual.

Pontoons represent a lackadaisical spiritual attitude in one's life.

Poolrooms symbolize dirty dealings.

Pools (indoor) symbolize the quality of an individual's inner goodness.

Pools (outdoor) symbolize the quality of an individual's outer goodness.

Porches suggest the extent of the distance an individual maintains.

    Enclosed porches indicate a desire to maintain maximum distance from others. The appearance of their image in a dream is a caution to the dreamer to open up more.

Open porches signify openness with others, a welcoming attitude.

Screened-in porches indicate a hesitant or cautious openness.

Porcupine Quills represent an individual's defense mechanisms.

Porcupines symbolize the dreamer's frequent use of subconscious defense mechanisms to obtain personal wants and goals. This symbol is a warning to stop manipulating others. It also represents a quickness to bristle and hide from new ideas or relationships.

Porpoises/Dolphins symbolize an individual's charitable nature.

Post Offices indicate communications are needed.

Potholders indicate awareness in the face of hot issues or relationships.

Potsherds denote those aspects in one's life that give partial validity to concepts or belief systems.

Potters represent creativity and talents, that is, individual expressions of self.

Power Plants signify one's inner drive and energies. Check the condition of the plant. Is it productive? Or are systems down?

Prayer Wheels represent an individual's tendency to place responsibility in God's hands. This is a warning to take responsibility for one's own life.

Preachers/Rabbis symbolize the various interpretations and translations of God's laws. They may also serve as a warning to stop preaching to others.

Pregnancy indicates the embryonic stage of spiritual awareness or enlightenment.

Pressure Chambers indicate the voluntary and involuntary pressures brought to bear on the spiritual journey. Practice acceptance and don't go deeper than you're able.

Pressure Cookers are a warning for the dreamer to prepare food in a manner that retains valuable nutrients. Of course, this symbol may also refer to a situation the dreamer is getting into that might not be best for his or her health.

Price Tags indicate what some aspect in the dreamer's life will end up costing him or her.

Primers (books) indicate a real need in an individual's life to begin at the beginning of an issue or relationship. This symbol is a clear warning for the dreamer to go back and learn the basics of something because he or she has not yet grasped them.

Printers signify the finality of the written word. This particular dream fragment is important because it is warning you that every thought, word, and deed is impressed, as in ink, upon your personal life record.

Prisms indicate the need for one to perceive from all angles.

Prisons signify self-imposed restrictions. A prison may also represent the dreamer's fear of being discovered and punished for a deed done. Are you inside a prison? Are you the guard? The warden?

Projectors (film) represent those aspects in one's life that serve to enlarge or magnify issues for clarification.

Promissory Notes represent one's responsibilities and the debts that need to be balanced out.

Propane Trucks signify the need to eliminate excessive bodily gases and the foods that are causing them. This dream fragment does not necessarily refer only to intestinal gases, but may instead indicate other gases within the system. Are you often a braggart? Are you full of hot air?

Propellers represent those spiritual forces that have the ability to propel you along your intended path and bring you into a higher level of enlightenment.

Prospectuses signify an individual's need to research an issue thoroughly before buying it.

Prostitutes symbolize ill-gotten gains.

Proverbs come in dreams to counsel the dreamer.

Psychiatrists indicate the dreamer needs to give deeper thought to belief systems. (There must be a thought process in error for this dreamscape component to appear.)

Psychics refer to the use of man's spiritual abilities.

Puffer Fish represent spiritual defense mechanisms. There is never cause for an enlightened individual to defend his or her beliefs! This symbol may indicate an individual's attitude of spiritual superiority (being puffed up with it). Nobody has the right to criticize another's private beliefs or to suggest that theirs alone is the correct and only way to God. Many, many roads lead to God.

Punching Bags represent the need to vent one's excessive energies and rid oneself of emotions such as anger or anxiety.

Purgatory appears in dreams to underscore the need for reparations and verify that earth itself is purgatory, for here we work to atone for our past transgressions.

Purple Hearts appear in dreams as high commendations for one's service.

Purses/Wallets represent the ideals that one expresses in his or her daily interactions with others. Is the purse empty? Stolen? Are you not carrying one at all?

Putty represents a personality that is indecisive and can be manipulated by others.

Puzzles signify one's tendency to complicate simplicity. This symbol may also indicate the dreamer's comprehension of certain spiritual concepts. Remember that all puzzles contain *all* the parts needed to make the whole.

Pyramids represent the more esoteric or hidden aspects of the Collective Wisdom.

Q

Quarantines are a warning for an individual to completely remove him- or herself from a situation or relationship.

Quarries represent those rich sources of information that are mother lodes of knowledge.

Quarters (coins) signify one-fourth of what is needed. This symbol usually refers to knowledge or insight.

Queens/Kings represent domineering or arrogant personalities.

Question Marks are from the Higher Self, who is questioning the individual's conscious choices.

Quicksand indicates the dreamer's inability to extract him- or herself effectively from sticky situations or relationships. This symbol may also refer to the hopelessness of your foundations; quickly move to firmer ground.

Quicksilver (mercury) represents the degree of one's advancement. Note the amount presented to you.

Quizzes appear in dreams to question and test the dreamer to see how much knowledge they've gained along their path.

Quotation Marks emphasize words in dreams to help the dreamer recall them upon awakening. These are most often words straight from the Higher Self or from one's personal Guide and are of great importance.

R

Rabbits indicate the dreamer's obsessive preoccupation with mental or physical sexual activities. This symbol is always a warning. Sexual obsession is spiritual suicide.

Race Car Drivers represent unawareness and foolhardiness. This symbol is a warning to the dreamer to stop racing through life and blindly rushing to attain material goods and reach goals.

Radar refers to intuition.

Radiation Suits indicate exposure to toxins. This dream fragment may refer to a physical situation, mental aberration, or spiritual belief. This symbol is a warning.

Radiators (vehicle) are a warning to the dreamer to monitor his or her daily intake of water. Is the radiator overheating? Remember, we require at least eight glasses of water a day.

This dream symbol may also refer to the individual's overheated temper. Clearly, if this symbol appears in your dream, you need to cool off.

Radios signify the need to tune in to one's Higher Self.

Blaring radios suggest that the dreamer is excessively boisterous or gabby—even a loudmouth.

Broken radios represent one who vacillates between talkativeness and silence.

Missing radios indicate the absence of communicativeness.

Soft radios indicate soft-spokenness and soothing, kind words.

Static Radios indicate unclear reception of communication. You are not making yourself clear in your daily interactions.

Radon symbolizes those forces in the dreamer's daily life or spiritual life that are hidden destroyers.

Rain represents the dreamer's methodical and steady search for truth.

Rainbows are always a sign from above that a spiritual accomplishment has been well done. A rainbow is a special symbol of acknowledgment and is the highest form of commendation.

Raincoats indicate an individual who desires to insulate him- or herself from spiritual talents or truths.

Rakes represent the need to rake through current information, to make a careful inspection.

Ramps symbolize the use of aids to ease your journey.

Rams represent the dreamer's argumentative nature. Stop challenging everyone about everything. Accept your own inadequacies.

Also, this dream fragment may refer to the dreamer's frequent tendency to bat his or her head against the wall. When circumstances cannot be changed, acceptance is then required. All the battering in the world cannot alter certain conditions or situations that we are meant to pass through.

Ranches represent control of others and a domineering personality. Are you herding cattle? Or herding sheep? Are you the boss man? Or a rustler? Are you branding? Slaughtering?

Ranger Stations represent self-restraint and self-imposed controls over the dreamer's nature.

Rats always symbolize a serious disease. This dream fragment may be referring to any one of the four facets of man's nature. Analyze your thoughts, your emotions, and your spiritual beliefs. Are you as healthy in all these areas as you could be? Do you rat on others by gossiping?

Rattles (baby) symbolize immature manners of getting attention or one's way in life.

Rattles (snake) represent harmful forces along one's path.

Ravens represent spiritual falsehoods. They may also indicate a personality that is ravenous in nature.

Ray Guns represent one's spiritual protection.

Rays (sun) symbolize commendations from the Highest Source.

Razor Blades represent the duality of life's situations. Razor blades signify the cutting edge.

Real Estate Agents represent the destruction of spiritual talents and their fragmentation and breakdown for commercial purposes.

Real Estate Offices represent the selection and fragmentation of one's talents. You cannot pick and choose abilities, so take this type of dream as a warning.

Red Carpets indicate a sense of inferiority. You should never have to put the red carpet out for anyone if you truly believe we all are equal.

Red Lights are warnings to stop something. The dreamer should know what this is referring to in his or her life.

Red Tape represents complexities that are self-created.

Referees represent the balance of life's positives and negatives. They refer to conditions, individuals, or situations that ease the negative forces in one's life.

Refrigerators are a warning to calm your emotions, to cool off. In some cases, they instead indicate a warning for the dreamer to stop being so cold. The details of the dream will reveal the precise meaning.

Rehearsals symbolize the need to practice what one believes or preaches.

Reindeer signify the dreamer's tendency to be easily led.

Reins are a caution to remember that only you can make choices about your life. The dreamer must be in total control and hold the reins of his or her own direction.

Reporters symbolize sensationalism and gross exaggerations.

Restaurants symbolize quality of diet.
Exclusive restaurants indicate a rich diet.
Fast-food restaurants symbolize insufficient nutrition.
Mom-and-pop restaurants symbolize homestyle cooking and a well-balanced diet.

Riddles symbolize self-created complexities.

Riding Hats indicate those individuals who do not take time to assimilate new ideas but rather prefer to ride along with the general consensus.

Ripples (in water) symbolize those spiritual actions that go out to create ripples in the world.

Rituals represent the extraneous baggage one attaches to one's spiritual beliefs.

Roadblocks are warnings from your Higher Self or Guide that you are not yet ready for a particular path and they have therefore blocked it to you.

Roadrunners signify impetuosity. Do you act before thinking? Do you frequently jump headlong into a situation before giving it careful consideration? Do you consistently make bad judgments because you rushed into a situation?

Robins symbolize rebirth. This may refer to a spiritual awakening, an attitude reversal, a personality change, or perhaps a dawning light to be shed on a formerly confusing concern.

Robots signify a creature of habit, one who never stops to think what he or she is doing.

Rock Shops represent natural talents and how they are shared or used for mankind's benefit.

Roller Skates indicate an individual who is inclined to skate or roll right through life without confronting the hardships that are required of him or her.

Rolling Pins represent the need to unroll concepts or ideas that the dreamer has balled up in his or her head. This symbol is a call for better understanding.

Rooftops represent an individual's highest ideals. Check the condition and color of the rooftop for further information.

Roosters symbolize an awakening.

Root Canals (dental work) indicate an individual's urgent need to dig out an infectious and dangerous manner of speaking.

Root Cellars represent how belief systems are preserved.

Rosaries indicate the fact that prayer works! Their appearance in your dream is a recommendation to talk to God.

Rosin symbolizes the individual's need to keep from slipping. The appearance of this symbol in your dream indicates you are not staying true to your path.

Roulette Tables symbolize chances taken in one's life.

Roundups indicate the need to gather together your beliefs instead of letting them stray far afield.

Roustabouts represent an individual with a diversity of talent.

Royalty (See QUEENS/KINGS)

Rubber Bands signify the extensions and furthest reaches of each spiritual concept.

Rubber Stamps are warnings from your Higher Self or personal Guide. Check closely to see just what the stamp spells out.

Ruins indicate a ruined situation, relationship, ideal, or belief. The appearance of this symbol in your dream may indicate you're heading toward ruination.

Rumors indicate the need to check facts.

Runners represent escape. What is the dreamer running away from?

Running suggests a state of urgency. Are you running to or from something? What? The details of the dream will serve to clarify the meaning of this symbol. Perhaps the dreamer needs to run?

Rust indicates spiritual atrophy. Since rust is caused by water and humidity (spiritual aspects), this dream fragment usually points to spiritual rustiness in the dreamer.

S

Sacrifices represent real-life sacrifices an individual makes for attainment of their spiritual goals.

Saddles symbolize one's control of his or her spiritual journey. Do you need to get back in the saddle?

Safaris indicate a life path or spiritual journey that is following a guide but wandering. This is a warning to leave the safari and strike out on your own.

Safes represent that which provides security for an individual. This may refer to a situation, relationship, attitude, or spiritual belief.

Sails symbolize a spiritual direction that is guided by the prevailing winds of destiny. This symbol suggests one who lets the Higher Self lead.

Salmon indicate a spiritual search in error, a denial of spiritual truths, or an impossible spiritual situation, for the dreamer is literally forcing him- or herself against the current. Examine yourself carefully after dreaming of this symbol, for the sign suggests a negative tendency to fight your spiritual destiny.

Salt symbolizes a gregarious personality. Depending upon the other details of the dream, this may also suggest someone is rubbing salt into his or her own wounds or the wounds of others.

Salvage Operations indicate value to something thought to be worthless.

Sand symbolizes people who tend to shift back and forth from one position to another, all the while never making any commitments that would advance them along their path. Such people wander aimlessly through life without a firm direction.

Sandals indicate an individual who desires to walk close to the earth but hasn't quite learned how to do so.

Sand Paintings represent spiritual healing knowledge.

Sandpaper indicates the need to smooth out your rough edges.

Sandwiches represent a relationship, belief system, or situation that is making the dreamer a middleman by sandwiching him or her in.

Santa Claus signifies an unrealistic personality that is overly optimistic.

Sap symbolizes the Life Force of Nature. The details of the dream may reveal how you relate to that bonding force.

Satellites (dishes) signify a need to pull in better communications. Improve your reception.

Satellites (man-made) indicate the dreamer's orbiting the truth. You need to stretch your seeking beyond the safe and charted confines of traditional dogma.

Satellites (planets) represent extraneous and peripheral factors on which an individual places importance.

Sauna Rooms indicate the need for inner cleansing in order to achieve spiritual advancement. You need to eliminate the negative attitudes and emotional impurities that serve as spiritual toxins.

Saws indicate the individual's urgent need to cut through a difficult aspect of his or her life or belief system.

Scaffolds represent the fail-safes we all build to protect ourselves from mishaps in our lives or spiritual journeys.

Scales signify balance. The meaning of this symbol is specified by the type of scale that appears in your dreams.

Scales of justice indicate the need for the dreamer to pay more attention to his or her attitudes about justice.

Produce scales signify the need to better balance one's nutritional intake.

Scales in the sky represent the need to pay spiritual debts.

Weight scales refer directly to physical weight.

Scanners indicate the need for greater awareness in life.

Scapegoats represent one's tendency to blame others.

Scarecrows are a warning for the dreamer to reinforce his or her spiritual protection.

Scarves represent a soft attitude toward new ideas. People with such an attitude accept new ideas quickly, but will also look deeply into the matter at their leisure.

Scepters symbolize a false prophet or spiritual belief.

Schools indicate the need for learning.
Business/trade schools indicate the need for the dreamer to expand his or her professional knowledge.

Elementary schools indicate the need for the dreamer to improve his or her understanding of the basics of a subject or concept.

High schools indicate more detailed study is needed.

Universities/colleges indicate extensive study should be done.

Scientists represent self-imposed intellectual confinements. Because scientists must see the proof of a theory before believing it, they represent an inability to expand personal consciousness to the finer realms of reality.

Scissors symbolize a permanent separation. What color are the scissors? If they are black, a death is indicated.

Scorecards represent an individual's personal spiritual balance sheet. Who is keeping score? What is the score?

Scorpions represent retaliations. This symbol indicates an individual or situation that will backfire on the dreamer. Also, this could well represent the retaliation of the self against others.

Scrapbooks represent the importance of recognizing the valuable aspects of one's life. Frequently we forget our accomplishments, and it serves one well to remember and treasure them.

Scrapers indicate the need for an individual to get down to the foundations of a situation, relationship, or belief system.

Screaming (silent) signifies retained emotions or calls for help. Please, release these, for as they fester they become toxins in your system.

Screws signify injustice.

Scrolls represent the Collective Wisdom or may appear in a dream to validate one's specific belief system. Check the condition of the scrolls to determine whether they are a positive or negative symbol for you.

Scrub Brushes indicate a less than clean condition. This may refer to any of man's four aspects. Clearly, something needs deep cleaning in the dreamer's life.

Scuba Divers represent the attainment of spiritual gifts. Watch for details of the dream that will serve to clarify this symbol. What is the condition of the water? What is the diver looking at, collecting, or searching for? How is the diver's apparatus working?

Seahorses indicate an illogical spiritual search or belief system. This symbol indicates the individual's beliefs are either contradictory or they are interspersed with errors. Frequently seahorses indicate spiritual beliefs that are more akin to fantasy than reality, and that hence remove individual responsibility for growth.

Sealing Wax represents confidentiality.

Seaquakes indicate spiritually shaky ground.

Search Warrants indicate an invasion of privacy. What is most important with this dream aspect is who is serving the warrant. Is it the dreamer? A friend? An authority figure?

Seashells symbolize spiritual gifts. Examine the quantity, quality, and disbursement of these shells. Are they beautiful and whole? Are they broken? Covered with barnacles? What are you doing with them? Stepping on them? Or picking them up and admiring them? Are you also sharing them with others?

Seat Belts represent protective measures.

Seaweed represents an individual's spiritual vacillation and an inability to discover the steadiness of truth. This symbol describes spiritual indecision generated by incessant weaving back and forth between varying currents of popular dogma.

Secretaries are symbols of helpfulness and one's support systems in life.

Seesaws represent life's ups and downs. This symbol is usually a comfort for the dreamer, because it reminds us that troubles and problems are temporary, and they strengthen us for advancement along our path.

Seismologists represent sensitivity to the earth. This symbol may also indicate our ability to sense when we are approaching unstable ground.

Semitrailers indicate a physiological overload.

Senior Centers signify wisdom.

Service/Repair Vehicles indicate the need for a physiological, psychological, or spiritual healing. Check the precise type of vehicle in your dream, as this is the key to its meaning.

Sewers indicate the basest aspects of life.

Sewing represents the desire to coalesce. Have you recently experienced a severed relationship that you now desire to repair? Have you turned away from a belief that you now wish to reembrace?

Sewing Machines signify the many tools and opportunities in life that can be used to correct a situation or relationship that has fallen apart.

Sex is a symbol that has multiple meanings, depending on the type of sexual activity presented.

Gentle sex indicates the need for the dreamer to get closer to his or her mate. This represents the need for more involved and deeper communication in the relationship.

Violent sex symbolizes a destructive relationship and warns the dreamer to be less possessive of his or her mate.

Homosexual sex is a warning to be more communicative with the opposite sex.

Unusual sex acts (as with animals) indicate an inability to communicate effectively. This symbol suggests a severe psychological aberration.

Shadowboxing indicates internal conflicts.

Shadows represent the Dark Forces that attempt to foil one's spiritual advancement.

Shamans symbolize the higher spiritual abilities and their sacredness.

Sharks represent the religious fanatics who prey on spiritually gentle people. Such fanatics have a driven need for the blood of those they perceive as not being religiously oriented. Children are especially vulnerable to such attacks.

Shawls represent ideals, thoughts, and belief systems that are gently covered.

Sheep indicate the dreamer's lack of individuality. This symbol suggests you need to be more of an individual thinker; assert yourself.

Sheepherders represent God's disciples and true spiritual teachers.

Shields represent spiritual protection. What condition and color are these? Are they broken? Penetrated? Left unused? Bright and whole?

Shipwrecks signify a spiritual wreck. Most often this refers to one's spiritual path rather than his or her belief system.

Shoemakers indicate someone in the dreamer's life who is instrumental in controlling the paths of others.

Shoes/Footwear (See specific shoe/ footwear types such as LOAFERS, MOCCASINS, SANDALS, etc. for further information.)

Shopping Centers/Malls indicate the need for more diversity in the dreamer's life. This recommendation may refer to your personal interests, attitudes, intellectual pursuits, or spirituality. What type of shops were in your dream? Did you purchase something? What? Did you shoplift? (See specific store/building types such as ROCK SHOPS, SPORTING GOODS, TOY SHOPS, etc. for further information.)

Shorts indicate a semiexposure of the belief system. This means that the dreamer is undecided if he or she wants to let others know of his or her ideas, thoughts, or beliefs.

Shrouds represent the covering of one's darker side.

Sick People symbolize mental dysfunctions or physical diseases. What are they ill with? The details of the dream will reveal the precise meaning here.

Sign Painters are a warning. Be sure to note what the sign says.

Signposts are path markers. Signposts are symbols that give a clear indication of whether the dreamer's life or spiritual direction is proceeding positively or negatively. Are you following the signposts? Ignoring them? What color are they? What exactly do these important signs say?

Silhouettes indicate a state of incompleteness. They are a sign of partial, not whole, understanding or experience. They most often appear in dreams as a warning. You need to get a complete look at a situation, relationship, or belief system instead of just perceiving the outline.

Silos indicate that which is stored. This may refer to any of the four aspects of man's nature. Are you storing talents instead of using them?

Silver symbolizes the spiritual gifts bestowed by God that are everyone's heritage. Are you denying these? Using them? Protecting them? Giving them away?

Singers represent vocal publicizing. This dream fragment may be a warning to stop gossiping and singing out other people's business. It may also indicate the need to sing (tell) something you know.

Singing suggests revelations. This may have a positive or negative meaning. Check the surrounding details of the dream for further information.

Siphons indicate the need to rid yourself of extraneous and irrelevant baggage. This symbol usually refers to spiritual aspects of the individual's belief system.

Sitting designates a lax attitude.

Skating (on ice) represents a voluntary disregard for high ideals. This activity suggests an individual who intends to breeze over spiritual concepts.

Skeins/Yarn symbolize foundations. This dream fragment may refer to physical or spiritual aspects.

Skeletons symbolize hidden negatives—the skeletons in one's closet. This may also indicate the need to get down to basics, as in getting down to bare bones.

Skiing indicates a wanton disregard for the personal efforts required of each of us for spiritual growth.

Skillets represent negative and destructive means to an end. This symbol is a warning to avoid frying or burning others to achieve your goals.

Ski Masks indicate those who have shallow thoughts and are in the habit of skimming over details and deeper concepts.

Skipping indicates one who willfully ignores important aspects of his or her spiritual path. Such a person is continually looking for shortcuts instead of taking one step at a time. This dream fragment comes to warn the dreamer to stop skipping over the challenging aspects of his or her path.

Ski Resorts indicate a shallow spirituality.

Skullcaps/Yarmulkes signify an individual's thoughts are grounded in a foundation of specific spiritual beliefs.

Skunks symbolize the dreamer's intense desire for justice to prevail in all aspects of society. This symbol indicates an individual's penchant to expose stinking situations.

Sleeping symbolizes unawareness or the frequent use of mental mechanisms to avoid confronting life's tougher challenges.

Sleepwalking indicates one who walks his or her path without awareness. This dream fragment may also reflect an out-of-body journey during your sleep.

Slides (lab) caution the dreamer to apply deeper analysis to a situation or concept.

Slides (playground) represent a caution to stop sliding through life without sufficient awareness and seriousness.

Slippers signify a path that is restful. This symbol indicates an individual who takes his or her journey slow and easy along the way.

Sloths indicate laziness or procrastination on the part of the dreamer or someone the animal is linked with in the dream.

Slow-motion Movements are a warning that is being emphasized by your Higher Self or Guide. It is emphasized in order to stress the importance for the individual to go much slower on his or her life path.

Smears represent slanderous deeds or words.

Smoke Screens symbolize defenses or deceptions.

Smoking is a sign of denied inner emotions. Where there's smoke, there's fire. You need to take an honest look at your feelings.

Snails signify cautiousness. This symbol suggests that the dreamer has been doing a commendable job of maintaining awareness in his or her daily life. Remember that, although the snail may be exceedingly slow, it advances just the same.

Snake Oil symbolizes deceptions.

Snake Oil Salesmen indicate those who would deceive others by trying to sell a phony product or concept.

Snakes represent underhanded dealings. This symbol may also indicate the dreamer's need to tread with caution.

Snow represents the dreamer's strong grasp of the truth. Note the surrounding details when snow appears in your dream, for it may have a negative meaning; are you the victim of a spiritual snow job?

Snowflakes symbolize the many beautiful and shimmering aspects of the spiritual truths.

Snowsuits indicate an individual who exposes him- or herself to those truths that are frozen and incapable of expanding to reach other realities or dimensions.

Soap Bars indicate a cleansing is required. This symbol may refer to the mental, physical, emotional, or spiritual aspects of man.

Soapboxes signify a fanatic who preaches to everyone around him or her.

Social Workers represent compassion and a personality that is eager to help others.

Soil represents the foundation you walk on. You will need to analyze its condition and color to get an accurate interpretation of its specific meaning in your dream.

Solariums symbolize the strong light that infuses correct spiritual belief systems. What color is the glass? Is it clouded or clear? Whole? Broken?

Solar Panels indicate the voluntary and purposeful admittance of God into the home. Are the panels broken? Missing? What color are the panels? If they are a specific color, this indicates that you are being selective in your beliefs. Avoid fragmenting the Truths!

Soot symbolizes negative forces an individual allows to contaminate his or her life.

Sorcerers indicate the negative use of spiritual talents.

Space Probes symbolize an individual's freedom to extend his or her spiritual search to the farthest reaches.

Sparks represent those challenges in one's life that provide opportunities for enlightenment. They also represent an individual's own sparks of wisdom or comprehension.

Spectators caution the dreamer to remember that he or she is never alone—someone, somewhere is always watching.

Spelunkers represent an individual who delves into the deeper aspects of concepts and belief systems to discover any hidden facets that will broaden his or her understanding.

Sphinxes are a sign that the dreamer is close to discovering or comprehending the totality of the Collective Wisdom.

Spiders signify conniving individuals. Take the appearance of this symbol in your dream as a warning. Do not be caught up in situations that you can't easily leave. Exercise extreme caution in all daily activities.

Spies indicate untrustworthy individuals. Is the spy the dreamer? A friend? Relative? Coworker?

Spiked Shoes indicate an individual who is resentful of the problems he or she encounters on his or her path and is intent on fighting back.

Sporting Goods Shops symbolize casual relationships. What were you looking at? A gun? A game? What was your emotional attitude while you were in the shop?

Sports Stadiums indicate procrastination. The dreamer prefers to sit and watch rather than to get out and *do*.

Springs (metal) symbolize an individual's tenacity—the ability to bounce back after adversity has been encountered.

Spring (season) symbolizes the time for new and fresh beginnings.

Sprouts indicate the birthing of new spiritual concepts within the individual.

Squirrels represent the act of hoarding. This dream fragment either cautions the dreamer to become more forthright or it indicates that the dreamer needs to be less of a braggart. The details of the dream should make the specific meaning of this symbol clear to you.

Stables symbolize attitudes toward personal talents. Are the stables unkempt? Unused? Dirty? Spotless?

Stains represent negative aspects in the dreamer's life. What colors are these? This symbol directly indicates one's spirit's record.

Stairs represent the ascent or descent of an individual's spiritual awareness.

Darkened stairs represent a wrong or evil direction.

Intermittently broken steps indicate the acceptance of partial truths.

Missing stairs indicate no search is being done.

Moving stairs represent your ease in attaining and absorbing the truths.

Tilted stairs indicate you've made errors or personal revisions in your understanding of the Law of God. This dream fragment is a dire warning, for such mistakes are more dangerous than any others.

Whole/sturdy stairs represent a sturdy path possessed of all the encompassing truths.

Standing signifies an adherence to one's convictions—a standing up for one's beliefs or ethics.

Staples indicate the immediate need to reestablish a belief, attitude, or relationship.

Starch indicates a stiffness of character.

Starfish represent spiritual truths. Are you searching for the starfish? Are you holding one? Burying them? Destroying one? What color are they?

Stars signify the search for Truth.

Colored stars represent a diversity of spiritual truths. Such a dream fragment indicates that the dreamer must continue the search for spiritual truth. There is only one bright Light of God and that will be represented by a brilliantly undulating *white* star. The dreamer must persevere.

Moving stars indicate the dreamer's search for the truth amid various spiritual doctrines. Stars that are in motion symbolize the constant changeability of man-made dogma.

Square configuration of stars indicates the dreamer has a closed mind regarding the matter of spirituality. The dreamer would not have this aspect appear within the dream unless his or her spiritual beliefs were presently in some form of serious disarray. The Truths encompass a vast field of material. The dreamer needs to expand his or her vision beyond the narrow confines of the familiar. Many times this dream fragment comes to a person who is prejudiced and clings to preconceived notions without allowing him- or herself to consider other intellectual concepts. Treat this symbol as a recommendation to become knowledgeable enough of other spiritual concepts to pass an informed and intelligent judgment on their possible value in your life.

Five-pointed stars (pentacles) symbolize spiritual attainment through selfless generosity and good works.

Six-pointed stars (hexagrams) represent spiritual attainment through effective use of God-given talents.

Seven-pointed stars represent the dreamer's full use of his or her awareness in spiritual life. The dreamer is developing the six spiritual centers through the controlled empowerment of his or her activated psychic Current Force.

Static (electricity) indicates an instability within the individual. This dream fragment most often refers to static action in one's aura that indicates confusion, anxiety, or hyperactivity.

Static (sound) indicates unclear comprehension.

Stealing represents personal inadequacies. What is being stolen? This will help pinpoint the void the dreamer feels requires filling.

Steering Wheels represent the control you need to follow any path you desire.

Broken steering wheels indicate a vacillating mind that makes confused choices.

Locked steering wheels suggest the dreamer's stubborn determination to go down the traditional paths.

Loose steering wheels indicate the dreamer's choice to go here and there without logical planning. The dreamer lacks a clear goal.

Missing steering wheels suggest a stagnant individual who chooses not to improve him- or herself or go anywhere.

Oversize steering wheels symbolize overblown plans that are premature.

Undersize steering wheels indicate an individual who is not spiritually, psychologically, or physically prepared for his or her journey.

Stereo Headphones caution the dreamer to stop listening selectively. You're only hearing what you want to hear, which won't teach you anything.

Stethoscopes represent emotional sensitivity and compassion. What is the condition of the stethoscope? Are you being cautioned to use it?

Stewardesses/Stewards symbolize the aides you use or have around you while walking the path to spiritual awareness.

Stew Pots are a serious warning to the dreamer that he or she is about to become involved in a boiling situation, relationship, or belief system.

Stingers (insect) represent aspects of one's life that will ultimately sting.

Stingrays signify false prophets. Remember that all true prophets caution their followers about the false ones. The stingray moves gracefully, yet its intent is deadly. However, the stingray can have a more positive meaning. It may indicate a spiritual truth that stings the individual into a new and heightened awareness. The dreamer must examine all details of the dream carefully to determine this symbol's true meaning.

Stockbrokers indicate risks taken with spiritual abilities.

Stones are most frequently indicative of life's little irritations. However, *to find beautiful stones* or *to have someone offer gemstones to you* would symbolize your discovery of life's intangible riches such as compassion and/or spirituality. If these stones are *pitted and ugly,* they represent the irritations. Who is doing the giving? Who is the recipient?

Stopwatches warn the dreamer to remember to follow *God's* time, not one's own. Remember, there is a time for everything in one's life.

Storytellers represent the preserving of truths. In the Native American way, the storytellers were those who kept the people's traditions and cultural history alive for future generations.

Stowaways symbolize unawareness. Your development is fragmented in such a way as to deny you total perception of each important stage of your journey. As a result, you're forced to hitch rides on any boat passing in the night.

Streams symbolize the ever-changing course the dreamer takes while searching for spiritual truths. Stay with the meandering stream. Follow its cheerful voice to the main body of water it leads you to, the ultimate One.

Students represent the need for additional knowledge, development, and experiences.

Stunt Actors are a warning to stop letting others do the hard or difficult tasks along your spiritual path.

Submarines signify an individual's tendency to expound outwardly on the depth of his or her spiritual comprehension, yet inwardly remain emotionally and intellectually removed from these beliefs. Submarines are a warning against spiritual hypocrisy.

Suckers (fish) represent spiritual gullibility.

Summer (season) signifies the time for giving more attention to one's life goals or spiritual journeys.

Summons Servers are a spiritual warning. This symbol serves notice to the dreamer regarding his or her erring ways.

Sun always represents God and the dreamer's personal relationship with Him.
>   *Bright sun* symbolizes the dreamer's sincere and true relationship with God.
>   *Clouded sun* symbolizes the dreamer's cloudy and uncertain beliefs in God. These problems need to be clarified before a true touching relationship can begin.
>   *Colored sun* symbolizes the inner attitudes that color the dreamer's relationship with God. (Refer to the COLOR section for further information.)
>   *Sun eclipse* symbolizes the dreamer's temporary fall from God's grace. More seriously, it might also indicate that the dreamer has denied God's very existence.

Sunbathing represents the purposeful absorption of spirituality and spiritual truths.

Sunburns indicate that an individual has been or will shortly be burned by a spiritual belief system.

Sunfish symbolize an individual's open spirituality. This symbol indicates that the dreamer takes quiet comfort in his or her beliefs and generously shares his or her spiritual gift.

Sun Hats indicate those who are reluctant to allow the Light of Truth into their thoughts.

Sunlamps symbolize an artificial manner of gaining spiritual knowledge. Be wary especially of so-called New Age methods that try to force such abilities. Spiritual knowledge must be developed naturally.

Surgical Caps/Masks symbolize an individual whose thoughts are intense and thorough.

Surgical Shoe Coverings indicate one who walks his or her path in fear of being touched by any negatives. This symbol indicates fear, which the dreamer should try to overcome. Remember, you gain strength and power through dealing with adversities.

Surveyors are a warning regarding the dreamer's intention to somehow fragment his or her life. The appearance of this symbol in your dream indicates that you're headed toward a path that will not provide you with complete knowledge. You are being warned to survey the intended path more carefully.

Suspenders are a symbol of holding up under adversity.

Swamps symbolize a weak foundation. You simply cannot construct anything of endurance in a swamp. This symbol warns and advises the dreamer to seek foundations elsewhere.

Swans symbolize man's beautiful inner talents, most often those of the spiritual nature.

Sweaters represent warmth of character. What color is the sweater? Is there a pattern?

Sweat Outfits signify the hard work expended by an individual to walk his or her paths.

Swim Fins/Swimming Flippers represent a desire to reach spiritual development as fast as possible. Be warned! Time is necessary for spiritual development.

Swimmers are spiritual seekers. The dreamer can gain insight from the style of swimming depicted in the dream. Are the swimmers racing? Are they flailing in the water? Are they playing or just treading water? Are they diving down deeper? Floating?

Swimming represents one's total submersion in the realm of the highest spiritual truths.

Swine represent the dreamer's excessive indulgences. This symbol may, of course, refer to any of the four aspects of man's nature.

Swordfish signify spiritual beliefs that need to be omitted or cut out.

Syrup symbolizes the honeyed and sugarcoated qualities of an individual's speech. This symbol is a warning against silver-tongued individuals.

T

Tadpoles represent spiritual immaturity or a novitiate seeker.

Talismans indicate an individual's tendency to misplace faith. This dream fragment suggests superstition.

Talmud symbolizes right living according to the spiritual truths and God's laws.

Tap Shoes symbolize an individual who thinks he or she is advancing along his or her path by tapping the resources of others. Be warned to avoid this practice.

Tar warns of a negative event that will be sticky for the dreamer.

Tarot Cards indicate an unhealthy fascination with the sensational side of spiritual talents. Remember, these special gifts are the natural benefits of spiritual development. They are not toys to be played with. This dream fragment warns the dreamer to stop being obsessed with the future and to pay more attention to the present.

Tattoos represent the dreamer's perceptions of him- or herself. What was the tattoo? What color was it?

Tattoo Shops symbolize pride in one's belief system.

Taverns indicate a reluctance to face life.

Tax Collectors indicate an individual who tends to be a burden and freeload on others. This symbol can refer to any relationship, situation, or person who taxes another's patience or resources.

Taxidermists symbolize shallow beliefs.

Teachers represent the Higher Self. This symbol may also refer to those whom the dreamer perceives as teachers, even though their lessons are not, in reality, of the highest caliber.

Teenagers symbolize those in transitional periods of their lives. This symbol suggests one is passing from ignorance into budding awareness.

Teeth represent an individual's manner of speech, which in turn speaks of one's inner personality.
> *Buck teeth* indicate one who speaks before thinking. Such people are usually quick to criticize.
> *Colored teeth* symbolize an aberration of speech. (Refer to the COLOR section for further information.)
> *Crooked teeth* represent slanted speech generated from the slanted thoughts of the individual.

Crowned teeth symbolize hypocrisy in speech. The natural teeth (or true words) lie beneath the beautiful false ones.
Decayed teeth represent abusive words or obscenities. Often this will indicate one who continually speaks negatively of others.
Falling-out teeth indicate a rhetorical individual, one who is verbose and exaggerates.
False teeth represent a new and beautiful manner of speech. This dream fragment indicates those who have found and adopted the language of truth.
Loose teeth indicate loose speech or a gossipy personality. Such people also tend to make other people's business their business. They cannot be trusted.
No teeth indicates an analytical thinker, one who measures his or her words carefully before speaking.
White/even teeth represent honesty and kind words. Truth comes from mouths with these teeth.

Telegraph Operators represent messages coming through the inner perceptions of yourself.

Telephone Operators indicate that physical messages are coming to the dreamer or have been placed by the dreamer.

Telephones signify communications. Is the telephone ringing? Is it broken? What color is it?

Telephone Trucks symbolize a hearing impairment. This dream fragment may refer to an actual physiological dysfunction, or it may indicate an individual's tendency not to listen well. If you are the driver of this vehicle, you may have the ability to be a spiritual messenger.

Telescopes indicate the need to look beyond the surface. You are close to the truth, but you must be more deeply involved if you want to understand it.

Television (watching) (See WATCHING TELEVISION)

Television Stations indicate the dreamer's desire to broadcast his or her talents or beliefs. Watch this!

Tellers represent one's use of spirituality. They refer to the saving or spending of spiritual traits such as compassion, sharing, and helpfulness.
> *Money deposits* indicate the dreamer is holding something back.
> *Money withdrawals* indicate the dreamer is sharing.
> *Green/gold money* represents monetary values. Is financial assistance being given or retained through the sharing or hoarding of money?
> *Silver money* represents spiritual values. Is spiritual assistance being given or retained through the sharing or hoarding of money?

Tenements symbolize an unsatisfactory state of affairs. This may refer to the physical, mental, emotional, or spiritual side of the dreamer.

Tennis Rackets indicate an individual who is irresponsible and has a tendency to hit the ball back to another instead of taking care of things him- or herself.

Tennis Shoes indicate an individual who is running him- or herself ragged trying to cover all angles.

Termites symbolize those aspects of life that serve to undermine an individual's moral, ethical, or spiritual foundation.

Tests (written) represent life's spiritual tests or challenges.

Thermometers indicate the state or level of an individual's temperament. Note the degree the thermometer reads.

Thermostats represent an individual's ability to regulate the intensity of a situation or relationship.

Tickets (driving) are warnings to correct certain aspects of your life that are breaking physical or spiritual laws.
> *Driving in the wrong lane* is a warning to change your path.
> *Ignoring railroad flashers* is a warning that you're currently set on a dangerous course and you're being reckless.
> *Illegal turns* indicate you're making incorrect choices about your life path.
> *Obstructed views* are a warning that you're proceeding without a full and clear view of what's ahead.
> *Speeding* is a warning to slow down your daily life so that you can become more aware. Also, don't try to speed through your spiritual journey.
> *Tailgating* warns against following the path of others instead of listening to your own Higher Self.
> *Weaving* is a warning to stop vacillating and being indecisive about your goals.

Ticket Takers indicate dues are required to achieve advancement. Each individual must pay his or her spiritual debts before advancing along his or her spiritual path. The ticket takers are key players in your life; they represent the people you need to pay back.

Ticks represent life's festering irritations. Avoid letting individuals or situations get under your skin.

Tigers symbolize the dreamer's aggressive nature.

Tight Clothing signifies constrictions that are self-generated by the dreamer. These are the self-imposed constraints that you need to shed in order to advance along your spiritual path.

Tightrope Walkers indicate that the dreamer is walking a tightrope. Check the surrounding details of the dream for further information about this symbol's meaning.

Timetables indicate an individual's need to attend to schedules.

Tires symbolize the condition of the dreamer's feet and the manner in which he or she walks his or her life path. Are the tires threadbare? Are they missing altogether?

Toe Shoes represent dancing and the tendency for an individual to tiptoe through life. This symbol is a warning to the dreamer to stop his or her nonchalant behavior and start taking life seriously.

Toilets indicate eliminations are required. This symbol may be a literal message for the dreamer to pay attention to his or her digestive system. It may also refer to psychological aspects of the dreamer's life and indicate the need to eliminate certain attitudes, insensitive comments, hypocrisies, or dishonesty.

Tollbooths refer directly to one's spiritual debts. You must pay your way before further advancement can be achieved.

Tools represent opportunities and talents.

Toolsheds indicate additional information or talents are needed.

Toothbrushes indicate the dreamer needs to clean up his or her manner of speech. Are you a braggart? A gossip? A defamer? Dishonest? Heretical? A hypocrite? Be honest with yourself and correct that which demands cleaning up.

Top Hats indicate an arrogant thinker. This refers to one who believes he or she has the best and greatest ideas.

Torahs represent an individual's high spiritual belief system. Please check the condition of the Torah. What color is it? Is it protected? Is it left exposed?

Tornadoes/Hurricanes symbolize great confusion and inner turmoil.

Tornadoes symbolize total mental breakdowns or intense emotional explosions. They warn of outbursts and devastating confrontations in tumultuous relationships.

However, remember that whenever a disaster (especially a natural one) appears in a dream, it could very well be a premonition.

Hurricanes represent dangerous fanatical spiritual beliefs that will eventually affect the physical negatively. Remember, hurricanes are swept onto land (physical) from off the water (spiritual). Spiritual beliefs are one's own private business, but they can, and often do, become so fanatical that they overpower the physical aspects of one's life.

However, remember this dream fragment may be a real premonition.

Totem Poles signify stacked spiritual belief systems. This symbol appears in your dream to remind you that one spiritual concept can lead directly into another without being in conflict.

Toupees indicate false thinking.

Tour Guides represent those we follow in life or while on our spiritual journey.

Towers symbolize the superconscious aspect of the mind, where the miraculous gifts of the spirit lie dormant. Inspect the condition of the tower. What color is it? Are you receptive to the abilities you possess?

Town Criers are a warning. What is the crier saying?

Tow Trucks indicate an individual who is carrying excessive and unnecessary responsibilities and worries with him or her.

Toy Shops symbolize the child in every adult. This symbol refers to man's frequently childish ideas or actions.

Trailblazers represent those who have gone before us to make our spiritual paths easier.

Train Engineers indicate individuals who will lead the dreamer along the smooth and established path through life. This symbol is a warning to the dreamer to seek out his or her own unique way. No right paths are smooth going!

Train Stations signify the need to either stay on track or get back on track.

Train Tracks indicate a straitlaced and narrow-minded personality. Such a person refuses to deviate from his or her own personal way and experiment with innovative ideas.

Train Whistles are a warning against reclusiveness. One who would voluntarily segregate him- or herself from others suffers from an ill spirit. The price of reclusivity is paid after physical death, so heed this warning now.

Tramps/Hobos represent nonconformists.

Transfers (tickets) indicate the need to take another path.

Transfusions indicate an urgent need to cleanse oneself of bad blood that has developed in a relationship. This is a warning to the dreamer to find a quick and satisfying resolution.

Translators represent understanding, and those who would bring it to the dreamer.

Trapdoors symbolize the result of unawareness.

Depending on the surrounding details of the dream, this symbol may instead indicate an opportunity for escape from a situation or relationship.

Trappers represent conniving personalities or situations that may backfire on the dreamer.

Traps symbolize the pitfalls in life. This symbol may also indicate a personality who uses entrapment for his or her own ends.

Travel Agencies represent social or spiritual inadequacies. This symbol cautions the dreamer not to let others dictate his or her life path.

Travel Agents indicate those individuals who would tell you how to live your life. Avoid them.

Treadmills indicate the futility of one's present path.

Triggers (grenade pins, gun) are a warning of an explosive situation or relationship. Beware of real danger here.

Trophies (animal) represent an insensitive, unaware, and egotistical personality. They may also indicate a predatory individual.

Trophies (sports) represent winnings. What are the trophies for?

Truck Stops represent necessary rest stops along the way. All paths, whether they be physical (occupational), mental (the search for knowledge), or spiritual, will frequently reach a plateau where one should assimilate all that has been gained. Such rests are necessary stopping points before further advancements can be made.

Trunks (baggage) symbolize important properties (physical or spiritual) that an individual believes are valuable to him or her.

Trunks (vehicle) represent hidden properties (physical or spiritual) that an individual carries with him or her along his or her life path.

T-shirts indicate the dreamer's need for shedding exterior attitudes and getting down to business.

Tsunamis represent spiritual overkill, a deadly flooding of doctrines that will drown the receiver. This symbol is a warning that the dreamer is being hit with too many spiritual concepts at once. You need more time to assimilate what you've learned so far.

Tugboats represent spiritual downtime or sluggishness. This symbol often appears in a dream when you've just had your belief systems disrupted or shattered and now you're in a state of semi-shock.

Tumbleweeds represent the shallow parts of an individual or a belief system.

Turbans indicate twisted thoughts. These thoughts are all wrapped up and turn around and around, but never go anywhere.

Turtlenecks indicate a reluctance or fear to expose yourself to the uncertainties of your path. This symbol means you are fearful of sticking your neck out to follow your path.

Turtles indicate that the dreamer frequently escapes from reality, mentally, emotionally, physically, or spiritually. Remember, you can't grow if you're not willing to face obstacles head-on.

Tutors signify those individuals in one's life who help to clarify one's comprehension.

Tuxedos symbolize arrogance or the desire to expose oneself to only the best aspects of one's life.

Twins represent the polarity and duality of life.

Twisting Roads represent one's perseverance in pursuing one's chosen goal in life. You are blessed with tenacity and stamina to forge ahead in the face of many unexpected adversities. You tend not to follow the smooth, paved path of others.

Typewriters represent preserved ideas.

U

Umbrellas represent skepticism and a voluntary insulation of the self from spirituality.

> *Black umbrellas* indicate no spiritual beliefs or protection against the Dark Truths.
> *Broken umbrellas* represent slanted beliefs and the tendency to accept a few and reject others.
> *Closed umbrella in rain* symbolizes a spiritually open mind.

Umpires represent one's Higher Self or Guide, who keeps one within the rules.

Undertows signify hidden spiritual beliefs that are in error and will serve to pull one under. Don't ever subject yourself to false beliefs. Be ever true to yourself.

Underwear symbolizes that which one covers up and is fearful of exposing.

Unidentified Flying Objects represent the totality of the brotherhood of all intelligent life. This symbol may also represent an actual unrecalled alien encounter.

Unidentified Sky Objects signify the ultimate, endless possibilities of the mind.

Unions represent those groups of people or belief systems that supply the dreamer with security.

Urns (funeral) signify an ignorant attitude or belief regarding death.

Ushers signify those who would be helpful in guiding one along his or her spiritual path. This frequently represents one's Higher Self or Guide.

Utility Companies indicate work needs to be done.
> *Electric companies* indicate the need for more knowledge to help the dreamer proceed toward advancement.
> *Gas companies* indicate more physical energy is required.
> *Telephone companies* indicate more communications are needed.

V

Vaccines represent that which provides protection. This symbol may refer to the dreamer's physical, mental, emotional, or spiritual life.

Vacuums indicate the need for an individual to clean up a negative attitude or situation quickly.

Valleys represent periods of rest along the course of your life path. These do not signify low spots, but rather cool and easy places to pause and revive energies.

Valves symbolize those controls the dreamer has in his or her power to regulate.

Vampires symbolize a user. This symbol is a warning to the dreamer to avoid a relationship or belief system that will drain his or her energies or life force.

Varnish represents the manner in which something is smoothed over. Check the color and condition of the varnish. Is it clear? Cracked? Peeling away?

Vaults (bank) represent that which is valued and treasured most in one's life. Be sure to note what is in the vault. Is it silver or gold? Family heirlooms? Pictures? Gems? This dream fragment shows the dreamer what he or she values most in life. If these things are material possessions, the Higher Self is warning you to reevaluate your priorities.

Vectors represent transmitters or carriers. This symbol is a warning to the dreamer of a negative relationship or situation. A vector carries something from one place to another. What is being passed along? A disease? A dangerous idea or concept?

Vegetable Steamers symbolize the dreamer's need to retain valuable aspects of his or her life. This symbol may refer to food nutrients, attitudes, ideals, or beliefs. Stop letting your valuables evaporate!

Vehicles symbolize the physiological system. Specific types of vehicles represent actions of the body or mind, and the separate vehicle components symbolize the body parts. (See specific types of vehicles such as AMBULANCES, CONSTRUCTION TRUCKS, GO-CARTS, etc. as well as specific vehicle components such as BRAKES, TIRES, WINDSHIELDS, etc. for further information.)

Veils indicate an individual who has veiled thoughts and prefers to conceal his or her ideas in shadow.

Veneers represent the self's false exteriors. What color are the veneers? Are they cracked? Fresh?

Venetian Blinds represent an individual's tendency toward selective perception. This indicates a manipulative person who frequently uses psychological mechanisms as ploys to defend or explain his or her lack of understanding on various issues.

Venom signifies a poisonous element in the dreamer's mental, emotional, physical, or spiritual life.

Vents represent opportunities. Are these outlets or inlets? What are the vents connected to? A furnace? An air-conditioning system? A sewer? A kitchen? A roof?

Vents appear in dreams to encourage the dreamer to use his or her options. They denote a way for the dreamer to either obtain something or get rid of something.

Vertigo indicates dizziness. This can be a dizziness in the dreamer's physiological system, relationships, or beliefs.

Vests represent extraneous baggage you're bringing on your life path. This symbol may also be suggesting that the dreamer needs to keep something close to his or her heart.

Veterinarians symbolize a deep and selfless compassion.

Video Shops represent unrealistic attitudes. This may also refer to the dreamer's desire to escape life.

Vineyards represent the fruit of one's spiritual labors. Check the condition of the vineyard and that of the grapes.

Viper Fish symbolize spiritual blindness and skepticism. However, this symbol may also refer to an individual's tendency to keep his or her personal beliefs hidden. Or this individual dabbles in the darker aspects of esoteric concepts. Be careful of your motives in any spiritual enterprise.

Visas signify an approval from higher sources for one's readiness to proceed to more advanced levels of spiritual learning.

Visor Caps indicate an individual whose thoughts are exposed to the light (truth), but whose perception is colored. Check for the specific color of the visor.

Vitamins indicate the need for nutrients. This need may be physical, mental, emotional, or spiritual. In any case, this is a warning to be wary of exhaustion, depression, or spiritual nonchalance.

Vixens symbolize a playfully cunning personality. Such people can be dangerous, for one never knows when they're serious.

Volcanoes indicate an explosive situation. This dream fragment suggests that a dangerous situation is brewing in the dreamer's life and may explode soon.

Voodoo indicates misunderstood spiritual concepts. Voodoo is a real and valid religion that is misunderstood by many. However, the effectiveness of many of its practices lies in the receptivity of the mind.

Vouchers signify the reasonings behind actions taken.

Voyagers represent independent spiritual seekers who follow their own paths.

Vultures indicate aggressive and greedy personalities. Such people are willing to take personal pleasure or gain at the expense of others. Simply stated, this dream fragment indicates a user.

W

Waitresses/Waiters represent servitude. Do you delegate your chores to others? Are you too frequently performing the menial tasks of others yourself?

Walking (on air) signifies one who possesses the godlike qualities of acceptance, contentedness, and happiness.

Walking (on water) represents spiritual arrogance. This dream fragment comes as a warning to those who believe they are as gods.

Wardens represent imprisoning aspects of life. This dream fragment may be referring to a specific individual, relationship, attitude, emotion, situation, or belief system that is, or will, imprison the dreamer.

Warehouses signify storage. This symbol may refer to the dreamer's memory, personality traits, or attitudes. Do you tend never to forget the least slight? Do you harbor and store resentment? Do you squirrel away your personal talents instead of using them for the benefit of others? Check carefully to discover what is stored in your dream warehouse.

Warehouse Workers represent order and organization. Are your mental and spiritual houses in order?

Warriors symbolize those who are devoted to their spiritual path.

Washing Hair signifies the cleansing of your thought processes.

Washing Machines indicate a cleansing is required.

Watching Television represents taking in thoughts and knowledge. Take note of what you are watching. Cartoons? News? Comedy? Mysteries? Documentaries? Preachers? Each of these gives the dreamer an indication of what he or she is filling his or her mind with. But is the dream trying to tell you that what you're watching is good or bad for you? It depends on the level of light the television emits.
> *Bright television* indicates the messages you're receiving are positive. You're watching something good.
> *Dark television* indicates that the messages you're receiving are negative. You're watching something you shouldn't be filling your mind with.

Water is the nature element that signifies man's spirituality. Spirituality does not necessarily refer to a religious doctrine, but rather to how closely the dreamer lives according to God's laws. (See specific water elements such as STREAMS, UNDERTOWS, WATERFALLS, etc. for further information.)

Waterfalls symbolize the refreshing and unselfish sharing of the dreamer's spirituality. This does not refer to the verbalization of dogma, but rather to the joyful interaction between the dreamer and others.

Water Pitchers represent an outpouring and sharing of one's awareness and gifts. Check the specific condition and color of the pitcher for an accurate interpretation here. Also, what color is the water? Is it pure?

Wax Museums represent the mask that people present outwardly. This dream fragment may indicate a past-life experience.

Weather Vanes indicate an individual who does not take his or her spiritual path seriously. Such people point their feet in whatever direction the wind is blowing.

Weavers represent the totality of spiritual truths, including the many-dimensional realities that are woven into them.

Wedges indicate an interference taking place.

Weeds represent false concepts added to the spiritual truths. Are you pulling the weeds up, thereby allowing the grass (truths) to remain pure? Are you allowing the weeds to thrive and choke out the grass? Watch your actions in the dream, for they reveal your true nature better than any mirror can.

Weights refer to negative forces you encounter on your path that weigh you down.

Welding Helmets indicate an individual who requires all thoughts, concepts, and ideas be properly connected. This is not a positive symbol, for many of the real connections are untouchable.

Well Drillers signify deep thinkers with analytical minds.

Wells Fargo Trucks indicate one's healthful riches. Is the truck being loaded or unloaded? Is it being robbed? Is the money inside silver (spiritual wealth), gold bullion (money), or greenbacks (talents)?

Wet Suits indicate one who insulates him- or herself from the spiritual truths.

Whales represent an individual's spiritual magnanimity. This symbol appears in a dream as a form of recognition from higher sources. It is an honor to receive such acknowledgments.

Wheelbarrows represent the shouldering of burdens. Who is pushing the wheelbarrow? Who is filling it? What are its contents?

Whirlpools symbolize overzealous spiritual actions. Do you preach your personal beliefs? Do you consistently try to convert others? If so, you are creating a spiritual whirlpool attempting to pull others down into your own obsession.

Whirlwinds signify a twisted manner of thinking.

White House symbolizes indecision. Its appearance in your dream indicates an inability to make a decision on your own; you tend to rely too heavily on advisors.

Whitewashing represents lies and cover-ups.

Wide-angle Views indicate a need for the dreamer to broaden his or her perspectives. This dream fragment may also indicate a need to expand one's knowledge on an issue.

Wildfires symbolize an out-of-control situation.

Winches represent forces that are capable of pulling us out of difficulties in life. These forces may even be spiritual in nature.

Wind symbolizes the mode of mental transmissions or the internal output of the brain's electrical circuitry. It is important for the dreamer to watch for subtle clues in the dream such as gently wavering tree leaves, wheat fields rippling softly, or the slant of a falling autumn leaf. (See specific wind types such as BREEZES, TORNADOES, WHIRLWINDS, etc. for further information.)

Windmills represent mental laziness or weakness. The dreamer's direction in life tends to be dependent on the way of the wind at any given moment.

Windows indicate an individual's perspective on the world. Check the condition and color of the windows.

Window Washers represent those who would assist in clarifying another's perspectives.

Windshields represent the physical eyes and what is seen through them. Many times windshields will also signify mental interpretations of visual stimuli.
  Cracked windshields indicate illogical thinking and faulty reasoning.
  Darkly-shaded windshields symbolize the dreamer's negative view of life.
  Green-tinted windshields mean one's perspective is colored by envy or greed.
  Pink-tinted windshields symbolize one's rosy outlook.
  Slanted windshields represent slanted viewpoints and perspectives.

Winemakers remind us of the two uses of wealth: It can be used negatively for only yourself, or positively for the welfare of others as well.

Winter Hats indicate those who generate heat with their thoughts. Such people come up with hot ideas and use them for the betterment of others.

Winter (season) symbolizes the time for contemplating one's spiritual beliefs.

Wiretaps are a warning that someone is always listening.

Wishbones represent an individual's desires and wishes.

Witches/Wizard Hats indicate those individuals who bring esoteric concepts into their daily thoughts.

Woolgathering represents daydreaming. Such daydreaming can be a waste of time, or spiritually constructive.

Workrooms represent quantity and quality of effort the dreamer puts into life. Is the workroom busy? Is it clean and bright, or disorganized and messy?

Work Uniforms symbolize the work applied to one's path. Check to see just what type of work uniform is represented here.

Worms indicate the dreamer's tendency to interfere in the lives of others, thereby creating a diseased relationship. Worming your way into something cannot result in anything positive.

Wounds symbolize the hurts of an individual. Such hurts can be physical, emotional, mental, or spiritual. Check who is injured.

Wreaths represent sentiments.
Baby's-breath wreaths symbolize a congratulatory message, usually a high spiritual acknowledgment.
Black wreaths symbolize sympathy and frequently signify a forthcoming death.
Grapevine wreaths represent encouragement.
Lily wreaths indicate joy of a birth or rebirth.

Wrestlers represent a manipulative personality. This symbol may also be indicating a specific situation or relationship that the dreamer is mentally wrestling with.

Writers symbolize the need to express inner thoughts, feelings, and sensitivities.

Writing symbolizes mental creativity gained through awareness. The act of writing indicates a personality who feels an inner prompting to get it down on paper.

X

X-ray Technicians indicate the need for close inspection and contemplation.

Y

Yachts represent the buying of one's spirituality. This symbol is a warning, for spirituality cannot be bought. Nor can anyone sell it.

Yard (back) symbolizes that which lies in one's past.

Yard (front) symbolizes that which lies in one's immediate future.

Yardsticks represent the measurement of one's advancement.

Yeast symbolizes expansion or extensions. Check the surrounding details of the dream to determine who needs to expand what.

Yield Signs are warnings for the dreamer to yield to something. This may indicate a situation, relationship, or belief system.

Yokes symbolize the weight of spiritual debts. These debts must be paid if the dreamer is to continue to advance spiritually.

Yule Logs indicate an individual's desire to stand on ceremony.

Z

Zealots represent fanaticism.

Zebras symbolize the polarity of good and evil, right and wrong. Closely examine the color ratio of the animal in your dream. This will clarify its message for you.

Zeniths indicate the pinnacle or fulfillment of one's purpose.

Zeros signify an emptiness.

Zippers indicate an individual's tendency to open and close issues at will. Such people tend to be domineering personalities.

Zodiacs represent a sign of commendation from the highest source.

Zombies represent those who allow others to control them through psychological ploys and the manipulation of fear. They are a warning to the dreamer to stop believing everything he or she is told.

Zookeepers symbolize an aggressive and repressive personality. Beware of those who don't allow your unique individuality or free will to be expressed.

Zoom Lenses indicate the need for a close-up look at something, whether a situation, relationship, or belief system.

Zoos symbolize those beautiful individual aspects in each of us that are being caged, either by others or by the self. Set them free!

DREAM RECALL METHODOLOGY

1. Before going to sleep, place a pen and a notebook in a convenient place beside the bed.

2. Turn out the light, lie very still, relax, and then work on programming your mental computer. Concentrate. Tell it to remember your dreams upon awakening. Instruct it over and over again. Say, "I will remember my dreams. I will remember my dreams." Sometimes your subconscious mind is resistant to new programs such as this, but if you stick with this routine several nights, you'll find it begins to work.

3. If you awake in the middle of the night with a vivid dream on your mind, immediately write it down. Record every detail that you can recall. *Don't wait until morning.*

4. Never, and I mean *never,* embellish one single aspect of the dream. You may be changing or confusing the meaning of the dream. Write down only what you actually recall.

5. Date the dream. Doing so will allow you to recognize premonitions. Some dreams may appear to be ordinary, but a few days, weeks, or

months later, you may realize they foretold events that subsequently took place.

6. Be patient. Oftentimes it takes practice to get your conscious commands through to the subconscious computer. Always be consistent, follow this simple method nightly, and you may soon be writing down as many as six dreams in *one* night.

7. Everyone dreams every night. The most visually active time of the night is around three in the morning. If after several serious attempts at recalling your dreams you are not successful, set your alarm for three in the morning and see if you awake in the midst of a vivid dream.

Such was No-Eyes' lengthy discourse on the "stuff dreams are made of."

We spent a long time afterward discussing the different facets of dreams and their symbols. The wise one explained that even though mankind had contaminated himself with his frequent indulgence in negative emotions and attitudes, he could heal himself with correct dream interpretation.

Man can use nightly dreams as a tool to *see* himself as he really is. That, in turn, will allow him to understand where his road to growth lies.

No-Eyes emphasized the healthful benefits of adults' encouraging their children, from a young age, to recall and discuss their dreams. I have found this practice to be an invaluable parental tool in determining my own children's daily problems, inner feelings, and fears.

Now you are also equipped with these same powerful tools. You possess the potent antidote to negative attitudes. Use it!

THE
S·P·I·R·I·T

The Blossom of
Eternal Life

THE CRYSTAL STREAM
The Meditation Way

On one especially balmy morning in early autumn when the fragrant mountain breeze wafted dreamily through my bedroom window, I experienced the familiar sensation of total love. As I lay unmoving, I allowed this euphoric emotion to creep into my being, bringing with it the heady sensation that a pure union with nature provides.

It is a completely selfless feeling, a sense of totally losing oneself in the Grand Design of Life. It is a perfect binding of separate spirits into one mystical brilliance. This beautiful union is a phenomenon that elevates a person's awareness of himself and his surroundings. It allows him a brief sensual glimpse into the wonders of the universe. It momentarily parts the gossamer veil that hangs between our reality and the next.

This warm feeling of oneness drifted over me like a gentle mist of an all-encompassing love. It was soothing and comforting. It eradicated all of my daily worries and petty problems. It gave me at once a sense of freedom and of being welcomed with open and embracing arms.

A beckoning whinny carried upon the wings of the wind entered my bedroom and shattered my sensuous reverie. Awaking, I knew with certainty how I'd spend my day.

The neighbors were grazing their horses down in the valley. This meant only one thing: The animals were free for the riding today. After calling for permission, I raced down into the dew-speckled meadow to greet Blue Boy.

Blue Boy was an ebony gelding of dubious parentage. But as far as I was concerned, he was all thoroughbred. He and I had ventured through many hidden mountain passes and lush valleys where the virgin forests rested peacefully in their primordial splendor.

When I reached the bottom of our hill, Blue caught my scent on the wind. His nostrils flared wide and he charged toward me, his long, coal-black mane waving in the breeze, his tail straight out behind him. He skidded to a stop in front of me and lowered his graceful neck to nudge my hand. He allowed me to lead him to a large boulder where I stood on nature's step stool and heaved myself onto his massive back.

For several sweet moments I leaned far forward, resting my weight upon his sleek neck and telling him softly how much I loved him. He turned his sculptured head around, and with his huge, soft eyes blinking, he snorted a like response. With a gentle nudge of my moccasins and a tug on his mane, we were off to places only he and I knew existed.

I gave Blue his head and he sauntered in and out of the various mountain crevices. Blue appeared to know exactly where he was going and I was alive with curiosity about where he'd take me.

After we cleared a natural corridor, the trail began to rise precariously. Blue continued to pick his surefooted way up along a ribbon of ledge carved out of the mountainside. We were climbing a considerable grade and I was becoming concerned that our dangerous trail was going to end in a dead one.

I peered over the sheer side of the cliff and came to the heart-sinking conclusion that Blue did not have the room he needed to turn around safely if we needed to.

But Blue confidently continued his slow advance. At one point he stopped to turn his head toward me and I nearly had a coronary, for I thought he was trying to turn around on that narrow ribbon of ledge.

He wasn't. He was just turning to assure me that he knew what he was doing. I breathed a little easier when I saw he turned back to the path. I sighed in a gesture of acceptance.

To the left side of us were jagged, craggy outcroppings of variegated granite. The wall was ragged and towered as high as I could see. It was a Tower of the Gods touching the very doorstep of Heaven. To the right of us was, well . . . nothing. A mere four feet or so separated Blue and me from a once-in-a-lifetime free-fall. I wasn't ready for that, not yet. I still had a heck of a lot of living to do.

I squinted up into the brilliant sapphire sky and wondered if the Great Spirit was aware of our precarious situation. I wondered if He knew whether I was ever going to walk within another pine-scented forest again. Then I caught myself up short when I realized that I certainly didn't even want to know the answer to that question. One's own ultimate square-off with Destiny is best left in the mind of the Great Spirit.

I was so deeply engrossed in my morbid thoughts, I never actually noticed when the angle of my riding changed. But I realized I was now leaning slightly backward. We were descending.

I couldn't predict where this ridge trail was leading. Blue boldly rounded several more alarming hairpin curves, descending all the while. As he came clear of the final bend, he halted with a decided stomp. As if to make clear that our perilous journey was concluded, he signaled with a violent shaking of his head and a whinny that echoed throughout the valley like an eerie banshee wail.

We were still considerably high up. Below us was the most captivating natural beauty I had yet to behold within the Rocky Mountains. This newly discovered valley was like the earthly mirror image of Eden two seconds after the Divine Creation. It was an enchanted land, so incredibly pristine, I almost expected it to vanish in wispy vapors like an imagined apparition. Perhaps my mind was hallucinating this illusion of paradise. Perhaps Blue and I had taken that dreaded free-fall after all and we were now actually experiencing the bliss of afterlife.

Yet I was so vitally alive, for my flesh was trembling with excitement, my blood rapidly surged through my arteries and veins in a deafening roar. My heart pounded like the thundering hooves of a thousand buffalo. Yes, I was alive, *alive!* And this valley was no phantasm teetering on the brink of vanishing like some winsome will-o'-the-wisp. It was touchable. It sent up myriad scents. It was as real as the noble peregrine that was soaring over its valley.

From my vantage point, I could see that the deep emerald green of the valley floor was blanketed in a dazzling rainbow of wildflowers. A distant rushing soothed my ears. A cascading waterfall spilled its glistening contents into the waiting fingers of a twisting stream. In turn, the translucent stream giggled merrily as it carried its waters this way and that before joining a shimmering lake of pure crystal prisms.

I sat astride Blue Boy while great breaths of awe involuntarily escaped from me. I didn't know how much time passed while we were on that lofty perch of ours, nor did I care. I stroked Blue's proud neck and he replied by pawing at the soft dirt of the trail ledge. I felt that time was standing still. I wondered if, indeed, Blue was some mystical specter that had whisked me through a veiled portal, up and down a path and into this high-hallowed valley of forgotten time.

But surely my very physical horse was nothing other than that. Surely he was no mythical Pegasus. Surely he had merely stumbled upon this natural passage and subsequently wandered into its beautifully pure meadow. Yet . . .

The two of us cautiously descended the final ramp of the trail, and Blue reverently set soft hooffalls upon the moist carpet of the meadow. As the pleasing potpourri of autumn scents floated dreamily about us, we moved silently through the vestal land. Our hearts throbbed in unison with a rhythmic chant, our spirits broke through their physical bounds, and our minds expanded with the awareness that we were now treading upon sacred ground.

A quiet hush escaped from Blue's hooves as they brushed through the tender blades of damp meadow grass. Together we moved through the center of the valley as though we were walking up an aisle of one of Rome's most magnificent cathedrals. The mountain peaks pointed up their sun-gilt spires to the heavens in eternal praise.

As we neared the meandering brook, its greeting coaxed us to tarry longer and to share fully in all its wonder.

I slid off Blue and let him wander wherever he wished. I stood at the edge of the swift-moving stream and deeply inhaled the sweet incense of the surrounding bushes. These scented shrubs shared their moist waterway with other bushes that were without blossoms. The wolf willow sent young orange twigs reaching up as fingers to mingle in a natural handshake with the tall mountain willows.

I stared into the mesmerizing watercourse. I left my moccasins on and stepped into the clear stream. It was knee-deep and sandy. A sandy stream is highly unusual for the Rocky Mountains. It didn't take long to appreciate the softness and rarity of this particular stream. The waters were rushing and bitingly cold, but so refreshing. I don't know how much time passed before I stepped up onto the far side.

The vibrant autumn colors and the fragrance of the thriving life around me were finely honed to saber-sharp clarity. I picked my way around the willows and approached the cool shade of the forest edge. Here I reclined among the aspen's fallen coins-of-gold to absorb the panoramic view of this sacred valley.

My soft bed was sheltered by a filigreed canopy of green. The mature lodgepole pines clustered around me, casting vibrating sunbeams of lace across my bedroom. I was as content as a babe in arms.

As far as I could tell, the valley was enclosed completely by the high mountains. It was as though I were in a medieval fortress, protected by the stone parapets and turrets of nature. There was no way in and no way out except along the dangerous path Blue had used. The lush valley was a playground for the vast array of wildlife that thrived naturally, enjoying the absence of man. Here, nature was in perfect balance.

I was hard-pressed to comprehend a region such as this in today's shrinking world. Ours is a world where the virgin forests and untouched lands are a thing of the past. At the same time, how can a rational mind dispute the proven, touchable reality? This valley was a real place.

I stopped trying to analyze the reasons for its existence. I knew that too many beautiful experiences were lost on people because they tried to pick them apart. No-Eyes had taught me the technique of becoming one with something by merely observing it, without the distraction of conscious thought. I did this now.

Suddenly I was one with the sweet valley entity. I was one with the mighty protective sentinels that guarded it. I was one with all the living creatures within its safe confines. I was the only human in this virgin land. I was a mystical being. And I was real. I was Summer Rain, and I was on Sacred Ground.

A shadow sliced the blue of sky. I watched the falcon soar across the mammoth backdrop of his azure domain. And I joined with it and flew with its magnificent free spirit. I observed the sparkling stream as its cascading waters danced and chanted. And I joined with its spirit and sang a new, sweet mountain song. I observed the hushed whisper on the breath of the breeze. And I joined with it and shared its ancient secrets. I observed the pulsating sun. And I joined.

I was jolted into wakefulness by a sudden wetness on my warmed face. Blue was gently nudging me. It must have been time to leave this enchanted place.

The blazing sun had calmed to a slow-burning glow. It threw down long fingers across the valley floor. A certain expectancy permeated the stillness. Nature awaited the entity of Dusk.

Blue and I walked side by side back through the meadow that time forgot. We retraced our steps until we reached the natural ramp of the trail. I took several steps up while Blue remained below me. Swinging myself up on the waiting animal, I glanced back upon the valley that had suddenly flared up with the magical fire of alpenglow. I studied the scene from boundary to boundary, imprinting it upon my mind. After releasing a deep sigh, I nudged my Pegasus forward and he carried me up and out of our mystical Sacred Ground, the same Sacred Ground that I would one day return to for my vision quest of the spirit.

A few days later, I drove out to No-Eyes' cabin. It was a crisp mountain morning and I had the road to myself. I took advantage of this and slowed the pickup in order to lengthen my journey.

Lining the roadsides were tall jack pines that swayed their heads in gentle unison. It was like driving through a tunnel of green. After rounding a curve, the massive evergreens were left behind and the roadside fell away into a deeply sloped valley that was ablaze with miles and miles of orange and yellow aspen stands that contrasted sharply with their vivid backdrop of turquoise sky. It was scenes such as this that took my breath away. I was in a euphoric mood when I greeted No-Eyes that wondrous autumn morn.

"Summer look like she be some drunk!" she teased while opening her door. "No-Eyes think maybe we have lesson outside today . . . but not now, not how Summer look!" She yanked me inside and slammed the door.

I whipped my serape over my head and flung it on the couch. I was excited from my beautiful drive. I was full of the particular warmth that comes with a special union, a touching.

"It's one of those days, No-Eyes," I crooned guiltily.

She lowered her head and shook it while trying to conceal her wide grin. "What No-Eyes gonna do with Summer?" she said, sighing heavily. "All times Summer let mountains snatch spirit away." She shook her head. "Some days Summer be like some skinwalker that can just take off."

"Shame on you, No-Eyes, I'm no skinwalker."

"No-Eyes know that. Summer's spirit just be too, too easy for mountains to call away, that all."

I fussed with her kindling and began building a graduated pyramid within her cold fireplace.

"What so!" I grinned.

The aged visionary pulled up her rocker in front of the hearth. "Tsk-tsk," she clucked. "Better open up that damper 'fore Summer light that match," she casually warned while bending into the old chair. "No-Eyes was gonna let Summer go 'head without checkin' . . . but I not like house all full of smoke like Summer's head. Summer need to see how autumn mountains steal mind away, too—fill it with that *woodsmoke!*"

I quickly opened the damper as cautioned, lit the fire, and watched it grow through the stack of piñon and juniper. I watched the licking flames for several minutes. I ignored No-Eyes' sarcasm. Behind me, I heard the familiar creak and thud of her rocking chair.

"Gonna stare in there all day?" she asked sharply.

I turned and smiled. She had not managed to steal away my wonderful mood. I gazed into the Old One's deep-set eyes and softly spoke.

"I love you, No-Eyes."

She fumbled with the tassels of the shawl I had given her. She examined her fingers and without looking up at me replied, "No-Eyes love Summer, too."

I leaned forward and placed a tender kiss on the gray, wispy hairs of her head before sitting near the fire in front of her. It began to crackle and snap. It added a comforting mellowness to our already glowing friendship. Silence passed between us as we listened to the lone voice that spoke from beyond the warming hearth.

I was mentally replaying the video of my day with Blue, for I had successfully imprinted every detail in vivid Technicolor. Suddenly the film went blank—the Old One had pushed the stop button.

"Where Summer gonna *be* today, anyway?" she barked. "Summer be so rude some days," came the exasperated sigh.

I looked up into the time-worn face. "I'm sorry, but that drive this morning really brought me up. It pulled me right out, and the feeling it left behind reminded me of a place Blue and I went during the week."

"Humph!" she mumbled with flaring eyes. "It be some big *secret?* Or Summer gonna share this great, wonderful place with old woman?"

I was glad she wanted to hear about it. All the initial wonderment welled within me as I told her about our beautiful untouched valley, our Sacred Ground. When I finished, I anxiously waited for her response.

The Old One sat without comment. She stared sightlessly past me into the firelight that flickered shadows across her deeply creviced face. Then she spoke softly.

"Summer be lucky she got place like that to go. No-Eyes was gonna talk 'bout certain stuff today, but now we gonna change all that."

The rocker began its metered rhythm.

"We been talkin' a lot 'bout Earthway to live. We speak 'bout bodies, we speak 'bout right way to think, an' right attitudes, an' 'bout all that dream stuff even. I think now be good time to speak 'bout place that be inside peoples, special place for spirit journey. It be like that Sacred Ground stuff of Summer's."

"My place made you think of that, didn't it?" I smiled.

"Yup. But mostly that *stream* in Summer's place make No-Eyes think of *different* stream, stream that run through Sacred Ground of *spirit.*"

My eyes lit up. "Are you talking about the kundalini stream?"

She simply nodded. "That be one all right, but it got no special name like that. No-Eyes see it be stream that spirit can ride right up through Power Point Gates into awareness, into enlightenment, right up to Great Spirit even."

And the wise sage began her lesson.

We so often read and hear about the severity of mankind's frequent depressed and despondent moods. People beat their breasts and wail that they have been forgotten by everyone—including God—and that they have been abandoned in a world full of apathy.

Why do people forever place blame on God? Why do people find it so easy to make Him their scapegoat for their disappointments and tribulations?

The physical body is merely a vehicle, an outer shell that encases the living core, the real self. That real self is the portion of Him that resides within each of us—our *spirit.* God does not forget anyone. Nor does He forsake His beloved children. Do not seek the Source only within the confines of worship buildings. Do not look for Him only within the dogma of a specific religion. God is *within* each of us, always. Always He is within us.

Mankind has been left an invaluable inheritance. This legacy encompasses many talents of the spirit, including a way each of us can communicate with the Source—the direct private line of meditation.

Meditation is not learned solely through the tutelage of an Eastern master. It is not a form of self-hypnosis, nor is it something to fool around with. What meditation is, is a *pathway* leading directly to the Source of all knowledge and enlightenment.

In perfect meditation, you will receive the answers you seek. Meditation is the opposite of prayer. While prayer represents the individual's *action* of speaking to the Source, meditation conversely represents man's inaction of silence—his *listening* for the Source's wisdom. One is active while the other is passive. Meditation is the process of learning to calm your thinking and activities so that you can pause and rest awhile within the Silence.

The Creator willed that mankind be created in His spirit likeness. Yet, people crush and smother that likeness with their continued doubts and skepticisms. Why is it so difficult for people to believe a child can perceive something that they cannot? Why is it so difficult for people to believe their child when he says that he heard something that they did not? These sensual perceptions are the fruit of an open mind. These spiritual sights and sounds are evidence of budding awareness. Perhaps you yourself saw and heard special things when you were a small child. Perhaps *your* elders disbelieved you, and you learned to ignore your perceptions rather than be ridiculed for them. Well, your ability to perceive is still there! It is just dormant, waiting for you. It is waiting for you to open up your mind and heart. *Look* for it. Know that it is there—waiting within yourself. *Believe* in it. *Cherish* it.

Within the physical body are ductless glands. There are six main glands. (Some like to include a seventh, the pancreas, which contains a cluster of island cells, but this is not a true gland in the sense of a spiritual Power Point. The awakened Stream of Force is considered the Seventh Aspect.) These six main glands serve as the body's Power Point Gates through which the meditative energy Force must flow. During meditation, these usually quiet glands will become active, each in turn, as the current of the Force approaches them. They awaken to become Power Points of highly potent activity.

The six Power Point Gates are, beginning from the lowest, the gonads, the adrenals, the thymus, the thyroid, the pineal, and the pituitary. We will examine each one individually.

The **GONADS** are Gates of the male and female sexual glands. These glands emit specific hormones that stimulate and awaken the stream of the Force. It is within these glands that the powerful Force lies dormant. The associated color for these glands is red.

The **ADRENALS** are Gates situated directly above the kidneys and are the source of positive and negative energy reservoirs. The adrenals are the life force of the entire physical, mental, and spiritual system. Yellow is the color to envision when concentrating upon this Power Point Gate.

The **THYMUS** gland rests just above the physical heart; hence it has been referred to as the heart center. It is this Power Point Gate that determines how celestial alignments at the time of birth affect the character and personality of an individual. It is the last Gate of the lower three that directly relates to the physical aspects of man's nature. The color associated with the thymus is green.

The **THYROID** gland is the Power Point Gate located within the throat area. It is from this Gate that the gift of tongues originates. The thyroid is associated with the color blue.

The **PINEAL** gland is located at the base of the physical brain and is the Gate through which all forms of psychic awareness stem. The color associated with this Gate is purple.

The **PITUITARY** gland is the Gate located at the frontal part of the physical brain and hangs from a membrane. It resembles a pearl. This Gate is extremely fragile and sensitive. It is when this final Power Point Gate is opened that you can become one with the Source. The color associated with this Gate is white.

Meditation is the only true way of connecting with the Source. The Force is there waiting within each and every individual. You don't need incense or music to activate it; you don't need drugs or special esoteric ceremonies. There is no need for any paraphernalia; such gadgets are only extraneous and bothersome trappings. Basically, all one needs to do is to reach out and activate the Force by having a pure mind, a strong desire, and a highly spiritual intention.

Once the current of the Force is awakened, it becomes a stream coursing up through the Gates. It is like a physical fire, for it can be used for positive or negative purposes, to destroy or to aid and save. You, within your mind, must determine in what manner you desire to use this most powerful Force.

If you choose to be a destructive force and have a negative intent, the Force stream will rise up through your Gates and you will direct it for negative purposes. But be ever mindful, if this is your tendency, that the evil that you perpetrate and unleash will indeed return to you tenfold, for when it reaches the pituitary Gate, the Source will not be waiting for you. . . . *Another* will be. This is not meant to frighten or threaten; this is merely the truth.

The first thing you must do to awaken the still waters that flow through the Gates is to be of pure intentions. Next, situate yourself in a comfortable position, sitting or reclining; just be sure your spine is straight. This allows the stream of the Force to flow smoothly.

You will not need to concentrate (which is a mental *action*), because for successful meditation passivity is required. You will at first experience many disassociated thoughts trying to assail your mental vision—let them have their say. *Allow them to pass* before your mind's eye without giving them any mental energies. After a time, you will be without visions and thoughts to distract your intended purpose. Soon you will be within a peaceful voice— the meditative Silence.

The amount of time you spend in meditation has no significance. You may sit or recline for only fifteen minutes or you may remain within the Silence for hours. Do not concern yourself with time; it is completely irrelevant.

What is relevant is that you are consistent. Routine practice is the key to success. Some people give up because they claim they "never *get* anything."

That attitude is an *active* one of expectation, and you'll never get anywhere with it. Meditation will eventually make your physical systems more relaxed. Meditation will bestow a calming effect upon your mind and bring you more tolerance with your fellow men. Meditation has a way of smoothing out man's rough edges and giving him an acceptance of life. Meditation will one day bring the words of the Source into your heart, but only if you are consistent, not expectant.

Now I'd like to share with you some words of caution.

The true meditative state opens the Gates of each Power Point as the Force approaches them. At such a time, the entire spiritual body is exposed to the finer elements of reality, elements that are oftentimes more harmful than good. Through this opening up, you are exposing your fragile psychic self (mental and spiritual) to a variety of outside influences that may wish, or have the capability, to affect you seriously in a negative way. To prevent this from happening you must erect safeguards around yourself. The only shield No-Eyes recommended is the White Light of Protection.

To erect this shield, you must visualize yourself (body) with a brilliant white light completely surrounding you. Some choose to visualize themselves within a cocoon of this White Light, which is very effective. Some like to see themselves within a bubble of White Light, which works equally well. And others seem to feel completely protected only when they visualize the White Light with speared rays emanating outward.

This White Light of Protection will prevent any negative physical, mental, or psychic harm from coming to you. You should do the visualization just before your affirmation of pure purpose at the beginning of meditation when you first assume your restful position.

During the course of true meditation, you may experience unnerving sensations. Many times your body may twitch or you may hear sounds such as a clicking or popping. You may feel a slight breeze waft across your face or hands, or you may have the sensation of being lightly touched. Other sensations are that of expanding or growing larger, drifting or floating. Sometimes a whispering will be heard near your ears, or you will notice the expansion and increase of echoes. These sensations often occur while the Gates are opening. They serve as clear indicators that all is progressing well. However, do not give these sensations any conscious attention. For your meditation to proceed, you must ignore them. If you do so, they will soon disappear altogether, leaving you alone within your quiet Silence of complete meditation where you will be able to receive incoming information.

Group meditation is to be avoided. Please understand the difference between group meditation and group healings. They are separate entities. Personal meditation is your private way of letting the current of spiritual energy, the powerful Force, flow up through you. Meditation is letting the crystal stream of the God-Force reach your highest Gate, thereby letting your cup overflow with His grace and essence. Meditation is a one-on-One touching with the Source's; it is the most intimate thing you'll ever do. True meditation can only be done alone . . . alone with the Source!

Be peaceful. Enter the Silence. Let your inner Crystal Stream flow freely through your Sacred Ground . . . the Sacred Ground where God awaits. All you have to do is open the Gate.

WARRIORS OF LIGHT
AND DARK
The Reality of Spirit Forces

My next visit with No-Eyes was going to be very different: for the first time Bill was invited to come with me. This day was special.

It was late autumn. The morning was perfect, the trees about to shoot off their final fireworks. The temperature was still mild for mid-October, giving us extra days to enjoy and celebrate nature.

The journey to the cabin was especially nice because I was now free to look around at the mountainside splendor. Bill was doing the driving this day and I loved having him with me.

We have always shared everything, and the Visionary's lessons were twice as easy having someone to practice them with. Bill was an adept learner and was finally going to meet his absentee instructor face-to-face. We were in high spirits and were both filled with a great anticipation.

My teacher had requested to see us together and we had agreed on this midweek date. She never gave me a reason for her strange request. I just supposed it would be natural for her to want to see Bill in person, to pick up on his personality and his essence of development. After all, I had bragged to her about how well he comprehended her lessons. He knew as well as I that this day could bring just about anything. We didn't know what she had planned for this very special meeting, but we did know that we wouldn't be disappointed.

Twice on our way to No-Eyes' cabin, Bill pulled the pickup over to the side of the road. We were traveling through some spectacular country and it was just too beautiful to pass up. We would sit by the wayside and silently

412

join in nature's celebration of life. No words were necessary. The fact that he had his arms around me was enough.

There wasn't much traffic on the highway. The hour was early and the misty morning light gently touched the sleeping entities of nature. They nodded in drowsiness and stretched their limbs in an effort to greet the newborn day. The spirit of the morning crept softly toward the eastern mountainsides while lovingly placing kisses of dew on the sleeping heads of all she passed over.

A reverent silence permeated all of life. Then, a bare breath of breeze provoked hushed whispers from the waking jack pines. The rising sun peered over a saw-toothed ridge, and a golden shaft of light shot down into the valley like a mystical cue stick, scattering the predawn shadows into the holes and crevices of the wide cottonwood canyon. It was now officially morning, and our world was once again teeming with the thriving wonders of life.

No-Eyes was waiting for us. She had moved the rickety rocker out into the morning sunshine. She loved to feel its warm spirit bathe her leathery face. The old woman remained motionless as we approached.

We said nothing. We stood off a ways, waiting for her to break her meditative state.

Silence.

Respectfully, we waited.

"You two gonna stand there all day?" barked the woman.

Bill gave me an incredulous look, as much as to say, "Oh, brother!"

I smiled back, to let him know "you ain't seen *nothin'* yet!"

And we walked up to the porch.

I introduced the two and Bill spoke first. "I'm very pleased to meet you, No-Eyes. Your friendship has meant a great deal to Summer. You've taught us both such beautiful things and I want to thank you."

"Humph!" came the clipped, unexpected reply.

I didn't understand her rudeness. She had requested to meet him and here she was being short with him. I had tolerated much humiliation from this old woman so that I could learn from her, but I never stood by for any unkindness directed at Bill—not from anyone.

"No-Eyes! This is my husband and—"

"Hush, Summer! I not be done. Where Summer's manners be?"

"I was about to ask you the same thing," I barked back.

"Summer be too quick to judge. Summer interrupt here."

"I apologize," I said, shooting Bill a quick glance.

No-Eyes leaned forward and reached out her knobby fingers toward Bill. "Come closer, Bill."

Bill climbed the gray, sun-bleached log steps and sat in front of the woman. He tenderly held the old hand between his own.

"Ahhh . . . ahhhh. Yup. Yup," she whispered in a long, drawn-out breath while her head slowly bobbed up and down. Her previous frown had turned into a bright grin. The deep crow's-feet at the corners of her eyes creased deeper and her nose wrinkled with a secret joy.

"No-Eyes knew. No-Eyes knew it," she chirped. "No-Eyes *knew* Bill gonna feel this way. You just like No-Eyes knew you'd be."

Bill laughed and I joined them on the warm porch. He was still grinning.

"How's that, No-Eyes?" he asked.

She hugged his hand and stroked it gently. She nodded. "Summer's man got white-man skin," she said while kneading it. Then one finger raised. "But he got warrior *spirit* . . . spirit that be one with all earth spirits. Summer an' Bill be like sun an' rain—earth need both to live." She giggled with her hand covering her mouth like a small child.

We smiled at her kind words.

Then she began again. "No-Eyes not be rude before when Summer interrupt. Bill, you say you thank No-Eyes for teaching beautiful stuff. And No-Eyes say 'humph' to that! Bill got it all backward! Bill an' Summer already *knew* words old woman speak to Summer. You only need way to *remember.* No-Eyes do that bringin' back stuff, that all."

Bill's brows furrowed. "Would you explain that a little more clearly?"

"What so? What to explain?" she asked, leaning back into her chair.

"Well, I don't want to appear ignorant, but I never knew of *all* the things you taught Summer before she relayed them to me. Yet you say I did."

"Yup!" she replied, displaying her famous toothless grin while gently rocking.

I was going into personal hysterics inside. Bill was now receiving a firsthand dose of attempting to get somewhere in a conversation with the Old One. True to his sense of humor, he took it in stride.

"If I already knew of these things, why did they appear so completely new to me?"

"*Think*, Bill."

My quiet mirth intensified over his increasingly sticky situation. He was digging himself in deeper and deeper. I listened as he attempted another approach.

"I think you have the best of me. I just don't understand," he gently admitted.

Deeper and deeper did he dig his hole. He had said the wrong thing.

The Old One shook one thin finger in his face.

"That be big *cop*-out! Bill try to *trick* No-Eyes!" Then she softened with wiseness. She slyly grinned. "No-Eyes say again, *think.*" And she smugly leaned back, closed her eyes, and began the wait as the rocker took up a patient pace.

He frowned over at me under lowered brows.

I simply shrugged my shoulders.

He opened his hands to me as if requesting some helpful input.

The Visionary shot one dark eye open. "Blah! Summer not gonna help Bill out! Bill not ever help Summer out when No-Eyes tell *Summer* to think!"

Bill had regrettably forgotten that even though the woman couldn't physically see, she had her own inner sight. Nothing escaped her fine mind. One had to conduct oneself in her presence as though the Old One was carefully scrutinizing every move.

"I'm sorry, No-Eyes," he began, "that was really rude of me."

"Not be rude. Maybe thoughtless," she replied matter-of-factly, "but not be rude."

Silence reigned for several minutes as we became serious and Bill gave her words deep consideration before he spoke again.

"My conscious mind didn't remember what my old spirit had known all along," he stated with assurance.

Her wide toothless grin brought a burst of laughter from all of us. The old woman was bubbling with excitement.

"Now Bill be cookin'!" With that, she bolted from her chair and ordered us inside.

The cabin was cool after our sitting out in the direct sun, and we trailed after her to the small kitchen.

The herbal supply no longer looked as imposing as it once had, for I was developing my own collection of jars and bottles, and hers were now a more familiar sight.

No-Eyes had brewed up one of her special tea blends and we returned to her cozy living room. She dragged in one of the kitchen chairs while Bill and I sank down into the lumpy couch.

Our teacher wasted no time in beginning her talk.

"All spirits know truths," she said. "Some people's minds not be ready, some not sure, an' some go seekin'. You two go seekin'. You know here," she said while placing her fist to her thin chest, "that there be much more to life. You doubt much, too. You search for words that feel right. You find . . . then you remember. I only give tiny push."

We knew she was right. The things she taught us did feel right, they were like coming home. However, Bill had a further question for her.

"No-Eyes, I know what you're saying is true. Once you jarred our soul memories, everything was relatively simple after that. What I'm wondering, though, is this: Why wouldn't *all* people be receptive to these same truths if they exist in the memory of their spirits?"

She grinned. "That be good one."

I winked over at Bill and we waited for the wisdom that we knew was forthcoming.

No-Eyes sipped her tea. "Want more tea?"

After we both said no, Bill jumped up and sprinted outside.

I was about to ask what was wrong when the Old One smiled at me. "He been worryin' 'bout No-Eyes in this stiff chair. He wanna go get my rocker."

Sure enough, Bill came back in carrying the cumbersome wooden chair. He set it down next to the stiff one and helped our teacher into it. After he returned the useless one back to the kitchen, he resettled himself down into the softness of the couch.

"That been nice, Bill."

He flushed. "I just didn't think you looked very comfortable in that other one. Now you look just like you're supposed to." No-Eyes was going to offer some criticism, but before she could get a word of it out, Bill finished what he was saying. "And I didn't mean that you were expected to look any certain way . . . with your rocker. All I thought was that you were uncomfortable without it."

She sighed and smiled. "Good thing Bill not be in expectation 'bout how peoples 'posed to look. Good thing Bill not done that."

"I wouldn't do that, No-Eyes."

"No-Eyes know."

A brief silence followed as the Old One settled herself into the well-worn rocker cushions. Soon the familiar creak and thud began.

"Now we gonna get back to what we be talkin' 'bout. Summer tell Bill of other side. Many, many spirits be there. It be like big school. They all at different levels. Some take many births to advance out of one level. Others go fast. Many peoples be like baby. Baby not gonna grasp big words, big meanings to ideas. They not understand. They not have *ability* to believe. Yet they seek comfort. They always seekin' somethin'. They not know what they want even. They not know what they seekin' even. Them baby peoples think they seek happiness. They think happiness be money or good job or fame. They be all wrong, all mixed up. They be just like babies.

"Spirits that be advanced on other side—spirits that be almost completed—they seek, too. They not seek money in life. They not seek material stuff or fame. They seek somethin' more. They have truths inside. They need bit of push to remember. Then they no seek again. See?"

We saw that it all boiled down to an awareness of the spirit. Some people were more spiritually advanced than others. It was that simple. She explained that the spirit had an awareness like the mind possessed intellect. A child couldn't mentally grasp the complex theories of a university psychology course just as a nonadvanced spirit couldn't comprehend the finer memories or abilities of the advanced spirit. These spiritually unaware people are the current skeptics and doubters. They are the ones who presently have no belief in anything but what they can touch, for they are not in any real contact with their spirits.

These thoughts weren't quite settling right with me.

"No-Eyes?"

"Yup."

"Being a skeptic, even a confirmed one, doesn't necessarily mean the door is closed on one's awakening. I mean, such people can still be exposed to the truths and then start wondering. Their wondering can lead to questioning and a lessening of doubts after some research is done."

The Old One nodded in agreement. "Yup. That happen sometimes. No-Eyes not say all them skeptics not be able to see an' know truth. But some not want to admit they been so wrong. Some not wanna know what be real—they be scared. An' some be just too, too cozy in their own simple belief."

Those words brought the die-hard groups to mind. She was talking about religious fanatics. We personally knew some of them, and their reasoning abilities were so faulty it was downright scary.

"I feel sorry for those ones, No-Eyes," I said. "They're led by exterior dogmas instead of what their spirit knows. They're like robots . . . no, more like lemmings that group together for support, and then they work themselves up into frightful states of hysteria that they think is God's power come into them." I shook my head. "It's really so sad how far off the mark they are."

The rocker creaked. Outside, the wind soughed through the pines. No words passed between the three of us in the cabin, for there was nothing left to say. Our shared silent sorrow for those who voluntarily chose ignorance said it all. The silence cooled to a physical chill.

"No-Eyes?" Bill said. "It's clouding up. Would you like me to start a fire?"

"That be nice, Bill."

He crossed the room to the hearth. And I watched our teacher.

Although she didn't turn to the fireplace, I felt her watching Bill's movements. An elfin twinkle sparked her eyes.

"Good thing Bill not got woodsmoke in head," she mumbled.

"What?" Bill asked, turning around.

Creak-thud. Creak-thud.

I explained the comment she'd made. "No-Eyes is glad to see you checked the damper before you started the fire."

"Oh. I always do that."

"Yeah, but one day I didn't."

"You always do, too."

"I was preoccupied at the—"

"Blah! Summer had that *woodsmoke* in head that time!"

I smiled at Bill and shrugged.

He grinned at me and then gave his attention to No-Eyes. "Yeah, I know what you mean. She's been known to do that now and then."

"Hey, you two! What is this?"

"Summer," came the soft voice. "No-Eyes hopin' that woodsmoke gonna always be there . . . now an' then."

"It will, No-Eyes. It will."

And with a newborn fire starting to test its voice, Bill returned to the couch.

Nobody spoke. Bill knew not to break the silence, for we needed to give the Visionary time to prepare for her next subject. Not that she needed to collect her thoughts. But she demanded the proper atmosphere to surround each lesson.

My thoughts were many during this quiet pause. Mostly they were ones of great contentedness, for my two best friends were finally in one room. And I loved the feeling that gave me.

Creak-thud. Creak-thud.

We heightened our attention.

"Summer, Bill, No-Eyes need to speak 'bout some important stuff now."

Bill leaned forward. "We're listening."

The Old One sighed a weighted breath. Her obsidian eyes slowly bored into Bill's, then mine.

"This gonna be serious stuff."

We didn't comment.

"It be serious spirit stuff."

I was about to ask if it involved the wayward spirits, but I thought better of it and held my tongue.

She sighed again, leaned her weariness back into the chair, and rocked with a decided meter.

"Summer, remember day we first meet?"

"Yes."

"Remember when No-Eyes tell how we gonna sneak Summer through like snake in grass?"

"Yes. Yes . . . I remember that." I also remembered why she had said that, and if her spirit stuff was going to be about that subject, this was indeed going to be a serious talk—a *very* serious talk. And if this was true, the wayward spirits paled in contrast.

Her black eyes bored into mine. "Yup. We gonna talk 'bout *them* ones now."

I turned to answer Bill's questioning look. "She means the Dark Ones."

His cheeks flushed.

She noticed. "Yup, Bill, we need to talk 'bout them now. It be right time 'cause you two gonna need all power you can get." She hesitated a moment. "It gonna be bad for you two . . . gonna be bad."

I swallowed hard.

Bill's attention became intense. "We know, No-Eyes. We've been involved for several years now."

The Visionary closed her eyes for a time. When she opened them again, they were filled with sorrow.

"That been baby stuff, Bill. That only been tiny games."

Bill and I exchanged surprised glances.

"Yup. They only been playin' with you two."

I rearranged myself on the couch and crossed my legs Indian style.

"But No-Eyes, if those were all just games, they play very seriously. They got us turned-down jobs, they fool with the truck all the time, they get my manuscripts rejected by putting doubts in editors' heads, they cause physical harm whenever they can. I could go on and on how they've foiled our lives and messed up every opportunity we've had to get the truths out to the masses. Our spiritual purpose has been just *full* of battles with them. How can you say they've been just games?"

Bill agreed. "They even put me in the hospital once. I needed a back operation and we had no insurance. Seems they love to keep us poor because we can't go anywhere with our purpose like that."

"Games. All games. That all been tiny stuff. They playin' with you two like some cat with mouse."

I sighed. If we'd been playing cat-and-mouse games all these years, what the hell were the real battles going to be like? Now I was getting very worried. I was getting scared.

"Scared gonna get Summer killed maybe. Strong power gonna get some stuff *done.*" The statement was delivered in soft words—a softness that felt like a hard slap in the face.

Bill asked why they'd step up their intensity.

"Remember what No-Eyes been askin' 'bout that snake in grass stuff? Summer gonna make it through with them books. Them books Summer been tryin' gonna finally get cross battle line. They not gonna like that. They gonna see they gotta play harder. They gonna bring in more warriors to watch Summer an' Bill. They no want truths out 'cause it make their work harder."

"I haven't written any book yet, No-Eyes."

"Books. Summer gonna write more than one."

"I hadn't planned on that. I was just going to do one about our times together and share a little of your wisdom. I'm planning on calling the book *Spirit Song.*"

She liked that title. "That be so nice name for first book. It fit. Summer got much song in heart."

I smiled. "I was thinking what was in *your* heart, No-Eyes."

"No-Eyes' song almost done. Summer got many left to sing 'bout. Summer do that singin' with *many* song books."

I wasn't about to argue. *Spirit Song* was all I was going to do. I was sure of it. I'd touch on all her lessons and that was that. I returned to our former discussion.

"All right. So I get snuck across the battle lines with *Spirit Song.* So?"

A wispy, gray brow rose. "What so? What so? So now they gonna see who one of main players be!"

My heart skipped a beat . . . several beats.

"Summer, once they know main players, players who find ways to win, they gonna get mean."

"They've been mean, No-Eyes."

"Summer not even seen enemy yet. They gonna start showin' themselves to Summer."

"Oh, No-Eyes," I sighed, "why me?"

Bill turned to me. "That's why we volunteered—*that's* why us."

I gazed over to the fire flames. I felt tired.

"Summer got Bill," came the whispered reply.

I turned and patted his leg. "Yeah, I got my Bill. We make quite a pair."

He rubbed my hand, then squeezed it before giving the Visionary his attention.

"No-Eyes, this whole thing has been quite a strain on us. Just as soon as it looks like we've got our heads above water, they strike again."

"No-Eyes know. That way it gonna be with all main players. The main warriors never gonna get coffee breaks, they gonna always have to be prepared . . . always."

"But sometimes the fight seems so futile. Every upcoming opportunity is a gamble. It's like a fifty-fifty toss-up if we win and—"

"Toss-up?" she repeated with a frown.

"A coin flip," I clarified.

She knew that one and quickly faced Bill again so he could go on.

"Well, sometimes we get to wondering why we even came back when every chance to get ahead with our work gets shot down."

Her face expressed her amazement. "Summer an' Bill wanna quit? Maybe even leave?"

We exchanged glances.

I lowered my head. "Sounds awful, huh? But No-Eyes, how much is one expected to endure anyway? Just how much heartache and defeat can one take?"

"As much as they give back," came the cold response.

"Give *back!* We can't fight enemies we can't even see! What are we supposed to fight back with?"

"Faith. Faith in purpose an' power in spirit. That be what powerful warrior be, Summer. That what *powerful* warriors be."

"No-Eyes, if we didn't have faith and powerful spirits we'd be long gone—*long* gone."

She merely glared at me.

My scalp crawled. "I just described your powerful warrior, huh, No-Eyes?"

Creak-thud. Creak-thud.

Bill had just witnessed his first real-life verbal circle dance. His expression was one of fascination, but he wasn't so enthralled that he'd lost his voice.

"So what do we need after the book is out and—"

"Books," came the correction.

". . . after the books are out and they intensify their efforts?"

"Determination. Summer an' Bill gonna need strong determination an' to remember why you both be here in first place. Them books be purpose . . . gonna get them books out so peoples wake up."

"Then?" he pushed.

"Then help people with them letters people gonna write you."

"Then?"

"Then help them dumb lost spirits."

Bill looked to me and back to No-Eyes. "Then?"

Silence.

"No-Eyes?" he whispered. "Then?"

"What so, then? Them books an' letters an' spirits gonna take up all time you two got. What more Bill wanna do?"

He grinned to soften the seriousness of the issue. "Oh, I don't know . . . a little fishing might be nice, or maybe time to read a book or two. Time for Summer to walk in the woods."

The lady smiled. "Time gonna be left," she said. "Time gonna be left to keep them battles goin'."

Silence.

"No-Eyes say this be serious stuff. That what old woman mean. Peoples gotta know what be goin' on here. This be serious time! Phoenix Days be here now. Dark Side warriors been so busy already. They been workin' with them phony prophets who tell peoples they can make their own realities. They been teachin' selfish spirit ways. That why they not want truths to be out. Light Side warriors been fightin' back hard. Battles been bad but they gonna get worse an' worse. Bigger fights. More battles. More an' bigger each day while Phoenix be risin'. Them Dark warriors gonna start showin' selves to Summer. They be so dark an' powerful, but Summer not gonna show fright—Summer gonna need to show her own power to them ones."

Silence.

"Warriors of Light an' Dark been fightin' so hard. There gonna be great battle times now over peoples' minds . . . souls. Each side gonna try to win most peoples over to their side of battle lines. Great war goin' on now."

Silence.

"Them spirits been fightin', too. They fight real hard for their warriors in physical dimensions. It goin' on all over . . . here an' over there, too. It just gonna get worse."

Silence.

"Sons of Light fightin' Sons of Dark. Each side know who main warriors be. Each side work extra hard on those ones. Them warriors gotta be so, so powerful in spirit, in heart an' head."

Silence.

"Summer an' Bill stay strong, huh?"

Two heads nodded.

"Gotta stay strong in power."

"No-Eyes?" I said.

"Yup?"

"Is all this fighting leading up to something?"

"Yup."

"Something real big?"

"Yup."

"Really big?"

"Yup."

"Will these battles ever be over?"

Her eyes twinkled with the thought. "Yup."

I was deathly afraid to ask. I almost left it at that, but I had to know.

"When . . . when will they be over?"

She was suddenly most grave. "When Phoenix be flyin' free!"

Oh, my God, I thought, the first skirmishes of Armageddon were already being fought . . . and nobody even had time to choose sides.

"They got time, Summer. If peoples wake up, they got some time."

I couldn't think straight. Only two questions unraveled themselves from my shocked consciousness.

"Will *He* come?"

"Yup."

"When?"

Creak-thud. Creak-thud.

"When, No-Eyes?"

Silence.

"How much time is left, No-Eyes?"

"Summer gotta get them books done."

"You didn't answer my question! You're changing the subject!"

Creak-thud. Creak-thud.

Bill touched my arm. Our eyes met. Mine were flaming, his were as soft as his voice.

"No, she didn't, honey. That *was* her answer. There's time left . . . there's still some time."

I slouched down into the couch and gave myself time to think. No wonder the Old One foresaw me doing more than one book. If that was the case, then books I'd do—lots of books. Maybe three. No, ten. Maybe two dozen. A *hundred* then! But I knew that those were just feeble wishful thoughts, for a grand timepiece had been set in motion. It wasn't mine to tamper with—it was God's . . . and the ticking made a mournful sound. Tick . . . Tick . . . Tick . . .

3

THE BROTHERHOOD
The Hoop of All Intelligent Life-forms

. . . Tick . . . Tick . . .

Finally I raised my eyes to the rocker. Sitting there was not an aged woman. She had no age. I saw no racial features. All those discriminating particulars were gone. What I saw was a Light Warrior. And what I felt was the passing of the coupstick. The elder warrior's days were numbered, her battles too numerous to count. I was her last student, so to me the war shield was passed. The shield and coupstick were not tangible objects; they were the nebulous power and purpose of one handed over to another. With great respect I accepted them, for in doing so I would greatly honor the one who had fought so fiercely before me. With love in my heart would I mix my own blood-and-tears coups with those already marking the trails of my teacher's long-suffered life.

Bill knew something important had just passed between No-Eyes and myself. He felt the electricity of it permeating the whole of the cabin, but respectfully he remained on the perimeter until the Old One was ready to bring him back into the circle again.

"We done talkin' 'bout them battles now," she said. "We got other stuff to talk 'bout."

The high intensity of our former discussion eased into a lighter vibration, and Bill and I were grateful. We readjusted ourselves on the couch and immediately felt more relaxed.

The Visionary directed her opening question to me.

"What Summer gonna write 'bout?"

423

"You. Your words. Some of what we've shared. Some things we've done together."

"Gotta tell 'bout Phoenix Days."

"Yes. That's one of the most important issues I'll cover. People need to know of your future visions."

Creak-thud.

Waiting.

The blacks of her eyes swirled like mercurial silver. "Gotta tell 'bout Gateway Healin' Way, too."

"I will."

"What else?"

"You. I have to tell a lot about you. Whenever I think about doing my book, I—"

"Books."

"Whenever I think about doing my books, I always have a strong feeling attached to it . . . them. I couldn't write without bringing those into play—they're just woven in too tightly." I glanced over at Bill.

He spoke then. "With all she's experienced with you, No-Eyes, with all the soul memories that have been stirred and brought to life, Summer needs to bring these feelings out."

The Old One thought on that for a moment. "Go on."

"Summer feels the need to awaken the other soul memories she senses so many people have. She hears the shuffling of many spirit moccasins that need a little direction toward inner understanding."

The rocker stilled its voice as No-Eyes paused to ask, "Bill mean them peoples who be confused 'bout why they love Indian way even though they not be Indian."

"Yes. Summer sees these carryover souls as being very helpful in the days to come because, although they're not Indian, they're the segment of the public that can be awakened to the current plight of the Native American race. She only wants to make people wake up to the reality of how the Indian people are being treated in today's world. It's real important for her to bring about a new public awareness of their cultural value and importance—especially the belief they have about man's being one with the land."

Silence.

"No-Eyes?" I said.

"Summer gonna tell 'bout sacred Indian lessons?"

Her question cut through to the quick—it hurt. "Those were *sacred*, No-Eyes. There'll be many, many things that I won't write about. All the times I came out here during the week when Bill was at work and the girls were in school, most of those were too sacred to even mention. No, I have to keep the high sacredness of those things within my heart." I paused as I thought about other books that were exposing so much sacredness. I felt as if the authors were traitors who had disrespectfully tossed diamonds around as if they were nothing more than common pebbles.

Bill nudged me out of my private thoughts. "Hon? You were saying?"

I looked to my teacher and realized she'd been in my head, for she was slowly nodding in agreement.

"No-Eyes need to warn 'bout other Indian stuff. No-Eyes see how many peoples gonna feel when they read this *Spirit Song.* Peoples gonna do that awake stuff an' understand why they always feel so Indian inside. They gonna then know why they feel drawn to Indian stuff an' culture. But then they gonna go off on wrong path with their new knowledge."

Bill frowned.

I made a stab at it, for I thought I understood her. "Let me see if I know what you mean by that. People who have had their carryover Indian souls awakened will want to be Indian. They'll want to seek out Indian teachers and do Indian ways—like Medicine Wheel and Pipe ceremonies."

"Yup. What so! Why that be wrong path?"

"Because they're trying to grasp onto the exterior Indian ways instead of bringing the *inner* Indian ways to their hearts. They're walking the Without Trail before the Within Path has been journeyed through."

"What so! Why that wrong?"

"It's wrong because they think they need the trappings instead of the ideals. Without the ideals in their hearts, all the other things like ceremonies and whatever else are shallow and meaningless. The Indian way is what's *inside.*"

The Visionary leaned far forward in her chair. Her eyes were like shiny hematite.

"That why Summer not gonna put great importance on No-Eyes' heritage."

I mulled that over while my teacher rested back in the rocker and set it in motion. If she was right in what she foresaw the public's doing with the knowledge I shared with them, I certainly understood her rationale. I could also envision full-bloods being more than a little upset with these whites trying to learn their sacred ways and ceremonies. That would just never do! There were age-old traditions to maintain here. Certain lines cannot be crossed. And I knew that better than anyone.

"No-Eyes? I'm wondering, though, if those with *true* Indian carryover souls wouldn't inherently recognize and respect the reality of their current ethnic difference. You know what I'm saying?"

"No-Eyes think so."

"I mean, I know I've lived before as Shoshoni and Anasazi, but I don't go into reservations or try to gain any Indian organization memberships because of that. My heart and mind are Indian and that's enough. You can't expect to be taken seriously by Indians when you're not currently Indian. I don't even know if I'm making myself clear on this."

"Summer be clear 'cept you *do* got Indian blood in them veins—it not be a lot, but it still be there anyways. Go on, Summer, talk some more."

I looked over at Bill. He urged me on, too.

"Well . . . I think those non-Indians with the *true* Indian memories will just naturally know their place. They'll cherish those special memories and make use of their recalled ways of living and knowledge to help bring about a better world. They'll comprise both Indian and non-Indian aspects—they shouldn't need to shoulder their way back into present-day Indian society. I think that would be all wrong."

"What should they do with their memories then?" Bill asked.

"Use them as they once did. Bring out their earth awareness, their high respect for all life. Use them to remember how well the Earth Mother provides for them and become active against pollution and other dangers. Their basic traditional beliefs of oneness are what can reverse what's been done in the world."

The rocker began to sing again as No-Eyes took the floor. "Summer got right idea 'bout this Indian stuff. No-Eyes gonna talk now, too, but No-Eyes needed to see how Summer was gonna write 'bout it. It be all so wrong if peoples follow wrong paths. That be part of Brotherhood stuff No-Eyes gonna talk 'bout."

The fire snapped and sent an extra measure of warmth into the room, encircling us in a loving aura. The kinship we each felt for one another enkindled a deep sense of serenity within my heart. A smile tipped the corners of my mouth while the sound of the wise one's voice brought music to my soul.

"This stuff 'bout peoples' path be so, so big. They not realize how big it be. All peoples lookin' for path to truths. Where truths be anyway? Truths be *inside* all peoples. What so then! Why they be lookin' under rocks or around bushes? Why they journey far to other lands? On top of mountains? Why they seekin' teachers? Or go this path an' that path? They think they need Indian path, or Summer's path or some foreigner's path. They runnin' round like rabbit from coyote! Peoples be leavin' pieces of themselves all over—they got nothin' left to bring inside!"

"Yes, No-Eyes," Bill agreed, "they think they have to run themselves ragged looking for their path. They fragment themselves all over the world running to ancient ruins and seeking teachers they think they need, when all their needs have been waiting for them on their own Within Path. I guess they don't believe their own spirits can teach them anything."

The Old One shook her head. "Tsk-tsk. That be so, so dumb. Peoples not see how big it all be. They not see fastest way be on the Within Path. They waste much time with all them others who gonna lead them back to Within Path anyway. Way to Great Spirit got no feathers, no wheels, no special words. Way to Great Spirit got no race, no outside nothin'."

"And the Brotherhood?" I asked.

"That what we been *talkin'* 'bout! The Way be same for all spirits in peoples. Peoples be one big Brotherhood! *All* peoples."

There was something in the way she chose to emphasize her words that gave me a new sense of what she was really talking about. I wasn't sure if my mate had picked up on it, but knowing him, he probably had.

"No-Eyes," Bill said, "are you talking about *all* people—as in 'intelligent *beings*'?"

"Yup. Earth peoples think so small. They not realize how big this Brotherhood stuff be. An' spirit path be same one for all in Brotherhood. That why only Indian way or other ways not be all peoples' way. All peoples' paths be inside—that be path of all in Brotherhood. See?"

"These *other* people, you mean aliens?" Bill asked.

"Bah! *Aliens!* That word mean 'strange.' See? Peoples not be thinkin' too right. Them other ones just be brothers, that all. They be aliens just 'cause they live out *there?*" she asked, pointing a knobby finger to the beamed ceiling. "They be aliens just 'cause they look different? We got red peoples an' black peoples on earth. They look different from yellow, brown, an' white peoples. *They* be aliens? Bah!"

"Whoa, No-Eyes, settle down," I said. "We know what you're saying. I've seen them, remember?"

Bill had just gotten a fast lesson on the importance of choosing his words carefully. He apologized for the indiscretion.

The Old One softened to him. "That okay, Bill. No-Eyes be sorry one. No-Eyes just gettin' too, too old to live more with peoples' dumb thinkin'." She quickly straightened her back and the wisdom sparked again in her eyes. "Peoples got many brothers. There be many, many kinds of brothers in this big Brotherhood. We all be brothers. Some live way far on other stars an' some live on Earth Mother an' share her."

I eyed her. "Share her? You mean our distant brothers who live here sometimes."

"Them, too," came the impish response that matched the expression.

Bill and I exchanged glances. He decided to go for it.

"You mean like the little one Summer saw."

"Yup. That be one, too. She been another kind of brother."

Silence.

Creak-thud. Creak-thud.

I could tell the Old One was enjoying this immensely, for she was purposely being evasive so we ourselves would think of who all our brothers were here on earth.

We sat in silence as we thought of all the possible brothers we had.

No-Eyes was nearly laughing at our futile efforts. Finally she felt sorry for us and gave us a hint.

"Other brother be bigger," she mumbled. "He be *big* bigger."

We smiled at each other, yet we still were frowning. This was some riddle.

Again the Old One took pity. "One night when Summer an' No-Eyes be in woods out there, Summer feel somebody watchin'."

My eyes lit up like full moons. "The Mountain Ones! The Woods-walkers!"

"Yup. See? See how many brothers peoples got? We all be one big Brotherhood. Big Brotherhood be all children of Great Spirit an' all got same path to truth—it be here inside everyone."

Bill had a huge smile on his face as he got up and crossed to the fireplace. "Need more wood," he explained. Then as he worked, he expressed his thoughts on the subject.

"I hope one day all our brothers will be able to come out of hiding. What I mean is, I hope humans will evolve to a more open level of awareness. We feel bad so many of our brothers have to fear for their lives just because humans are so threatened by things they don't understand."

"Mmmm, that day gonna come, Bill. After Phoenix Days be done, some brother friends No-Eyes got say vibrations gonna be little different. They mean mental vibrations, too, not only body ones. Earth peoples gonna see many new brothers in Phoenix Days 'cause they gonna come to help out. Then earth brothers gonna be ready to meet other brothers who been livin' here all the time. See? It gonna work out okay."

Bill finished up, and as he returned to the couch, I had another thought on the subject.

"Speaking of brotherhood, I had an awful time coming up with the name for our information center. Sometimes when I thought of this or that name, 'brotherhood' kept returning—just as if it couldn't be anything else. But I worried about the word because there are some negative organizations that have 'brotherhood' in their title. Yet I just couldn't get away from it either. Could you shed some light on why that was?"

"Yup, No-Eyes could."

Waiting.

Silence.

"Well?" Bill prompted.

"What so? It not be some big mystery. Summer an' Bill know stuff. Summer seen stuff . . . some brothers. It be natural, that all. That Mountain Brotherhood mean *the* Brotherhood. Maybe Summer an' Bill not know it at time, but that what it mean anyways. It gonna be up in mountain woods where all earth brothers be, right?"

I grinned. "Yeah. I like that. Thanks, No-Eyes. I like that a lot."

The Old One's smile widened, too. There was a moment of specialness that seemed to stop time. Our deep love for each other was starting to break through as our eyes locked. My heart welled and a lump lodged in my throat.

The Visionary's eyes began to mist just before she jumped up and turned her head. "No-Eyes be hungry. We gonna go eat now."

THE KNOWING AND
THE GREAT ALONE
The Side Effects of Wisdom

And so the spell was broken.

We followed No-Eyes into her kitchen and helped make cold cheese sandwiches and chicory coffee. During the meal, we shared some of our daily life with her. I told stories of our girls' awakening talents, and Bill recalled some of his more humorous experiences in his service work. These last were good medicine, for the Old One laughed so hard tears fell from her wizened eyes. I'd never before seen her laugh so hard and it made my heart shine with happiness.

With the meal concluded, I insisted on cleaning up. Bill took care of the fireplace and No-Eyes pulled her rocker closer to the hearth. When we were ready to resume our discussions, I grabbed a couch pillow and propped it up on the hearthstones. Motioning for Bill to rest his back against it, I snuggled down between his bent knees. We were facing the rocker and we were ready for our teacher's next lesson.

For a few moments she stared at us and I could feel Bill becoming uncomfortable. I patted his knee to reassure him. It took time to get used to the Visionary's quiet staring spells, but once you realized the wonderful thoughts that went on behind them, all sense of unease vanished.

Then she smiled. "Summer an' Bill feel so good. You be so right together. You gonna be good spirit helpers. That love be what make such strong power. You two gonna make fine warriors."

429

We expressed our appreciation of her words.

Then the mood deepened as her smile faded. The cloud-darkened day brought shadows into the cabin room. Firelight illumined the woman's deeply creviced face, softening its time-worn lines. Wispy gray hairs were highlighted like a heavenly halo. Aged fingers toyed with the fringe of her shawl.

"There be one more important stuff No-Eyes gonna talk 'bout this day. No-Eyes thought maybe it not be needed. It not been needed with any other student No-Eyes have 'cept Many Heart. But No-Eyes see how it gonna be for Summer later on, so Summer gonna need to hear some stuff."

"What does it concern, No-Eyes?" Bill asked.

"It concern many stuff like other peoples an' how they gonna think of Summer—how they gonna make Summer feel inside."

The critics, skeptics, and doubters came to mind.

"No-Eyes be talkin' 'bout all them believers, Summer."

I was visibly surprised. "I want people to believe in you, No-Eyes. I want them to realize what a wonderful wise one you are." I innocently smiled. "You're going to have students lined up from here to the road out there."

She knew that that would never be, but I didn't. I had no idea she'd be gone by the time that first book reached the first reader's hands.

"No peoples come to old woman's woods unless they meant to. Nobody else gonna come to this old cabin. No-Eyes *see* that. We be talkin' 'bout Summer now, not old woman."

Bill squeezed his arms around me.

"What are the believers going to think of Summer? What will they make her feel about herself that she doesn't feel now?" he asked.

"They gonna think many things. They gonna—"

"No-Eyes, I'm sorry to interrupt, but I just had a thought that I don't want to lose."

"Go on."

"I want the Indian People to see my books with clarity. I want them to understand that these are not written by a white author just trying to make a buck off their plights or culture. I want them to see that I'm desperately trying to bring the general public into a higher conscious awareness of how the Indians are being socially shoved under the carpet. The public has got to wake up and realize the beautiful value of Indian culture. Right now, when minorities are spoken of, people mention Mexicans, blacks, Cubans, Asians, Vietnamese, and Nicaraguans . . . but the Native American seems to be so much of a minority that people don't even include them. They've become sort of a nonentity in the public consciousness—people don't even *see* them. I need to change that, No-Eyes. Above all, I need to bring attention to the Indian People because the general public has kept them buried for too long."

Bill nudged my arm. "You need to get to the point." Then he looked to No-Eyes. "She tends to get carried away a lot."

The Old One nodded in understanding. "That 'cause she got so much to say."

I grinned. "Sorry. My point is that I want the Indian People to see my books for what they are—an effort to enlighten the public, not a commercial vehicle that uses their culture, not one that exposes sacred ways. I think that—"

"The point?" Bill reminded. "Can't you say anything in one sentence?"

"I want the Indian People to be glad I wrote the books."

No-Eyes closed her eyes in a long blink. When she opened them, they rested on mine.

"Summer not gonna tell no Sacred Way stuff. Summer gonna write from heart. Peoples gonna know what to think. Summer got no need to worry 'bout that stuff."

I breathed a deep sigh of relief. "I just didn't want to look like someone else taking advantage of the Indians."

"It all gonna work out fine. Explain your Indian blood in *Spirit Song,* and people gonna understand."

Silence.

Creak-thud. Creak-thud.

"So getting back to the believers," Bill said. "What will they think?"

"Many stuff. They gonna be in expectation of Summer. They gonna think she need to go here, go there . . . talk here, talk there. But that not be Summer's purpose. Besides, that not be Summer's way. They gonna think she be their teacher. But that not be Summer's path either. An' there be somethin' else that gonna get in way of all that expected talkin' an' teachin'."

"What, No-Eyes?" I asked. "What gets in the way?"

She looked as though she was mentally searching for a nice way to say a bad thing.

"No-Eyes need few minutes here. No-Eyes not used to tellin' student 'bout this stuff."

We waited in respectful silence.

The fire crackled behind us. We felt a wonderful serenity watching the shadows flicker across the smoky walls of the tiny log cabin. And our teacher finally found the right words.

"Summer, Bill, there be somethin' called The Knowing. You know what that be?"

Bill tried first. "Inner vision? Like Summer's premonitions, our daughter Aimee's spontaneous vision flashes, and her sister Sarah's nature bond, and your constant visionary sight?"

"Nope. That only be tiny bit of The Knowing, but that not be all of it."

I took a stab at it. "Is it knowing a spiritual teacher? The relationship and learning between student and teacher?"

"Nope. That only be tiny bit, too, but that not be all of it either."

I pulled away to look back at my mate. We both had quizzical expressions. I turned to face the Old One in the rocker.

"Is it knowing about all our different brothers and being on friendly terms with them?"

"Nope. That be tiny part, too."

"I guess we don't know then."

She wasn't surprised. Now when she spoke she carefully chose her words. Her speech was slow and deliberate.

"When peoples take the Within Path to truths, they get there faster 'cause that path got no extra trapping stuff to take attention from truth. See?"

We said that we did.

"The Within Path opens up spirit Gates so spirit sees an' knows truths. When spirit see an' know truths, it lives them truths. See?"

"Yes."

"We're with you," Bill confirmed.

"So when peoples' spirits be ready to live them truths, the mental consciousness rises up to that higher spirit understanding level." She paused then to check for any questions. There weren't any.

"When conscious mind an' spirit's highest knowledge be equal, that be called The Knowing."

I wanted to be sure I understood this. "You're saying that The Knowing is when a person's mental understanding of the truths has reached the total comprehension level of their spirit's higher self-knowledge."

"That be right. That why Summer an' Bill's first guesses be only pieces of it. The Knowing be all spirit learnings that lead to complete comprehension, plus the conscious awareness of all higher self's knowledge."

I grinned. "People who have The Knowing are like you, Two Trees, and Many Heart, huh, No-Eyes?"

"Yup."

"And Dreamwalkers, of course," Bill added.

"Yup. An' peoples who can be easy friends with all brothers in Brotherhood got The Knowing, too."

I sighed. "That must really be something."

"Nope. It not be."

"Why?"

" 'Cause peoples who got The Knowing . . . they also got The Great Alone."

I ran those last words through my head a few times. They brought to mind visions of my one day with Many Heart when we'd talked of No-Eyes' need for solitude—her aloneness.

"You have The Great Alone, don't you, No-Eyes?"

"No-Eyes got that. Yup. It be somethin' that just come with The Knowing. That be why Many Heart not be able to find right mate. He not be able to be shut up in any house. He need to be outside an' all time freedom for spirit voice to lead him here an' there."

I felt a little sad. "And that's why you can't bear being among crowds or in towns."

"Little bit why. Mostly 'cause when mind be on same spirit level all the time, mind be too fragile—too tuned to peoples' thoughts an' dumb un-awareness. Noises even hurt new vibration mind an' body. Everything be raised up higher . . . body, mind, an' spirit be extra sensitive an' they need silence of woods an' maybe desert even."

"Ah, I think we missed something here," Bill interjected. "What's this about vibrations?"

"When mind be same level as higher self of spirit, physical-body vibration get pulled up, too. That be natural way. That why body need plenty restful place to live. They all be connected, see?"

We saw.

"That why No-Eyes need to tell Summer this stuff."

We didn't see.

"Now we're confused again," I told her.

Creak-thud. Creak-thud.

"You lost us, No-Eyes," I said. "My sense is that you're warning *me* of The Great Alone, but I don't have The Knowing."

"No-Eyes not say Summer did."

Bill gently moved me away from him so he could change his position. He stretched out on the braided rug and I took his vacated cushion by the hearth. I tried to sort this all out.

"Okay. The brothers said that all those who carry on after the Phoenix Days will have raised bodily vibrations. I take it that's because of technical operations they'll do to right the earth's condition and reverse pollution. Is that right?"

The Old One nodded. She looked so weary.

"And I also figured these raised vibrations would naturally have to include mankind's mental attitudes, ideas, and beliefs—his con-sciousness—his collective consciousness."

"Go on," the Visionary prompted.

"Is that correct so far?"

"Yup. That be right."

"Okay . . . so if those remaining on earth have raised bodily vibrations and their collective consciousness is raised, too, wouldn't they also have The Knowing?"

She nodded.

"Well, where does The Great Alone fit in then?"

"There not gonna *be* any Great Alone after Phoenix rise up . . . only *before*. Them ones who got The Knowing *before* Phoenix be flyin' free gonna also have The Great Alone 'cause they not gonna be able to live with ones who still got lower vibrations. See? Them two levels not mix. That just be way of it."

Silence.

"It not be so bad."

Bill sat up. His eyes were intent on the Old One's. "Is Summer going to want to live alone?"

No-Eyes gave him a sympathetic smile of warmth. "Yup . . . but only if Bill be with her."

"What about the kids?"

"This be *later*, Bill. It not be now. It gonna all work out. Summer not gonna want to leave nobody she love—just gonna need some solitude and aloneness."

This was not good news.

"I could never be a recluse, No-Eyes, too many people need me! I would never want to live anywhere without my family . . . ever!"

"No-Eyes not say Summer gonna ever live without family. No-Eyes see Summer an' Bill in one cabin an' grown girls in others . . . all still side by side. It gonna be in mountains—in woods."

That sounded much better. When the girls were grown they'd naturally want their own cabins anyway. And I envisioned them all clustered together—just as we always had been.

"But Summer," the Old One cautioned, "never, never say stuff you 'never' would do. Some stuff gonna come anyway . . . it be natural way of path. Them raised vibrations be natural. The Knowing be natural, too."

She left one natural out: The Great Alone.

5

IN SEARCH OF RAINBOW'S END
The Purpose of Life

The Visionary abruptly changed the entire subject; evidently there was nothing more to say on the issue. She had done her duty to warn me of a condition she foresaw entering my life, and like the wise one that she was, she felt she needed to prepare me for that eventuality.

"Summer, Bill, remember before we talked 'bout how peoples lookin' all over? The searchin's they do?"

"Yes," I said.

"Summer ever think what they really be searchin' for?"

"Their truth. No, not their truth, but *the* truth. They look all over for it. They make it very difficult for themselves."

"But it be so simple," she said with a grand smile. "Everybody's lookin' hard for somethin'. Everybody's searchin' for end of rainbow. It never there for them. They lookin' for all wrong stuff in all wrong places.

"Peoples think they need new job. They not be happy with it. They think they need new house or car. They not be happy with them either. They think they need love. They not be happy. They search an' search. They still not be happy. They *die* not happy. They only be happy when they find Great Spirit here," she said, pointing softly to her heart and the center of her forehead. *"Then* they not search more. They be happy an' content when they find Truth in Great Spirit."

The wise one had brought the lesson full circle to close the hoop. We had started out with this aspect of one's spiritual searching and we were closing with it. Her choppy sentences couldn't have been more eloquent.

Her words were beautiful. So many, many people wasted their happiness. They sweated out two or three jobs attempting to gain the sacred dollar—the golden calf that would buy them all the material things that, in the end, wouldn't make them happy at all. They would then discover that happiness had eluded them and they would begin the search once again, only with a more intense obsession to obtain the elusive golden ring.

For others, the nebulous pot-o'-gold is fame. Yet, once achieved, happiness again vanishes from their grasp like vapors. All manner of ends were strived for. People blindly leave grief, anger, disrespect, and hate in the wake of their relentless searchings. Yet, the beginnings and the ends of their rainbows are within themselves all along. The elusive pot-o'-gold, the greatest treasure of all, is centered within everyone. It is God's own loving spirit of truth and the Force that opens the Gates to His door. All one needs to do is to perceive the beautiful rainbow that gently arcs above and ends where one stands.

Simply stated, these were the words of No-Eyes. And the words were pure and sweet—they were eloquent and simple, as all the truths are.

Quickly the Old One rose from her rocker. "We gonna go out into fresh air now," she said.

We followed her out into the golden light that speared down from the separating clouds.

"We gonna go to woods. We gonna finish this now."

There was a chill in the autumn air and I wondered if the frail lady would be cold. I thought about running back into the cabin to grab her serape. Her shawl wasn't much cover.

No-Eyes caught my arm just as I was turning. "I not need it, Summer. I be fine."

Well, that was that. I should've known better. Bill and I walked on either side of her while we chatted casually about how crisp the weather was becoming. Bill was thinking about the coming winter.

"No-Eyes, would you like me to stock up some wood for you?"

Ordinarily I think she would've declined the offer. She rarely accepted outside help, even though she did have a few close friends who checked on her regularly.

Her answer came as a surprise to me. "That be nice, Bill. No-Eyes get old, not be strong like old days. That be real nice."

We entered the forest and the old one wasted no time.

"What you see?" she asked, directing the question at no one in particular.

We questioningly looked at one another, not certain of her meaning. I attempted a reply.

"The pine and aspen, all of nature, the spirit of nature."

"Anybody see that! What *you* see?"

After searching for a deeper meaning, Bill tried.

"Nature is preparing for winter. All of nature is busy with it."

She shrugged her narrow shoulders. "That one be better. How nature do this busy thing?"

We talked as we strolled her well-worn woodland paths. I spoke next.

"They gather and store a season's supply of food. They insulate their nesting places for hibernation and warmth."

"Good!" she spat. "What store they get fur coats from? How they gonna chop wood for warmth? Where the market where they buy food, huh, Summer? Huh, Bill?"

We grinned at her simple point and Bill replied, "All their needs are amply provided. The Great Spirit gives them all they require and the spirit of the woods makes sure they are distributed."

She sighed with a decided nod. When she looked up into our faces, her eyes were misty.

"Peoples be dumbest animals of all," came her tired voice. "Great Spirit provide all for *them*, too. Great Spirit give good food, powerful medicine that grow on Earth Mother's breast, great powers for peoples' energy needs. But they no see this good Earth Mother stuff. She give all beautiful life stuff . . . for all peoples . . . for all times. She give all she got to give, but peoples take an' take all wrong stuff from her. They be so blind, they no see this."

She paused before continuing.

"Great Spirit be so loving to His peoples. He give four great things. He give love. He give truth an' way to it. He give faith. He give bounties of Earth Mother for peoples to live good Earthway lifes."

Her obsidian eyes glistened as she looked to the turquoise sky that peeked above the moving clouds. She looked up for the Great Spirit.

"Peoples can find end of rainbow with them four things. They never need more."

Eyes closed, head lowered, she continued.

"But peoples be so dumb. They not realize that they be big, big part of all life; life of nature . . . life of Great Spirit . . . that they be one brother to *all* brothers. They not see how they be part of life of spirit of *all* living things."

We walked into the jewellike forest while the wise visionary softly spoke of mankind's need to raise their collective consciousness to the reality of the greatness of the living hoop of life.

"Peoples need to understand," she nearly pleaded with a voice barely above a whisper. "Peoples need to understand what they be seekin' be in own hearts, deep down in own spirits. When peoples run to end of rainbow for big pot of gold, they say, 'It not be here!' They cry, 'It *never* be here for me.' But they need to see that big pot of gold *is* there. It be standing at end of rainbow . . . it be *in* peoples' hearts an' *in* peoples' *own* spirits. It be *inside* all 'long."

Our old friend slowly shook her head. She whispered in her great tiredness. "Peoples need to wake up. When they ever gonna see that the Great Spirit be livin' *inside* them? When they ever gonna see that the Great Spirit *be* that rainbow end?"

And there was nothing left to be said, for she had said it all.

AFTERWORD

We spent the remainder of that autumn afternoon strolling through No-Eyes' mountain woodlands. Most of the time we walked on in silence, each one deep in private thoughts.

I thought about her last words. As always, she was so clear in her perceptions.

Man did have everything provided for him. But what a pity he didn't see it. He was too caught up in the hectic rush of life, the breakneck pace that modern civilization carries him on, the high-speed treadmill that he allows himself to be controlled by.

Man was no longer close to the Earth Mother, who so lovingly gave of Herself. Man didn't take the precious time to inspect the tiny golden aspen leaf and perceive the thriving universe within its tender veins. He didn't calm his energies enough to hear the touching sounds around him, like the gentle heartbeat of the breathing mountains, or the soft approach of the Dawn Spirit or the quiet footfalls of the Spirit of Night. Did he even hear the music of falling snow?

Yes, the Old One was absolutely within her right when she frequently became upset with man's voluntary unawareness of his God-given surroundings.

Man continues to defile and desecrate the Earth Mother through his ignorance of her tender spirit. Man continues to harm himself and others through his negative attitudes and emotions. When will man take the time to raise his head to the heavens and understand that he is a living part of all the

439

shimmering celestial beauty he sees? When will man comprehend that he is the sum total of all of nature that surrounds him? When will man comprehend that he is a child of the earth who is nurtured through the cosmic bond of genetic coding that pulses through the Earth Mother's nourishing umbilical?

People are so involved in their surface lives that they don't ever take their shoes off to feel the soft give of the forest floor. They're too busy to watch a mother robin lovingly feed her sightless fledglings, too hurried to stop along the scented wayside to take note of the Earth Mother's intense beauty and to sniff the sweet fragrance of the crisp mountain air, too busy to smell the meadow's glistening wildflowers. They are too busy to realize that their airplanes, cars, shoes, all serve to separate them from their birthland . . . and in their ignorance do they cut the cord.

I am absolutely convinced that everyone who reads this book can obtain the clarity of awareness that I've achieved through the enlightened teachings of my wise visionary friend, No-Eyes. There is nothing mysterious about them. It is an ingrained aspect of our spiritual heritage to feel a oneness with nature and to benefit from its healthful bounties.

I hope that this book has brought you a unique sensitivity to the inner essence of nature, that it has given birth to an intensified awareness of the Spirit of Life, that it has brought you an openness of heart that, in turn, enables you to live an enriched and peaceful life—an Earthway life.

May you always walk upon sunlit trails, and may warm friendships be drawn to the open hearthside of your hearts.

Mary Summer Rain
Colorado Rockies
9,500 feet

APPENDIX: BOTANICAL SOURCES

Through the letters I've received from readers, I've seen a common belief that in order to obtain the healing herbs and plants one must become field-wise. In other words, it appears to be the general consensus that each individual must go up into the high mountains, down into the valleys and plains, and learn to recognize and harvest the growing botanicals. But this is hardly the case. Botanical remedies are much more readily available than most people realize.

The easiest place to get most healing plants is your local corner health-food store. Most all botanical remedies mentioned in this book can be purchased locally. They come in many forms and can be packaged individually or in combination with other herbs. Most often they're in capsule form or loose bulk.

For those of you who don't have a local health-food store, I've also provided the following list of mail order suppliers:

Heritage Store
P.O. Box 444-MR
Virginia Beach, VA 23458
1-804-428-0100

The Herb & Spice Collection
P.O. Box 118, D35
Norway, Iowa 52318
1-800-365-4372
(Suppliers of a full line of quality herbs and spices—bulk and packaged—and pure essential oils.)

Lorann Oils, Inc.
P.O. Box 22009
Lansing, Michigan 48909
1-800-248-1302

Aphrodisia Herbs
282 Bleecker Street
New York, New York 10014
1-212-989-6440
(catalog $2)

Larsen's Old-Fashioned Country Herb Shoppe
P.O. Box 253
786 South State
Orem, Utah 84058
1-801-225-4111
Grace Larsen, owner

AUTHOR'S NOTE

Any readers interested in contacting Mary Summer Rain directly, concerning *Earthway* or any of her previous titles, may write her at:

P. O. Box 6699
Woodland Park, CO 80866

Please include a stamped, self-addressed envelope.